AUDITORY MANAGEMENT OF HEARING-IMPAIRED CHILDREN

Auditory Management of Hearing-Impaired Children: Principles and Prerequisites for Intervention edited by **Mark Ross, Ph.D.,** and **Thomas G. Giolas, Ph.D.,** is a volume in the new PERSPECTIVES IN AUDIOLOGY Series—**Lyle L. Lloyd, Ph.D.,** series editor. Other volumes in this series are:

Published:

Communicating with Deaf People: A Resource Manual for Teachers and Students of American Sign Language by Harry W. Hoemann, Ph.D.

Language Development and Intervention with the Hearing Impaired by Richard R. Kretschmer, Jr., Ed.D., and Laura W. Kretschmer, Ed.D.

Noise and Audiology, edited by David M. Lipscomb, Ph.D.

Supervision in Audiology by Judith A. Rassi, M.A.

In preparation:

Elements of Hearing Science edited by Lawrence J. Deutsch, Ph.D., and Alan M. Richards, Ph.D.

Psychology of Deafness by Harry W. Hoemann, Ph.D.

Rehabilitative Audiology (Part I: The Adult/Part II: The Elderly Client) edited by Raymond H. Hull, Ph.D.

Introduction to Instrumental Phonetics by Colin Painter, Ph.D.

A Primer of Acoustic Phonetics by J. M. Pickett, Ph.D.

Hearing Assessment edited by William F. Rintelmann, Ph.D.

American Sign Language and Sign Systems by Ronnie Bring Wilbur, Ph.D.

Publisher's Note
Perspectives in Audiology is a carefully planned series of clinically oriented, topic-specific textbooks. The series is enriched by contributions from leading specialists in audiology and allied disciplines. Because technical language and terminology in these disciplines are constantly being refined and sometimes vary, this series has been edited as far as possible for consistency of style in conformity with current majority usage as set forth by the American Speech and Hearing Association, the *Publication Manual of the American Psychological Association,* and *The University of Chicago Manual of Style.* University Park Press and the series editors and authors welcome readers' comments about individual volumes in the series or the series concept as a whole in the interest of making **Perspectives in Audiology** as useful as possible to students, teachers, clinicians, and scientists.

A Volume in the Perspectives in Audiology Series

AUDITORY MANAGEMENT OF HEARING-IMPAIRED CHILDREN

Principles and Prerequisites for Intervention

Edited by

Mark Ross, Ph.D., and
Thomas G. Giolas, Ph.D.

Department of Speech
University of Connecticut

University Park Press

Baltimore

UNIVERSITY PARK PRESS
International Publishers in Science and Medicine
233 East Redwood Street
Baltimore, Maryland 21202

Copyright © 1978 by University Park Press

Typeset by American Graphic Arts Corporation.

Manufactured in the United States of America by
The Maple Press Company.

Library of Congress Cataloging in Publication Data

Main entry under title:

Auditory management of hearing-impaired children.

(Perspectives in audiology series)
Includes bibliographical references and indexes.
1. Deaf—Education—Addresses, essays, lectures.
2. Deaf—Means of communication—Addresses, essays,
lectures. 3. Children, Deaf—Addresses, essays,
lectures. I. Ross, Mark. II. Giolas, Thomas G.
III. Series. [DNLM: 1. Hearing disorders—In infancy
and childhood—Congresses. 2. Hearing disorders—
Rehabilitation—Congresses. 3. Education, Special—
Congresses. WV270 A916 1977]
HV2430.A9   371.9'12   78-6114
ISBN 0-8391-1246-7

CONTENTS

CONTRIBUTORS

Thomas R. Behrens, Ph.D.
Bureau of Education for the Handicapped
U.S. Office of Education
400 Maryland Ave., S.W.
Washington, D.C. 20202

Arthur Boothroyd, Ph.D.
Clarke School for the Deaf
Round Hill Road
Northampton, Massachusetts 01060

Knud Børrild, M.S.
Director, Audiology Unit
Fredericiaskolen
Merkurvænget 2
7000 Fredericia
Denmark

Richard J. Dowling, J.D.
Government Affairs Department
American Speech and Hearing Association
9030 Old Georgetown Road
Washington, D.C. 20014

Dennis B. Fry, Ph.D.
Department of Phonetics and Linguistics
University College
Gower Street
London WCIE 6 Bt
England

Thomas G. Giolas, Ph.D.
Department of Speech
University of Connecticut
Storrs, Connecticut 06268

Ira J. Hirsh, Ph.D.
Central Institute for the Deaf
818 South Euclid
St. Louis, Missouri 63110

Harry Levitt, Ph.D.
Doctoral Program in Speech
and Hearing Sciences
City University of New York
33 W. 42nd Street
New York, New York 10036

Daniel Ling, Ph.D.
School of Human Communication
Disorders
McGill University
1266 Pine Avenue West
Montreal, P.Q. H3G 1A8
Canada

Mark Ross, Ph.D.
Department of Speech
University of Connecticut
Storrs, Connecticut 06268

Edgar Villchur, M.S. Ed.
Foundation for Hearing Aid
Research
Woodstock, New York 12498

PREFACE TO PERSPECTIVES IN AUDIOLOGY

Audiology is a young, vibrant, dynamic field. Its lineage can be traced to the fields of education, medicine, physics, and psychology in the nineteenth century and the emergence of speech pathology in the first half of this century. The term "audiology," meaning the science of hearing, was coined by Raymond Carhart in 1947. Since then, its definition has expanded to include its professional nature. Audiology is the profession that provides knowledge and service in the areas of human hearing and, more broadly, human communication and its disorders. As evidence of the growth of audiology as a major profession, in the 1940s there were no programs designed to prepare "audiologists," while now there are over 112 graduate training programs accredited by the Education and Training Board of the American Board of Examiners in Speech Pathology and Audiology for providing academic and clinical training designed to prepare clinically competent audiologists. Audiology is also a major area of study in the professional preparation of speech pathologists, speech and hearing scientists, and otologists.

Perspectives in Audiology is the first series of books designed to cover the major areas of study in audiology. The interdisciplinary nature of the field is reflected by the scope of the volumes in this series. The volumes currently in preparation (see p. ii) include both clinically oriented and basic science texts. The series consists of topic-specific textbooks designed to meet the needs of today's advanced level student. Each volume will also serve as a focal reference source for practicing audiologists and specialists in many related fields.

The Perspectives in Audiology series offers several advantages not usually found in other texts, but purposely featured in this series to increase the practical value of the books for practitioners and researchers, as well as for students and teachers:

1. Every volume includes thorough discussion of all relevant clinical and/or research papers on each topic.
2. Every volume is organized in an educational format to serve as the main text or as one of the main texts for graduate and advanced undergraduate students in courses on audiology and/or other studies concerned with human communication and its disorders.
3. Unlike ordinary texts, Perspectives in Audiology volumes will retain their professional reference value as focal reference sources for practitioners and researchers in career work long after completion of this series.
4. Each volume serves as a rich source of authoritative, up-to-date information and valuable reviews for specialists in many fields, including administration, audiology, early childhood studies, linguistics, otology, psychology, pediatrics, public health, special education, speech pathology, and speech and hearing science.

While the field of audiology is based upon accurate assessment of hearing impairment and the design and implementation of appropriate habilitative and educational programs to remediate and/or compensate for hearing impairment, the field has developed without a single volume specifically designed to provide the rationale for the aural rehabilitation aspects of audiology. This volume, *Auditory Management of Hearing Impaired Children: Principles and Prerequisites for Intervention,* was selected as one of the initial volumes in this series to fill this major void in the professional preparation of individuals providing clinical and educational services for the hearing impaired.

The contributors' primary goal has been to discuss the importance of hearing in the language acquisition, educational achievement, and social development of the hearing-impaired child. It is the editors' contention that successful mainstreaming of hearing-impaired children is contingent upon appropriate auditory management of these children; the chapters that follow provide a discussion of the concepts prerequisite to an understanding of the role of audition in primary language development and the issues involved in the integration of hearing-impaired children into the regular classroom.

The scope of this topic required the collective efforts of a number of professionals from diverse backgrounds. Therefore the editors Mark Ross and Thomas Giolas selected scientists and practitioners on the basis of their previous international contributions to this critical area to develop this monumental volume. These top experts were asked to develop papers on assigned topics, which then were discussed extensively at a conference convened especially to ensure that the goals of the book were met. Extensive integrating and editing of the material was undertaken by the editors after the conference. Their product is a volume that provides an integrated rationale for aural rehabilitation based upon some of the best current thinking on the topic. *Auditory Management of Hearing-Impaired Children* is designed as a text for the professional preparation of clinical audiologists and educators of the hearing impaired. However, the fundamental nature of this work makes it useful to speech pathologists and others concerned with communication problems in a broader sense.

Lyle L. Lloyd, Ph.D.
Chairman and Professor of
Special Education
Professor of Audiology and
Speech Sciences
Purdue University

FROM PROMISE TO REALITY: A FOREWORD

Government's interest in the learning needs of hearing-impaired children is long standing. At the state level, for example, government-run residential institutions for deaf and hard-of-hearing children were in operation as far back as the post–Civil War period. The federal government's entry into the field of education for the hearing impaired also dates back to the Civil War and the 1864 establishment in Washington, D.C., of a national school for the deaf: Gallaudet College.

Regrettably, however, an interest does not a commitment make. The purpose of the state-run asylums of more than a century ago was, in every instance, the provision of custodial care, not educational services. Not until 1917 did a state (Michigan) legally declare its special "school" for the deaf to be an educational institution. And at mid-century, there still were a dozen states without public education programs for hearing-impaired children. At the federal level, significant follow-up to the 1864 initiative was 100 years in coming.

What finally got government on track was the application of tremendous pressure by parent organizations and other advocacy groups. Their first target was state legislatures; their first major achievement, beginning in the early 1960s, was a spate of state statutes making educational opportunities for hearing-impaired and other handicapped children not merely permissive but mandatory. In the early 1970s, they turned their attention to the courts, where they cited constitutional guarantees of due process and equal protection of the laws, and from which they emerged with a veritable avalanche of decisions mandating equal access to education for handicapped children.

Taking its lead from the states, the federal government renewed its long dormant interest in the learning needs of deaf, hard-of-hearing, and other handicapped children. In the early to mid 1960s came legislation covering such matters as captioned films for the deaf and support for training teachers and other education specialists for the deaf, the hard of hearing, and the speech impaired. There followed, in relatively quick succession, Public Law 89-313, which provided federal financial support for state-operated schools for the deaf; Public Law 89-750, which created a special Bureau of Education for the Handicapped within the United States Office of Education and established a grant program designed to strengthen state programs for handicapped children; and Public Law 93-380, which authorized higher levels of federal aid to the states for special education, specified due process requirements protecting the rights of handicapped children, and required each state to establish a goal of providing full educational services to all handicapped children and to develop a plan detailing how and when it would achieve its goal.

Then, in November of 1975, came the most important federal initiative of all, the landmark Education for All Handicapped Children Act, Public Law 94-142. The new statute authorized in perpetuity (i.e., designated no expiration date for) massive increases in federal funding support for state special education efforts. Significantly, it represented more than just another act in a series of federal expressions of interest in special education programming; it was a specific commitment to all handicapped children. Together with state legislative directives and court mandates, Public Law 94-142 guaranteed to the handicapped, as a fundamental right of citizenship, a free and appropriate education.

The principal elements of the new act's guarantee are as follows:

1. Federal payment to the states of an escalating percentage of the national average expenditure per public school child, multiplied by the number of handicapped children being served in the school districts of each state (the percentage escalates through 1982 and remains constant thereafter). Based on current pupil-count figures, federal authorization levels through 1982 are as follows: fiscal 1978, at 5%—$387 million; fiscal 1979, at 10%—$775 million; fiscal 1980, at 20%—$1.2 billion; fiscal 1981, at 30%—$2.32 billion; and fiscal 1982, at 40%—$3.16 billion. By comparison recent past annual federal appropriations for assisting state special education efforts have been in the $100–$200 million range.

2. A written "individualized education program" (IEP), jointly developed by a qualified school official, the child's teacher and parents, and when possible the child himself, and including an analysis of the child's present level of achievement, short range and annual goals, and an identification of specific special education service needs.

3. The education of handicapped children with nonhandicapped children to the maximum extent possible, reverting to special classes or separate schools "only when the nature or severity of the handicap is such that education in regular classes cannot be achieved satisfactorily."

4. The assignment of priorities in making education available to all handicapped children; first, to children not receiving any education (including preschoolers) and, second, to the most severely handicapped within each disability who are receiving an inadequate education. (Note that under federal law the disabilities "deaf" and "hard of hearing" are separate and distinct.)

5. The preparation and administration of placement tests and evaluations that are neither culturally nor racially discriminatory and the presentation of such tests and evaluations in a given child's native tongue.

6. Prior consultation with a handicapped child's parents or guardian regarding school placement procedures and other major decisions concerning the child's schooling.

7. Due process procedures (specified earlier by Public Law 93-380, but greatly "clarified and strengthened" by Public Law 94-142) through which a child's parents or guardian may seek administrative and judicial remedies for the inappropriate identification, evaluation, or educational placement of the child, or for the failure, generally, to provide a free and appropriate public education.

8. State compliance with the requisites of the act by "dates certain" (failure to comply could mean a cutoff of federal special education funding). A free public education must be made available to all handicapped children between the ages of 3 and 18 by September 1, 1978, and to all those between 3 and 21 by September 1, 1980.

The new law has been called "blockbuster legislation," "a Bill of Rights for Handicapped Americans," "the most significant development in federal school legislation since the enactment of some of the more revolutionary provisions of the Elementary and Secondary Education Act of 1965," and "the herald of a new era for American education." Public Law 94-142 is very likely all of these.

As the National Advisory Committee on the Handicapped has pointed out, however, there may be "a serious difference between actual practice and what state and federal laws supposedly require." This lamentable difference, in the committee's words, makes "the basic challenge in special education today . . . the conversion of promise into reality" (United States Department of Health, Education, and Welfare. 1976. The Unfinished Revolution: Education for the Handicapped. Annual Report. Washington, D.C. p. 6.)

The achievement of that most desirable conversion will indeed be a challenge, and a great one. Although the guarantees of government's new commitment are laudable and their attainment crucial to the interests of handicapped children, there is considerable question as to whether they can be achieved fully. Even the most enlightened educators and special educators will face implementation problems, for example. Some will refuse to accommodate the involvement of parents and guardians in placement and planning activities. Others will fail to recognize that significantly increased responsibilities necessitate substantially increased manpower, training, equipment, and other resources. Still others will fail to appreciate the genuinely extraordinary education needs of secondary school handicapped pupils, the severely handicapped, handicapped children from nonmajority cultures, and handicapped children living in inner cities, rural locales, or sparsely populated areas. Not all education and other public program administrators will list special education among their priorities. And there will be other hurdles between the promise of a universally free and appropriate education and the full and efficacious achievement of that bright promise, hurdles neither fewer nor less high for hearing-impaired than for other handicapped children.

This book, developed with foresight and a keen understanding of the present state and the prospective needs of education for the hearing impaired, concerns the most imposing of the hurdles confronting hearing-handicapped children: the preparation of skilled professional personnel sufficient in number to ensure the ultimate fulfillment of Public Law 94-142's commitment.

According to the most recent United States Office of Education estimates, 70% of the nation's 377,000 deaf and hard-of-hearing children and an incredible 80% of the 328,000 nondeaf hearing impaired are educationally unserved. The Office of Education has no estimates regarding the additional thousands of hearing-impaired youngsters who, although "served" in education settings of one kind or another, receive services that are inadequate or inappropriate. Clearly, if we expect to see the commitment of Public Law 94-142 fulfilled for hearing-impaired children, we must commit ourselves to significant alteration of this abysmal service-delivery record. Assuming that commitment, we may look to this volume for the benchmarks we will need on our way from the promise of the new law's guarantee to the reality of significantly upgraded educational services for hearing-impaired children.

Richard J. Dowling

PREFACE

The hard-of-hearing child is considered by many persons as the most likely among the handicapped to succeed in the mainstream of education. Although mainstreaming of handicapped children has become a central issue, little has been done by specialists in the field to define or describe the specific needs of the hard-of-hearing child integrated into a public school setting. Educational programming for these children has been haphazard or inappropriate, with no solid theoretical or practical basis. It is an empirical fact that many hard-of-hearing children, by the time they finish their elementary education, have become underachievers and fail to enter secondary school programs. This reflects not their innate potential for growth and learning but rather a lack of skilled educational management and support.

A thorough investigation to clarify and delineate the needs of these children is long overdue. The educational needs of the hard-of-hearing child have never been considered sufficiently serious to warrant professional specialization in this area, as, for example, has been the case with the care for all other handicapped children. Past reliance on occasional and sporadic inservice programs for teachers and speech clinicians dealing with these children has proved insufficient.

The Rand Corporation (1973) study "Improving Services for Handicapped Children" (Services for Handicapped Youth: A Program Overview R-1220-HEW) estimated that, of the 83.8 million youths under 21 years old in the United States, approximately 8 million had some type or degree of hearing impairment (15 dB or more), 440,000 were hard of hearing (40–90 dB), and 50,000 were deaf (more than 90 dB). Furthermore, 379,000 hearing-handicapped youths needed some form of assistance in education, ranging from provision of hearing aids to education in a residential institution. Basically the above statistics refer to youths who have frequent difficulty in understanding normal speech.

In the same study it was estimated that only 83,000 hearing-handicapped youths (21% hard of hearing and 72% deaf) were being serviced by special education agencies, with reported expenditures from $500–$3000 per child in various states. The problem most often cited was inadequate resources (financing, personnel, and facilities).

Until recently, all children who exhibited a moderate degree of loss or more were considered "deaf," and thus were candidates for special educational settings designed for deaf children. The advent of powerful acoustic amplification devices has made this concept dated in theory; in practice, however, too many children have been considered and are becoming "deaf," because of our inadequate and unintelligent use of these amplification systems. Many young hearing-impaired children—used here in the generic sense to mean any degree and type of hearing loss—can travel one of two roads with respect to the implications of their hearing loss: they can become functioning "deaf" individuals, primarily dependent upon some form of visual communication system, or hard-of-hearing persons, functioning primarily auditorally in our society, albeit imperfectly.

The maximum development of residual hearing is a time-limited function. By starting early, and by practicing our profession efficiently, we can arrange the required conditions for the young hearing-impaired child to use audition as his communication avenue, that is, to become "hard of hearing." We provide the child, and the adult he grows up to be, with an alternative. The obverse is not possible; we cannot ignore a child's residual hearing, require him to depend upon a visual form of communication, and then later, as an adult, give this individual the alternative to become a hard-of-hearing person. This is not to say that being hard of hearing is not a handicap, just that it provides opportunity and options not available to a functionally deaf person.

Taking into consideration the fact that profound differences exist between hard-of-hearing and deaf children, these two types of children must be divided into separate groups, each with its own specialized resources. It is recognized that there are many children who fall into a "gray" area; nevertheless, a conceptual separation is possible. This is not an academic or a bureaucratic exercise. Better management for both groups of children requires an accurate portrayal of their primary handicap. In the last few years, the Bureau of Education for the Handicapped has instituted a number of conferences and workshops designed specifically to deal with the education of hard-of-hearing children. The funding for projects designed to improve their educational management has been increased. Coinciding with and intensifying the increased awareness of their unique needs has been the mandates set forth by Public Law 94-142. For the most part, these children have always been "mainstreamed" in our public schools, the least possible restrictive environment for them. They have not, however, been mainstreamed adequately. They have been called *Our Forgotten Children: Hard of Hearing Pupils in the Schools* in the title of a book published by the University of Minnesota Press, Leadership Training Institute, under funding by the Bureau of Education for the Handicapped.

A major need concerning the optimum management of hard-of-hearing children in school relates to the increased level of competencies required of the professionals who deal with them. The first requirement in the educational management of these children is to ensure that their residual hearing is exploited to the maximum extent possible. Based upon this foundation, other modes of therapeutic intervention would prove much more effective. This volume is intended to provide practitioners in schools and prospective practitioners in training programs with the basic information necessary to manage the auditory and educational needs of the hard-of-hearing child. This volume is an outgrowth of a symposium supported in part by the Bureau of Education for the Handicapped, but it goes beyond the usual symposium format. Each of the contributors is a nationally or internationally recognized figure who spent two days discussing with the other participants the basic issues contained in this volume. The Bureau of Education for the Handicapped is pleased to have been able to play a role in, and to contribute to, the development of this excellent document. Our ultimate goal is to serve children, and we are hopeful that this work will also serve this purpose.

Thomas Behrens

CHAPTER 1

INTRODUCTION

Mark Ross and Thomas G. Giolas

CONTENTS

The current educational trend for hearing-impaired children is placement in a "least restrictive" educational environment, with "mainstreaming" representing the least restrictive of all educational environments. It seems that mainstreaming will be with us for a long time. Professionals working with hearing-impaired children are obliged to help make this experience optimally valuable.

The rationale for placing a child in a regular school is that the total educational and social experience will be more valuable than segregated placement in a special school. This rationale is based on a number of assumptions, an important one being that the child is receiving proper auditory management so that he can make optimum use of the sounds around him. A hearing-impaired child is not being mainstreamed if he simply sits alongside a normal hearing child but does not interact or comprehend what is being said by the teacher or his classmates.

The editors of this book contend that successful mainstreaming of hearing-impaired children is dependent on appropriate auditory management of those children. It is the goal of this book to provide the reader with some basic information as a foundation for solid practicum procedure.

DEFINITION OF TERMS

In that the educational procedures prescribed for a particular child can be greatly influenced by the diagnostic label applied to him (Ross and Calvert, 1967; Wilson, Ross, and Calvert, 1974) it is important to

1

define a few terms used to identify the child with a hearing problem. The terms "hard of hearing," "deaf," or "hearing impaired" are not synonymous, and educational programs designed for one category may not be appropriate for another category. The often interchangeable use of these terms suggests an inadequate understanding of hearing impairment and its implications. We must first define our terms and the child being so labeled before the most appropriate educational program can be planned.

Hearing Impaired

We suggest we use the term "hearing impaired" generically, to refer to any child with any type and degree of hearing loss. Sometimes the term is used with certain qualifier adjectives, such as mild, moderate, severe, or profound, to denote the degree of the impairment. We prefer to use "hearing impaired" to label young children for whom we have, as yet, an inadequate understanding of the degree of hearing loss or auditory functioning.

Deaf

The term "deaf" has a more specific meaning and should be used in a fairly precise manner. Basically, it means that the person has minimal or no hearing. This is an important definition, because much of our thrust in managing the educational needs of hearing-impaired children deals with the exploitation of residual hearing, which most of them possess in differing degrees. It is an apparent contradiction of terms to talk about exploiting residual hearing in a deaf person. The improper application of the descriptive label "deaf" can lead to an educational placement, and therefore achievement and behavioral expectations, consistent with the connotations of the label rather than the potential of the child. In practice, the term "deaf" is used to denote any person whose auditory channel is sufficiently damaged so as to preclude the auditory development and comprehension of speech and language, with or without sound amplification. This does not negate the possible value of amplification for deaf children; it does imply that for them sound is a secondary and supplemental channel to vision.

Hard of Hearing

The book's major concern is with the "hard-of-hearing" child. This child hears and uses sound. Deviant though his speech and language skills may be, they were developed primarily through an auditory base (Dicarlo, 1968). In this respect, he is much more like a normal hearing child than he is like a deaf child. This is opposite to the conception held by many professionals and lay people. The hard-of-hearing child is frequently treated as a high achieving deaf child rather than as a lower (usually) achieving normal hearing child. Many of the educational aberrations he is exposed to follow from this erroneous, limiting, and basically pessimistic conception. Educationally, because he is considered more like than unlike the deaf child, the visual channel is primarily stressed in language and communication development, to the detriment of the overwhelmingly more powerful (for language development and communication) auditory channel. This point of view, which is discussed in more detail below, holds that for the hard-of-hearing child it is necessary first to ensure that the educational situation optimally exploits his residual hearing, and then to employ the visual channel in a secondary, supplemental, and supportive manner. What we are implying here is that for the hard-of-hearing child the effective use of the impaired auditory channel can better serve the child's primary educational needs than a primary dependence on the unimpaired visual channel.

It would not be difficult to criticize these terminologic distinctions. There are children who seem to fall somewhere in the gray area between the categories of deaf and hard of hearing. In our view, ignoring the real distinctions between these categories because of occasional exceptions is an educationally self-defeating exercise. Moreover, it is an exercise that undervalues hearing and helps create more of these "exceptions." We would opt for an optimistic interpretation, viewing these gray area children as potentially hard of hearing, and then take the correct measures to fulfill this prediction. On the other hand, we would not suggest that a deaf child be exposed to frustrating and fruitless efforts to create a hard-of-hearing child, when there is insufficient residual hearing to accomplish this goal. We should not belabor the physiologically impossible. Moreover, although the amount of residual hearing is the most important indicant for separating the hard of hearing from the deaf category, it is not the only one. The age at which the hearing loss is detected, the effectiveness of the early habilitative measures, and the capacity of the child in many nonauditory dimensions are all important influences on the child's ultimate status. There are many hearing-impaired children who are functionally deaf, although they apparently possess ample residual hearing to operate auditorially. This may be true because of delayed or ineffective habilitative measures or because of the deleterious interaction of other handicaps or problems. These children are not helped by prolonged and zealous efforts to make them primarily auditory communicators when the optimum time for this has long since been passed. The recognition of an individual's needs and unique status must transcend any categorical attempt to define or describe him. Categories such as hard of hearing and deaf are guidelines, not specific prescriptions for services or proscriptions of exclusion from certain other services.

The evidence currently available suggests that the physiologic separation between the deaf and hard of hearing categories occurs around the 90- to 95-dB hearing level (HL). A discontinuity in either speech reception or production has been found as the hearing loss exceeds 90–95 dB HL (reported in Stark, 1974). Our own formulation is that this figure is low, that with early and effective auditory management (including early binaural hearing aids, which provide about an extra 6-dB loudness sensation), this presumed physiologic borderline can be increased to the 95- to 100-dB hearing level, averaging across the speech frequencies (500, 1000, and 2000 Hz are considered to be the most important frequencies for the understanding of speech, and thus are termed the "speech frequencies").

It is not, however, only at these high threshold levels in which problems of definition occur. We must also be concerned with the distinctions between the normal and the hard of hearing. How much of a hearing loss is it necessary to have before one can assume hearing-related deviances in some academic and behavioral performance? The answer is not as much as is generally believed. As one observes group data, it is apparent that even a relatively minor hearing loss can produce problems. In a very interesting study, Quigley and Thomure (1968) evaluated the academic performance of children in relation to their degree of hearing loss. At first, they used a traditional formulation and assumed that any child with less than a 26-dB hearing loss in the better ear would demonstrate no resultant academic problems. As they looked at their data, they found that not only were most of their subjects in this category (82.7%) but that they had to further separate this group into two subgroups (14 dB or less and 15–26 dB) in order to analyze their data better. They report that even the group with the least loss showed some academic retardation relative to what would be expected. These results were in part corroborated by studies reported by Ling (1972) and Holm and Kunze (1969), in which relatively minor (15–26 dB) and sometimes fluctuating hearing losses negatively impacted upon language development and academic performance. It is important to note again that what are reported here are group averages. As one observes the performance of individual children with minor hearing losses, it is quite possible that some may display average or above average performance.

Given this qualification, the evidence suggests that a child with a 15-dB hearing loss or more in the speech frequencies in the better ear is at risk regarding the potentially negative impact of a hearing loss on some aspect of his performance.

Audiometric contour also plays an important role. It is quite possible for two children to demonstrate the same average hearing loss, but to display markedly different threshold configurations, with quite different adjustment implications. Thus, a child with a hearing loss of 20 dB at 500, 1000, and 2000 Hz would have an average hearing loss of 20 dB; the child with zero thresholds at 500 and 1000 Hz and a 60-dB threshold at 2000 Hz would also show an average hearing loss of 20 dB. However, the implications regarding speech intelligibility, language and academic performance, and behavioral consistency of these two hearing losses are not at all alike. The high frequency hearing loss has more negative implications.

INCIDENCE OF HEARING LOSS

Keeping in mind that we are making generalizations that must be applied cautiously in specific instances, the hearing level limits that encompass the category "hard of hearing" extend from 15 dB HL at the low end to about 90 or 95 dB HL at the upper end. Conservatively speaking, there are at least 15–30 times more children in the hard of hearing category than in the deaf category. The most frequently cited number of deaf persons is usually 1/1000 population. Actually, this may be high, if one accepts the notion that to be deaf one cannot hear and understand most spoken words, and only school age children are considered (National Center for Health Statistics, Series 10, Number 35). Even if we accept a little flexibility in this figure, we can still observe that being deaf is a relatively rare occurrence in our society. This is not the case with the hard of hearing. The Eagles et al. (1973) study indicates that about 50 school children per 1000 demonstrate hearing levels, in one or both ears, at one or more frequencies beyond the range of normal hearing. Of these children, perhaps one-half have hearing losses of sufficient magnitude and permanency to be at risk regarding the potential impact of the hearing loss upon them. What these statistics suggest is that there are probably several hard-of-hearing children in every school building in the country. Certainly, there are enough of them to warrant more attention than they have heretofore received.

SPECIAL NEEDS OF THE HARD-OF-HEARING CHILD

Psychosocial Description

What does it mean to be hard of hearing? What are the implications of the phenomenon signified by the label? Superficially, the hard-of-hearing child does not look or act very different from the other children in the classroom. He may be a bit of a problem, but so are many of the normal hearing children. He may be withdrawn or aggressive; socially adjusted or maladjusted; performing adequately or inadequately in some or all academic areas; his speech may be perfectly intelligible, grossly unintelligible, or just a bit "different." Rarely does the hard-of-hearing child exhibit specific behavior that is not also found in some of his normal hearing classmates. Even the one invariable characteristic of his condition, that he does not hear very well, does not uniquely mark him. Remember he is not deaf; he can and does respond to environmental sounds, including speech. When he does not respond or, as most often happens, responds incorrectly or inappropriately, his behavior is not necessarily associated with his hard-of-hearing condition. It is dismissed as "not listening," "not paying attention," or "daydreaming." This child is accused of "hearing when he wants to," and deliberately and willfully being provocative by misunderstanding or ignoring the teacher. Professionals (and parents) dealing with him cannot understand how it is possible for a child to comprehend speech in some situations but not in other superficially comparable situations. The effect of language complexity, dialectical or poor speech, distance from the speech source, room acoustics, and competing noises may have a devastating effect upon the hard-of-hearing child's ability to comprehend the spoken message. At the same time, these conditions may minimally or not at all interfere with a normal hearing child's communication. Although he may often be aware of being spoken to, he very often does not understand what was said. Adults assume that he does "understand" because he quite evidently heard. For the same reason, normal hearing children tend to find him an undesirable playmate and neither really quite comprehend why. The resultant, reciprocally reinforcing conflicts between 1) the expectations of the adults and the performance of the child and 2) between the needs of the child and the elusive and blocked gratification of these needs by a hostile, poorly informed or suspicious environment may impact upon him throughout his school life (Reynolds, 1955; Elser, 1959; Steer et al., 1961; Goetzinger, Harrison, and Baer, 1964; Fisher, 1966; Kennedy and Bruininks, 1974; Kennedy et al. 1976).

The pity of it all is that rarely is the "minimal" or "moderate" hearing loss pinpointed as the genesis of the problem; instead, the secondary and overlaid problems are often considered primary. The root of the child's problems is sought in the emotional or neurologic spheres, with the application of esoteric diagnostic labels substituted for diagnostic economy. Some of the labels with which these children have been afflicted include aphasic, central auditory disorder, minimal brain damage, specific language disability, and emotional disorder (Merklein and Briskey, 1962; Rosenberg, 1966; Ross and Matkin, 1967; Kleffner, 1973). It is not that these disorders do not also occur, but that their relevancy can be doubted if a hearing loss exists and its effects are either discounted or unknown.

SPEECH, LANGUAGE, AND ACADEMIC STATUS

The behavioral and psychosocial problems that the hard-of-hearing child manifests have their counterparts in the speech, language, and academic domains as well. Except for the children with the most minimal hearing losses, the probabilities are that the hearing impairment will be responsible for deviancies in speech production and speech perception (Goetzinger, 1962; Goetzinger, Harrison and Baer, 1964; DiCarlo, 1968; West and Weber, 1973; Ollder and Kelly, 1974) with the more severe losses responsible for the more severe problems (Markides, 1970). Some types of hearing impairment may affect just the articulation of certain consonants, leaving voice quality and prosody intact; others may affect both articulation and prosody. Very mild losses may not have an observable effect upon speech or language competencies, but in reference to language one cannot be sure of this until this dimension is explicitly evaluated. Vocabulary and information deficiencies may exist in spite of superficially "normal" receptive and expressive communication skills.

In the language and academic performance areas, hard-of-hearing children invariably score much lower than their normal hearing counterparts. The discouraging aspect of this research is that results reported more than 30 years ago (Caplin, 1937; Pintner and Lev, 1939; Pintner, Eisenson, and Stanton, 1946) mirror those obtained more recently in this and other countries (Young and McConnell, 1957; Steer et al., 1961; Kodman, 1963; Brannon, 1968; Hine, 1970; Davis, 1974; Wilcox and Tobin, 1974; Davis and Blasdell, 1975). There is little merit in this book in reviewing or citing all the studies on this topic, because the same discouraging news is found in them all. Just for illustration, however, the results of a few typical findings will be noted. Kodman (1963) and Quigley and Thomure (1968) both found that elementary school children with moderate losses (from about 40–55 dB) performed on academic achievement tests an average of 3 years behind their normal hearing age peers. Davis (1974) looked at the scores of young hard-of-hearing children on the Boehm Test of Basic Concepts and found that 75% of the hard-of-hearing children scored at, or below, the 10th percentile on this test, with two-thirds of them scoring at the first percentile. In regards to their language performance, it should be noted that scoring the hard-of-hearing children's performance on age-derived norms will probably underestimate their actual problem, because the nature of the language breakdown is not observable in this kind of analysis.

In summary, the hearing-impaired child's language performance, compared to his normal hearing peers, demonstrates an ever increasing gap in vocabulary growth, in ability to express and understand colloquial expressions and verbal nuances, and in comprehension and production of complex sentences. For example, many hard-of-hearing children interpret passive sentences as active, and negative sentences as positive. They are unable to process and comprehend embedded phrases and sentences from a larger utterance, and are completely lost if too many grammatical transformations occur in a single sentence. The casual observer, engaging such a child in social conversation, may not be aware of these problems. They are observable, however, when one considers such a child's performance on standardized tests of language and academic achievements.

THE ROLE OF HEARING

What this sad litany should communicate is that the hard-of-hearing child is handicapped precisely because he has a hearing impairment. We are making this point not to be simplistic or facetious, but as preliminary to the orientation that remediation measures can be most effective only if the significance of the point is fully comprehended. This child demonstrates speech and language problems because it is through the auditory mode that speech and language is normally, and usually effortlessly, developed. Possessing an impaired auditory channel, his consequent development of speech and language is likewise impaired. Furthermore, and an important generalization to consider, is that the problems he exhibits in speech and language production and perception, and academic achievement, are related to the degree of his hearing loss. Hearing is the key; it is the major cause of his handicap and the major avenue through which the handicap can best be minimized or overcome.

Although the speech and language deviations manifested by hard-of-hearing children can be considered a direct consequence of the hearing impairment, not so the problems in academic achievement. The academic lag is secondary to, and reflects, the language deviations and retardations. It is well to note that, for the normal hearing child, reading skills, the foundation academic area, are not visually but auditorially based. Children learn to read by associating the orthographic symbols with known auditory/verbal language competencies. The basic components of their grammar (the phonologic, morphologic, syntactic, and semantic) are already highly developed by the time the children are expected to learn how to read. They do not learn (although they may refine) these grammatical components by reading. Reading is therefore a somewhat parasitic skill based upon hearing, and of clearly secondary importance in regards to language development.

What is primary for the hard-of-hearing child is the full use of his hearing. By our definition of what constitutes a hard-of-hearing child, he needs to hear in order to learn and the better he hears the more he will learn. With this child, we must first ensure that the educational situation maximizes the use of his residual hearing and then proceed to remediate the remaining problems. Instead, what is done is that the child may receive (if he is lucky) a great deal of individual attention in response to his obvious lacks, but often this attention acts as a substitute for appropriate auditory management. The child may very well require this extra assistance, but it should supplement appropriate auditory management and not replace it. Given effective, consistent, and continuing auditory management, we will find that most hard-of-hearing children can be educationally programmed similarly to their normal hearing peers. The consequent need for special education intervention procedures should then be greatly diminished, although not eliminated.

Most educators would recognize the primary role audition plays in learning to read and the consequent impact upon other academic areas, but may argue that this is a moot issue in that "most of our hard-of-hearing children wear hearing aids" and are scheduled for audiologic intervention once a year. As we shall see later, however, this is a gross oversimplification of what constitutes "appropriate" auditory management.

Up to now the hard-of-hearing child has been a bit of an orphan, sometimes belonging to no one, sometimes claimed by everyone. We do not, in our judgment, have to create a new profession in order to best provide for his educational needs. The most important fact for us to consider is that he is not "deaf" and should not be exposed to educational methods that rely primarily upon vision. When we do this, when we treat a severely hard-of-hearing child as if he were deaf, when we fail to open up the auditory channel to the maximum extent, we as educators are then responsible for the functional creation of another "deaf" person. Consider an analogy with vision: if we deprived a child who was moderately visually impaired from birth of glasses, then provided him with a poorly fitting monocle, then with a random choice of refraction, then smeared the glasses with mud while asking him to learn to read small print in very dim light, he would not do very well. As a matter of fact, he very likely would wind up in a special program for the visually impaired and be taught how to read with a braille rather than a visual system. We are somehow certain that this horrendous chain of events never occurs with visually impaired children; it is hoped that it does not. However, its counterpart with hard-of-hearing children happens almost every day in almost every school building in the country.

In summary, we must remain cognizant of the role of audition in primary language development, the fact that most hard-of-hearing children possess adequate residual hearing (by definition), and that we have not exploited these facts in practice, and furthermore, if we do, we can work with and treat most hard-of-hearing children like normal hearing kids rather than something "special."

The primary goal of this book is to discuss the essential concepts necessary to understand the significant role hearing plays in the optimum development of speech and language, educational achievement, and social growth of the hard-of-hearing child. To accomplish this goal a number of well known scientists and educators were each invited to contribute a chapter dealing with an assigned topic relating to the auditory management of the hard-of-hearing child. Each chapter was circulated to all contributing authors before a 2-day conference. The conference discussion provided feedback to each individual author with the object of ensuring that the most pertinent information was included and that the overall mission of the book was met. A number of chapters were modified after the conference.

The conference discussion was transcribed in its entirety. An analysis of the transcript and the chapters revealed that several issues pertinent to the book's mission were not included. Consequently, Chapter 9 entitled "Issues and Exposition" was written after the conference to provide a more complete product. Additionally, a chapter based on the edited transcripts was included in highlight interchanges between participants on specific topics.

A word should be included here about what seems to be some content overlap in several of the chapters. Each time the editors attempted to eliminate the apparent redundancy by excluding coverage of some topics in one or more of the chapters, it became evident that something was lost in the process. It seemed we were not reducing overlap as much as we were eliminating different perspectives on the same topic. For example, Fry, Boothroyd, and Ling all discuss some aspects of the process of speech perception; yet each one, coming from the background of linguistics, physics, and deaf education, respectively, contribute unique insights to a comprehensive view of the process. In all cases of apparent overlap of material we opted to include all material that would present to the reader either different perspectives or insights on a topic.

It is hoped that the net result of this approach has resulted in the compilation of a set of chapters that provide in one volume the salient facts and issues facilitating the mainstreaming of the hard-of-hearing child into the regular classroom. Although the inclusion of practical suggestions and procedures per se is minimal, it is thought that many of these procedures will naturally evolve from a solid grasp of the book's content.

A word or two should be written regarding the intended audience of the book. It is aimed primarily at the practitioners who are confronted daily with the reality of working with a hearing-impaired child. It was felt that the book would have its greatest impact on this reality-based person. The student in training should also find it useful in preparing for a career in working with the hearing impaired, and will want to use it as a reference book as he commences his professional career.

REFERENCES

Brannon, J. B. 1968. Linguistic word classes in the spoken language of normal, hard of hearing, and deaf children. J. Speech Hear. Res. 11:279–287.

Caplin, D. 1937. A special report of retardation of children with impaired hearing in New York City schools. Am. Ann. Deaf 82:234–243.

Davis, J. 1974. Performance of young hearing-impaired children on a test of basic concepts. J. Speech Hear. Res. 17:342–351.

Davis, J., and R. Blasdell. 1975. Perceptual strategies employed by normal-hearing and hearing-impaired children in the comprehension of sentences containing relative clauses. J. Speech Hear. Res. 18:281–295.

DiCarlo, L. M. 1968. Speech, language and cognitive abilities of the hard-of-hearing. Proceedings of the Institute of Aural Rehabilitation, pp. 45–66. SRA Grant #212-T-68, University of Denver.

Eagles, E. L., S. M. Wishik, L. G. Doerfler, W. Melnick, and H. S. Levine. 1973. Hearing sensitivity and related factors in children. (NINDH Grant NB-02375-07) Laryngoscope, June 1973.

Elser, R. P. 1959. The social position of hearing handicapped children in the regular grades. Except. Child. 25:305–309.

Fisher, B. 1966. The social and emotional adjustment of children with impaired hearing attending ordinary classes. Br. J. Educ. Psychol. 35:319–321.

Goetzinger, C. P. 1962. Effects of small perceptive losses on language and speech discrimination. Volta Rev. 64:4808–4814.

Goetzinger, C. P., C. Harrison, and C. N. Baer. 1964. Small perceptive hearing loss: Its effects in school-age children. Volta Rev. 66:124–131.

Hine, W. D. 1970. The attainment of children with partial hearing. Teach. Deaf 68:129–125.

Holm, V. A., and L. H. Kunze. 1969. Effect of chronic otitis media on language and speech development. Pediatrics 43:833–839.

Kennedy, P., and R. H. Bruininks. 1974. Social status of hearing impaired children in regular classrooms. Except. Child. 40:336–342.

Kennedy, P., W. Northcott, R. McCauley, and S. N. Williams. 1976. Longitudinal socio-metric and cross-sectional data on mainstreaming hearing impaired children: Implications for preschool programming. Volta Rev. 78:71–82.

Kleffner, F. R. 1973. Hearing losses, hearing aids, and children with language disorders. J. Speech Hear. Disord. 38:232–239.

Kodman, F. 1963. Educational status of hard of hearing children in the classroom. J. Speech Hear. Disord. 28:297–299.

Ling, D. 1972. Rehabilitation of cases with deafness secondary to otitis media. In A. Glorig and K. W. Gerwin (eds.), Otitis media, pp. 249–253. Charles C Thomas, Publisher, Springfield, Ill.

Markides, A. 1970. The speech of deaf and partially-hearing children with special reference to factors affecting intelligibility. Br. J. Disord. Commun. 5:126–140.

Merklein, R. A., and R. J. Briskey. 1962. Audiometric findings in children referred to a program for language disorders. Volta Rev. 64:294–298.

National Center for Health Statistics, Series 10, No. 35.

Ollder, D. K., and C. A. Kelly. 1974. Phonological substitution processes of a hard of hearing child. J. Speech Hear. Disord. 39:64–74.

Pintner, R., J. Eisenson, and M. Stanton. 1946. The Psychology of the Physically Handicapped. Appleton-Century-Crofts, New York.

Pintner, R. and J. Lev. 1939. The intelligence of the hard of hearing school child. J. Genet. Psychol. 55:31–48.

Quigley, S. P., and R. E. Thomure. 1968. Some effects of a hearing-impairment on school performance. Institute of Research on Exceptional Children, University of Illinois, Urbana.

Reynolds, L. G. 1955. The school adjustment of children with minimal hearing loss. J. Speech Hear. Disord. 20:380–384.

Rosenberg, P. E. 1966. Misdiagnosis of children with auditory problems. J. Speech Hear. Disord. 31:279–283.

Ross, M., and D. R. Calvert. 1967. The semantics of deafness. Volta Rev. 69:644–649.

Ross, M., and N. Matkin. 1967. The rising audiometric configuration. J. Speech Hear. Disord. 32:377–382.

Stark, R. E. (ed.). 1974. Sensory capabilities of hearing impaired children. University Park Press, Baltimore.

Steer, J. D., T. D. Hanley, H. E. Spuehler, N. S. Barnes, K. W. Burk, and W. G. Williams. 1961. The behavioral and academic implications of hearing losses among elementary school children. Project number P.U. 0240, Purdue Research Foundation.

West, J. J., and J. L. Weber. 1973. Phonological analysis of the spontaneous language of a four-year-old, hard-of-hearing child. J. Speech Hear. Disord. 38:25–35.

Wilcox, J., and J. Tobin. 1974. Linguistic performance of hard of hearing and normal children. J. Speech Hear. Res. 286–293.

Wilson, G. B., M. Ross, and D. R. Calvert. 1974. An experimental study of the semantics of deafness. Volta Rev. 76:408–414.

Young, D., and F. McConnell. 1957. Retardation of vocabulary development in hard of hearing children. Except. Child. 23:368–370.

CHAPTER 2

THE ROLE AND PRIMACY OF THE AUDITORY CHANNEL IN SPEECH AND LANGUAGE DEVELOPMENT

Dennis B. Fry

CONTENTS

The child born with a severe loss of hearing or who suffers such a loss before he has acquired his mother tongue presents a most serious educational problem. It is a small wonder that those whose task it is to seek workable solutions to the problem should have ranged far and wide in their exploration of methods designed to enable the hearing-impaired child to progress educationally at a pace comparable with that of his more fortunate hearing fellows. The crux of the difficulty is self-evident: it lies simply in the fact that we have developed the auditory, acoustic method of communication called speech, and early hearing impairment presents an obstacle, although not necessarily an insuperable one, to the acquisition of speech and language. It is conceivable that our history might have been different and that we might have evolved a visual system of signals as our basic means of communication; had this been so, the situation of the child born deaf and the child born blind would have been completely reversed and it would be the latter who would present such grave problems with regard to language acquisition and all the educational processes that depend upon it. As it is, we remain confronted with the task of discovering effective ways of making good the deficit that any considerable hearing loss entails in the sphere of communication.

One thing we can be certain of is that our methods are unlikely to succeed if they transgress the principles that underlie the normal processes of speech and language acquisition. To put it more positively, our best hope of success lies in looking as closely as we can at the stages by which a normal child acquires his native language and using knowledge gained in this way to improve our management of the hearing-impaired child. All too many of the techniques put forward fail to recognize the indispensable conditions for language acquisition or are based on misconceptions of them. All too often the fact is simply overlooked that nature has evolved a miraculously successful routine for developing communication skills in the normal child. The proportion of children who do not learn to talk and to perceive speech is infinitesimally small, so we should digest the fact that we are not going to invent a superior method in a hurry. What we need to do, and what this chapter attempts to do, is to think in a very fundamental way about the conditions necessary for language acquisition. We need to see whether there are respects in which these conditions cannot be met in the case of the hearing-impaired child and to examine what modifications will give such a child the best chance of joining his normal hearing contemporaries in the educational system.

LANGUAGE ACQUISITION:
THE RESULT OF SENSORY EXPERIENCE

The first principle that underlies language acquisition is practically never formulated but is nonetheless the most important of all: the mother tongue cannot be taught, it can only be learned. Every individual child learns the whole language system of his native community for himself and from scratch, and he does so by abstracting the information he needs from the mass of sensory inputs relevant to language by which he is surrounded. In all ordinary circumstances the sensory channel is the auditory one and the sounds are the sounds of speech, but the principle is independent of the sensory mode. Any child will learn his first language only if he is continuously exposed to the relevant sensory inputs; a normal hearing child will not learn through speech if he is not constantly in situations where the sounds of speech reach his ears and where they are clearly linked with the context of ordinary life. If the medium for language acquisition were the visual mode, then language stimuli would have to reach his eyes in an unending stream just as speech sounds reach the ears.

MOTIVATION

The most vital qualification of these sensory inputs, and as we are for the moment concerned with the normal child we will talk in terms of speech sounds, is that they are relevant to language and to life. It is this property alone that supplies the motivation for a child to acquire language at all. This is another question that does not get the attention it deserves when the management of the hearing-impaired child is under consideration. Why should any child learn to talk and to understand speech? The baby begins his life in an environment where he is completely passive, where food, warmth, comfort and, incidentally, discomfort arrive without any action on his part. However, at a very early stage he begins to notice the features of the world around him; these include the phenomenon of speech. It becomes clear to him quite soon that the strings of noises issuing from the mouths of the adults around him are in some strange way a powerful force that influences what happens in his small world; as a matter of fact, there is comparatively little that does happen without this apparently magical activity. Food and drink appear and they disappear, clothes are put on and taken off, a whole range of sensations, some pleasant and some not so pleasant, are provided for the child to the accompaniment of speech sounds. It is not surprising that the baby develops a strong urge to qualify himself for admission to what is very obviously a powerful club, that of *Homo loquens*. Social pressures of this kind supply the motivation for learning one's native language. Where they are absent, language acquisition will not take place. In the various reported cases of "wild boys" who have been deprived of an ordinary environment, it is not only the absence of the sensory input but also the lack of any pressure to interact in a communicative way that keeps them speechless. Again, in some cases of autism in children, the inhibition of all contact with the human environment is so strong as to cancel out the social pressure, and language is not acquired.

The motivation for language acquisition is ordinarily generated through the auditory channel. Spoken language is seen to work, or its effects are experienced in some other way, for the blind child encounters no difficulty in developing language. The essential factors are the auditory input and its relation to the events of real life. Is it impossible then that there should be any substitute for the auditory input? The answer is that a substitute in any sensory mode will work provided that the necessary conditions are met. A visual input will furnish the motivation for language acquisition if it is continuously available to the child in contexts in which it is firmly linked to happenings that concern him personally and if there is very little in his everyday life that proceeds without the accompaniment of the visible language signals. If these requirements are not fulfilled, we cannot expect successful language acquisition; we shall achieve at best a poor substitute for real language capacity. Where they are fulfilled, as for example in some communities of deaf people, there will be language acquisition through the visual sense. The usefulness of the language so acquired, like that of any language, is limited to communities where the language is current.

The motivation we are discussing is not simply that required to start the baby off on the process of language acquisition; it has to be maintained throughout the process, that is, until the child has mastered the whole framework of his mother tongue, which is achieved by the ordinary child when he is about 5 or 6 years old. In a later section, the stages by which this end is attained are outlined briefly, and it is clear that the auditory input is an essential component in all of them. The child's experience during the early stages of language acquisition is closely linked with his parents, particularly his mother, and if the situation is such that the parents are unable to supply the auditory input, this is bound to interfere with language acquisition. The relative importance of parents and other adults changes considerably at later stages of language learning, and it is a statistical fact that a child ordinarily encounters many more adults who can provide auditory speech input for him than can provide an alternative language input.

This is an appropriate point at which to consider the question of a "critical" period for the acquisition of language and the development of speech. The child's capacity for developing new forms and new patterns of behavior during the first few years of life is dependent upon maturation in the nervous system and on myelination of the neural tracts involved. While these processes are going on there is a special facility for acquiring new behavior. Language and speech require not only this maturation but also as we have seen, the continuous supply of external stimuli so that learning and maturation are blended together. There is no doubt at all that the greatest success in language acquisition and speech development is achieved if the sensory inputs are available and the motor practice is carried out during the normal period of development, from the age of about 6 months to 6 years. For the hearing-impaired child, it is of the utmost importance that his condition should be diagnosed early so that the special treatment and management can be begun that will give the best chance of normal or near normal language development. The longer this is delayed, the slower progress is likely to be and the less satisfactory the result.

It is not the case, however, that if this early period is missed altogether the development of language and speech through the use of the auditory channel becomes impossible; very many individual cases have been recorded that indicate the contrary. Not only children of 5 or 7 years of age, but young people in their teens or twenties have learned to use their hearing for language purposes when given enough auditory training and practice of the right kind. The major obstacle to progress in such cases of a late start is largely a social one: a child of 3 without speech who is diagnosed as deaf may well revert to the stage of babbling when provided with hearing aids without seeming to be particularly abnormal. He can for some years continue to pass nearly all his time in his mother's company and so gain experience of the speech of a single speaker before he is faced with a wider circle. However, these conditions are denied to the older person; he is likely to have to interact with a variety of speakers instead of just one. It will not be so easy for him to go through the stages of using single word utterances, then two-word utterances and so on, which would constitute the normal procedure for a younger child. Thus, in the matter of language and speech, the biologically favorable period for development coincides with the socially favorable period. The auditory channel is infinitely better adapted than any possible substitute to take full advantage of this favorable period.

RECEPTION PRECEDES PRODUCTION

The importance of the sensory input for language acquisition becomes even more evident through its relevance to the next basic principle: in the process of language learning, reception always precedes production. Whatever the child is learning in language and at whatever stage, he learns to recognize and identify given language elements before he can use them in his own speech productions. This is a fundamental fact about language acquisition that has to be digested if the process is to be understood; it is a logical and a practical necessity that arises out of the very nature of language functioning.

Any language provides primarily a set of symbols that represent objects, persons, and events in the world external to the language user. The beginning of language acquisition depends first of all upon the child's noticing differences between objects and people, and then upon his perceiving differences in the way they are symbolized. His only basis for this lies in the signals sent to him by other people; he must begin by hearing differences in the sounds, or seeing differences in the signs associated with differences in the external world. Every individual builds up the system of his native language for himself. He does so by detecting differences in the auditory or visual signals that reach him, and by establishing the relations between these signals and the events they stand for. Only when a particular distinction has been noted in reception can a child make use of the knowledge in controlling the signals he himself produces. This order is never reversed and it characterizes all the stages of language acquisition and development.

One consequence is that there is a marked time lag between a child's learning to recognize a given linguistic distinction and his implementing this distinction in his own speech. Nearly all mothers notice this time lag, which they frequently comment upon by saying that their baby understands everything that is said to him; this remark means that the child is capable of making a wide range of distinctions when receiving speech, although he himself can say only a few words. The time lag is illustrated in two cases cited by Illingworth (1963): the first, a child of 15 months who could say only four or five words but could readily point out 200 common objects in picture books in response to questions such as "Where is the drum?" The second was a child of $2\frac{1}{2}$ years who could say only four or five different words but who 3 weeks later was speaking freely in sentences of five words.

There is an understandable tendency for parents and teachers to be much more interested in the variety of utterances a child can produce at any stage than in the amount of speech he can take in, and it is not uncommon for those professionally concerned with language acquisition to believe that the former are a true measure of the child's language development. In fact, the extent of the language elements and structures that a child can recognize gives a much better picture of his progress in language and this will always exceed the range of what he himself is able to say at the same point in time.

The relation between reception and production is discussed in a later section; the point made here is simply that of the priority in time of reception. Successful language development requires that production of language signals follow reception and there is inevitably interaction between the two processes in the individual learner.

NATURE OF SPEECH RECOGNITION

Before discussing the functioning of speech sound recognition in the linguistic system it is necessary to consider in a general way what is implicit in the recognition or identification of a sound. In everyday life we are constantly dealing with things that are familiar, with things and with people that we have seen before and that we have heard before; recognition seems to be a matter of sensations that recur. This is only half the story, however, for it is only in laboratory conditions that we can ensure that our sensory apparatus receives the same input on successive occasions. Extreme measures have to be taken to cause the same pattern of light and color to fall on the retina, the same acoustic wave form to reach the eardrum repeatedly. In ordinary life there are always changes in what we see and what we hear when we recognize the "same" sight or sound, so that recognition involves not only experiencing similar sensations in some degree but also the disregarding of many actual differences in the sensory information that is coming in. In order that we should recognize an acquaintance, the brain has stored a pattern of criteria that are applicable to the particular person: height, build, gait, hair color, style of dress, and so on. If the fresh visual impressions show enough similarities to meet these criteria, we recognize the person; if not, we fail to do so, or we experience a delay in recognition. By the use of this technique we are able to give differential weight to the various features of a scene, and thus to disregard many real changes that take place in the visual input in favor of features that do recur with the "same" person or object.

The reliance upon features or cues is very much greater in the recognition of speech sounds than in the case of visual inputs or of other kinds of sound. This is because the variability of speech sounds far exceeds that of any type of sensory input about which judgments of sameness or difference have to be made. The functioning of the whole linguistic system, at all levels, rests upon decisions as to the sameness or difference of incoming speech sounds but in the case of speech, the decision that two language elements are the same entails disregarding the myriad acoustic variations introduced by changes of speaker, acoustic environment, voice quality, intensity, fundamental frequency, and duration. In order that the English language system should function, for instance, listeners must decide that the word *short* is the same word every time it is uttered, no matter whether by man, woman, or child, in a high level of noise or in comparative quiet, in fast or slow tempo, in tones of anger or approbation, with rising, falling, or level intonation, in the accents of the east or the west, the north or the south, of Britain or Australia, of Canada or Central Europe, by individual X or individual Y, and so on. Furthermore, listeners must decide, over the same range of possible variation, that *sort* is a different word from *short* and all these decisions must be made with a high degree of reliability. For such decision-making routines the only possible basis is acoustic cues, that is, specific acoustic features of speech sounds that can be noted by the individual listener despite the presence of a mass of additional acoustic information. These features tend to recur with the same sound in the speech of different speakers and in different conditions and can be used diagnostically by the individual listener to identify and to distinguish between the sounds in a given language system. The totality of acoustic information we receive when a spoken message comes in is far in excess of what is needed for the linguistic decisions; if we paid equal attention to all of it, we would probably fail in our linguistic decoding of the message. This is not to say that everything except the cue information is lost, but simply that we use different types of acoustic information for different purposes. We can and do, for example, recognize a familiar voice no matter what words and sentences it may be saying. Here we are abstracting another kind of information in order to decide that this is the same voice. We perceive that a speaker in making a particular remark is irritated or exhilarated, while also recognizing perfectly readily what the remark is, much in the same way as, when an orchestra is playing, we may register that a given musical phrase has been correctly played by the clarinet and also register either like or dislike for the tone in which it was played. The acoustic cues that are used for language purposes occupy a special place only because they have to function in the face of far greater variability than any other kind of cue.

ACOUSTIC CUES IN SPEECH

The major part of the research that has been carried out on acoustic cues refers to their functioning in the English language system. The published reports are far too numerous and extensive for any attempt to be made here to review them (see Fry, 1976), but it is necessary for the present purpose to give a brief account of the types of acoustic feature that may serve as cues in speech reception. Their function is to enable the listener to decide that what he has heard is the first sound of *sort* and not of *short*, of *boat* and not of *coat*, of *chop* and not *shop*, or the last sound of *win* and not *wing*, of *cab* and not *cap*, and so on. Because the cues have to operate regardless of great variability, a primary requirement is that an acoustic cue should refer to relations between sounds and not to any absolute value. A very gross example will make this clear. Suppose, for the sake of argument, that the pitch of some sound were to act as a cue: the cue must be effective for the speech of men, women, and children alike and although there is some overlap of the pitch ranges of men and women, and also of women and children, it would not be possible to find any point on an absolute scale of pitch that would be available to all three classes of speakers. Such a cue would therefore have to depend on a pitch relation, of the form that sound A is lower than sound B, regardless of the location of this difference on an absolute scale and regardless too of the exact size of this pitch difference. Whatever acoustic cues we find operative in speech reception, they will all have this relational character.

Acoustic cues may be classed very broadly as being time cues, frequency cues, or intensity cues. For example, in the continuous stream of speech sound there are times when the vocal cord mechanism is vibrating and producing the sound of voice, and times when this mechanism is switched off. The moments in time when this switching takes place afford a very powerful cue for differentiating between sounds. While the vocal cords are vibrating, the sound issuing from the mouth is periodic; at other times it is aperiodic. In the word *cab*, the change from periodic to aperiodic sound will tend to take place later than in the word *cap*. Notice that it is not a matter of switching so many milliseconds after the word begins; this obviously would not work because the absolute time difference would vary in fast and slow speech: the cue depends on a time relation. Again, the fricative noise that begins the word *shop* is of relatively longer duration than that in *chop*, that is, longer in relation to the whole word or the whole utterance.

Frequency cues form the largest class and are somewhat varied in character. Most frequency cues are a consequence of the fact that the resonances of the vocal tract are varying continuously during speech so that as time passes different frequency bands rise and fall in prominence. This is most easily exemplified by the cues for vowel distinctions; in a word like *seesaw*, during the vowel of the first syllable the two major resonances of the vocal tract, formants 1 and 2, will be widely separated on the frequency scale; during the second vowel, formants 1 and 2 will be much closer together in frequency, with formant 2 having dropped considerably. It is the frequency relations that form the cue because the formant values in cycles per second and the distance between the formants will vary from speaker to speaker.

Rather rapid frequency shifts in the resonances of the vocal tract, and hence in formant frequency, are occasioned by the comparatively swift movements of the articulators, particularly the tongue. These formant transitions provide another class of powerful acoustic cues. The articulation of the first sound in *boat*, for example, causes a rapid rise in frequency in the second formant, a minus F2 transition, whereas that in *coat* involves a rapid fall in frequency, a plus F2 transition.

A frequency cue of a slightly different kind may be used in differentiating the two words *sort* and *short*. In the first word, the fricative noise is restricted to a fairly narrow frequency band in the highest part of the speech range; in the second, the fricative noise spreads over a much wider band stretching down to something in the region of 2000 Hz. Because both sounds last an appreciable time, even in rapid speech, the difference can be registered by listeners as a difference in pitch: *s* is relatively high pitched and *sh* relatively low pitched.

If we contrast another pair of fricative noises, in the words *thought* and *sought*, for example, we find another opportunity for the use of a frequency cue because *th* is likely to contain noise energy in a band even higher than *s*, but the major cue here would undoubtedly be an intensity cue; *th* is of much lower intensity than *s*, a difference that is more readily noted by a listener than the frequency difference.

All the examples given so far have been of phonemic distinctions. Acoustic cues are equally necessary for the recognition of differences in intonation and rhythm that form an important part of the language system. Intonation and rhythm are very much interlocking components in the system and the relevant cues can scarcely be thought of as independent, but intonation differences are cued mainly by the variations in vocal cord frequency, that is, in the fundamental frequency pattern of the periodic stretches of speech sound. Distinctions between a statement and a question, a request and a command, depend principally on the direction and the extent of these frequency variations. Rhythmic patterns are also cued partly by fundamental frequency, but depend very much on the cues of duration and intensity as well. The distinction between "*I* do" and "I *do*" is carried for the listener by shifts in fundamental frequency, duration, and intensity from the first to the second syllable.

These examples do no more than illustrate the kind of acoustic feature that a listener is likely to pay attention to when he is perceiving the sounds of English. We shall see later on that in the actual processes of decision making he is usually not obliged to rely on a single cue for any decision; there are always a number of cues at his disposal and he may use a combination or all of them as the situation demands.

DEVELOPMENT OF A CUE SYSTEM

It will be clear that the use of acoustic cues in the reception of speech is not the work of the ear mechanism, but of the brain, which has learned to process the information fed to it by the ear so as to deal effectively with speech inputs. In the simplest terms this means to know what word has been said, but the listener can achieve this only by operating with the complete phonologic system of the language: in English the 43 phonemes, the half-dozen functional intonation patterns, and the two variants of stress. The function of acoustic cues is to put the listener in a position in which he can distinguish unfailingly among all these language units, that is to decode incoming messages and reach the right solution. It cannot be too strongly stressed that every individual evolves methods for doing this by himself; no one teaches him how to do it, no one can teach him how to do it. When he learns, he does so through the reception of speech first; we discuss later the interaction of speech reception and speech production. The process of language acquisition is clearly a process of development and we now look briefly at some of the important stages in this development.

We said earlier that the child learns his mother tongue because of social pressures that oblige him to link the experience and the events of the world around him with their linguistic formulation. In the early stages the baby learns to recognize a word because the person or thing that it stands for has become of interest to him. As more words are added, his only possible method of keeping them distinct is to pay attention to the sound differences that are in fact the basis of the phonemic system. By the time the child is about 5 years old, he will be operating in speech reception with the complete adult phonemic system. It is essential to realize that this system has been built up gradually, step by step; it is in the nature of phonologic systems that they cannot evolve and cannot be acquired in any other way.

The phonemes of a language are a set of sound classes used to differentiate words from each other; the functioning of any one class, for instance, the *s* phoneme in English, is entirely dependent upon the existence of the other classes in the system, on the fact that the word *sin* must be recognized as different from *shin* and also from *thin, fin, tin,* and so on. The acoustic cues that an individual listener evolves for himself are determined entirely by the range of these oppositions that his native language demands. An English listener must discover cues to distinguish *sin* from *shin*, otherwise his phonemic system will not work. The Spanish language system, on the other hand, does not make use of this particular opposition of *s* and *sh*, consequently the Spanish speaker does not evolve an acoustic cue for the distinction and indeed remains incapable of hearing the difference between the two sounds unless he receives a great deal of training in some foreign language such as English. The complete phonemic system in Spanish comprises some 25 phonemes compared with over 40 in English; the Spanish listener therefore forges for himself a cue system that is enough to take care of all these units but no more.

The English child is operating with the adult system of over 40 phonemes by the time he is about 5 or 6 years old, but during the learning period he is working with a gradually expanding system, beginning with very few phonemic units and gradually adding to them. The important point is that at each succeeding stage the phoneme system works as a whole and the child will have developed only the acoustic cues that are called for. At a very early stage suppose that he recognizes only two words, *mama* and *dada*; he now has a complete phoneme system of only three units: the vowel plus *m* and *d*. The vowel is readily identified as the loud stretches of the utterances but because the child does not confuse one word with the other, he must have an adequate acoustic cue for differentiating *m* and *d*. In *dada* the consonant makes an interruption in the flow of sound whereas *m* does not and this difference would be perfectly effective as an acoustic cue in this small system of three phonemes. Perhaps a grandmother is the next person to take on a particular interest for the baby and let us say she is referred to as *nana*. To recognize this new word consistently, that is, to expand his system to four phonemes, the child must evolve a fresh acoustic cue because the *n* is like the *m* in providing continuous sound. Research with very young infants has shown that the ability to distinguish sounds on the basis of a difference in formant transition is present very early (Eimas et al., 1971), and it is therefore likely that the child develops the use of the second formant transition cue to differentiate *n* and *m*. Simply in order to illustrate the principle that is at work, we will assume that a second grandparent is referred to as *baba* and that this is the next word added to the baby's vocabulary, increasing the complete phoneme system to five units. The question is whether the child now has to discover an additional cue in view of the fact that *b* is an interrupting sound like *d*. In fact he will not need to do so because the formant transition cue that has been found to differentiate *m* and *n* will work equally well for the distinction between *b* and *d*.

This shows us something of the economy of phonemic systems generally; an inventory comprising a considerable number of phonemes is generated by the crossing of a relatively small number of dimensions of differentiation. Sometimes a new word recognized does call for an entirely new cue and often this cue splits an existing class, as the formant transition cues split the class of continuous sounds; at other points in the development of the system existing cues can operate adequately on a fresh distinction, as in the case of *b* and *d*. The subset of phonemes formed by the fricative sounds in English offers a good example of the kind of progression that takes place. The first word containing such a sound that is recognized entails the finding of a new acoustic cue; if the word were *shoe*, for instance, the initial sound would probably be registered as a long-lasting but undifferentiated noise. At later stages other fricatives have to be recognized and then the class of undifferentiated noises must be split up with the aid of additional cues: *sh* will differ from *f* because it is very strong (high intensity) whereas the latter is weak (low intensity); when *s* enters the system, it also is strong but it is high pitched where *sh* is low pitched; *th* is weak like *f* and is also high pitched like *f*, so the distinction here is likely to depend once more on a formant transition cue. In the few short years from birth to about 5 years of age, the child's brain evolves for itself all the acoustic cues required to operate the complete adult phonologic system, only in the reception of speech, however, for speech production necessarily lags somewhat behind.

One of the principles that is the most difficult to grasp, and one of the most vital from the point of view of the use of residual hearing by the hearing impaired, is that any individual learner is quite free to employ any acoustic cues he likes provided they do the job of differentiating sounds in accordance with the phonemic system. The only requirement is that when speech comes in, his brain should make the right decisions and reach the right solutions. As long as it does this, it does not matter what acoustic cues are put to use. Research work on speech recognition in the last decades has made it clear that there is a strong tendency for normal hearing language users to use the same cues for certain phonemic distinctions; however, the same work has also shown that among such language users there are some who do not use a given cue for a particular distinction. They operate in a perfectly normal way with the phonemic system and decode speech like everybody else but they happen to have evolved a different acoustic cue for the purpose, or to be applying cues in a different way. To take one example, most English listeners use the different pitch of the friction noise to differentiate *s* from *sh*; the two sounds involve, however, a difference in second formant transition and each of them can be identified by registering first the high intensity noise and then the transition, rather than the difference in pitch. There was strong evidence for the use of this alternative in the case of one hearing-impaired girl who not only identified the sounds consistently but also pronounced them perfectly. When tested with synthetic speech containing friction noises differing in frequency band but with no formant transitions, she answered randomly and was incapable of assigning the noises to the *s* and *sh* categories. In another test based on second formant transitions (not with fricatives), her responses were almost up to the level of a normal hearing person, suggesting very strongly that this was her cue for dealing with *s* and *sh* (Fry, 1975).

This matter of the freedom of the individual brain to develop its own cue system is so vital to an understanding of the use of residual hearing that it is worthwhile to draw the parallel of the color-blind person. In extreme cases of this condition, the subject perceives the whole visual world in monochrome, and even in less serious cases there are ranges of color over which the subject perceives no differences of hue and can discriminate objects and shapes only on the basis of their monochromatic tone values. Yet such people navigate the visual world with the same ease as those with normal color vision; they are not continually bumping into things or knocking them over. They are no more likely than the next person to be killed at traffic intersections and in fact it is only in very exceptional contexts that their abnormality is revealed. Many of the visual cues available to normal people are simply not available to them so they must clearly have evolved for themselves other cues, which work equally well.

In many respects the recognition of speech sounds is not comparable with visual recognition, nor is the situation of the hearing-impaired very similar to that of the color-blind person. We should have to add the factor of reduced visual acuity to the distortion caused by color blindness in order to approximate the conditions in any realistic way. Nonetheless the most essential component is common to the two conditions, namely the capacity of the brain for shaping its processing of incoming signals in accordance with the demands of the external world. A hearing loss undoubtedly means a distortion of the acoustic input of speech and a reduction in the amount of acoustic information that this input supplies, but it does not mean that acoustic cues cannot be found for operating the phonemic system. There are thousands of hearing-impaired people who demonstrate the truth of this. What is important is not so much the degree of hearing loss as the amount of speech that the child hears. Speech for the hearing-impaired child must be brought up to a usable level of loudness but provided this is done, the effectiveness with which the phonologic system of the language is developed and used will be a function of the child's exposure to real speech inputs, that is, speech linked with the events and interests of everyday life.

INTERACTION OF SPEECH RECEPTION AND PRODUCTION

The phonologic system, which includes all the functional intonation and rhythmic patterns as well as the inventory of phonemes, is established in the first place through the reception and recognition of speech. It is indeed possible for the system to function fully without the production of speech at all, as happens in some cases of severe neurologic deficit where the subject remains throughout life incapable of producing the sounds of speech. Normally, attempts to produce speech follow very soon upon the beginnings of the phonemic system and they are again the fruit of the social pressures upon the child. Naturally he wants to wield the power of speech and he can do this only by speaking himself. His first word is amply rewarded by the approval and attention of his mother and other adults and it is not long before his speech productions are reinforced by getting what he wants or at least evoking a verbal response. To benefit to the full from this situation his speech must be readily decoded by more and more people. There is always the period during which the mother acts as interpreter between the baby and the world, but this arrangement places a severe limitation on his sphere of influence. There is continual pressure on the child to shape his pronunciation so as to bring it more and more in line with that of adults. That he is able to do so is just one more result of his use of acoustic cues.

The baby's attempts at speech are efforts to make active use of the words he has learned to recognize, but he can produce different words only by implementing phonemic differences. As we have said, throughout language acquisition production lags behind reception; this means quite literally that at the moment when he has expanded his phonemic system to, for example, 10 units, his own speech may embody no more than six. Speech movements, whether in the child or the adult, are under the control of auditory feedback, that is, we govern our articulations by reference to what we hear of our own speech. We do this by applying the acoustic cues that we have evolved for speech reception to the monitoring of our own movements. During the learning period, the child is trying to reproduce the sound patterns that he receives from adult speakers, primarily from his mother. The match can never be very exact, however, because his larynx and vocal tract have different dimensions and, most important of all, the bone-conducted feedback he gets from his own speech has a very different characteristic from the air-borne signal coming from other speakers. What he must do therefore is to shape his own articulations so that the acoustic cues that he uses in recognition are appropriately reproduced in his own productions; if he does this successfully, his speech will be readily decodable by others. It takes considerable practice and hence time for this process of adaptation to take place, and this is why the number of phonemic distinctions embodied in the child's speech productions is always less than he uses in speech reception. This time lag persists throughout the period of language acquisition. The normal child will have the phonemic system complete by the time he is 5 or 6 years old, but it may be some considerable time, even years, before he can implement all the distinctions in the adult manner. In fact some speakers go through life without having really mastered some articulatory differences, usually in *r* and *s* sounds.

The time lag between recognition and production may be exemplified by the class of fricative sounds referred to earlier. At the moment when a child first recognizes a word containing a friction noise, his own speech will probably consist entirely of vowels, stops, and nasals. He will then learn to produce just a single undifferentiated friction noise but by this time his receptive system may include both a strong and a weak fricative sound, as in *sock* and *foot*; he *pronounces* both of these with the same sound. With practice he succeeds in producing both a strong and a weak fricative, but has already advanced to the stage of recognizing the difference between a high pitched and a low pitched strong fricative as in *sock* and *shoe*, which are, however, pronounced with the same strong fricative. At succeeding stages he will be able to produce different sounds for *s* and *sh*, then to recognize the *f* and *th* distinction, and finally to articulate all four members of the fricative class adequately.

During such a sequence of developments it is often possible to demonstrate that reception is in advance of production by deliberately presenting the child with a wrong form. For instance, at the period when he is able to discriminate between *s* and *sh*, but pronounces them the same, if you say to him "Where's the *fis*?", he will protest and reject this form time and time again until you correct it to "Where's the *fish*?", showing that he is perfectly able to recognize the difference although he cannot produce it as yet.

It must be emphasized, however, that there is a strong interaction between reception and production throughout the process of language acquisition and particularly during the time when the phonemic system of the mother tongue is being built up. The ability to pronounce a particular sound difference, which has already been recognized, goes a long way toward confirming and stabilizing the operation of this distinction in the child's language system. One direction in which the interaction is very important is in fixing the distribution of sounds in the language. For example, a child may learn to recognize the difference between the initial sounds of *chain* and *train*, but there will then be a long lag before he is able to produce this difference successfully. When he does so, he will go through another stage of discovering which words require the one sound and which the other. He may, for instance, say *treeks* for *cheeks* or *satrel* for *satchel* while he is establishing through his own speech productions the appropriate distribution of the two sounds.

SPEECH PRODUCTION IN THE HEARING-IMPAIRED CHILD

The interaction between speech reception and speech production is thus a very important factor in stabilizing the working of the phonologic system, and we may ask whether the same mechanisms can possibly operate in the case of the hearing-impaired child. Here, as with the reception of speech, it is exposure to speech sounds that is the vital factor and it cannot be repeated too often that if a child hears speech loud enough and often enough, he will develop to a remarkable degree the speech and language skills exercised by the normal child. It is perhaps understandable that those who have little direct experience of this fact are sometimes prepared to accept that the hearing-impaired child may learn to take in speech but are quite incapable of understanding or indeed believing that such a child can produce intelligible speech. They tend to say in effect that they are being asked to believe that a child can produce speech sounds that he cannot hear. The situation is admittedly a complex one, and in order to clear up this misconception it may be helpful to review again the steps that lead to the production of acceptable speech.

We will assume that our hearing-impaired child has been provided from an early age with suitable hearing aids, amplifiers that make the major part of the speech going on around him easily audible. We know that the speech signals he is getting are distorted in comparison with those transduced by the normal ear, but the important thing is that they should provide an input great enough for the brain to work on. The child will now proceed in the same way as the normal child: he will be interested in his surroundings and will pick out words that he will learn to recognize. To do this he must evolve his own acoustic cues and these are quite likely to differ from those found by the normal hearing child, but this has no importance because the cues work and enable him to differentiate sounds that the phonemic system keeps distinct. With his own cues he begins to build the system and quite soon he starts to produce speech himself. It is this step that is particularly hard to visualize. Like the rest of us he will control his own pronunciation on the basis of what he hears. He will strive to produce in the course of his own speech sounds precisely those acoustic cues that he uses when recognizing the sounds made by other people. We need to remember that his speech is subject to basically the same distortion in his ears as other people's speech. When he pronounces a sound in which the cues are a good match with the cues he hears in that sound coming from others, because of the physical properties of the speech mechanism, he is very likely to be producing a sound that is a good match overall. To take the particularly complex example of the English fricatives *s* and *sh*, the hearing-impaired child who has a severe high frequency loss will not be receiving the level of noise, particularly in the higher frequency bands, that most of us depend on for recognizing and producing the difference between these sounds. However, both of them contain noise energy spread over quite a wide range and given adequate amplification the child will perceive that noise is present. For purposes of recognition he may use the second formant transition cue and when he pronounces the sounds himself, he will reproduce this cue, making for *s* a strong noise with one transition pattern and for *sh* a strong noise with another transition. These transitions will only be the right ones when he makes the noise with a further forward, narrower air passage for *s* and a further back, wider air passage for *sh*; in other words he will make a higher frequency noise for *s* and a lower frequency noise for *sh*. This seems to be the technique actually used by the girl referred to earlier who, despite a threshold loss of 60 dB and greater for frequencies from 1000 Hz upward, produces the sounds *s* and *sh* in a manner that is indistinguishable from normal. Not all hearing-impaired speakers can achieve this degree of success and it is generally noticeable that the noises they employ for these sounds are lower pitched than the normal speaker's, but the important thing is that they can produce two different sounds with the aid of their own cue system.

This method works for the complete phonemic system and during the learning period the hearing-impaired child, like the normal child, is shaping his own pronunciations in order to make a better and better match with incoming sounds. The normal hearing child goes through the stage when *w* and *r* are represented by just one sound, or where one noise is used for any fricative that turns up. These things change as the child extends his cue system and applies new cues to his own speech. The same process can go on in the hearing-impaired child, provided he hears enough speech and has the chance of developing his processing techniques in speech reception.

IMPORTANCE OF BABBLING FOR SPEECH PRODUCTION

One vital factor in the development of speech production that remains to be mentioned is babbling. From the age of about 6 months a baby will indulge in the obviously pleasurable occupation of babbling, sending out streams of sounds and noises, most of them the result of repetitive articulatory patterns. Periods of babbling generally occur when the child is alone and the activity starts spontaneously.

Babbling is undoubtedly a preparation for the motor side of speech; the baby is in fact exploring the possibilities inherent in the speech mechanism and practicing a wide range of articulations. By far the most important function of the activity is the establishing in the brain of circuits that link together auditory and kinesthetic feedback. The high degree of muscular coordination and the fine control that we exercise in speaking are possible because we both hear and feel ourselves speak. The speech centers of the brain develop the capacity for combining these feedbacks during the learning period and it is through babbling that the necessary links are set up. The baby who lies babbling is learning that if he repeats a certain movement over and over again, he will hear the same sound repeated; conversely, if he wants to hear a sound repeated, then he has to repeat the same movement. In this way the control mechanism is set up that is vital to the motor activity of speech; without it the interaction between reception and production and the shaping of articulation in accordance with the requirements of the phonologic system would not be possible.

Language acquisition, like other developments in the young child, proceeds by stages but in the individual child the stages are not marked off from each other in time; one type of activity does not cease at the moment when another begins. This is particularly true of babbling, which persists for some considerable time and overlaps with the next stage of development. This is no doubt the reason why many people find it hard to appreciate that of itself babbling is a prelinguistic activity; it precedes the learning of the mother tongue. The evidence on this point is extensive and reliable and has been summarized in a number of publications (see, for example, McNeill, 1970, pp. 130–133). The movements a child makes and the sounds he produces during babbling are not tied to a specific language system; the articulatory practice he is indulging in is of a much more general kind and he will make a number of sounds that do not figure in the system of his native language. The most convincing demonstration of the discontinuity between babbling activity and language development is the fact that during babbling a child will successfully articulate a range of sounds that will be needed in the system of his mother tongue but at a later stage. When these sounds are required to fulfill a function in the phonologic system, he will have lost the capacity to produce them and it will cost him a great deal of learning and practice to reacquire it.

Thus babbling is a spontaneous, preparatory activity, which is independent of the language system and is in no sense the fruit of imitation of adult speakers. Some time after the babbling period has begun, however, the child reaches a stage when the sound of adult speech will act as a trigger to start the babbling activity. This is an important moment because it is the first sign that the baby is getting to the point of beginning work on the language system. The sounds of speech coming from outside himself has impinged upon the child, and although his babbling remains unchanged, a link has been forged between it and the language-based speech of those around him.

It has frequently been noted that babies with hearing impairment enter the babbling stage in the normal way and their babbling is not perceptibly different from that of hearing babies (Lenneberg, Rebelsky, and Nichols, 1965; Lenneberg, 1966). What is reported almost equally often is that after the lapse of some time the babbling fades. This is usually at about the time when the trigger action of incoming speech begins to take effect. Because the sound of adult speech is not loud enough to the child to start him babbling, this motor activity ceases before the control mechanism in the brain has been established. A contributory factor is that this stage is often reached just about the time when the baby begins to crawl and to increase the normal distance between himself and his mother. While he is in her arms or on her lap, her speech may be loud enough to affect him but when he crawls away, the distance interposed brings the sound of the mother's speech below his threshold. For this reason alone, therefore, the early diagnosis of a hearing loss and the providing of adequate amplification at an early stage are essential to the proper management of the hearing-impaired child. If these requirements are met, then the normal development of speech from the babbling period onward becomes a real possibility. In some cases it has been reported that, even where babbling has faded, the provision of a hearing aid after an interval has resulted in a resumption of babbling activity.

BRAIN WORK AND EAR WORK IN SPEECH AND LANGUAGE

Language acquisition begins through the child's need to collect words that stand for things and people. His quest for words leads him at once into the realm of sounds and phonemes, of intonations and rhythms; in other words, he learns the phonologic system of his mother tongue because it is only in this way that he can recognize different words when he hears them and send them out so that other people can recognize them. The language includes very much more than the phonologic system, however. The child has also to acquire all the information needed for dealing with the grammar and syntax of the language. He has to learn the grammatical elements, the morphemes, and to discover how to string these together to make words; he has to construct the routines necessary for putting words together to make sentences and has to extend his dictionary of words continually in order to be able to express what he wants to say.

We shall not attempt to outline the stages by which all this development takes place; it is enough to underline two important facts about the process. The first is that the mechanics of language use are completely mastered during the period of language acquisition; all the information required for controlling the form of spoken messages is collected by learning finite sets of language elements. This is the case, as we have seen, at the phonologic level; the list of phonemes and functional intonation and rhythm patterns is finite, and the child has learned them all by the time he is 4 or 5. It is equally true, although it may be less obvious, that the use of grammar and syntax also depends on restricted sets of elements. To deal with the grammar of English a child has to learn a small set of bound morphemes: *-ing, un-, -ed*, etc.; several sets of form words: pronouns, prepositions, conjunctions, articles; and a restricted number of laws concerning word order. All this the child will usually have acquired by the time he is 7 or 8 years old. Thereafter he will be learning new words for the rest of his life and these will afford the means of greatly extending the content of what he says, but he will not learn any new prepositions or pronouns or develop any new grammatical apparatus for use in his native language. The use of a natural language depends on the possession of a relatively small body of information that makes possible the expression of an infinite variety of contents. Were it not for this feature, a language would scarcely be learnable and would certainly not be acquired in the comparatively short time in which a child masters his native tongue.

The second fact is even more important from the point of view of the hearing-impaired child: the process of language acquisition is nine-tenths brain work rather than ear work. When taking in speech we hear sounds and on the basis of these sounds we recognize the string of phonemes, the intonations and rhythms that make up the spoken message. Everything else is inferred and constructed by the brain. The morphemes, the words, and the sentences are reconstructed by the speech centers of the brain on the evidence supplied by the phonologic decoding of the message. The only part played by the ear in speech communication is the perceiving of sounds, the application of acoustic cues in placing these sounds in phonemic classes, and the use of those same cues in the control of articulation through the medium of auditory feedback. This ear work is indispensable to speech, which is why the auditory channel is so vitally important during the learning period; it supplies the foundation of the language system. The superstructure that is erected on this foundation is much larger than the phonologic system and all of it is the work of the brain. The hearing-impaired child in most cases has a normal brain and if the ear work can be efficiently done in his case, in the conditions already outlined, he is well equipped to acquire grammar, syntax, and vocabulary.

The normal process of language acquisition shows very clearly this interaction between ear work and brain work. Not only the child's phonemic system but also his distribution of phonemes and the finer details of his articulations are the direct result of what he actually hears from others. His accent will resemble most closely that of his mother or of anyone who looks after him, and he is also likely to take from them some idiosyncrasies of pronunciation, the pronunciation of certain words in a way that is atypical of the larger community. Characteristic intonations will also be acquired in the same fashion, all demonstrating the close links between what is heard and what is produced. At levels above the phonologic, the story is very different. When the development of syntax begins with the stringing together of two word utterances, the child's brain evolves for itself a syntactic technique that results in the well known *all-gone milk, bye-bye car* type of construction, which plays no part in the speech that comes into the child's ears. The same phenomenon is apparent at a later stage when the child's brain abstracts rules for the use of bound morphemes and leads him to use forms like *standed* and *badder*. These are forms he has never heard from adult speakers and their production is purely the result of brain work.

This does not mean that at any stage ear work becomes less important, but it does mean that ear work is supplemented by an enormous amount of brain work. For the normal and the hearing-impaired child alike, the continued and continuous provision of the sensory input of speech is essential. Obviously, the normal child eventually discards such things as *standed* and *badder* by reference to incoming speech. Just as the individual brain evolves for itself the phonemic system of the language, so it infers the grammatical and syntactic structure. The brain of the hearing-impaired child is perfectly equal to this task but it needs, if anything, more speech input than normal in order to do the job; all too often it receives less.

ROLE OF REDUNDANCY IN LANGUAGE

One further aspect of brain activity in speech has a bearing on the situation of the hearing-impaired child. The brain of the adult speaker carries a mass of information about his native language: it contains a large dictionary of words, the lists of form words, the list of bound morphemes, the inventory of phonemes and of functional intonations and rhythms, the routines for forming words from morphemes and sentences from words. All of this is instantly available when speech is being taken in or sent out. The existence of all this information in the individual brain constitutes what we call "knowing a language." Much of our reception of speech is in reality a process of prediction based on our knowledge of the language system at all its levels. We hear a stream of sounds, which we recognize as representing a string of phonemes and on this scaffolding we construct the morphemes, the words, and the sentences of the message. A great deal of this reconstruction is done by guessing because at every point in the message it is possible to predict with varying degrees of certainty how the speaker will continue what he has to say. He is never completely free to choose, if he wants his listeners to understand him, for he is constrained by the context, both the language context and the social context. We can predict with certainty the end of the message "A stitch in time saves . . . ;" there are infinitely more choices in "The scientist's name was . . . ," so much so that we can hardly make any guess as to what the continuation will be. An extension of the linguistic context might alter the situation completely, for example, if we knew that the speaker had said: "A famous scientist developed the 'Special Theory of Relativity.'" The scientist's name was . . . ."

All languages exhibit the property of redundancy, that is, of predictability, in all their forms and at all levels. Knowledge of a language includes not only the stores of information and of routines we have already spoken about but also the capacity for computing probabilities as to the continuation of a message. At any point in a string of phonemes, a listener's brain knows which phonemes cannot occur next, which are unlikely to and which are most likely to, and similarly with sequences of morphemes and words. In English the string *spr-* would have to continue with one of the 20 vowel phonemes and of these only about 10 would be possible continuations in English words. If the message had proceeded up to the morpheme *thought*, it is certain that the next morpheme cannot be *-ing*, and so on. Through the continual reception of speech the brain learns to make a running computation of probabilities and to reconstruct the incoming message in accordance with this computation. The part played by the actual hearing of the sounds of speech is confined to the provision of the rough scaffolding of the message and to the confirmation or correction of the predictions the brain makes. In fact if we hear about half of what is said to us we can guess the rest and reconstruct the message without any errors.

This exploitation of the redundancy of natural languages, because it too is a matter of brain work, is open to the hearing-impaired just as it is to the hearing, but once more it is a function of experience in dealing with speech. The hearing-impaired child who builds an adequate acoustic basis for this will be just as efficient in guessing and predicting as the normal child; his brain will become equally skilled in computing probabilities. However, the normal hearing person must get enough acoustic input to base his guessing on, and this is even more the case for the hearing-impaired; this input must be there during the time when the brain is learning how to carry out these very complex operations.

Redundancy is not limited to the linguistic aspects of speech communication; it takes effect also in the acoustic domain, where we have already seen it at work, although without labeling it explicitly as redundancy. The articulations taking place during a speech sequence are the physiologic transform of the phoneme string; the movements themselves are continuous and are necessarily influenced by the articulatory context, that is, an articulation performed at one moment will determine the way in which a later articulation is carried out. Hence the latter is in some degree predictable from the former. Such variations in articulation are inevitably reflected in the sound waves so that some features of the acoustic continuum are constrained by preceding or indeed following sections of the wave. This is seen particularly clearly in the case of formant transitions whose precise form is bound up with the acoustic sequence: the frequencies of long-lasting formants, the frequency location of noise bands and of noise bursts, and the presence of low frequency (nasal) resonances. This is all information the listener is able to make use of in the application of acoustic cues to speech reception. Furthermore, acoustic information carried by one part of the frequency spectrum may be inferred from that contained in another part, as has been shown by the many experiments with filtered speech. Speech filtered so that all frequencies below about 1800 Hz are transmitted to listeners gives a syllable articulation score of 70%, which means that running speech is highly intelligible. However, speech filtered so that all frequencies above 1800 Hz are transmitted also gives a syllable score of 70% (Fletcher, 1953), showing that sufficient cues for the decoding of running speech may be found in the frequency bands below and above 1800 Hz. In other words, the acoustic redundancy of speech is such that relevant information in the upper band can be inferred from the lower band and vice versa. This is another way of expressing the facts that lie behind the hearing-impaired child's capacity for achieving near normal performance in speech reception and also in speech production.

LANGUAGE SYSTEM AS A BASIS FOR READING

Long before he sets foot in a school, a child's education begins with the interactions with life and the world around him that have been stressed throughout this chapter. Any degree of failure or delay in learning to understand speech and to talk interferes very seriously with this educational process during the early years and all the school years that follow. A barrier to the child's progress that is second in importance only to failure with speech is a failure to learn to read. Practically all of the information not presented to the child in the form of speech will reach him in printed form, despite a trend in recent years toward the exploration of alternative modes of presentation, and it is obviously important that the skills of speech should be backed up by the skills of reading and writing.

All the cultures in which reading is of primary social importance use an alphabetic writing system, and in these cases there is clearly a strong link between the phonologic system of the language and the method of writing. The latter is basically a technique for recoding in visual form the phoneme strings of the spoken language. Confusion over this point has been generated in the past by some of the most doctrinaire linguists who have asserted, for example, that natural languages do not operate with phonemes and that the whole idea of the phoneme arises only among people who have learned to read an alphabetic script. This is seeing the world upside-down; it is because language systems are based on a restricted inventory of phonemes that are commutable in the strings that constitute different words that we have alphabetic writing. The principle of a limited number of letters to represent the closed set of phonemic units works admirably over a very wide range of languages. The anomalies of spelling that are thought to be so prevalent in English tend to blind us to the efficiency with which the phoneme strings of the spoken language are encoded in the written form. It follows from this that the best possible basis for learning to read is the kind of familiarity with the phoneme system that we have seen to be the fruit of language acquisition through the auditory channel.

Just as the ear work of speech is limited to perceiving sounds and their assignment to phoneme classes, so the eye work of reading is restricted to perceiving visual shapes and their assignment to alphabetic classes. From this point onward, as in the parallel case of listening, the decoding process is pure brain work and, more than this, the stores of morphemes and words and the routines for word and sentence building that it involves are substantially the same as those evoked in the auditory mode. This does not mean that learning to read is easy; the evidence from normal children is more than enough to dispose of this notion. It does mean, however, that the difficulties are confined to a comparatively low level of operation, that of deciphering the visual signals and learning their relation to the phonemic system. Learning one's native language is itself a trick, the essence of which is the realization that strings of noises stand for things in the world; learning to read is a second trick, requiring the child to digest the fact that visible shapes may stand for sound units. Once this has been grasped and the inventory of shapes mastered, progress with reading can be very rapid.

The eye language exhibits just as much redundancy as the ear language. We do not read the separate letters in a word any more than we hear words sound by sound. While the eye is running along the lines and down the printed page, the brain is predicting as it does with speech, and it only checks the actual letters closely if these predictions run into trouble or seem nonsensical. This is why it takes a certain amount of practice to read proof and detect printing errors efficiently, for the brain is only too ready to see what it expects to see in print. As the child learns to read and becomes more proficient at it, he makes more and more use of redundancy until he is able to read, not separate letters, but the outlines of whole words and phrases, in the way that the adult reader does. This is one reason why the anomalies of English spelling, which are bothersome during the learning period, cease to cause us any trouble, more especially because the majority of them affect the representation of vowel sounds that convey relatively little information.

The normal sequence is that the child learns first to deal with speech and then, some time later, to read and also of course to write. If the first of these processes is not thoroughly well established, then learning to read is not likely to be very successful, as has been shown in the case of profoundly deaf children with little or no experience with audible speech (Myklebust, 1964). It is clear that the normal sequence cannot be reversed, that is, it is not possible for a child to learn to read and to acquire knowledge of the language system in this way and then to apply this knowledge to the reception of speech. The reason for this is that nothing in the process of learning to read would equip him to deal with the extreme variability of speech inputs, unless indeed he learned to read from a variety of manuscripts, a possibility so remote that it need not detain us. The advantage of the natural sequence is precisely that the child learns first to deal with the highly encoded system of speech, in which a single category or unit, a phoneme, is represented by a wide variety of forms in the acoustic medium, and learns to abstract from this variety of inputs the limited number of phonemic classes that the language requires. The problem of reading is then that of learning a set of ciphers, a system with approximately a one-to-one relation with the units of the phonemic system. The order of the two operations cannot be reversed.

However, it is sometimes suggested that in dealing with the hearing-impaired child it is wise to concentrate very much on reading and writing because the auditory pathway is deficient. Apart from the fact that the phonologic system is the soundest basis for learning to read, this method encounters again the difficulty of motivation. The child who is already thoroughly at home with speech has every reason for wanting to read because it opens up a whole new field for the application of the language skills he has acquired. Where these are missing, it is not possible to provide the same degree of motivation directly for the learning of reading and writing because, as we said earlier, they cannot be linked closely and continuously with all the things in everyday life that interest the child. Without these links, the child has little incentive to develop reading and writing as a primary means of communication.

USE OF RESIDUAL HEARING

In this chapter we have tried to show the many aspects of language acquisition that point to the primacy of the auditory mode for the normal hearing child. It furnishes adequate motivation for language learning through the continuous speech activity of the adults who surround the child and the evident connections between this and the baby's life environment. Through the auditory channel the child is trained to deal with the highly encoded signals of speech and to abstract from them the complex system of his mother tongue, based on the phonologic system and including the higher level units of morphemes and words, together with the grammatical and syntactic routines that sentence building involves. The development of acoustic cues enables the child not only to operate eventually with the complete adult phonemic system but also to control his own speech production so as to make his speech intelligible to people around him. No other sensory mode or alternative set of signals can adequately replace speech as a medium for language acquisition and this remains true for the hearing-impaired child, despite deficiencies in the auditory signals he receives. Because every individual evolves acoustic cues for speech that suit his own mode of operating, and because this work is predominantly brain work, the hearing-impaired child is also able to acquire language through the auditory channel and, in the best conditions, to perform satisfactorily in both speech reception and speech production. In conclusion we review very briefly these necessary conditions.

The first requirement is early diagnosis of the hearing impairment; in cases of congenital hearing loss it is very desirable that the condition should be discovered by the age of 3 months and certainly not later than 6 months, although it should be understood that later diagnosis does not preclude the chance of a satisfactory outcome, if the further requirements are met. Second, the baby must be provided with suitable amplification, preferably fitted binaurally, so that all speech inputs within a reasonable distance reach the child's ears well above threshold. This is particularly important so that the prelinguistic activity of babbling may be continued into the next stage of language development without interruption. Third, the mother must be fully informed as to the needs of the situation and trained to maintain the continual input to the child of speech that is firmly linked to everyday activities. This process must be continued not only through the stages of development of acoustic cues and establishment of the phonologic system but also through the acquisition of grammar and syntax and the building of a substantial vocabulary.

This is very far from being a theoretical statement or the specification of ideal conditions; very many hearing-impaired young people and adults are the living demonstration that near normal speech functioning is possible even for those with severe loss of hearing. There is certainly as yet very little evidence to show that any sensory pathway other than the auditory channel or any input other than speech can serve as well for the acquiring of language and for the development of all those mental capacities that spring from this first step in the psychologic growth of the human being.

REFERENCES

Fletcher, H. 1953. Speech and Hearing in Communication, p. 288. Van Nostrand Reinhold Company, New York.

Fry, D. B. 1975. Acoustic cues in the speech of the hearing and the deaf. Proc. R. Soc. Med. 66:959–969.

Fry, D. B. (ed.). 1976. Acoustic Phonetics. Cambridge University Press, Cambridge.

Fry, D. B. 1977. Homo Loquens: Man as a Talking Animal. Cambridge University Press, Cambridge.

Illingworth, R. S. 1963. The Development of the Infant and Young Child. Livingstone, Ltd., London.

Lenneberg, E. H., F. G. Rebelsky, and I. A. Nichols. 1965. The vocalizations of infants born to deaf and to hearing parents. Vita Humana (Human Development) 8:23–37.

Lenneberg, E. H. 1966. The natural history of language. In: F. Smith and G. A. Miller, (eds.). The Genesis of Language, pp. 219–252. The MIT Press, Cambridge, Mass.

McNeil, D. 1970. The Acquisition of Language: The Study of Developmental Psycholinguistics. Harper & Row, Publishers, New York.

Myklebust, H. R. 1964. The Psychology of Deafness. 2nd Ed. Grune & Stratton, Inc., New York.

Whetnall, E., and D. B. Fry. 1971. The Deaf Child. Heinemann Medical Books, Ltd., London.

CHAPTER 3

THE ACOUSTICS OF
SPEECH PRODUCTION

Harry Levitt

CONTENTS

SOME BASIC PHYSICAL PRINCIPLES

Sound is produced by the vibration of molecules. These could be molecules of air, water, metal, or any other medium in which the sound is produced. There are three basic ways in which sound vibrations may be generated. These are:

1. Controlled periodic vibrations, as may be produced by a buzzer or siren. If the frequency of vibration is in excess of 30 Hz (and less than the upper frequency limit of hearing, which can go up to 20,000 Hz), then the resulting sound has a distinct tonal quality.
2. Random vibrations. Turbulent air flow is a common source of random vibration that is of sufficient intensity to be audible. Everyday examples are the hissing of steam escaping from a hot water radiator, or the more pleasant sound of wind whispering through the trees.

3. Plosion, the sudden release of acoustic energy. A common example of plosion occurs when the cork from a champagne bottle is successfully pried loose and the built-up pressure within the bottle is suddenly released with a distinct popping sound.

Sound is transmitted from one point to another when the molecules set into vibration cause neighboring molecules to vibrate, which in turn cause their neighboring molecules to vibrate, and so on. In this way sound can be transmitted over long distances. It is important to note that the molecules remain fixed in essentially the same position, and that it is the vibration per se that is transmitted. A vibration may be described in terms of three fundamental physical characteristics: the frequency of vibration, the intensity of vibration, and the relative time of onset (or phase) of the vibration. The first two characteristics, frequency and intensity, are of particular importance in describing the acoustics of speech production. It can be shown that any sound vibration, no matter how complex, can be viewed as the sum of many simpler vibrations, each of which is defined in terms of its frequency, intensity, and phase.

Typically, when sound is transmitted through an acoustic system, certain frequencies of vibration are transmitted more efficiently than others depending on the physical characteristics of the acoustic pathway. For example, when the vocal tract of an adult male is shaped so as to produce an /i/ vowel (as in *beet*), vibrations at frequencies in the vicinity of 300 Hz, 2300 Hz, and 3000 Hz, typically, are transmitted through the vocal tract with much greater efficiency than vibrations in the intervening frequency regions. Those frequencies at which sound vibrations are transmitted with high efficiency (as opposed to those frequency regions in which sound vibrations are transmitted with low efficiency) are referred to as the resonant frequencies of the sound transmission system. As shall be seen later, the concept of resonant frequencies plays a particularly important role in describing the acoustic characteristics of speech.

In summary:

1. Sound is produced by vibration of molecules.
2. There are at least three basic ways in which sound can be produced: controlled periodic vibrations, random vibrations, and impulsive vibrations.
3. The most complex vibrations may be considered as being made up of a large number of simple periodic vibrations.
4. The three basic components of a simple periodic vibration are frequency, intensity, and phase.

5. Sound travels by means of the transmission of vibration from one set of molecules to the next.
6. The efficiency of sound transmission will typically vary for different frequencies of vibration depending on the physical characteristics of the sound transmission system.
7. For a sound transmission system that is highly frequency dependent, there will be certain frequencies at which sound is transmitted with relatively high efficiency; these frequencies are referred to as the resonant frequencies of the sound transmission system.

ANALYSIS AND REPRESENTATION OF ACOUSTIC SIGNALS

There are two basic ways in which acoustic signals, and speech signals in particular, are commonly represented: the time wave form and the frequency spectrum. The latter method of representation is based on an extremely important theorem derived by the mathematician Fourier. Fourier showed that any complex periodic wave form can be represented by the sum of a set of simpler periodic wave forms. An illustration of the theorem and its application to the representation of acoustic signals is given in Figure 1.

Figure 1 is divided into two parts. The *left* shows the time wave form representation of several different signals; the *right* shows the corresponding frequency-spectrum representation of these signals. Of the various physical properties of sound, acoustic pressure is the easiest to measure. Consequently, acoustic time wave forms are usually specified in terms of the variation in sound pressure as a function of time.[1] The term "instantaneous sound pressure" is sometimes used to distinguish between the time-varying nature of the sound-pressure wave form and the average sound-pressure level, which is a measure of the intensity of the sound.[2] It is also important to distin-

---

[1] Another equally important, but less commonly used representation is that of volume velocity as a function of time. Volume velocity is the instantaneous rate of flow of air through a specified cross-sectional area of 1 unit. Unfortunately, it is difficult to measure volume velocity directly and, for practical purposes, acoustic wave forms are typically described in terms of the more easily measured quantity, pressure (see Appendix I). The relationship between pressure and volume velocity in an acoustic system is analogous to that between voltage and current in an electrical system. For further information, see Beranek (1954) or other texts in acoustics. For the purposes of this introductory treatment of speech acoustics, time wave forms specified in terms of pressure are sufficient.

[2] Appendix I of this chapter describes the relationship between sound power, sound pressure level, and instantaneous sound pressure.

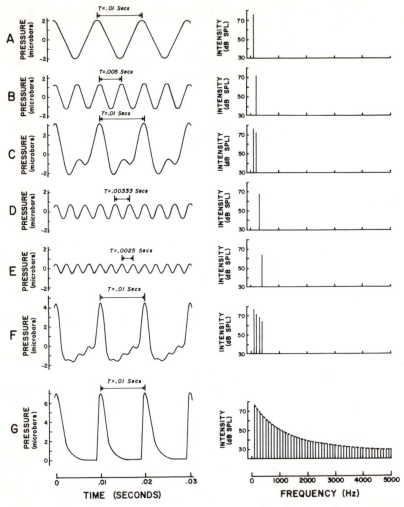

Figure 1. Time and frequency representation of a sound. A sound may be represented by either its time wave form or its frequency spectrum. The *left* side of the figure shows time wave forms, in this case the variation of instantaneous pressure with time. The *right* side shows the power-frequency spectrum; in this case the intensity (in decibels SPL) of each sine wave component of the wave form is shown as a function of frequency. *A, B, D,* and *E* of the figure each show individual sine waves, the frequencies of which are exact multiples of the lowest frequency sine wave (the fundamental). The amplitude and phases of these sine waves have been chosen such that when the sine waves are added they approximate, as well as possible, the triangular-pulse wave form shown in *G.* The quality of this approximation may be assessed by comparing the wave forms shown in *C,* which is the sum of two sine waves, to that shown in *F,* which is the sum of four sine waves, to that shown in *G,* which is the sum of an infinite number of sine waves. Note that for a periodic wave form, such as that shown here, the frequencies of the sine wave components making up the wave form are exact multiples of the fundamental frequency.

guish between the pressure variations that constitute sound and the steady ambient pressure (i.e., atmospheric pressure for airborne sound) upon which the sound-pressure variations are superimposed. The unit of sound pressure is the microbar, which is about one-millionth of normal atmospheric pressure.

Figure 1A shows a simple periodic wave form known as a sine wave. This wave form is the basic component used in representing complex signals according to Fourier's method. A sine wave is completely defined by three parameters: amplitude (A), frequency (f), and phase (ϕ). As shown in the figure, the amplitude, A, is the maximum value of the sinusoidal pressure signal. The frequency, f, is the rate at which the wave form repeats itself and is inversely related to the period, T; i.e., $f = 1/T$. The unit of frequency is the Hertz (Hz), where X Hz means that the wave form repeats itself X times per sec. As is evident from older textbooks, the unit of frequency used to be cycles per sec. However for purposes of international standardization, it has been replaced by the Hertz, where Hertz and cycles per sec are numerically identical. The phase, ϕ, defines the relative time location of the wave form. If the sine wave shown in Figure 1A were to be shifted along the time axis, i.e., if it were delayed by a fraction of a period, then this would represent a change in the phase of the wave form, the frequency and amplitude remaining the same.

The ear is sensitive to both the amplitude and the frequency of a sine wave signal, but is relatively insensitive to its phase. Consequently, methods of representing the frequency spectrum of acoustic signals often specify only the power (or intensity) of each frequency component in the signal. Such a specification is incomplete in that phase information is omitted, but is sufficient for many practical purposes and is commonly used in the specification of speech signals.

Before discussing the concept of a frequency spectrum, it is necessary to describe what is meant by the intensity of a sound. The *left* side of Figure 1A shows the sinusoidal variation in instantaneous air pressure as a function of time. The greater the amplitude of this variation, the greater the power. The power of a sound, however, is distributed over an area perpendicular to the direction of sound travel; the intensity of the sound is the power transmitted per unit area. In most cases of interest in speech research the intensity of a sound is proportional to its amplitude squared, the constant of proportionality depending on a property of the sound-transmission medium known as the acoustic impedance. A discussion of acoustic impedance and pressure/intensity relationships is beyond the scope of this chapter. (See Appendix I for a brief review of the issues involved. For a detailed treatment of the topic, the reader is referred to Beranek

(1954).) However, it is important to remember that the intensity is proportional to the pressure squared and also that the power of a sinusoidal signal is independent of its phase; i.e., two sine waves with the same amplitude but different phases will have the same power.

It is common practice to use a decibel scale in specifying intensity. In order to do this, it is necessary to define a reference intensity; i.e., by definition, intensity in dB = 10 log (intensity in linear units/reference intensity). Unfortunately, several different reference quantities are used in acoustics, leading to several different scales, which in turn are a constant source of confusion. The various ways of specifying sound level are described in Appendix I of the chapter. In the discussion of speech acoustics that follows, interest does not center on the absolute intensity values of speech sounds but rather on their relative values.[3] Hence, it does not much matter what reference intensity is used in defining the decibel scale, provided the same reference is used throughout. The important consideration to bear in mind is that the decibel scale is logarithmic; i.e., adding a fixed number of decibels on the intensity scale is equivalent to multiplying the intensity (measured in absolute linear units) by a corresponding fixed amount. A simple way of remembering the essential difference between a linear and decibel scale is to consider the effect of doubling sound intensity several times. The magnitude of the increase becomes progressively larger with each doubling on the linear scale (e.g., from 1-2-4-8 μW/cm^2). In contrast, the increase on the decibel scale is equal to a fixed amount, 3 dB, independent of the number of times the signal has already been doubled. (e.g., from 0-3-6-9 dB, etc.).

According to Fourier's theorem, any complex periodic signal can be represented by a sum of sine waves. Each component sine wave in this sum will have its own frequency, amplitude, and phase. The characteristics of the component sine waves are usually specified as functions of frequency, the resulting method of specification being known as the frequency spectrum. For the complete specification of a complex wave form, it is necessary to specify both the amplitude-frequency spectrum and phase-frequency spectrum. However, as noted earlier, it is sufficient in many cases to omit the phase information and to specify only the power or intensity of each frequency component. The specification of intensity as a function of frequency is known as the power-frequency spectrum and that is the spectrum shown on the *right* side of Figure 1. The vertical axis shows relative intensity in decibels; the horizontal axis is frequency.

---

[3] Absolute intensity values vary as a function of talker-to-listener distance and other factors not of direct interest in this discussion (see "Summary of Gross Frequency and Intensity Characteristics").

Figure 1*A* shows a 100-Hz sine wave. The period corresponding to 100 Hz is 0.01 sec and the *left* side of Figure 1*A* shows a sinusoidal pressure wave form with a period of 0.01 sec. Because the wave form consists of a single frequency component, it is represented by a single bar in the power frequency spectrum shown on the *right*. The height of this bar is the intensity of the sine wave in decibels sound pressure level (dB SPL). Note that a sinusoidal pressure wave form with an intensity of 0 dB SPL has an amplitude of 0.000282 μbars, which corresponds to a root mean square (rms) pressure of 0.0002 μbars.

Figure 1*B* shows a sine wave of frequency 200 Hz and amplitude equal to 0.65 of the 100-Hz sine wave shown in Figure 1*A*. As before, the frequency spectrum shows a single bar, this time at a frequency of 200 Hz, and with an intensity that is 3.7 dB less than that of the frequency component shown in Figure 1*A*; i.e., a proportional reduction of 0.65:1 in the amplitude of the instantaneous pressure wave form corresponds to a 3.7-dB reduction in relative intensity.

Figure 1*C* shows the sum of the wave forms in *A* and *B*. The summed wave form is no longer sinusoidal; however, it is periodic, with *T* equal to 0.01 sec, the period of its lower frequency component. The frequency spectrum of this wave form contains two bars, one for each frequency.

Figure 1, *D* and *E* show sine waves with frequencies of 300 Hz and 400 Hz, respectively. The amplitudes of these frequency components are equal to 0.40 and 0.26, respectively, of the amplitude of the 100-Hz sine wave. The relative intensities of these frequency components are, respectively, 8.0 and 11.7 dB lower than that of the 100-Hz component.

Figure 1*F* shows the sum of the sine waves in *A*, *B*, *D*, and *E* (or alternatively, the sum of the wave forms shown in *C*, *D*, and *E*). The wave form in *F* bears a rough resemblance to a triangular pulse wave form. As shown by the four bars in the power-frequency spectrum, this wave form consists of four components, at frequencies of 100, 200, 300, and 400 Hz, respectively.

Figure 1*G* shows a triangular pulse wave form that is an idealization of the type of pressure wave form produced by the periodic opening and closing of the vocal cords during voicing.[4] In this case, the

---

[4] The wave form shown in Figure 1*G* was actually generated by a digital speech synthesizer. It was obtained by exciting with a unit impulse a digitally simulated single-pole resonator having a resonance frequency of 0 Hz and a moderately large bandwidth. Note that the resulting impulse response has a sharply rising leading edge and a less rapidly falling trailing edge. Although triangular in shape, the pulse is not a true triangle in that the leading and trailing edges are not exact straight lines and there are no sharp corners.

power-frequency spectrum consists of an infinite number of components, the intensity of these components becoming progressively smaller with frequency. The *dashed curve*, known as the "envelope," traces out this reduction in intensity with frequency. Note that the signal power is concentrated at those component frequencies shown by the *vertical bars*; there is no power in the intervening frequency regions and the *dashed line* shows the way in which the intensity of these frequency components varies as a function of frequency.

The triangular pulse wave form is periodic, with a period of 0.01 sec. This corresponds to the period of the lowest frequency component in the power-frequency spectrum. The lowest frequency component is known as the "fundamental." The higher frequency components, known as "harmonics," all have frequencies that are exact multiples of the fundamental frequency. If the time wave form were not periodic, the frequency components would not be harmonically related. In this case, the frequency representation would be more complex in that an infinitely large number of frequency components spaced extremely closely together would be needed. The power-frequency spectrum for aperiodic signals generally takes the form of a smooth curve showing the relative density of frequency components, rather than a separate vertical bar for each frequency component.

In summary, Figure 1, *A–F* show how a triangular pulse wave form can be approximated by several sine wave components. Figure 1 *G* shows that many more sine wave components are needed to obtain a close approximation to this wave form. The *left* of the diagram shows the time wave form representation; the *right* shows the power-frequency spectrum for each wave form. Whereas a linear scale is used to represent the time wave form (e.g., instantaneous sound pressure measured in microbars), a decibel scale is usually used to measure the relative intensity of each component in the power-frequency spectrum. The intensity of each sine wave component is proportional to the square of the amplitude of the time wave form.

The frequency representation of a periodic wave form consists of a set of equally spaced frequency components. The lowest frequency component is known as the fundamental. The remaining frequency components, known as harmonics, have frequencies that are exact multiples of the fundamental. The way in which the harmonics vary in relative intensity as a function of frequency is known as the envelope of the power-frequency spectrum. The triangular pulse wave form shown in Figure 1*G* is an idealization of the variation in instantaneous sound pressure produced by the periodic opening and closing of the vocal cords during voicing. The envelope of the power spectrum of this wave form decreases with increasing frequency. The rate of attenuation also increases with frequency, approaching a maximum rate of 12 dB/octave[5] for the frequency region above the fourth or fifth harmonic.

Finally, it should be remembered that a complete, exact specification of the frequency spectrum requires that both the phase-frequency spectrum and amplitude-frequency spectrum be specified. However, because the ear is relatively insensitive to phase information it is sufficient, for many practical purposes, to specify the frequency spectrum of speech signals in terms of the relative intensities of its frequency components (i.e., the power-frequency spectrum) and to omit phase information.

THE SOUND SPECTROGRAM

The method of analyzing and representing speech signals described in the preceding section assumes that the spectrum of the signal does not change with time. This is patently not true for speech signals, because different speech sounds are known to have different spectra. How then does one apply the very powerful method of spectrum analysis to speech signals, which are known to violate one of the fundamental assumptions of spectrum analysis? One approach is to analyze the speech signal over short intervals in time assuming, in this case with some degree of reliability, that the spectrum of the speech signal is constant over this time interval. The spectrum analysis is then repeated on the next time interval, and the next, and so on. In this way a sequence of spectrum analyses is obtained as a function of time. This method of analysis is known as "short term spectrum analysis."

The instrument commonly used for short term spectrum analysis of speech is the sound spectrograph. Two sound spectrograms are shown in Figure 2. In these diagrams frequency is shown on the *vertical axis*, time on the *horizontal axis,* and relative intensity by the degree of *gray.* Dark regions in the spectrogram indicate a concentration of sound intensity. The spectrograms shown in the figure show two quite different analyses of the same acoustic signal, a periodic

---

[5] It is customary to specify the rate of attenuation of the spectrum envelope in terms of decibels per octave, i.e., in terms of the reduction in intensity with each doubling of frequency. In going from the 100- to the 200-Hz component, the reduction in intensity is 3.7 dB. In going from the 200- to 400-Hz component the reduction is 8.0 dB, and in going from 400 to 800 Hz, the reduction is 10.7 dB. As frequency is increased, the rate of attenuation approaches 12 dB/octave. Note that, theoretically, the triangular-pulse wave form shown in G has an infinitely large number of components. However, the intensities of the higher harmonics are extremely small (becoming even smaller with increasing frequency) and for practical purposes only those frequency components within a reasonable intensity range are used in the analysis of the signal.

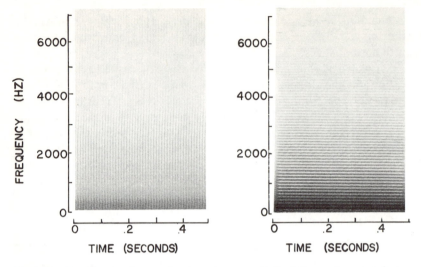

Figure 2.   Broadband and narrowband spectrograms. Both of the spectrograms shown here are of the same acoustic wave form, the triangular-pulse train shown in Figure 1 *G*. The spectrogram on the *left* side is a broadband spectrogram and was made with an analyzing filter bandwidth of 300 Hz. The narrowband spectrogram on the *right* side was made with a 45-Hz analyzing filter bandwidth. The broadband spectrogram has good time resolution and the individual pulses of the pulse train are clearly evident, as shown by the vertical striations. There are 10 striations for every 0.1 sec, corresponding to a pulse repetition rate of 100 Hz. The harmonic structure of the periodic wave form is not evident from the broadband spectrogram, but is clearly evident in the narrowband spectrogram. In this case, each harmonic is shown by a *horizontal bar*. Because the pulse repetition rate is 100 Hz, the harmonics (i.e., the *horizontal bars*) are spaced 100 Hz apart. The time resolution of the narrowband spectrogram is poor and there are no vertical striations corresponding to individual pulses. Both spectrograms show a systematic reduction in degree of grayness with increasing frequency, indicative of a spectrum envelope that is decreasing with frequency.

pulse train of the type shown in Figure 1*G*. The spectrograms differ, however, in terms of the analyzing time, or bandwidth, used in the analysis.

An inherent limitation of short term spectrum analysis is that if the time interval over which each short term analysis is performed is short, the frequency resolution of the resulting analysis is limited. Conversely, the longer the time interval for analysis, the more precise is the resulting frequency analysis. This limitation is often expressed the other way around. In order to perform a precise frequency analysis it is necessary to use an analyzing filter of narrow bandwidth. However, the narrower the bandwidth of the analyzing filter, the poorer is the time resolution of the resulting spectrum analysis. It is important to recognize that the inverse relationship between analyzing time and analyzing bandwidth is inherent to all forms of short term spectrum analysis and is not a peculiarity of any single instrument or method of analysis.

Two analyzing bandwidths are typically used in speech analysis, 300 Hz and 45 Hz. The spectrogram on the *left* of Figure 2 was obtained with an analyzing bandwidth of 300 Hz. This is a relatively broad filter bandwidth and this type of spectrogram is known as a "broadband spectrogram." As a rough rule, the time resolution of a filter is approximately equal to the reciprocal of its bandwidth.[6] Thus, with an analyzing bandwidth of 300 Hz, the broadband spectrogram should be able to track temporal events within 1/300 sec. Because the pulse train analyzed in Figure 2 has a period of 1/100 sec, the broadband spectrogram should be able to track individual pulses in the wave form. This is indeed the case, as shown by the *vertical striations* in this spectrogram. Each striation corresponds to a separate pulse in the periodic wave form. An inherent consequence of the good time resolution is that the frequency resolution of the spectrogram is relatively coarse. The harmonic structure of the periodic signal is not evident from the spectrogram; however, the spectrum envelope is evident. The systematic reduction in degree of grayness on the vertical axis (i.e., decreasing with increasing frequency) is indicative of a falling spectrum envelope. As shown by the *dashed line* on the power-spectrum diagram of Figure 1G, the spectrum envelope for this pulse train decreases with increasing frequency, approaching a rate of 12 dB/octave at the higher frequencies. It should also be evident from this power-spectrum diagram that because the harmonics are spaced at 100-Hz intervals, a 300-Hz analyzing filter will combine the intensity of three adjacent harmonics at a time, hence averaging out the harmonic structure.

The spectrogram on the *right* in Figure 2, known as a narrow-band spectrogram, was obtained with an analyzing filter bandwidth of

---

[6] The resolving power of a narrowband filter depends in a complex way on the bandwidth, the attenuation introduced by the filter, and the sensitivity of the instrument measuring the output of the filter (Gabor, 1946; Kharkevich, 1960). As a general principle, (time resolution) × (frequency resolution) = a constant. The value of this constant depends on how the time and frequency resolution are specified. For the instrumentation and method of specification used here, the constant has been assumed to equal unity resulting in the simple, but nevertheless approximate, rule that (time resolution) = 1/(frequency resolution). This rule seems to work well, albeit conservatively, for commercially available spectrographs. Greater resolution in both the time and frequency domains can be obtained by using more sensitive instrumentation, but the trading-relationship between time and frequency resolution cannot be avoided because it is a fundamental characteristic of short term spectrum analysis. For a discussion of the resolution limits of practical analyzers see Corliss (1963).

45 Hz. In this case the filter bandwidth was sufficiently narrow to separate out the individual harmonics of the periodic wave form and these appear as the dark *horizontal bars* on the spectrogram. The vertical location of each *horizontal bar* indicates the frequency of that harmonic. Note that the degree of grayness of these *horizontal bars* decreases with increasing frequency, indicative of a gradual reduction in signal intensity with increasing frequency. The time resolution of the 45-Hz analyzing filter is roughly 1/45 sec, which is substantially greater than the period of the pulse train. The filter thus averages out the effect of individual pulses and consequently the narrowband spectrogram does not show any *vertical striations* corresponding to individual pulses.

The resolution of the intensity scale in a sound spectrogram is usually relatively poor. The range of the gray scale is very limited and only a few levels of grayness can be determined reliably from the spectrogram. Caution should thus be excercised in interpreting those regions of the spectrogram that are either entirely white or entirely black. A white region does not necessarily mean that there is no acoustic power, but rather that there may be some sound in that frequency-time region at an intensity below the threshold of detection of the spectrograph. The dynamic range of the ear is substantial and many sound components that are not visible on the sound spectrogram may well be quite audible. Similarly, there may be important variations in relative sound intensity that are not visible within the black regions of the spectrogram. For example, the low frequency harmonics shown in Figure 2 are equally black. However, as can be seen from Figure 1G, the relative intensities of the first five harmonics cover a range of 15 dB. Because the range of the gray scale is limited and since the relative intensities of the high frequency components of speech are usually much less than those of the low frequency components, most spectrographs include some form of frequency-selective amplification as an option so that the high frequency components of speech can be brought within the range of the gray scale. Without this high frequency boost, spectrograms of many of the speech sounds would show only the low frequency components. Because of the difficulties encountered with the gray scale, the sound spectrogram is seldom used for obtaining quantitative information on relative sound intensity. Unlike the limitations on the resolution of the time and frequency scales, the poor resolution of the intensity scale is not a fundamental limitation, but is rather a consequence of the method of instrumentation. In order to provide reliable quantitative information on relative sound intensities, many sound spectrographs have the facility to display power-frequency spectra in the form shown in Figure 1 (i.e., relative sound intensity on the vertical axis and frequency on the horizontal). These spectra are sometimes referred to as "cross-sectional spectra" in the context of short term spectrum analysis in that they represent a cross-section, at a given instant in time, of the three-dimensional representation of time, frequency, and intensity.

In summary, the sound spectrogram provides a three-dimensional representation of time, frequency, and intensity. There are fundamental limitations on the resolution of the time and frequency scales and practical limitations on the resolution of the intensity scale. The limitations on time and frequency resolution take the form of a trading relationship in that greater frequency resolution can be obtained at the expense of time resolution, and vice versa. As a result, two types of spectrogram are commonly used in representing speech sounds, the narrowband spectrogram, which has good frequency resolution and is useful in displaying the harmonic structure of speech sounds, and the broadband spectrogram which has relatively good time resolution and is also useful in displaying the spectrum envelope of speech sounds.

SOME BASIC PERCEPTUAL PRINCIPLES

When the intensity of vibration of a sound is sufficiently high such that the sound is transmitted to the eardrum of a listener who, in turn, perceives an auditory sensation, then the listener is said to "hear" the sound. The perceptual and physical characteristics of sound are two distinctly different entities and it is important to keep the distinction in mind at all times. For example, the perceptual correlate of intensity is loudness and that of frequency is pitch. Altering either of these physical parameters will produce a change in the corresponding perceptual dimension of the sound. However, there is not necessarily a one-to-one correspondence between the physical and perceptual dimensions. For example, the intensity of a tone will also affect the pitch to some extent (Stevens and Davis, 1938). Similarly, speech of a fixed intensity will sound louder when heard in quiet than when heard in noise. In complex stimuli, the same percept can be produced by different stimulus combinations. A well known example of this effect is the perception of voice pitch on the telephone although the physical variable directly associated with voice pitch, fundamental frequency, is actually not transmitted over the telephone.[7] Thus, although there is

---

[7] The frequency range usually transmitted over the telephone is from 300–3500 Hz. The fundamental frequency of a normal adult male voice is usually well below 300 Hz.

a close correspondence between frequency and pitch (as there is between intensity and loudness, and other stimulus-percept pairs), there is no invariant one-to-one correspondence between the physical and perceptual correlates.

The distinction between the physical and perceptual domains is particularly important in speech in that the processing of speech involves several levels (psychoacoustic, phonetic, linguistic, semantic) and the correspondence between the physical stimulus (i.e., the speech signal reaching the ear) and each of the corresponding perceptual correlates becomes increasingly more complex at the higher perceptual levels. For example, the vibration of the vocal cords is heard as the pitch of the voice at the psychoacoustic level, as an important (but not the only) cue to voicing at the phonetic level, and as one of several correlates of stress and intonation at the linguistic level.

This chapter is concerned with the acoustic characteristics of speech. Where appropriate, reference is made to the perceptual correlates of the acoustic stimuli, and the above mentioned distinctions between acoustic and perceptual correlates should be kept in mind. Suggested readings on various aspects of speech perception are Denes and Pinson, 1963; Liberman et al., 1967; Lehiste, 1967; Flanagan, 1972; Studdert-Kennedy, 1974. Similarly, the articulatory gestures associated with specific speech sounds are described briefly when appropriate; a detailed description of the articulatory aspects of speech production may be found in Haycock (1933); Bronstein (1960); Minifie, Hixon, and Williams (1973); Ladefoged (1975); Ling (1976); and other texts.

ACOUSTICS OF SPEECH PRODUCTION

The production of speech involves the basic acoustic mechanisms described under "Some Basic Physical Principles." A sketch of the human vocal apparatus is shown in Figure 3. Speech is produced while exhaling. Air from the lungs is forced through the larynx, into the mouth and nose, then finally escapes into the surrounding acoustic medium. The vocal cords are situated roughly in the middle of the larynx. The region above the larynx consisting of the pharynx, nose, mouth, and lips is known as the "vocal tract."

Voiced sounds are produced by a voluntary tightening of the vocal cords. The space between the vocal cords is known as the "glottis," and when the cords are pulled taut, the flow of air through the glottis is blocked. This causes a build-up of air pressure behind the glottis. After a while, the build-up of this subglottal air pressure is so

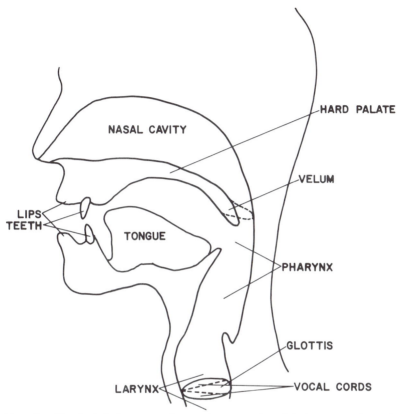

Figure 3.   Sketch of the human vocal tract. A cross-section of the human vocal tract is shown during production of the vowel /i/. The vibration of the vocal cords generates a quasiperiodic train of air pulses that enter the vocal tract at the larynx and travel through the tract exiting through the mouth (or nose for nasal or nasalized sounds). For the /i/ vowel, as shown here, the mouth is open and the arch of the tongue is placed high up and forward in the mouth. The velum controls the acoustic coupling between the mouth and nasal pathway. In the case of a nasalized vowel, the velum does not form a tight seal and the sound travels through both the oral and nasal pathways.

great that the vocal cords are forced to fly apart, allowing some air to escape. With the release of air, the subglottal air pressure falls and the cords are pulled back together, blocking the glottis once again. This sequence of events is repeated cyclically as long as voicing continues. The opening and closing of the glottis is almost, but not quite, periodic in time. The result is a sequence of quasiperiodic air pulses flowing into the vocal tract.

The vocal tract is effectively an acoustic enclosure with distinct resonances. The shape of the tract is easily changed by movements of the articulators, i.e. the jaw, tongue, teeth, lips, and velum. The velum, as shown in Figure 3, controls the entrance to the nasal cavity. By changing the shape of the vocal tract, the resonant frequencies are changed. For most practical purposes, the vocal tract may be regarded as having three major resonances. These resonances are often referred to as "formants," and this terminology is used here. However, there is a subtle distinction between vocal-tract resonance and formant, which should be noted (Halle, Hughes, and Radley, 1957). A resonance is a property of only the acoustic enclosure; a formant is a measured concentration of spectral energy and involves both the sound source and the acoustic enclosure. Numerically, formants and vocal-tract resonances have very similar, but not necessarily identical values. The formants are usually labeled in terms of their relative frequencies. The formant with the lowest frequency is referred to as the "first formant," that with the second lowest frequency as the "second formant," and so on.

Voiceless sounds are produced by relaxing the vocal cord muscles so that there is no major obstruction to the air flow through the glottis. At some later point in the vocal tract, however, a constriction is introduced so as to cause turbulence in the air flow. Sounds produced in this way have a characteristic hiss, such as the fricative sounds.

It is important to bear in mind the distinction between the source of sound and the acoustic system through which the sound is transmitted. In the case of voiced sounds, the train of air pulses generated by the vocal cords (referred to variously as the "glottal wave form" or "glottal pulses") is the source of sound; the vocal tract through which these pulses travel is the acoustic system that modifies the sound. As the shape of the vocal tract is changed, so are the acoustic characteristics of these pulses. Figure 4 provides an idealized representation of how the glottal pulses are modified by the vocal tract when in the position for producing the vowel /i/.[8]

As noted earlier, signals may be specified either as functions of time or as functions of frequency. Both of these representations are shown in Figure 4. The *left* half of the diagram shows the time wave form representation; the *right* half shows the frequency-spectrum representation. Figure 4*A* shows an idealization of the glottal pulses entering the vocal tract. This signal is identical to that shown in Figure 1*G*. To recapitulate, the wave form on the *left* shows the

---

[8] The phonetic representation of a sound is usually shown between two slashes of the type shown here. Appendix II of this chapter provides a summary of the phonetic symbols used in this text. The symbols used are based on those recommended by the International Phonetic Association.

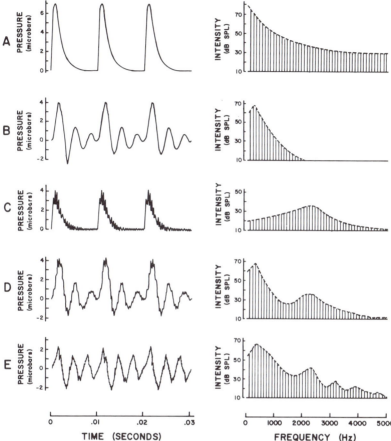

TIME (SECONDS)   **FREQUENCY (Hz)**

Figure 4.   Effect of vocal tract resonances on the acoustic characteristics of a vowel sound. Following the format used in Figure 1, the *left* side of the diagram shows time wave forms and the *right* side shows the corresponding power-frequency spectra. *A*, which is identical to Figure 1 *G*, shows an idealization of the glottal pulses entering the vocal tract (as obtained from a computer-simulated speech synthesizer). *B* shows the effect of passing these glottal pulses through a simulated vocal tract having only a single resonance at 300 Hz. *C* shows the effect of passing the glottal pulses through a simulated vocal tract with a single resonance at 2300 Hz. Note that in both cases the pulses produce damped oscillations in the vocal tract at roughly the resonant frequency and that the spectrum envelope shows a major peak at the resonant frequency. *D* shows the effect of passing the glottal pulses through a simulated vocal tract having resonances at both 300 and 2300 Hz, corresponding to the first two formants of the vowel /i/. The sound produced in this way is identifiable as an /i/ vowel, but has a harsh, machine-like quality. *E* shows the wave form and power-frequency spectrum of an actual /i/ vowel produced by a normal male speaker. Note that this spectrum has several resonances in addition to the two major resonances at 300 and 2300 Hz. Because the relative intensity of the spectrum at these higher frequency resonances is relatively low, the damped oscillations corresponding to these resonances are not visible to the naked eye on the acoustic wave form. However, the effect of these resonances is nevertheless audible.

instantaneous pressure as a function of time. the spectrum on the *right* shows the relative intensities, on a decibel scale, of the harmonic components making up the wave form. Note that the harmonics are spaced 100 Hz apart (which is the repetition frequency of the glottal pulses), and that the relative intensity of successive harmonics decreases at the rate of about 12 dB/octave, as indicated by the *dashed line* known as the spectrum envelope.

Figure 4*B* shows the effect of passing the glottal pulses into an acoustic tube or hypothetical "vocal tract" having a single resonance at 300 Hz. The *left* side shows the effect of the resonance on the time wave form. After each glottal pulse, there is a sequence of damped oscillations at the resonant frequency. (A damped oscillation is one in which the amplitude of the oscillation decreases systematically with each period. The rate at which the oscillations die down is a measure of the degree of damping). Because the fundamental frequency of the pulse train is 100 Hz and the damped oscillations occur at the resonant frequency of 300 Hz, there are three damped oscillations per period. The decrease in amplitude between successive oscillations is typical of the damping occurring in the human vocal tract. The power-frequency spectrum corresponding to this damped pulse train is shown on the *right*. As before, the power is concentrated at the harmonic frequencies. The spectrum envelope in this case shows a large peak in the vicinity of the resonance at 300 Hz. The spectrum envelope shown in Figure 4*B* can be derived by adding (in decibels) the frequency response of the acoustic tube producing the resonance to the spectrum envelope of the glottal pulses shown in Figure 4*A*.

Figure 4*C* shows the effect of passing the glottal pulses into an acoustic tube with a resonance at 2300 Hz. As before, each glottal pulse produces damped oscillations at the resonant frequency. In contrast to the previous case, the resonant frequency is much greater than the fundamental frequency of the glottal pulse train and there is time for a relatively large number of damped oscillations between glottal pulses. The power spectrum of the damped pulse train is shown on the *right* side of the diagram. It is similar in form to that shown in *B*, except that in this case, the spectrum envelope has a peak at 2300 Hz, rather than 300 Hz. Because the resonance in the latter case is in a frequency region far removed from the fundamental frequency, the spectrum envelope is more clearly defined. In some cases, when the fundamental frequency is not very different from the lowest resonant frequency, as might occur with a high pitched female or child's voice, it may be very difficult to separate out the spectrum envelope from the harmonic components.

Figure 4*D* shows the effect when the glottal pulses are fed into an acoustic tube having resonances at both 300 Hz and 2300 Hz. These two resonances are representative of the two major resonances that occur when the vowel tract is shaped so as to produce the vowel /i/. The sound produced by this acoustic system will be identifiable as an /i/ vowel, but will have a machine-like or synthetic quality. Because there are two resonances, the wave form between the glottal pulses will be a combination of the damped oscillations shown in Figure 4, *B* and *C*. As before, the power spectrum will have discrete concentrations of acoustic power at the harmonic frequencies. The spectrum envelope, however, will have two major peaks, one at 300 Hz and the other at 2300 Hz.

Figure 4*E* shows an actual acoustic pressure wave form for a male voice producing the vowel /i/. The pressure wave form was measured at a distance of 1 m from the lips of the speaker. The wave form shown in *E* is similar, but not quite the same as that shown in *D*. If the two wave forms were identical, then this would imply that the simple two-formant model of vowel production is entirely accurate. This is not the case, but the two-formant model is nevertheless a moderately good approximation. The power spectrum shown on the *right* side of *E* is also very similar to the synthetic vowel spectrum shown in *D* in the frequency region up to about 2500 Hz, which encompasses the first two formants.

PRODUCTION OF VOWELS

Each language has its own set of vowels. English, for example, has roughly a dozen distinct vowels. Variations of these vowels can be tolerated, provided the intended vowel is not lost or confused with another vowel. For example, when we speak with a blocked or stuffy nose, the vowels we produce have a nasal quality, but they may still be identified as the intended vowels. The term "nasal" is used colloquially; the vowels are actually denasalized, because there is no flow of air through the nasal cavity. (For further discussion of vowel nasalization, see "Nasals and Nasalized Sounds.")

Associated with each vowel is a normative configuration for the vocal tract. Although slightly different configurations may produce essentially the same vowel, the normative positions are those most often used or aimed at by skilled speakers. Because movements of the articulators (i.e., tongue, jaw, teeth, lips) bring about extensive changes in the shape of the vocal tract, the normative positions are usually defined in terms of these articulators.

Of the 12 or so vowels in English, four are of particular interest because they correspond to extreme positions of the tongue. For the vowel /i/, as in *seen*, the arch of the tongue is placed high up and forward in the mouth; that is, in the front of the mouth, just behind the teeth and approaching the hard palate. For the vowel /u/, as in *soon*, the arch of the tongue is again placed toward the hard palate, but at the back of the mouth. For the vowel /æ/, as in *sat*, the tongue is placed at the front of the mouth, but is kept low behind the lower teeth. Finally, for the vowel /a/, as in *father*, the blade of the tongue is placed at the back of the mouth and low down. The four vowels, /i/, /u/, /æ/, and /a/, are classified, respectively, as high front, high back, low front, and low back, according to the position of the tongue. Other vowels may fit these same categories, such as /ɪ/, as in *bit*, which is also a high front vowel, or may involve intermediate categories, such as /ʌ/, as in *up*, which is a central vowel. When the tongue and other articulators are held in a relaxed position, a neutral, schwa vowel /ə/ is produced, such as the initial vowel of *above*. This vowel is frequently used in place of other vowels in unstressed syllables.

Although convenient for purposes of classification, the position of the tongue is not the only determinant of vowel type. There are important concomitant changes in lip and jaw positions, as well as changes in the shape of the pharyngeal cavity and other variables. For example, for the front vowels, the lips tend to be spread out, showing the teeth. For the back vowels, the lips tend to be rounded. At the same time, the jaws are relatively close together for the high vowels and far apart for the low vowels.

Normative vocal tract configurations for the four vowels, /i/, /u/, /æ/, and /a/ are shown in Figure 5, together with typical power-frequency spectra. As noted earlier, the almost periodic train of glottal pulses produced by the action of the vocal cords causes vibrations at only those frequencies that are harmonics of the average repetition rate of the glottal pulses. Each of the power-frequency spectra in Figure 5 thus consists of a sequence of *vertical bars*, where each bar corresponds to a separate harmonic and the height of each bar represents the relative intensity of that harmonic. An identical repetition rate for the glottal pulses has been assumed for each vowel. The spectrum envelope shows how the vocal tract configuration tends to emphasize certain harmonics and reduce the intensity of others. The peaks of the envelope correspond to the resonances or formants of the vocal tract.

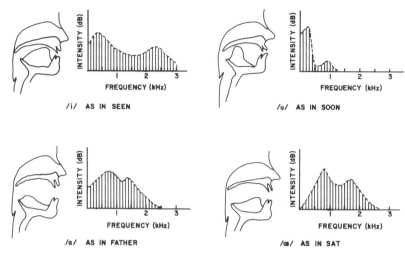

Figure 5. Vocal tract configurations and approximate power frequency spectra for the vowels /i/, /u/, /æ/, and /a/. For each vowel, a cross-sectional sketch of the vocal tract is shown alongside an approximate idealization of the corresponding power-frequency spectrum for an adult male speaker. The power-frequency diagrams are approximate in that only the first two formants are shown. For the vowel /i/, a high front vowel, the arch of the tongue is placed high up and forward in the mouth. The first two formant frequencies of this vowel are typically on the order of 300 and 2300 Hz. For /u/, a high back vowel, the arch of the tongue is placed toward the hard palate, but at the back of the mouth. In this case, the first two formant frequencies are typically 300 and 900 Hz. For /æ/, a low front vowel, the tongue is placed at the front of the mouth, but is kept low behind the lower teeth, the first two formant frequencies being on the order of 800 and 1800 Hz. For /a/, a low back vowel, the blade of the tongue is placed at the back of the mouth and low down; for this vowel the first two formant frequencies are typically 700 and 1300 Hz.

The shape of the vocal tract and the location of the formants are closely interrelated. Three characteristics of the vocal tract that are of particular importance in determining the formant frequencies are, 1) the diameter of the vocal tract at the point of maximum constriction between the tongue and roof of the mouth, 2) the distance of this tongue constriction from the glottis, and 3) the area of the mouth opening relative to the degree of lip rounding (Stevens and House, 1955). The last variable is expressed mathematically as the ratio of the area of the mouth opening over the length of the front portion of the vocal tract. If there is no lip rounding, as in the vowels /i/ and /æ/, this length is approximately 1 cm. If there is lip rounding, such as in the vowel /u/, the front portion of the vocal tract is extended up to about 3 cm in length.

A narrow tongue constriction towards the back of the mouth and a large mouth opening, as is the case for the back vowel /a/, will produce a high first formant, a typical value for a male speaker being 700 Hz, as shown in Figure 5. Conversely, a small mouth opening with lip rounding, as in the vowel /u/, or a narrow constriction near the mouth opening, as in the vowel /i/, will produce a low first formant. Both /u/ and /i/ have essentially the same first formant frequency, which is approximately 300 Hz for an adult male. The frequency of the second formant is increased as the point of maximum constriction is brought forward in the mouth and the relative area of the mouth opening is increased or the degree of lip rounding is reduced. Thus, for the back vowel /u/, which has the tongue constriction relatively far back in the mouth, a mouth opening that is small, and a good deal of lip rounding, the second formant is quite low, typically about 900 Hz. Conversely, the front vowel /i/, which has the tongue constriction close to the front of the mouth, a large mouth opening, and no lip rounding, has a relatively high formant, typically about 2300 Hz. For the front vowel /æ/, which has a tongue constriction a little further back in the mouth, but a large mouth opening and no lip rounding, the second formant is sightly lower in frequency, typically about 1800 Hz. Greater detail on the link between shape of the vocal tract and the frequency-power spectrum may be found in Stevens and House (1955, 1961), Fant (1960), and Flanagan (1972).

The power-frequency spectrum diagrams shown in Figure 5 are idealizations in which it is assumed that the frequency of vocal cord vibration and the shape of the vocal tract remain absolutely steady over a long enough time interval for the frequency-power spectrum to be measured with the precision shown in the diagram. In practice, both the frequency of vibration and the shape of the vocal tract vary with time, and in order to track these time-varying changes, a short term spectrum analysis is used (see under "The Sound Spectrogram"). Spectrograms of the eight English vowels, /i, ɪ, ɛ, æ, a, ɔ, ʊ, u/, are shown in Figure 6. Frequency is shown on the *vertical axis*, time on the *horizontal axis*, and relative acoustic power by the degree of *gray*. The bandwidth of the frequency analyzer used in obtaining the spectrograms shown in Figure 6 was 300 Hz, the conventional bandwidth used for broadband spectrograms. For these spectrograms, the harmonic structure of the power-frequency spectrum has been averaged out. Most normal speakers have a fundamental frequency well below 300 Hz and, as a result, each analyzing bandwidth contains at least one harmonic, usually two or three harmonics. The dark bands in the spectrogram indicate regions of acoustic power spread

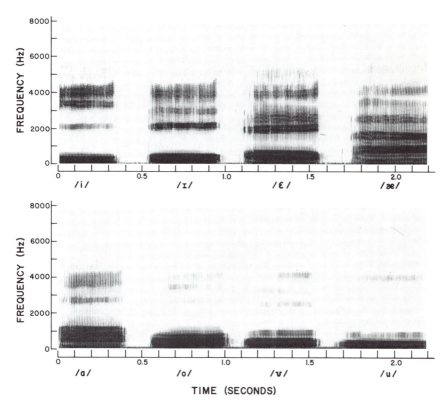

Figure 6. Broad band spectrograms of eight English vowels. Spectrograms of the vowels /i, ɪ, ɛ, æ, a, ɔ, ʊ/ and /u/ produced as isolated, steady sounds are shown. The bandwidth of the analyzing filter was 300 Hz. The vertical striations correspond to individual glottal pulses of the voiced sound. The dark *horizontal bands* represent formants. For the vowel /i/, for example, at least four formants can be discerned at frequencies of 400, 2000, 3100, 3500, and 4000 Hz. The first two formant frequencies correspond roughly to those of the approximate idealized power-frequency spectrum of this vowel shown in Figure 5. On the average there are roughly 11 vertical striations over a 0.1-sec time interval, indicating that the speaker had a fundamental frequency of approximately 11/0.1, i.e., 110 Hz. The speaker was a young adult male with a British accent (a composite South London and educated South-Eastern English accent).

out over several adjacent harmonics. These are the so-called formants referred to earlier.

For the rather special situation in which the voice frequency is well in excess of 300 Hz, there will be no smoothing out of harmonic structure and the spectrogram will show dark bars corresponding to individual harmonics. This can occur with a voice that is very high pitched, as is sometimes the case with deaf children. Alternatively, if a narrow analyzing bandwidth (e.g., 45 Hz) is used on normal speech, the resulting narrowband spectrogram will clearly show the harmonic structure of voiced sounds.

Figure 7 shows both a broadband and narrowband spectrogram of the vowel /i/ produced with a gradually falling fundamental frequency. The formants are clearly visible in the broadband spectrogram, as are the vertical striations corresponding to individual pulses of the voiced sound. The narrowband spectrogram shows up the harmonic structure. No vertical striations are evident here because of the longer averaging time of the narrowband filter. Because the fundamental frequency is falling with time, all of the harmonics show a related decrease with time. The rate of decrease increases systematically with each harmonic because the harmonics are exact multiples of the fundamental frequency. Concomitantly, the spacing between the harmonics also decreases as the fundamental frequency is reduced. Although the harmonics are clearly evident, the contour corresponding to the fundamental itself is not easy to measure and is of poor resolution because of its relatively low frequency. A practical way of obtaining the fundamental frequency contour is to measure the contour for the 10th harmonic, which is relatively high in frequency and for which the resolution of measurement is high because any variations in the fundamental frequency is multiplied by a factor of 10. The measured frequency contour is then divided by 10 in order to obtain the fundamental frequency contour.

In comparing the spectrograms of the vowels shown in Figure 6 with the idealized power spectra shown in Figure 5, it may be noted that the spectrograms show several horizontal bars for each vowel, indicating that each vowel has several formants, whereas the idealized power-spectrum diagrams show only the lowest two resonances. For example, the spectrogram for the vowel /i/ shows formants at frequencies of 300, 2300, 3300, and 4000 Hz, whereas the idealized power-spectrum diagram shows resonances only at 300 and 2300 Hz, respectively. This was done because the lowest two formants play a dominant role in identifying the vowels. The higher formants, although useful in vowel identification, affect vowel quality primarily.

Peterson and Barney (1952) measured the formant values of American English vowels for a fairly large number of speakers (33 men, 28 women, and 15 children, for a total of 76 speakers). Their data are summarized in Table 1. Average formant frequency values are shown separately for men, women, and children. Also shown in the table are the average amplitudes of each formant and the average fundamental frequency for each group of speakers on each vowel.

Although there is considerable overlap in the average formant frequencies obtained for different speakers on different vowels, the

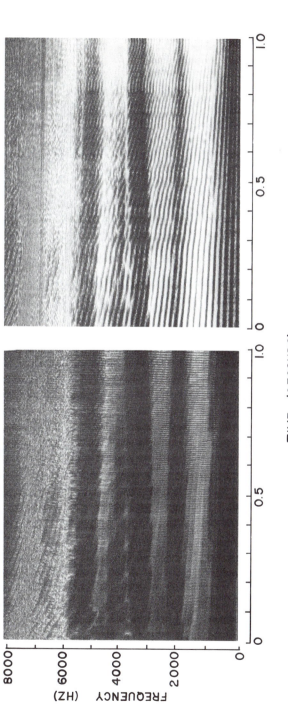

TIME (SECONDS)

Figure 7. Broadband and narrowband spectrograms of the vowel /i/. The vowel was produced in isolation with a gradually falling fundamental frequency. The broadband spectrogram is shown on the *left*. The formants are clearly visible as dark, *horizontal bands*. Note that the formant frequencies remain relatively steady with time, although there is evidence of two formants merging into one formant toward the end of the utterance. The speaker producing this vowel was not the same one who produced the vowels in Figure 6 and there are slight between-speakers differences in the values of the formant frequencies for this vowel. The *vertical striations* corresponding to individual pulses of the voiced sound are clearly evident. The rate of occurrence of these striations can be seen to decrease systematically during the utterance, indicative of a gradually falling fundamental frequency. The narrowband spectrogram is shown on the *right*. The narrow, slightly downward sloping *bars* correspond to the harmonics of the voice fundamental frequency. The formants of the vowel are also partially visible in that the *harmonic bars* are darker within the region of a formant. Note that the dark regions corresponding to the formants are roughly horizontal indicating no change in formant frequency with time, whereas the harmonic bars slope downward indicating a gradually falling fundamental frequency. Because the harmonics are exact multiples of the fundamental frequency, the spacing between harmonics also decreases with time and thus the slope of the harmonic bars is greater for the higher harmonics. A convenient way of measuring the fundamental frequency is to measure the frequency of the 10th harmonic bar, which is easier to read off the spectrogram, and then to divide the measured value by 10.

Table 1.   Fundamental frequencies and formant-characteristics of 10
American English vowels[a]

	i	ɪ	ɛ	æ	a	ɔ	U	u	ʌ	ɝ
Fundamental frequencies (Hz)										
Men	136	135	130	127	124	129	137	141	130	133
Women	235	232	223	210	212	216	232	231	221	218
Children	272	269	260	251	256	263	276	274	261	261
Formant frequencies (Hz)										
F_1 Men	270	390	530	660	730	570	440	300	640	490
Women	310	430	610	860	850	590	470	370	760	500
Children	370	530	690	1010	1030	680	560	430	850	560
F_2 Men	2290	1990	1840	1720	1090	840	1020	870	1190	1350
Women	2790	2480	2330	2050	1220	920	1160	950	1400	1640
Children	3200	2730	2610	2320	1370	1060	1410	1170	1590	1820
F_2 Men	3010	2550	2480	2410	2440	2410	2240	2240	2390	1690
Women	3310	3070	2990	2850	2810	2710	2680	2670	2780	1960
Children	3730	3600	3570	3320	3170	3180	3310	3260	3360	2160
Formant ratios										
F_2/F_1 Men	8.48	5.10	3.47	2.61	1.49	1.47	2.32	2.90	1.86	2.76
Women	9.00	5.77	3.82	2.38	1.44	1.56	2.47	2.57	1.84	3.28
Children	8.65	5.15	3.78	2.23	1.33	1.56	2.52	2.72	1.87	3.25
Formant amplitudes (dB)										
L_1	−4	−3	−2	−1	−1	0	−1	−3	−1	−5
L_2	−24	−23	−17	−12	−5	−7	−12	−19	−10	−15
L_3	−28	−27	−24	−22	−28	−34	−34	−43	−27	−20

[a] Average values of fundamental frequency, formant frequencies, formant frequency ratio, and formant amplitudes are shown for each of 10 American English
speakers. The data were obtained by Peterson and Barney (1952) for 76 speakers: 33
men, 28 women, and 15 children. Note the relative invariance across speakers of the F_2/F_1 formant-frequency ratio for each vowel.

ratio between formant frequencies is relatively constant for each
vowel. For example, on the vowel /i/, the average value of the first
formant frequency is 270 Hz for the adult males and 370 Hz for the
children; the latter value is almost the same as the average first formant frequency observed for adult males on the vowel /ɪ/. In
contrast, the ratio of the second over the first formant frequency is
essentially the same for each vowel, for all three groups of speakers.
For the vowel /i/ this ratio is 8.48, 9.00, and 8.65, for men, women,
and children, respectively; for the vowel /ɪ/ the ratio is 5.10, 5.77, and
5.15 for men, women, and children, respectively. As can be seen, there
is relatively little variation in the formant-frequency ratios between
the different groups of speakers. Further, the formant-frequency ratios
for different vowels are distinctly different.

   An effective method of representing formant frequencies so as to
show up the invariance of the formant-frequency ratio between

speakers is to plot the frequency of formant 2 against that of formant 1 (formants 1 and 2 being the lowest and second lowest formants, respectively). Figure 8 is a plot of this type for all 76 of the speakers in the Peterson and Barney (1952) study. The data for each vowel cluster are in distinct regions of the diagram. The region associated with each vowel is enclosed by an elliptic[9] contour which encompasses well over 90% of the data points corresponding to that vowel. Passing through the center of each vowel region, along the major axis of the encompassing elliptic contour, is a straight *dashed line*. Each *dashed line*, when extended, passes through the origin and has a slope equal to the average value of the formant-frequency ratio (F_2/F_1) for the associated vowel. If the ratio of the first two formant frequencies (F_2/F_1) is a constant for a given vowel, then the data for each vowel should fall on the corresponding *dashed line*. As can be seen from the figure, the data for each vowel fall reasonably close to their respective *dashed lines*.

The width of each elliptic contour about the *dashed line* on its major axis represents the extent to which the ratios of the measured formant frequencies differ from the average ratio for each vowel. For the majority of vowels, the elliptic contours are long and thin indicating that despite wide variations in the measured formant frequencies, the formant-frequency ratio is relatively invariant. Only the back vowels /u/, /ʊ/, and /ɔ/, and the central vowel /ɝ/, show a relatively large variation in the measured formant-frequency ratios; the elliptic contours for these vowels are short in length and are comparatively broad. There is also a fair degree of overlap between the regions associated with each of these vowels and adjacent vowel regions.

As an aside, it may be noted that the method of representing the data in Figure 8 differs slightly from that used in the classic paper by Peterson and Barney (1952). In their figure, Peterson and Barney used a special frequency scale that is linear up to 1000 Hz and logarithmic above 1000 Hz. This choice of frequency scale, although useful for certain applications (Koenig, 1949), tends to obscure the inherent invariance of the F_2/F_1 ratio. Both axes in Figure 8 use a linear scale. By so doing the invariance of the F_2/F_1 ratio is emphasized and the estimated value of this ratio for each vowel is represented by a straight (*dashed*) line passing through the origin with a slope equal to $\bar{F}_2/\bar{F}_1$, where $\bar{F}_1$ and $\bar{F}_2$ are the average values of the first two formant frequencies for the 76 speakers.

---

[9] The contours are ellipse-like in their shape, but are not true ellipses in the geometric sense.

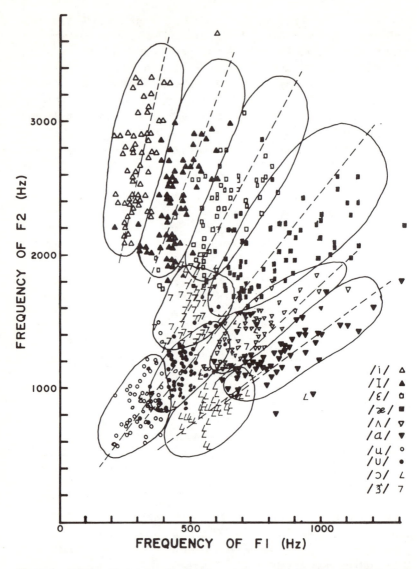

Figure 8. Relationship between first two format frequencies. The frequency of the first formant (F_1) is shown on the *horizontal axis*, that of the second formant (F_2) on the *vertical axis*. Data for 10 vowels produced by 76 speakers (33 men, 28 women, and 15 children) are shown. The data for each vowel cluster in distinct regions. Each of these regions is enclosed by an ellipse-like contour, which encompasses well over 90% of the data points corresponding to that vowel. Passing through the center of each vowel region, along the major axis of the encompassing elliptic contour, is a straight *dashed line*. Each *dashed line*, when extended, passes through the origin and has a slope equal

Aside from the spectrum or formant structure of vowels, another important acoustic characteristic is that of duration. For example, as may be seen in Figure 9, the /ɪ/ in *bit* has formant values that are similar to (but not the same as) those of /i/ in *beet*. A major acoustic difference between these two vowels is in their relative durations, the /i/ being longer than the /ɪ/. The reason for the similarity in formant structure is that the two vowels have nearly the same tongue, lip, and jaw positions. In terms of an articulatory characteristic, the terms "tense" and "lax" (referring to muscle activity) are sometimes used to distinguish between these two vowel types, /i/ being the tense vowel. There is, however, some controversy as to the accuracy of this description (Lisker and Abramson, 1975).

Vowel duration is also an important cue in signaling whether a vowel is stressed or not. The third spectrogram in Figure 9 is that of the word *beet* produced with added stress. Note the considerable lengthening of the vowel compared to the unstressed production of *beet*. Vowel duration is also affected by the phonetic environment as are other aspects of vowel production (House and Fairbanks, 1953; House, 1961). The effect of phonetic environment and other context effects are discussed under "Production of Speech Sounds in Context."

Longer vowels tend to be less steady than the shorter vowels and may drift into other vowels. For example, the vowel sound in *see* is commonly heard as two connected vowels, /ɪ/ and /i/. This process of gradually shifting from one vowel to another without abrupt change is know as "diphthongization." In American English there are two vowels that are almost invariably diphthongized, /eɪ/ as in *day* and /oʊ/ as in *soap*. Three other common diphthongal forms are /ii/ in *see*, /ʊu/ as in *shoe*, and /ju/ as in *few*. Vowels that come at the end of a word, as in *be* or *boo*, are known as "free" vowels. Vowels that are terminated by a consonant, as in *bit* or *bet*, are known as

---

to the average value of F_2/F_1 for the associated vowel. If the ratio of the first two formant frequencies (F_2/F_1) is a constant for a given vowel, then the data for that vowel should fall on the corresponding *dashed line*. The width of each elliptic contour about the *dashed line* on its major axis represents the extent to which the ratios of the measured formant frequencies differ from the average ratio for each vowel. For the majority of vowels, the elliptic contours are long and thin indicating that despite wide variations in the measured formant frequencies, the formant-frequency ratio is relatively invariant. Only the back vowels, /u/, /ʊ/, and /ɔ/, and the central vowel /ɝ/, show a relatively large variation in the measured formant-frequency ratios; the elliptic contours for these vowels are short in length and are comparatively broad. There is also a fair degree of overlap between the regions associated with these vowels and adjacent vowel regions. The data shown in this figure were obtained from Peterson and Barney (1952).

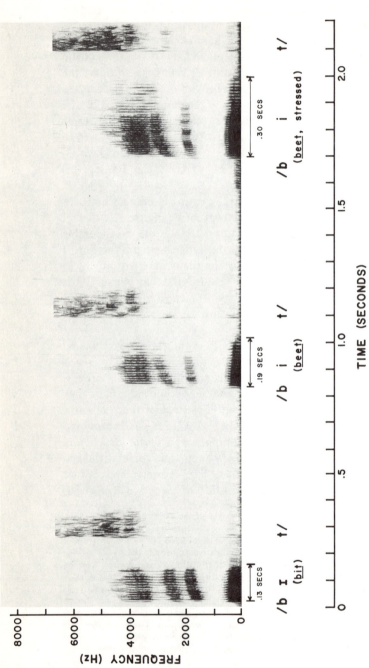

Figure 9. Duration as an acoustic cue. Spectrograms of the words *bit*, *beet*, and *beet* produced with added stress are shown. Although the frequency spectra of the three vowels are similar, they differ markedly in relative duration. Of the three vowels, the /ɪ/ in *bit* has the shortest duration (0.13 sec). The /i/ in *beet* is almost 50% longer (0.19 sec) and more than another 50% longer again (0.30 sec) if the word is produced with added stress. In comparing the two versions of *beet*, note that the effect of adding stress is to increase the duration of the vowel with relatively little change in the durations of the surrounding consonants. There is also an increase in the fundamental frequency of the voice during the stressed vowel. This effect is not obvious from the broadband spectrograms shown here. However, careful examination of the voiced portions of the spectrograms shows a greater density of *vertical striations*, i.e., a higher rate of glottal pulses per sec, during the stressed version of *beet*. A narrowband spectrogram should be used if the fundamental frequency contour is to be examined in any detail.

"checked" vowels. The free vowels are invariably longer and are prone to a greater degree of diphthongization than checked vowels.

When a vowel is diphthongized its identity as a phoneme is not changed. However, there are three complex vowel-like sounds in American English that are identified as separate phonemes, /aʊ/ as in *now*, /aɪ/ as in *sigh* and /ɔɪ/ as in *toy*. These sounds are known as "diphthongs." The essential difference between a diphthongized vowel and a diphthong relates to the meaning of what is said. If only the major, stressed component is produced then there will be no change in meaning for the diphthongized vowel, but the diphthong will be changed into another phoneme with a concomitant change in meaning. For example, both /sɪi/ and /si/ represent the same word, *see*, whereas /sɔɪ/ and /sɔ/ represent two different words, *soy* and *saw*, respectively. The /ɪi/ in *see* is a diphthongized vowel and thus there is no change in meaning if only the major component is produced. The /ɔɪ/ in *soy* is a diphthong and thus there is a change in meaning if only one component is produced.

Spectrograms of diphthongs and diphthongized vowels are shown in Figure 10. For reasons discussed in the next section, each of these sounds is preceded by an /s/. The first two spectrograms show the diphthongized vowels /ɪi/ in *see* and /eɪ/ in *say*. The next two spectrograms show the dipthongs /aʊ/ in *sow* and /ɔɪ/ in *soy*. Note how the formants change their values during the vowel or diphthong, beginning with values appropriate to the first component and moving systematically, but not too rapidly, toward values appropriate for the second component.

There is some evidence of triphthongization (i.e., diphthongization of a component within a diphthong) in the production of *soy*. The initial formant values are not quite appropriate for the /ɔ/ component, but there is movement into the /ɔ/ position (shown by a small downward shift of the second formant) followed by a major shift towards formant values appropriate for the /ɪ/ component. Because of the initial variation in formant values, the diphthong produced may not sound quite like /ɔɪ/ but rather as if an additional vowel-like component (possibly /a/) precedes the diphthong.

CONSONANTS

There are three major groups of consonants: plosives, fricatives, and the frictionless consonants. The last group, which is all voiced, may be further subdivided into nasals, glides, the lateral /ℓ/, and the rather special /r/ sound. Appendix II (this chapter) shows how the consonants of English may be classified.

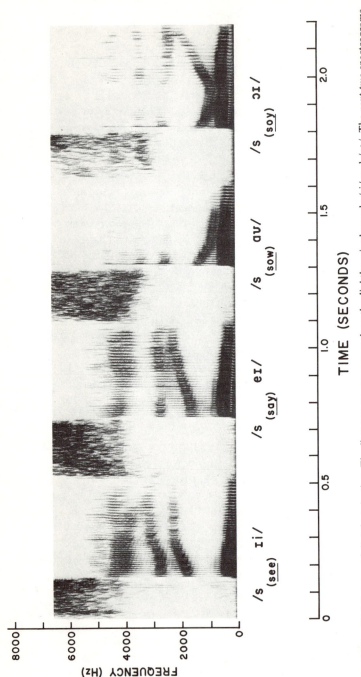

FREQUENCY (Hz)

8000 — 6000 — 4000 — 2000 — 0

/s ii/
(see)

/s ɛɪ/
(say)

/s aʊ/
(sow)

/s ɔɪ/
(soy)

0   0.5   1.0   1.5   2.0

TIME (SECONDS)

Figure 10. Diphthongs and diphthongization. The first two spectrograms show the diphthongized vowels /ii/ and /ɛɪ/. The next two spectrograms show the diphthongs /aʊ/ and /ɔɪ/. Although the diphthongs and diphthongized vowels have a similar acoustic structure, both exhibiting gradual movements of the formants, they differ phonetically in that the diphthongs have a distinct identity as separate phonemes. This distinction is best clarified by considering the effect on meaning if only one component of a diphthong or diphthongized vowel is produced. There is no change in meaning if only the major component of a diphthongized vowel is produced; e.g., both /sii/ and /si/ are identified as the word see. However, there will be a change in meaning if only one component of a diphthong is produced; e.g., /sɔɪ/ and /sɔ/ are identified as separate words, soy and saw, respectively. In examining the spectrograms, note how the formants change gradually from values appropriate to the first component of the diphthong or diphthongized vowel to values appropriate to the second component. Note also that the spectrum of the preceding voiceless consonant is affected by the voiced component and there is some evidence of the /s/ sound sharing one or more formants with following vowel or diphthong.

Fricatives

Fricatives, as the name suggests, are produced by frication or turbulence in the air stream. Turbulence is caused by forcing the air to flow through a narrow constriction, and it is convenient to classify fricatives primarily in terms of the place where the constriction is narrowest. The fricative /θ/, as in *thumb*, is produced by forming a constriction between the tongue and the gum ridge behind the upper front teeth. The /ʃ/, as in *ship*, is produced by forming a constriction between the blade of the tongue and the mid region of the mouth roof. A second important classification is whether or not voicing occurs in addition to frication. The voiced fricatives, /ð/, as in *that*, /z/ as in *zoo*, and /ʒ/, as in *treasure*, are produced in essentially the same way as their unvoiced counterparts, /θ/, /s/, and /ʃ/, respectively, except that the speaker uses his vocal cords as well to provide a combination of voicing and frication.

Figure 11 shows spectrograms of the most common fricative sounds. The voiceless fricatives, /f/, /s/, /ʃ/, and /θ/, are shown in the *upper half* of the diagram. Their voiced cognates, /v/, /z/, /ʒ/, and /ð/, respectively, are shown in the *lower half* of the diagram. The spectrograms of the voiceless fricatives are characterized by a relatively broad distribution of acoustic power with frequency. As with the vowels, the vocal tract has distinct resonances that show up as dark regions on the spectrograms, but unlike the vowels, these formants are relatively broad and not as clearly defined.

There are several reasons for the differences in the formant characteristics of the vowels and voiceless fricatives. The source of sound for the vowels and vowel-like sounds is at the glottis and all of the vocal tract serves as a sound-transmission path for this sound source. The source of sound for the voiceless fricatives is at the point of constriction and there is a complex interaction between the resonances of the vocal tract behind the point of constriction, which affect the characteristics of the sound source, with those resonances in front of the point of constriction, which affect the transmission of sound through the remainder of the vocal tract. Also, turbulence in the flow of air through the vocal tract, because of the absorption of sound power to maintain the turbulence, has the joint affect of reducing the efficiency of sound transmission through the vocal tract and increasing the damping of the vocal-tract resonances. As a result, there is a less intense concentration of acoustic power within the resonant frequency regions and, consequently, the formants are of much greater width. Another consequence is that the power of the voiceless fricatives is generally much less than that of voiced sounds.

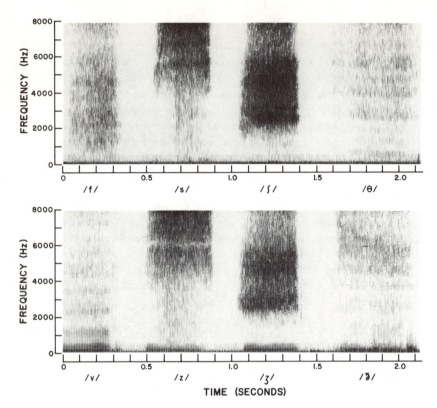

Figure 11. Spectrograms of the fricative sounds. Spectrograms of the most common fricative sounds are shown. The voiceless fricatives /f/, /s/, /ʃ/, and /θ/ are shown in the *upper half* of the figure. Their voiced cognates, /v/, /z/, /ʒ/, and /ð/, respectively, are shown in the *lower half* of the figure. The spectrograms of the voiceless fricatives are characterized by a relatively broad distribution of acoustic power with frequency. As with the vowels, the vocal tract has distinct resonances that show up as dark regions on the spectrograms, but unlike the vowels, these formants are relatively broad and not as clearly defined. The spectrograms of the voiced fricatives are essentially the same as their voiceless cognates except that an additional voiced component is superimposed on the fricative component. The voiced component manifests itself as a dark region in the vicinity of the fundamental frequency with *vertical striations* indicative of the quasiperiodic pulsive nature of the sound source. All of the fricatives shown here were produced in isolation. See Figure 10 for an example of a fricative produced in context.

The fricatives /f/ and /θ/ show the greatest spread of acoustic power with frequency, the spectrum of /f/ being slightly broader. As shown in Figure 11, the spectrogram of /θ/ shows less power in the low frequency region than that of /f/. In terms of overall power, both /f/ and /θ/ are relatively weak. Because these two sounds have similar spectra and are also of relatively low power, they are frequently misheard, the one often being heard in place of the other.

The fricatives /s/ and /ʃ/ are more powerful than the other voiceless fricatives and are marked by very distinct spectral characteristics. Most of the acoustic power in /s/ is concentrated in the high frequency region. For the spectrogram of /s/ shown in Figure 11, almost all of the acoustic power is distributed in the region above about 3000 Hz. Because there is relatively little acoustic power in the low frequency region, many hearing-impaired children simply do not hear the /s/ sound. However, contextual cues can be very effective in indicating whether or not an /s/ is present. The spectrum of /ʃ/ is similar to that of /s/ in that the bulk of the acoustic power is in the high frequency region. The major differences are that the upward spread of the high frequency power begins at a lower frequency (from about 2000 Hz for the spectrogram shown in Figure 11) and there is a greater relative concentration of power in the 2000–5000 Hz region.

The spectrograms of the voiced fricatives /v/, /ð/, /z/, and /ɛ/ are essentially the same as their voiceless cognates, /f/, /θ/, /s/, and /ʃ/, respectively, except that superimposed on the fricative component is an additional voiced component. The voiced component manifests itself as a dark region in the vicinity of the fundamental frequency with vertical striations indicative of the quasiperiodic, pulsive nature of this sound source. The voiced fricatives shown in Figure 11 were produced with some emphasis on the fricative component of the sound with the intended result that both the frication and voicing components are clearly evident. In many cases, the voicing component is much more powerful than the fricative component and spectrograms of such voiced fricatives will look more like vowels or vowel-like sounds with some added frication.

The articulators used in forming the constriction for the fricative sounds are not generally the same as those used in shaping the vocal tract for the vowels, or other continuant sounds. Consequently, when a fricative leads into a vowel, or vice versa, those articulators that are not critical for the production of the fricatives may take on positions appropriate for the adjacent vowel. The shape of the vocal tract during the fricative is thus affected by its phonetic context and this effect is shown spectrographically by context-dependent changes in the power-frequency spectrum of the fricatives (Hughes and Halle, 1956).

The spectrograms shown in Figure 11 are of fricatives produced in isolation, and thus these spectrograms show the inherent characteristics of the fricatives. Spectrograms of these fricatives produced in context would be modified somewhat, taking on some of the characteristics of adjacent phonemes. An example of the effect of phonetic context is shown in Figure 10. In this diagram spectrograms of various diphthongs and diphthongized vowels are shown, each preceded by the fricative /s/. Note how the spectrum of /s/ changes depending on the characteristics of the following vowel sound. The most marked contrast is between /sɪi/ and /sɔɪ/. The spectrogram of the latter shows a much broader spread of the high frequency power in the /s/, going downwards in frequency to at least 3000 Hz. There is also some evidence of the /s/ sound sharing some formants with the following vowel. Contextual effects are not peculiar to the fricative sounds. The mutual interactions between sounds produced in context are discussed under "Production of Speech Sounds in Context."

Plosives

The plosives, particularly those at the start of a word or phrase, are produced by blocking the flow of air through the vocal tract at some point and allowing pressure to build up and then, by a sudden movement of the articulators, unblocking the tract with sufficient speed to cause a minor acoustic shock wave: hence the name plosive. Plosives at the end of a word or phrase are produced by blocking the vocal tract, but not necessarily with the subsequent build-up and sudden release of air pressure. These plosives do not have the characteristic plosion of the initial plosives, but are nevertheless classified as plosives because of the similarity in vocal tract configuration.

The plosives may be classified according to the place at which the vocal tract is blocked. The plosives, /p/, /t/, and /k/, as in *pea, tea,* and *key,* for example, are produced by closure at the lips, hard palate, and soft palate, respectively. As with the fricatives, a second important variable is whether or not voicing occurs. The plosives /b/, as in *bash,* /d/, as in *dash,* and /g/, as in *gash,* are the voiced counterparts of /p/, /t/, and /k/, respectively. However, unlike the fricatives, which are of relatively long duration, the plosives are produced by rapid movements of the articulators and are of short duration. Voicing may not actually occur during the period in which the tract is blocked, but the timing of events, particularly the time taken before the onset of voicing, as well as the duration of the preceding vowel, play an important role in determining whether a plosive is heard as voiced or unvoiced.

Figure 12 shows spectrograms for three plosive-vowel combinations. In the first there is a long delay (95 msec) between the release from closure and the onset of voicing. This delay is known as the voice onset time. During this period some aspiration, i.e., turbulent airflow, occurs and the plosive that is heard is the voiceless, aspirated plosive /pʰ/. The aspiration is seen as a broad gray region with some slightly darker regions that are indicative of the formant structure. The for-

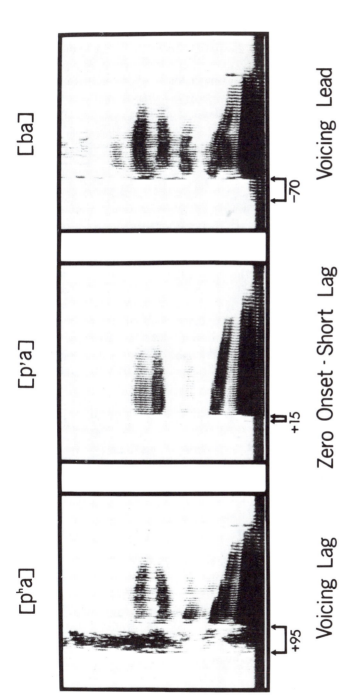

[pʰa]   [p'a]   [ba]

+95   +15   -70

Voicing Lag   Zero Onset - Short Lag   Voicing Lead

Figure 12. Voice onset time in plosive-vowel combinations. Three conditions of voice onset time are shown. The first spectrogram shows a relatively long delay (95 msec) between the release from closure and the onset of voicing. Some aspiration is evident during this period and the plosive that is heard is the voiceless, aspirated plosive /pʰ/. The aspiration is seen as a broad gray region with some slightly darker regions that are indicative of the formant structure. The formants become clearly visible after the onset of voicing. The voiced portion of the spectrogram also shows the *vertical striations* typical of a pulsed sound source. The second spectrogram shows a short voice onset time (15 msec). The plosive in this case is voiceless but unaspirated, /p'/, in that there is no audible aspiration before the onset of voicing. Since the vocal tract is already open and in the approximate position for the vowel at the onset of voicing, the formant transitions indicative of a change in vocal tract shape are not evident. The third spectrogram shows a negative voice onset time (−70 msec) for the voiced plosive /b/. In this case voicing begins before the release, as shown by the small low-frequency *bar* close to the baseline during the closure period.

mants become clearly visible after the onset of voicing. The voiced portion of the spectrogram also shows the vertical striations typical of a pulsed sound source.

The next sound spectrogram shows a short voice onset time (15 msec). The plosive in this case is voiceless, but unaspirated, /p′a/, in that there is no audible aspiration before the onset of voicing. As before, the formant structure is clearly evident during the voiced portion of the spectrogram. Because the vocal tract is already open and in the approximate position for the vowel at the onset of voicing, the formant transitions showing movement of the vocal tract configuration are not evident.

The third spectrogram shows a negative voice onset time (-70 msec) for the voiced plosive /b/. In this case voicing begins before the release, as shown by the small low frequency bar close to the baseline during the closure period. Because the vocal tract is blocked, voicing can continue for only a short period before the build-up of air pressure in the vocal tract is such that a plosive release must occur. This effect can be demonstrated quite easily by blocking the nostrils, keeping the lips closed, and producing a voiced sound for as long as possible. At the instant of the release, the spectrogram shows a narrow vertical striation indicative of plosion, followed by the usual, less intense striations, representing individual glottal pulses. Immediately after the release, the shape of the vocal tract changes from its closed configuration to an open configuration for the vowel /a/. This movement of the vocal tract is evident from the formant transitions that occur immediately after the release.

Plosives occurring at the end of a word or phrase may be released or unreleased. If they are released, the characteristic differences in voice onset time help distinguish between the voiced and voiceless plosives. If the final plosive is not released, the voice onset time and aspiration cues are not available and the listener will need to depend on other available cues. Duration of the preceding vowel is a particularly important cue for distinguishing whether a final plosive is voiced or voiceless. As a rule, vowels preceding a voiced plosive are longer than those preceding a voiceless plosive. For further information on this topic, see Raphael (1972).

A number of cues are used in helping the listener identify the place of articulation of plosives. These include the formant transitions that occur just before or just after closure, the temporal and frequency characteristics of the aspiration burst following the release, and the relative timing of events from the phoneme preceding to the phoneme following the plosive. Of these cues, the formant transitions that are characteristic of plosive-vowel combinations are of particular importance.

A summary of formant transitions for the plosives /b/, /d/, and /g/ into a range of different vowels is shown in Figure 13. These data are from a perceptual study on the identification of synthetic speech stimuli (Delattre, Liberman, and Cooper, 1955), and are idealizations in the sense that they are not the only acoustic cues characterizing these plosive-vowel combinations. The cues shown are nevertheless perceptually important. The central acoustic cue, at least for the stimuli shown in Figure 13, seems to be the direction of the second formant transition. For the voiceless plosives, the location on the frequency axis of the aspiration burst following the release seems to be an important cue for distinguishing between /p/, /t/, and /k/ (Cooper, et al., 1952; Halle, Hughes, and Radley, 1957).

The formant transitions shown in Figure 13 follow a relatively simple pattern. During the closure period the vocal tract has a characteristic set of resonances, depending on the place at which the vocal tract is blocked. These resonances are not visible on the spectrogram since there is negligible acoustic output during closure. After the

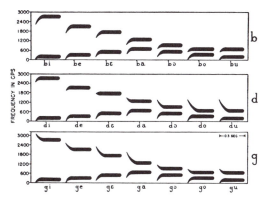

Figure 13. Synthetic spectrograms showing second formant transitions for various plosive-vowel combinations. A summary of formant transitions for the plosives /b/, /d/, and /g/ into a range of different vowels is shown. These data are from a perceptual study on the identification of synthetic speech stimuli (Delattre, Liberman, and Cooper, 1955), and are idealizations in the sense that they are not the only acoustic cues characterizing these plosive-vowel combinations. The cues shown are nevertheless perceptually important. The central acoustic cue seems to be the direction of the second formant transition. Note that for each plosive the two formant transitions seem to be emanating from a common pair of points on the *frequency axis*. Although not shown on this diagram, an important cue for distinguishing between the voiceless plosives, /p/, /t/, and /k/, is the location on the frequency axis of the aspiration burst following the plosive release (Cooper et al., 1952; Halle, Hughes, and Radley, 1957). (From Delattre et al., 1955; reprinted with permission.)

release, the vocal tract changes its shape rapidly toward the target configuration for the following vowel. For the voiced plosives, there is periodic excitation (i.e., voicing) of the vocal tract during this transitional period and the spectrogram shows the characteristic dark contours corresponding to the formants in a state of transition. A simple rule for these formant transitions, as exemplified by the idealized formant patterns shown in Figure 13, is that the transition is from an initial value that is characteristic of the place of constriction of the plosive toward the steady, target formant frequency of the following vowel. The very early portion of the transition may not be visible from the spectrogram because of the negligible acoustic power generated during closure and the interference from the impulsive sound generated during the plosive release; however, the direction of the formant transition is usually evident from the spectrogram. These transitions are not always obvious in spectrograms of voiceless plosives, as shown in Figure 12, if the onset of voicing occurs after the transitional period.

The formant patterns shown in Figures 12 and 13 are for plosive-vowel pairs produced in isolation and, as a result, the formant values for the vowel portion are relatively steady with time. Furthermore, the formant frequencies for each vowel during this steady state portion are consistent with those measured by Peterson and Barney (see Figure 8). In running speech, there is seldom sufficient time for the formants to reach their target values for a given vowel before a new transition is initiated towards the next sound. This effect is evident from Figure 9, which shows spectrograms of an entire word and in which the formants never quite reach a steady state condition. Even though the target formant values may not be reached, the intended sound may well be heard by the listener. It is thus important in interpreting spectrograms to pay attention not only to the steady target values reached by the formants, but also to those incomplete formant movements in the direction of a targeted value.

Nasals and Nasalized Sounds

Nasals are produced by blocking the air path through the mouth and allowing air to escape through the nose. For example, /m/, as in *mom*, is produced by blocking the vocal tract at the lips and lowering the velum to allow air to escape through the nasal cavity (see Figure 3). The /n/, as in *nun*, is produced by blocking the vocal tract with the tongue placed against the upper gum ridge. The nasal /ŋ/, as in *sing*, is produced by blocking the vocal tract toward the rear of the hard palate.

Both the oral and nasal cavities are involved in the production of the nasals. Sound is transmitted through the nasal cavity, the blocked oral cavity acting as a closed resonant tube that is acoustically coupled to the main sound-transmission path. The acoustic interaction between the oral and nasal cavities is complex and not fully understood (Flanagan, 1972). One factor contributing to this complex interaction is that at certain frequencies, when the oral cavity is resonant, the nasal cavity shows an antiresonance, and vice versa; i.e., in certain frequency regions one section of the vocal tract may be transmitting acoustic power with high efficiency (resonance), while another section may be absorbing acoustic power (antiresonance). The result is a complex interaction that depends critically on the exact values of the resonance and antiresonance.

As shown in Figure 14, the spectrograms of the nasal sounds are similar to those of the vowels with certain important differences. Because the nasals, like the vowels, are continuant voiced sounds, the spectrograms show a distinct formant structure that is relatively steady with time; they also exhibit the narrow vertical striations typical of voiced sounds. Unlike the vowel spectrograms, the formants are broader and there is some evidence of a greater degree of acoustic power between the formants. Both of these effects are attributable to the interactions resulting from the acoustic coupling of the oral and nasal cavities. The nasals also show a relatively large concentration of acoustic power in the region of 250–300 Hz (Malecot, 1956). This low resonance is caused by the greater overall size (both length and volume) of the vocal tract which, in this case, includes the oral and nasal cavities. As a rule, the greater the length of an acoustic tube, the lower the first resonant frequency.

Another sound type that involves both the oral and nasal cavities is the nasalized vowel. These vowels are produced in much the same way as other vowels except that the velum does not completely block the entrance to the nasal cavity and sound is thus transmitted through both the oral and nasal cavities. The effect of the acoustic coupling of the nasal and oral cavities produces systematic changes in the vowel spectrum (Curtis, 1970; Flanagan, 1972). The spectral changes caused by nasalization are quite subtle and not immediately obvious from the spectrogram. The differences are nevertheless clearly evident when the cross-sectional spectra (i.e., the power-frequency spectra) of nasalized and non-nasalized vowels are compared (Curtis, 1970). Typically, the frequency of the lowest formant is raised slightly and some additional low-level high-frequency formants are introduced.

A contrast between a nasalized and non-nasalized vowel may be

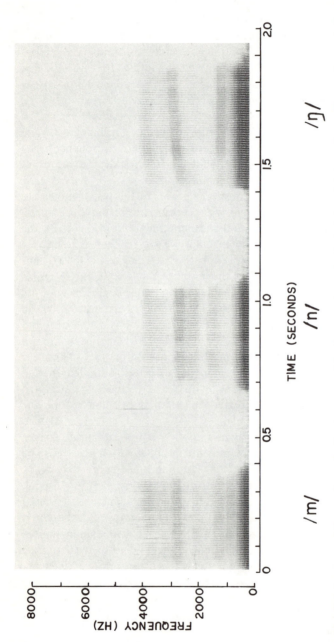

Figure 14. Spectrograms of the nasal sounds. Spectrograms of the three nasal sounds, /m/, /n/, and /ŋ/ are shown. The nasals are similar to the vowels in that they are continuant voiced sounds and the spectrograms show a distinct formant structure that is relatively steady with time; they also exhibit the narrow *vertical striations* typical of voiced sounds. Unlike the vowels, the formants of the nasal sounds are broader and there is relatively more acoustic power in the intervening region between formants. Both of these effects are attributable to the interactions resulting from the acoustic coupling of the oral and nasal cavities. The nasals are also characterized by a relatively large concentration of acoustic power in the low frequency region. This low frequency resonance is attributable to the greater overall size of the vocal tract which, in this case, includes both the oral and nasal cavities.

obtained by comparing the /i/ vowel in the words *be* and *me*. The /i/ in *me* is nasalized because the velum typically does not return completely to its position for non-nasal sounds thereby leaving some acoustic coupling between the oral and nasal cavities at the end of the /m/. Perceptually, the differences between the two productions of /i/ are very subtle. However, the fact that nasalization is taking place can be demonstrated quite easily by holding the nostrils closed during the production of *be* and *me*. The former is unaffected by blocking the nostrils, whereas the latter is markedly affected even during the vowel, although phonemically both words contain the same vowel.

Nasal-vowel interactions are quite common in normal speech. In general, any voiced sound can be nasalized if the velum does not form a tight seal between the oral and nasal cavities. In certain regions of the United States it is quite common for vowels and vowel-like sounds to be nasalized routinely and not only as a result of nasal-vowel interactions.

Glides

The glides are produced by vocal-tract movement from one articulatory position to the next. The glides generally precede vowels and the resulting motion is from an initial vowel-like position to that of the intended vowel. For example, the word *we*, which starts with the glide /w/, is produced by initially holding the tongue and lips roughly in position for the vowel /u/, as in *boot*, and then, while the sound is being produced, moving tongue, jaw, and lips to the position for the /i/ vowel. Similarly, the glide /j/ is produced by initially holding the articulators roughly in position for the vowel /i/ and then gliding into the position for the following vowel.

Spectrograms of the glides are shown in Figure 15. Because the acoustic characteristics of the glide are critically dependent on the following vowel, each of the two glides in English, /w/ and /j/, is shown in combination with the vowels /i/, /a/, and /u/. These three vowels cover a wide range of formant spacings and thus provide a good illustration of the range and magnitude of formant transitions that occur with the glide sounds. The most notable contrasts are between /wi/ and /wu/ and between /ji/ and /ju/. For /wi/ the articulators are initially in position for the vowel /u/ and the spectrogram begins with formant values appropriate to this vowel, gliding rapidly to values for the vowel /i/. Because /i/ and /u/ have similar first formants, but differ markedly in the location of their second and higher formants (see Table 1 and Figure 8), the spectrogram for /wi/ shows a relatively steady first formant, but a substantial transition in the value of the second (and higher) formants.

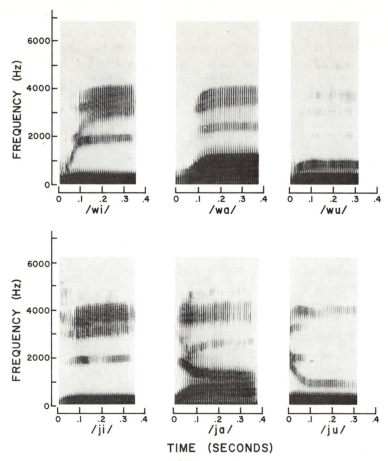

TIME (SECONDS)

Figure 15. Spectrograms of various glide-vowel combinations. The glides generally precede a vowel and spectrograms are shown of the glides /w/ and /j/ in combination with the vowels /i/, /a/, and /u/; respectively. These vowels cover a wide range of different formant spacings. For the glide /w/, the initial positioning of the articulators is similar to that for the vowel /u/. Each of the spectrograms in the upper row thus begins with formant values appropriate for the vowel /u/ (see Figures 7 and 8), gliding rapidly to formant values appropriate to the following vowel. Because /i/ and /u/ have similar first formants, but differ markedly in the location of their second and higher formants, the spectrogram for /wi/ shows a relatively steady first formant but a substantial transition in the value of the second (and higher) formants. In contrast, for /wu/ the articulators begin in positions roughly appropriate for the vowel /u/ and then stay in essentially the same positions for the following vowel. The spectrogram thus shows relatively minor changes in formant values. For the glide /j/, the initial positioning of the articulators is similar to that for the vowel /i/ and each of the spectrograms in the lower row begin with formant values appropriate to this vowel. Because for /ji/ the initial positioning of the articulators is essentially the same as that for the following vowel, there are relatively minor changes in formant values during this utterance. In contrast, the spectrograms for /ja/ and /ju/ showed marked formant transitions as the articulators move from their initial /i/-like positions to those for the vowels /a/ and /u/, respectively. The formant transitions in these glide-vowel combinations are less rapid than those of the plosive-vowel combinations (see Figures 12 and 13) but more rapid than the formant movements occurring in diphthongization (see Figure 10).

88

In constrast, for /wu/ the articulators begin in position roughly appropriate for the vowel /u/, and then stay in essentially the same position for the following vowel. The spectrogram thus shows relatively minor changes in formant values. Similarly, there is relatively little movement of the articulators in /ji/ and the corresponding spectrogram shows formant values that are relatively constant with time. For /ju/, however, the articulators start in position for /i/ and rapidly glide to that for the vowel /u/. As before, there is relatively little change in the value of the first formant, but the second and higher formants undergo a substantial transition. The magnitude of the transition is roughly equal to, but opposite in direction to that shown in the spectrogram for /wi/.

Thus far, three types of sound have been described that involve movements of the formants. These are the plosives, glides, and diphthongs. It is instructive to compare the different rates of formant movement that characterize these sound types. For the plosives, as shown in Figures 12 and 13, the formant transitions are quite rapid. For the glides, Figure 15, the rate of transition is less rapid, and for the diphthongs, Figure 10, the formant movements are comparatively slow.

Slowing down or speeding up speech without regard to phonetic structure, as can be done quite easily with a speech synthesizer or even a simple tape recorder, will alter the rate of change of the formants, which in turn will alter the nature of the sounds that are perceived. For example, a sufficient slowdown in playback can make a plosive sound like a glide and a glide sound like a diphthong. When a human speaker changes his or her rate of speaking, the changes in timing are made selectively, the vowels and other continuant sounds absorbing the major changes in duration, and the noncontinuant consonant sounds being affected only slightly.

Affricates

The affricates are a rather special group in that they are a combination of a plosive and fricative pronounced as one sound. This occurs when a stop[10] is released relatively slowly into a fricative that is produced in the same area of the mouth. Although there are several such combinations, only two are recognized in American English. These are /tʃ/, as in *church*, and /dʒ/ as in *judge*. Other combinations, such as in the words *hats* and *bids,* are recognized as two distinct sounds in sequence since the plosives may be separated from the following fricatives.

---

[10] The terms stop and plosive are used interchangeably in this chapter.

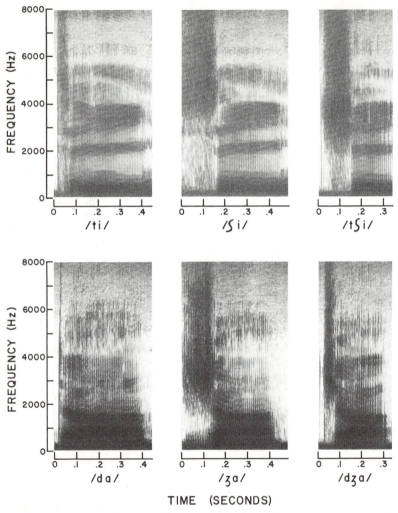

TIME   (SECONDS)

Figure 16.   Spectrograms of affricate-vowel combinations and related consonant-vowel combinations. The affricates are a combination of a plosive and a fricative produced as one sound. Spectrograms of the two English affricates, /tʃ/ and /dʒ/, in combination with the vowels /i/ and /a/, respectively, are shown. Also shown are spectrograms of each plosive component and each fricative component in combination with the same vowel. One of the effects of producing a plosive and fricative in combination is that the burst of aspiration typical of the released plosive is absorbed by the following fricative. The burst of aspiration is usually quite marked for the voiceless plosive /t/, as is evident in the spectrogram of /ti/. However, there is no evidence of such a burst in the spectrogram of /tʃi/. In comparing the spectrogram of /ʃi/ with that of /tʃi/ (and that of /ʒa/ with /dʒa/) it may be noted that the duration of the fricative alone is greater than that of the corresponding fricative component of the affricate.

Spectrograms of the affricates are essentially the same as those of a stop followed by a fricative, as shown in Figure 16. Because the stop and fricative are produced in combination, the burst of aspiration typical of released plosives has been absorbed by the following fricative. This burst of aspiration is usually quite marked for the voiceless plosives and for /t/, in particular. However, in the spectrogram of /tʃ/, as in that for /dʒ/, the plosive release is followed immediately by frication appropriate to the fricative component of the sound and no separate burst of aspiration is evident.

Lateral /ℓ/ and Glide /r/

The lateral /ℓ/ is produced by placing the tip of the tongue against the upper gum ridge with the sides of the tongue free from contact with other parts of the mouth so that air can flow out laterally. The /ℓ/ is a voiced sound similar to a glide and is partially devoiced when following a voiceless plosive in a stressed syllable (e.g., *play, clean*) or when following a voiceless fricative (e.g., *flew, sly*).

There are two important variations of the /ℓ/ sound. A "light" /ℓ/ occurs before a voiced sound, as in *like,* and a "dark" /ℓ/ occurs after a voiced sound, as in *fool.* The light /ℓ/ is made with the tongue forward in the mouth, the tongue blade touching the upper gum ridge. The "dark" /ℓ/ is made with the tongue farther back in the mouth, with the body of the tongue being raised toward the velum.

The consonant /r/ is perhaps the most complicated of the speech sounds. It has a number of different forms that vary with dialect and pronunciation. Two important cases for general American English are the glide /r/ and the vowel-like /r/. The glide /r/ generally occurs before a vowel, e.g., as in the word *red*, and is produced like a glide with an initial position similar to that for the vowel /ɜ/, as in *turn*. The vowel-like /r/ may precede a consonant or occur at the end of a word or phrase, as in *bird* or *mother.* It is produced in a manner similar to a vowel with the tongue pulled back slightly towards the center of the mouth. In some parts of the country the /r/ sound is dropped altogether and the preceding vowel is lengthened, sometimes forming a diphthong. Space does not allow for a detailed discussion of the various forms of /r/, and the reader is referred to Bronstein (1960, pp. 114–122) for further details.

Spectrograms of /ℓ/ and /r/ are shown in Figure 17. Because of the marked interaction of these sounds with adjacent phonemes, the spectrograms show /ℓ/ and /r/ in a vowel context consisting of /i/, /a/, and /u/. The second and higher formants of both /ℓ/ and /r/ are lower than those of /i/ and the first spectrogram shows marked transitions for these formants into and out of /ℓ/ and /r/, respectively.

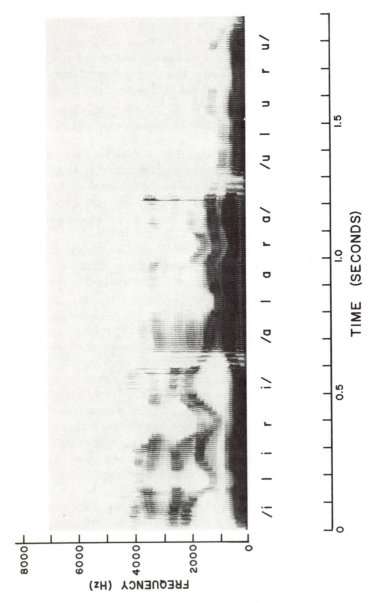

Figure 17.   Spectrograms of /ℓ/ and /r/ in a vowel context are shown for the three vowels /i/, /a/, and /u/. The second and higher formants of both /ℓ/ and /r/ are lower than those of /i/ and the spectrogram shows marked formant transitions for /ℓ/ and /r/ into and out of this vowel. The effect is not quite as marked for /a/, and there is relatively little variation in formant values when /ℓ/ and /r/ are each bracketed by the /u/ vowel.

The effect is not quite as marked for /a/, and there is relatively little variation in formant values when /ℓ/ and /r/ are each bracketed by the /u/ vowel.

SUMMARY OF GROSS
FREQUENCY AND INTENSITY CHARACTERISTICS

The preceding sections provide a brief description of how the sounds of speech are produced and the major acoustic characteristics of these sounds. The detailed acoustic structure of each speech sound is quite complex and, as discussed in the next section, subject to substantial modification depending on how it is produced in context. It is nevertheless very useful to have a summary of the gross acoustic characteristics of speech sounds, in addition to the fine detail contained in the spectrograms shown in Figures 6–17. Such a summary is provided in Figure 18.

Figure 18 shows the spectral regions occupied by the major components of the various speech sounds. The *vertical axis* shows sound pressure level (see Appendix I for a discussion of the relationship between sound intensity and sound pressure level). The *horizontal axis* shows frequency plotted on a logarithmic scale (e.g., the distance from 50–100 Hz is the same as that from 100–200 Hz, which in turn is the same as that from 200–400 Hz, etc.). The data summarized in this diagram are only to be used as a rough guide because there are many complicating factors that can effect the relative levels and spectral composition of speech sounds.

As shown in Figure 18, the most intense components of speech are the first formants of the vowels and nasals, and the fundamental frequency of the voiced sounds. The higher formants become progressively less intense with increasing frequency, the average sound pressure level of the formants in the vicinity of 3000 Hz being some 20 dB less than those in the vicinity of 500 Hz. The consonants are, on the average, less powerful than the vowels and the sound pressure levels of the major components of these sounds occupy a region just below that occupied by the vowel formants. There is, of course, some overlap between these two regions, the formants of the nasals, glides, /ℓ/, and /r/, being almost as powerful as those of the vowel sounds. The frequency region of the fricatives extend well beyond that of the other consonantal and vowel sounds.

The sound pressure levels shown in Figure 18 are derived from measurements taken at a distance of 1 m from the speakers lips in a quiet, nonreverberant room. Under these conditions all of the speech sounds are clearly audible. As shown in the diagram, even the least powerful components of the consonantal sounds lie well above the

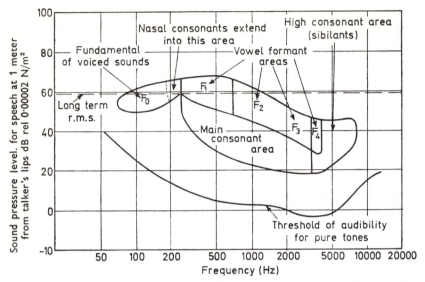

Figure 18. Spectral regions occupied by the major components of various speech sounds. The *vertical axis* shows sound pressure level in decibels, the *horizontal axis* shows frequency plotted on a logarithmic scale. The sound pressure levels shown in the figure are derived from measurements taken at a distance of 1 m from a male speaker's lips in a quiet, nonreverberant room. The data summarized here should only be used as a rough guide, however, because there are many complicating factors that can affect the relative levels and spectral composition of speech sounds, As shown in the figure, the most intense components of speech are the first formants of the vowels and nasals, and the fundamental frequency of the voiced sounds. The higher formants become progressively less intense with increasing frequency, the average sound pressure level of the formants in the vicinity of 3000 Hz being some 20 dB less than those in the vicinity of 500 Hz. The consonants are, on the average, less powerful than the vowels and the sound pressure levels of the major components of these sounds occupy a region just below that occupied by the vowel formants. There is some overlap between these two regions, the formants of the nasals, glides, /ℓ/, and /r/ being almost as powerful as those of the vowel sounds. The frequency region of the fricatives extends well beyond that of the other consonantal and vowel sounds. (From Richards, 1973; reprinted with permission.)

threshold of audibility for pure tones. However, if there is background noise in the room, or if the distance between speaker and listener is well in excess of 1 m, then the less powerful sounds or important components of these sounds may not be audible. Note that there is only a 20-dB difference between the bottom of the main consonantal area and the threshold of audibility.

The range between the most intense components of speech and the least intense components that are perceptually important is close to 50 dB. The most intense components occur in the region of 500 Hz. The least intense components occur at much higher frequencies, from about 3000 Hz and up. Within a given frequency region, however, (e.g., within an octave bandwidth), the range from the most intense to least intense components is approximately 30 dB.

Data on the relative levels of individual speech sounds[11] as heard by the ear are summarized in Table 2. The first column shows relative levels as measured with respect to the threshold of audibility for that sound. The second column shows relative levels measured with respect to that level at which the sound is just recognizable, i.e., the level at which the sounds were correctly identified 90% of the time in a syllable articulation test of the type developed by Fletcher and his coworkers. For further information on how the relative levels shown in Table 2 were derived, see Fletcher (1953). Because the data shown in Table 2 are in terms of relative sound levels it is necessary to define a reference intensity. For convenience, the intensity of the least intense sound, $/\theta/$, has been chosen as the reference; i.e., the relative sound level of this sound has been set to 1 dB and the levels of the other sounds are specified relative to this sound.

The relative sound levels shown in Table 2 reflect the ear's sensitivity to these sounds. By far the most intense sounds (whether measured in terms of relative sensation level or in terms of their relative level above the threshold of recognition) are the vowels and diphthongs. The next most intense sounds are the laterals, nasals, and affricates. These are followed by plosives and the voiced fricatives and the plosives, with some overlap between individual members of these two groups of sounds. The least intense sounds are the voiceless fricatives (with the exception of $/\int/$, which is a moderately intense sound). Because the voiceless fricatives are, on the average, of relatively low intensity with most of their power in the high frequencies, they are the sounds that are most easily misheard by the hard of hearing. The vowels and nasals because of their high relative sound levels and low frequency content are usually the sounds for which the hearing impaired have least difficulty.

Finally, it is useful to have some idea of the overall acoustic power of speech in absolute rather than relative terms. Unfortunately, an exact, absolute specification is very difficult to provide because of the many factors that affect speech levels. These include speaker-to-listener distance (Beranek, 1954), effects of room reverberation (Beranek, 1954; Kryter, 1970), effect of background noise level on speaker's voice level (Lane and Tranel, 1971; Pearsons et al., 1976), age and sex of speaker (Pearsons et al., 1976), and individual dif-

---

[11] The specification of the relative levels of individual speech sounds raises a number of complex issues, which are discussed in Appendix I of this chapter.

Table 2.   Relative levels of speech sounds as heard by the ear[a]

Relative sensation level (dB)	Relative level re: threshold of recognition (dB)	Average (dB)	Speech sound	
26.0	26.0	26.0	ɔ	(sought)
25.6	26.0	25.8	a	(calm)
25.5	26.0	25.8	aɪ	(sigh)
25.2	26.0	25.6	aʊ	(now)
25.6	24.9	25.3	oʊ	(soap)
23.4	26.3	24.9	a	(half)
25.2	23.2	24.2	æ	(sat)
23.1	24.1	23.6	ʊ	(foot)
24.4	19.5	22.0	ɛ	(set)
19.3	24.2	21.8	eɪ	(day)
22.0	21.5	21.8	ɝ	(third)
21.9	20.3	21.1	u	(food)
18.6	21.5	20.1	ɪ	(sit)
19.5	18.6	19.1	l	(low)
15.4	22.3	18.9	i	(seat)
14.9	19.8	17.4	ŋ	(sing)
14.9	19.2	17.1	ʃ	(shed)
13.2	15.7	14.5	tʃ	(child)
12.8	12.7	12.8	n	(no)
9.7	15.7	12.7	dʒ	(jump)
11.4	11.1	11.3	m	(me)
10.1	12.4	11.3	t	(ten)
8.9	12.9	10.9	g	(gate)
9.8	11.3	10.6	k	(key)
10.2		10.2	ð	(then)
4.9	13.8	9.4	d	(den)
9.9	7.7	8.8	h	(home)
7.6	7.6	7.6	z	(zero)
4.8	9.7	7.3	b	(bend)
6.6	7.4	7.0	p	(pen)
7.4	6.1	6.8	v	(vine)
9.6	3.7	6.7	f	(fine)
8.4	4.1	6.3	s	(said)
4.7	−2.8	1.0	θ	(thin)

[a] Two measures of relative level are shown. The first column shows relative levels as measured with respect to the threshold of audibility. The second column shows relative levels measured with respect to that level at which the sound is just recognizable. The third column shows the average of these two measures. All data are in decibels. Since relative levels are shown, the least intense sound, /θ/, was chosen as the reference and its average level was arbitrarily set to 1 dB. The data shown in the table were derived from measurements reported by Fletcher (1953), and represent average values for these sounds produced in various contexts.

ferences between speakers. In order to separate out the effects of these variables it is common practice to specify speech levels in terms of a standard set of conditions. One set of conditions that is commonly used is to measure the sound pressure level at a distance of 1 m from the speaker's lips in an anechoic room (such that there are no significant reflections off walls or other surfaces that might affect the measured speech level). Under these conditions the long term average speech level for a typical male speaker is about 65 dB sound pressure level. This value should be interpreted with caution because of the very large variation between individuals and in speaking habits (Pearsons et al., 1976).

PRODUCTION OF SPEECH SOUNDS IN CONTEXT

Although the sounds of speech may be classified into minimum distinctive units known as phonemes, the flow of speech involves more than simply articulating a sequence of such units. There are important variations in how a phoneme is produced depending on interactions with neighboring phonemes, as well as on the overall structure of the utterance. In this section we review briefly the overall structure of speech and discuss variations in the production of sounds in context.

Speech has both a segmental and suprasegmental structure. The segmental structure refers to the features and characteristics of individual phonemes. The suprasegmental structure refers to those features and characteristics that do not relate to specific phonemes, but to two or more phonemes, up to entire phrases or sentences. There are two basic groups of suprasegmental features: those that directly affect the meaning of what is said, and those that have little effect on meaning but relate primarily to that elusive property known as speech or voice quality.

The key suprasegmental characteristics that affect meaning directly are intonation, stress, rhythm, and phrasing. Intonation is the modulation of voice pitch. The pitch[12] of the voice is determined primarily by the frequency of vibration of the vocal cords, which in turn is controlled by the tension on the vocal cords and the air pressure developed by the lungs. Rhythm refers to the pattern in which certain syllables are stressed and others are left unstressed. A stressed syllable is one that is spoken in such a way as to make it perceptually more prominent. This may be done by raising the pitch of the voice or by

---

[12] As noted under "Some Basic Perceptual Principles," the distinction between frequency and pitch should be kept in mind.

increasing the duration or loudness of the syllable. Usually some combination of these factors is used.

Phrasing refers to the process whereby words are grouped together according to the linguistic structure of the utterance. A basic unit in phrasing is the "sense group," which is a group of one or more words forming a distinct linguistic entity such as a phrase or clause. Sense groups are bounded by breaks in the flow of speech. Several sense groups may be linked together before the speaker finds it necessary or convenient to pause for breath. The portion of an utterance between pauses for taking breath is known as a "breath group."

Intonation is perhaps the most important variable used by a speaker to link the separate sounds of speech into a unified whole. Even with voiceless sounds, the orderly change in pitch before and after the sound compensates for any short term variations in the overall pattern. Because the mechanics of voicing require a flow of air through the larynx, the basic unit for characterizing intonation contours is the breath group. At the start of a breath group, air pressure in the lungs is high and the voice frequency typically increases rapidly to reach a comfortable pitch and, as in the case of simple declarative statements, the voice frequency remains roughly steady until the last portion of the breath group, when the voice frequency begins to fall, ending in a downward glide.[13] In the case of a question, the voice frequency rises and may end in an upward glide. There are important modifications to these basic contour shapes, depending on the linguistic structure and meaning of what is said. Superimposed on the basic contour for an utterance are prominences and valleys that reflect the pattern of stressed and unstressed syllables. There are also breaks in voicing caused by short pauses or voiceless consonants. The contour follows its overall characteristic pattern by means of inflections and glides during the voiced portions and by means of jumps between breaks in voicing.

Space does not allow for a detailed examination of how a speaker modulates his voice frequency in keeping with the phonemic and linguistic constraints set by a given utterance. There is also some divergence of opinion as to the interpretation of intonation contours. The reader is referred to Bronstein and Jacoby (1967) for an excellent introduction to the subject, and to Pike (1946) for a classic study on

---

[13] Glides in the intonation contour should be distinguished from glides in the formant frequencies that characterize the glide sounds (see under "Glides"). The two effects are perceptually quite distinct and occur independently of each other.

the intonation of American English. For a good pedagogical treatment of English intonation, see O'Connor and Arnold (1963). See also Kingdon (1958), Bolinger (1958), and Liberman et al. (1967) for alternative approaches.

Having briefly reviewed the most important variables governing the suprasegmental structure of speech, we can now return to consideration of how the production of individual phonemes is affected by neighboring phonemes. Generally, phonemes within a sense group interact, but there is little, if any, interaction between adjacent phonemes belonging to separate sense groups.

One of the major causes of interaction between phonemes is that the required movements of the articulators for each sound are not initiated at the same time. Some articulators are moved earlier than others in anticipation of the phoneme to follow. The effect is to change the quality of the ongoing phoneme, as well as that of the following phoneme. Several simple examples of coarticulation have already been described for the case of fricative-vowel, plosive-vowel, and nasal-vowel combinations (see under "Fricatives," "Plosives," and "Nasals and Nasalized Sounds"), respectively.

Coarticulatory effects are most pronounced for the plosive sounds. The articulatory mechanisms involved in the production of the plosives are such that plosives cannot be produced in isolation, but must necessarily involve another sound. A good example of anticipatory interaction occurs in the word *plan*. Unlike the usual form of plosive release, the release of air for the plosive /p/ occurs laterally, because the tongue is already in position for the /ℓ/ by the time the release occurs. This effect is common to all the plosives when followed by an /ℓ/. Some illustrative examples are *pan-plan, bud-blood, care-Clare, gory-glory.*

A similar anticipatory interaction occurs when nasals follow a plosive. In this case the air is released nasally. Several examples occur in the sentence "Agnes woul*d n*ot ru*b m*y ho*t n*ose." If the entire sentence is spoken as a single sense group, the plosive-nasal interaction occurs between the italicized pairs. If, however, the speaker introduces a break between a pair, such as between the words *would* and *not*, so as to emphasize the word *not*, then the /d/ and /n/ belong to separate sense groups and are articulated separately.

Another common anticipatory interaction occurs when a plosive leads into a vowel. Typically, those articulators not required for the plosive move toward the vowel target positions well before the plosive is actually released. To demonstrate the effect, the reader may articulate the syllables *dee* and *doo* in front of a mirror. The lip positions should be quite different for *dee* and *doo* even before the /d/ is produced.

In the case of the plosives /k/ and /g/, the place of articulation can be varied over a fairly wide range and the effect of the following vowel is to move the place of articulation to a location more in keeping with the target position of the vowel. The effect is demonstrated in the words *keep, cope,* and *coop.* In *keep,* the transition is to a high front vowel and the /k/ is produced by placing the hump of the tongue in a fairly high position behind the hard palate. In *cope* the transition is to a mid back vowel, and the place of articulation for the /k/ is moved down toward the velum. In *coop,* the transition is to a back vowel, and a low velar position is used in articulating the /k/.

Anticipatory movements are very pronounced when an /ℓ/ or /n/ precedes either of the dental fricatives, /θ/ or /ð/. In this case the /ℓ/ or /n/ is produced with the tongue tip placed against the upper teeth, which is the characteristic position for the fricative. The following pairs demonstrate the changes in tongue position during /ℓ/ and /n/; *on a day, on the day*; *Anthony, Antony*; *all at, all that*; *will throw, will row.* The articulation of /ℓ/ is also affected by its position relative to adjoining vowels, as evidenced by the distinction between the "light" /ℓ/ and "dark" /ℓ/, discussed in the preceding section.

Interactions tend to increase when sounds using the same articulatory mechanism follow each other. Plosives, especially voiceless plosives, are marked by aspiration (i.e., a turbulent outward flow of air) after their release. If the following sound is a fricative, which requires aspiration for its production, then much of the plosive release is absorbed by the fricative. For example, compare the following pairs: *hippy-hipsy, tar-tsar, big ape-big shape.* Even if the fricative precedes the voiceless plosive, the aspiration during the release is greatly reduced, such as in *tar-star, par-spar.* Plosives leading into plosives also have marked interactions. Generally, the release of the first plosive is absorbed into the release of the second plosive. Several illustrative examples are *topcat, topdog,* and *topboy.* The effect is most marked when the two plosives use the same articulators, as in *topboy.*

Not all articulatory interactions result in the reduction or absorption of one sound into another. Sometimes an additional, unintentional sound is introduced. This effect usually occurs when the articulators, in moving from their positions for one sound to the next, pass throught the characteristic positions of a third sound, which may be produced unintentionally. Thus, *sense* may be produced as *scents, prince* as *prints, do in* as *do win* and *see am* as *see yam.* The inverse also happens in that the intermediate sound may be intended, but is not produced, such as the /d/ in *hindsight*. It should be noted that the paired examples cited above are perceptually very similar, and it is frequently difficult even for a trained listener to determine which phoneme sequence was produced.

Another form of interaction results from poor timing in the control of voicing. The facility with which we can control the movements of our articulators greatly exceeds that with which we can control the onset and termination of voicing. Thus, it is to be expected that when voiced and voiceless sounds are produced in sequence, a voiceless sound will occasionally be voiced and voiced sounds occasionally devoiced. The voiced-voiceless confusion frequently occurs when a voiceless sound of brief duration, such as a plosive, is surrounded by strongly voiced sounds. Typical examples are *bicker* pronounced as *bigger, batter,* as *badder,* and *beetle* as *beadle.* The voiceless fricative /h/ is also frequently voiced when in the intervocalic position, such as in the word *mayhem*.

A typical speaker usually provides additional cues as to whether a consonant is intended as voiced or voiceless. Subtle changes in timing play a key role. The duration of a vowel is longer before a voiced consonant than before a voiceless one. Also, voiceless plosives are strongly aspirated when leading to a stressed vowel. These subtle changes in timing and manner of production are lost, however, when both syllables surrounding the consonant are unstressed. Voiced-voiceless confusions are most marked during the unstressed portions of speech.

Devoicing, or partial devoicing, of voiced sounds tends to occur before pauses such as at the end of sense groups or breath groups. The voiced fricative is a common candidate for devoicing when in this position, or when preceding a voiceless consonant. Typical examples are the /v/, /ð/, and /z/ in the sentence, "I lo*v*e *s*moo*th s*eas and mountai*n*s." If the speaker pauses between *seas* and *and*, the /z/ in *seas* may also be partially devoiced.

All of the preceding examples dealt with interactions involving adjacent phonemes. Coarticulatory effects, however, can involve several phonemes at a time. As noted earlier, the plosives necessarily involve a good deal of coarticulation and thus multiple coarticulatory effects are to be expected for phoneme sequences involving plosives. Spectrographic data showing such effects in vowel-plosive-vowel sequences have been obtained by Ohman (1966). Coarticulatory effects extending over several phonemes at a time also occur in consonant clusters where one or more phoneme pairs within the cluster involve interactions of the types described above.

At a more global level, a major factor affecting interactions between sounds is the subordination of articulatory behavior to maintain the natural rhythm of speech. Stressed syllables are generally of fairly long duration, and in order to maintain a smooth, rhythmic flow, unstressed syllables tend to be very short in duration. A common effect in unstressed syllables is that of vowel reduction (Lindblom, 1963), in which the articulators do not have the time to reach their targeted positions before movement to the next phoneme is initiated.

The rules governing the timing of speech sounds are complex and much research is currently in progress to help further understand timing patterns in speech (Bolinger, 1963; Goldman-Eisler, 1968; Huggins, 1972; 1976; Lehiste, 1973; Cooper, 1976; Klatt, 1976). One relatively simple interpretation of speech timing (Huggins, 1976) is that each phoneme has an intrinsic duration consisting of two components, a minimal duration below which the phoneme cannot be shortened and a duration beyond the minimum, which is adjusted according to a hierarchy of rules. These rules are hierarchical in that "phoneme duration is affected by the other phonemes within a syllable, syllable duration is affected by the number of other syllables within a word, and word duration is affected by the number of words in the phrase, clause, or sentence" (Huggins, 1976).

The major factors affecting the duration of sounds in context seem to be:

1. Intrinsic durations. Data on the intrinsic durations of speech sounds may be found in Peterson and Lehiste (1960), House (1961) and Klatt (1976). The consonants are on the average effected less by shortening rules than the vowels. This suggests that consonants have minimum durations that are closer to their intrinsic durations than do the vowels.
2. Rate of speaking. Speech can be produced at various rates depending on the speaker's accent, emotional state, and other factors (Goldman-Eisler, 1968). Speeding up the rate of speech will obviously shorten the durations of the component speech sounds, but certain sounds will be affected more than others. Typically, the consonants are shortened far less than the vowels (Kozhevnikov and Chistovich, 1965) and, in certain cases, the duration of a vowel may be reduced to the point where it is heard as an indistinct neutral sound, although other phonemes in the utterance are clearly distinguishable.
3. Stress pattern. Unstressed syllables are of shorter duration than stressed syllables. As noted above, most of the adjustment in

duration is carried by the vowel (Lindblom, 1963). Stress operates at both the word and sentence level. Every multisyllabic word has a distinct stress pattern that is determined largely by relative syllabic durations. In cases where a word has more than one meaning, the difference meaning can often be conveyed by adjusting the stress pattern within the word, the major acoustic cues being the difference in relative syllable durations. For example, compare relative syllable durations in the word *refuse*, as a verb meaning "to reject" and as a noun meaning "rubbish." At the sentence level, a stress pattern is superimposed on the word stress pattern, depending on the meaning of the sentence and whether or not emphasis is to be placed on one or more words. For example, compare the stress pattern in "*You* will sing." (as opposed to someone else), with that in "You will *sing*." (as opposed to dance). Stress at the sentence level is conveyed not only by the lengthening of the stressed syllables, but also by marked variations in the intonation contour.

4. Prepausal lengthening. The last syllable in a phrase or sentence just before a pause is usually lengthened quite substantially, quite often by a factor as large as 2 or more. Lengthening of the final syllable in a phrase can also occur even if the phrase does not terminate in a pause (Klatt, 1975).

5. Phonetic environment. The duration of a phoneme is affected by the phonemes that precede or follow it. For example, vowels are generally longer before voiced than voiceless consonants and free vowels are longer than those that are checked by a consonant (see Figure 9). Similarly, consonants in clusters are of shorter duration than consonants bounded by vowels. See House (1961), Klatt (1976), and references cited therein for data on the effect of phonetic environment on duration.

6. Relative position. The duration of a phoneme is affected by its location in the syllable and the number of other phonemes in the syllable. The duration of a syllable, in turn, is affected by its location and the number of other syllables in the word. Similarly, the duration of a word is affected by its location and the number of other words in the phrase or sentence. As a rule, the greater the number of components within the unit (syllable, word, phrase, or sentence), the shorter the durations of the component parts.

It is beyond the scope of this chapter to engage in a detailed discussion of all the phonemic interactions that occur in speech. This section has been concerned primarily with representative examples of the major types of interaction in general American English. Interactions that are heavily dialect-oriented have not been discussed and the reader is referred to Gimson (1952), McDavid (1958), and references cited therein, for a detailed treatment of dialectal differences.

Almost all interactions between phonemes spoken in context involve subtle variations in articulatory movements, and most talkers are quite unaware of these variations when speaking. Their main concern is that the sounds produced should be heard as the intended sounds. Variations and adjustments in articulatory movements that produce distorted or erroneous sounds are corrected with time, but articulatory adjustments that do not cause noticeable or unacceptable changes gradually become part of the speaker's speech habits. Hearing-impaired children are at an obvious disadvantage in this process in that they are unable to effectively monitor their speech production and hence to learn the rules of normal speech production in the conventional way.

APPENDIX I

ENERGY, POWER, INTENSITY, SOUND PRESSURE LEVEL AND THEIR UNITS OF MEASUREMENT

The distinction between energy and power is a common source of confusion. Energy is the capacity for doing work; power is the rate at which work is done. Power is thus the rate at which energy is expended.

The relationship between energy and power is illustrated by the following example. A motorist runs out of gas a short distance from a service station. The motorist, being a strong and energetic young man, decides to push his automobile the rest of the way to the service station. In pushing the automobile, he applies a force to the vehicle thereby causing it to move. The force multiplied by the distance moved is the work done; it is also the energy expended. The time taken to push the automobile was roughly 30 min. Had the motorist not run out of gas, the time taken to drive the same distance would have been less than a minute. The energy expended in moving the automobile to the service station is the same whether it was pushed by the man, or driven by its own engine. However, the automobile engine is clearly more powerful than the man in that it did the same work (force × distance) in less than one-thirtieth of the time. Power is measured in terms of work done per unit time or, alternatively, in terms of the energy expended per unit time.

Which of these two measures, energy or power, is better suited for describing the relative physical magnitude of a sound? Power is usually the more appropriate measure except for the important case of a single sound of short duration. Consider, for example, a sound consisting of only one of the pulses shown in Figure 4A. During the early part of the pulse the power, i.e., the energy expended per unit time, is relatively high but as the pulse dies down the energy expended per unit time also decreases, reaching zero at the termination of the pulse. The power thus varies as a function of time, which leads to difficulties in its measurement.

Most power-measuring instruments measure the energy expended over a finite time interval and thus power measurements of short-duration stimuli, as obtained on conventional instruments, will be critically dependent on the averaging time of the instrument. It is well known, for example, that changing the response time of the meter on a conventional sound-level meter will result in different readings for impulsive sounds. In brief, for sounds of short duration reliable measurements of power are difficult to obtain and are critically dependent on extraneous variables such as the averaging time of the meter.

The measurement of the energy of short duration sounds is not subject to the above constraints because the energy of a stimulus of finite duration is a constant and does not vary with time. Under these conditions, energy rather than power is the more appropriate measure. The situation is reversed for sounds of long duration. The energy of a sound is dependent on its duration, but for ongoing sounds of long duration the overall duration of the sound is a variable of marginal interest. For these sounds, power rather than energy is the more appropriate measure. For the case of periodic stimuli, such as the pulse trains shown in Figure 4, the average power measured over one or more periods provides a stable, consistent measure.

Given that it is more appropriate to specify short duration sounds in terms of their energy and long duration sounds in terms of their power, where does one draw the boundary in practice between sounds of "short" and "long" duration? The answer depends, in part, on the intended application.

In the case of speech analysis, the majority of speech sounds are relatively steady for durations well in excess of that for an individual pitch period. These sounds can thus be specified in terms of their average power, provided the averaging time is equal to at least one pitch period. Ideally, the averaging time should equal an exact number of pitch periods, but this requirement is not important if the averaging time is well in excess of a pitch period, nor does it apply to the voiceless sounds, which can be measured with an instrument having an averaging time appropriate for voiced sounds. Although the majority of speech sounds may be regarded as being relatively steady with respect to a viable averaging time, these sounds will nevertheless exhibit variations in average power with time depending on the phonetic context, how the sound is produced, and on the characteristics of the talker. Also, there are several sounds for which a power description may be inappropriate. In particular, the plosives consist of a sequence of discrete events (e.g., closure, release, onset of voicing) occurring in rapid succession. The "average power" of such a sound is critically dependent on how the duration of the sound is specified. In this case if may be wiser to specify the physical magnitude of the sound in terms of the energy of its individual components, such as the energy generated during the closure period, the burst of aspiration, the formant transitions, etc.

In another application, experiments in psychoacoustics have shown that for sounds of less than about 300 msec in duration, audibility and loudness are determined primarily by the energy of the sound. For sounds of longer duration, audibility and loudness are more closely related to power. Most speech sounds, excluding certain stressed vowels and sounds in the sentence final position, have a duration of less than 300 msecs. Thus, in specifying speech sounds with a view to examining the acoustic correlates of their perceptual prominence (e.g., relative detectability, loudness, perceived stress) it would seem more appropriate to use an energy rather than a power description.

Because of the above mentioned difficulties, data on the power of individual speech sounds must be interpreted with caution. In order to circumvent some of the problems, Table 2 of the text shows the relative levels (the measurement of relative level is discussed shortly) of the sounds of English using the ear as the basic measuring instrument. In this case, the relative levels of individual speech sounds are shown with respect to the detectability (and also the recognizability) of the weakest sound /θ/. These measurements are not easily related to purely physical measures of power or energy because of our incomplete knowledge of the temporal integration and frequency-weighting characteristics of the ear.

The power of speech may also be measured without regard to the detailed phonetic structure of its component sounds. In this case average power is measured in the same way as that for any long term, ongoing sound and the difficulties inherent in specifying the power of short duration sounds do not arise. However, a new problem has to be contended with. Are the measurements to be averaged across the pauses and breaks in voicing that typically occur in normal speech, or is power to be measured only when speech is present? If the latter approach is used, it then becomes necessary to specify a criterion for determining whether or not speech is present. Unfortunately, there is no simple answer to this problem.

The relationship between energy and power is the same whether we are dealing with the minute amount of work done by a sound wave in causing the eardrum to vibrate or the considerably larger amount of work done in lifting a rocket ship off the earth's surface. There is, however, an important additional factor that needs to be considered when dealing with the energy or power of sound waves. In the illustrative example given earlier the force used in pushing the automobile was applied at a single point. In a sound wave, force is distributed over an area and is not concentrated at a single point. It is thus more convenient when dealing with sound waves to use force per unit area (i.e., pressure) rather than the total force generated by the sound source. Similarly, the power generated by a sound source is distributed over an area and it is thus more convenient to specify the intensity (= power propagated per unit area) of a sound rather than its total power. By analogy, in dealing with energy it may be more convenient to use energy density (= energy propagated per unit area) rather than total energy.

In specifying the intensity (or power density) of a sound it is necessary to also specify the direction of power flow. By definition, the intensity of a sound in a specified direction is equal to the power propagated through a unit area (e.g., 1 cm²) at a right angle to the specified direction.

The above definition contains a number of nuances that need to be explained. Consider the example of a sequence of stones being thrown into the center of a quiet pool. The disturbance created by the stones is carried by a series of ripples radiating outward from the source of the disturbance and the diameter of each ripple becomes progressively larger as it moves away from the source. However, as the diameter increases, the height of each ripple decreases such that the ripples gradually die out at some distance from the source of the disturbance.

The power generated by the disturbance (i.e., the sequence of stones thrown into the pool) is propagated outward by the ripples in the water. As the ripples move further away from the source, their intensity becomes progressively smaller. That is, as the ripples expand in diameter the power propagated is spread out over a greater area and the power flow per unit area (i.e., the intensity) is systematically reduced. It is also important to note that the power is being propagated in a specific direction, i.e., outward from the source of the disturbance, and that there is no power flow in a direction tangential to the outward movement of the ripples. In setting up this illustrative example a sequence of stones was used so as to create an ongoing disturbance at the center of the pool. Had a single stone been used to create a single disturbance of short duration, then energy and energy density would have been used in place of power and intensity, respectively.

Finally, it should be added that the distinction between power and intensity is important for sounds in space. Once a sound has been converted into an electrical signal the distinction between power and intensity becomes redundant because all of the power is constrained to the electrical conductor carrying the signal. This may help explain the apparent inconsistency in terminology when referring to the intensity of speech sounds but to the power-frequency spectrum of these same sounds when presumably the intensity-frequency spectrum is intended. Techniques for the spectrum analysis of speech were developed by electrical engineers dealing primarily with electrical signals. The terminology developed for this application has come to be accepted in speech analysis and it is used in this chapter rather than introduce new terms for the sake of terminologic exactitude.

Having explained the distinction between power and intensity, the next question is, what units should be used in specifying these quantities? At least two choices are available, the CGS (centimeters, grams, seconds) system of units and the MKS (meters, kilograms, seconds) system. A third system of units the British foot-pound-second system is rarely used in acoustics. Historically, the CGS system has been used for scientific purposes and the MKS system for engineering purposes. In acoustics, the CGS system was formerly the system of choice, but the MKS system is now being used on a much wider scale. For purposes of simplicity, the CGS system is described here. The units corresponding to the two systems are shown in Table I-1.

The unit of force in the CGS system is the dyne. It is the force required to accelerate a mass of 1 g at the rate of 1 cm/sec^2. The unit of acoustic pressure is the microbar which is equal to 1 dyne/cm^2. A microbar is equal to one-millionth of a bar, which is roughly equal to normal atmospheric pressure. The unit of work or energy is the erg, which is equal to the work done by a force of 1 dyne applied over a distance of 1 cm. A more convenient unit is the joule (see Table I-1) which is equal to 10^7 ergs. The unit of power in the CGS system is that of ergs/sec. A more convenient unit is the watt, which is equal to the work done at the rate of 1 joule/sec. In electrical terms, 1 watt is equal to the product of voltage and current measured (in volts and amperes, respectively) across a pure resistance.

Unfortunately, it is not a simple matter to measure acoustic power or intensity directly. In order to understand the problem, consider the basic components of power. Power is defined as the rate at which work is done and is equal to force × distance per unit time. Thus, in order to measure power it

Table I-1. Relationship between CGS and MKS units[a]

Quantity	Components	CGS units	MKS units	Relationship
Length		centimeters (cm)	meter (m)	1 m = 100 cm
Mass		gram (g)	kilogram (kg)	1 kg = 1000 g
Time		second (sec)	second (sec)	
Force	mass × acceleration = mass × distance/time^2	dyne = g · cm/sec^2	Newton (N) = kg · m/sec^2	1 N = 10^5 dynes
Energy (or work done)	force × distance = mass × distance^2/time^2	erg = dyne · cm	joule = N · m	1 joule = 10^7 ergs
Power	energy/time = mass × distance^2/time^3	ergs/sec	watt	1 watt = 10^7 ergs/sec.
Intensity	power/area	ergs/sec/cm^2	watts/m^2	1 watt/m^2 = 10^3 ergs/sec/cm^2
Pressure	force/area = mass/distance · time^2	microbar (μbar) = dyne/cm^2	N/m^2	1 N/m^2 = 10 μbar

[a] Note that the reference pressure of 20 μN/m^2 is equivalent to 0.0002 μbar or, alternatively, 0.0002 dynes/cm^2.

is necessary to measure both the applied force and the velocity (i.e., distance per unit time) of the particles set into vibration by the sound. If pressure rather than force is measured then the expression for power reduces to:

power = (force/unit area) × (velocity × unit area)

The first term on the right is the pressure; the second term is a quantity known as the volume velocity. Whereas pressure can be measured relatively easily, it is difficult to measure particle velocity or volume velocity directly.

There is an added complication in the measurement of power in that, at any given frequency, the pressure and volume velocity may not be in phase. This phase difference must be taken into account in deriving the power or intensity of a sound. An analogous problem occurs in electrical systems in that voltage and current are not necessarily in phase, except across a pure resistance. In the general case,

$$\text{electrical power} = \text{voltage} \times \text{current} \times \cos \phi \qquad (1)$$

and

$$\text{acoustic power} = \text{pressure} \times \text{volume velocity} \times \cos \phi, \qquad (2)$$

where ϕ is the phase difference between voltage and current in Equation 1 or between pressure and volume velocity in Equation 2.

Because of the difficulties encountered in measuring sound power or sound intensity directly, an alternative method for specifying the physical magnitudes of sounds has been developed that depends solely on the measurement of pressure. According to this system of measurement, sounds are specified in terms of pressure *levels* (e.g., sound pressure level, sensation level, hearing level). Pressure levels are specified in terms of a decibel scale and in order to understand this system of measurement it is necessary to know what is meant by a decibel.

A decibel scale is essentially a logarithmic scale usually used in expressing power ratios. Specifically,

$$R = 10 \log W_1/W_2 \qquad (3)$$

where W_1 is the power of Sound 1, W_2 is the power of Sound 2, and R is the power ratio in decibels. Unless otherwise stated, common logarithms (i.e., to the base 10) are used. Because W_1/W_2 is a ratio, the unit of power that is used is immaterial, provided the same units are used for both W_1 and W_2. Similarly, intensity rather than power can be used since both numerator and denominator are both divided by the same quantity, i.e.,

$$W_1/W_2 = (W_1/A)/(W_2/A) = I_1/I_2$$

and

$$R_I = 10 \log_{10} I_1/I_2 \qquad (4)$$

where A is an infinitesimally small area, I_1 is the intensity of Sound 1, I_2 is the intensity of Sound 2, and R_I is the intensity ratio in decibels, which is numerically equal to the power ratio R of Equation 3. It can be shown that power is proportional to pressure, i.e.,

$$W = kP^2 \tag{5}$$

where W is the power of the sound, P is the pressure of the sound, and k is a constant depending on the characteristics of the acoustic medium in which the sound is propagated. In the case of a sound with a fluctuating wave form it is recommended that the root mean square (rms) pressure be used. The rms value of a wave form is obtained by taking the square root of the average squared value of the wave form. For a sine wave, the rms value is equal to 0.707 of the amplitude; i.e., 0.707 of the maximum value reached by the sine wave.

The ratio R can be expressed in terms of a pressure ratio by substituting Equation 5 into Equation 3; i.e.,

$$
\begin{aligned}
R &= 10 \log (kP_1^2)/(kP_2^2) \\
  &= 10 \log (P_1/P_2)^2 \\
  &= 20 \log P_1/P_2
\end{aligned} \tag{6}
$$

where P_1 is the pressure of Sound 1, P_2 is the pressure of Sound 2, and R is the power ratio in decibels. Equation 6 provides the basis for specifying sounds in terms of pressure levels. In order to do this it is necessary to assign a reference value for P_2. Depending on the reference that is used, levels of various kinds can be derived.

Sound pressure level (SPL) is obtained by using $P_2 = 0.0002$ μbar (or 20 μN/m^2 using the MKS system of units) as the reference quantity in Equation 6; i.e.,

$$L_{\text{SPL}} = 20 \log (P/0.0002) \tag{7}$$

where P is rms pressure in microbars and L_{SPL} is sound pressure level in decibels. In obtaining the sound pressure level it is necessary that the sound level meter have a flat frequency response. If another frequency response is used, the measurement obtained is referred to as a sound level.

Sensation level (SL) is obtained by using the pressure at which the sound is just audible for the reference pressure P_2 in Equation 6. Hearing level (HL)[14] is obtained by using the normal threshold of hearing as the reference quantity. In using Equation 6, the same units must be used for both P_1 and P_2.

The scales described above are used primarily for convenience. Pressure is easier to measure than power or intensity and a decibel scale, which is logarithmic in form, is better suited than a linear scale for expressing relative sound levels given the remarkably wide dynamic range of the ear. However, the use of pressure on a scale designed primarily for expressing power ratios (the decibel scale) raises inherent problems. Specifically, the relationship expressed by Equation 6 is valid only if both pressures have been measured across the same acoustic impedance. Thus, if the pressure at one point in an acoustic system is doubled, the sound intensity at that point will be quadrupled and the sound pressure level will be increased by 6 dB. (It is assumed

---

[14] Also known as Hearing Threshold Level (HTL).

that the acoustic impedance of the system is constant at a given point.) However, if the pressure at point A in an acoustic system is twice that at point B, the sound pressure levels will differ by 6 dB, but the sound intensity at point A will not necessarily be four times that at point B, unless the acoustic impedances at these two points happen to be identical. In order to specify the relative intensities at these two points, it is necessary to know the phase difference between pressure and volume velocity at each point.

A related problem occurs when sounds are added. If two sounds of equal intensity are added and there are no frequency components common to both sounds, as would occur if the bandwidth of a flat spectrum noise is doubled, then the overall intensity of the sound is doubled and the sound pressure level is increased by 3 dB. (Note that doubling of pressure leads to a quadrupling of intensity and hence a 6-dB increase in sound pressure level, there being a 3-dB increase for each doubling of intensity.) If, however, the added sounds have frequency components in common, then it is necessary to take the relative phases of the common frequency components into account. Consider, for example, the addition of two tones having the same frequency and equal intensity. If the two wave forms are in phase, the resulting tone will have an amplitude that is twice that of either component; i.e., the pressure will have been doubled and the sound pressure level will have been increased by 6 dB. If the two wave forms are in opposite phase, they will cancel when added. Even if perfect cancellation is not obtained, which may happen in practice, the intensity of the resulting sound will be close to zero and the sound pressure level will be considerably less than that of either component. In general, in order to obtain the sum of two tones of the same frequency it is necessary to add them vectorially so as to ensure that the phase difference between the two tones is taken into account.

One way of avoiding the problems associated with the use of sound pressure levels is to use intensity levels instead. By definition

$$L_I = 10 \log I/I_o \qquad (8)$$

where L is intensity level in decibels, I is intensity in absolute, linear units (e.g., $\mu W/cm^2$), and I_o is the reference intensity in the same units as used for I. The use of intensity level thus depends on the proper measurement of intensity, which is difficult. It should be remembered that most commercially available sound measuring instruments measure pressure and not intensity.

APPENDIX II

THE PHONEMES OF AMERICAN ENGLISH

Throughout this text, the phonetic representation of a sound is shown between two slashes of the / /; e.g., the vowel in the word *seat* is represented by /i/. The symbols used here are based on those recommended by the International Phonetic Association. See Bronstein (1960, Appendix B) for a discussion of methods of phonetic representation. The phonemes of American English are listed in the following chart.

The phonemes of American English

Consonants

Plosives	Affricates
/p/ as in pen	/tʃ/ as in child
/b/ as in bend	/dʒ/ as in jump
/t/ as in ten	
/d/ as in den	**Nasals**
/g/ as in gate	/m/ as in me
/k/ as in key	/n/ as in no
Fricatives	/ŋ/ as in sing
/f/ as in fine	
/v/ as in vine	**Glides**
/θ/ as in thin	/w/ as in win
/ð/ as in then	/r/ as in red[a]
/s/ as in said	/j/ as in yes
/z/ as in zero	
/ʃ/ as in shed	
/ʒ/ as in measure	**Lateral**
/h/ as in home	/l/ as in low

Vowels

/i/ as in seat	/ʊ/ as in foot
/ɪ/ as in sit	/u/ as in food
/ɛ/ as in set	/ə/ as in alone
/æ/ as in sat	/ʌ/ as in shut
/a/ as in half	/ɚ/ as in mother
/ɑ/ as in calm	/ɝ/ as in third
/ɔ/ as in sought	

Diphthongized Vowels

/eɪ/ as in day	/oʊ/ as in soap

Diphthongs

/aʊ/ as in now	/ɔɪ/ as in toy
/aɪ/ as in sigh	

[a] See text under "Lateral /ℓ/ and Glide /r/" for other forms of /r/.

ACKNOWLEDGMENTS

I would like to thank Dr. Claude Simon for his help in preparing the speech spectrograms, all of which (excluding Figures 7 and 12) are of his own voice. I am also particularly grateful to Mr. Harvey Stromberg for writing the computer programs to generate the wave forms shown in Figures 1 and 4 and to

Mr. Cecil Redmond for preparing the spectrograms of the computer-generated stimuli. Special thanks are due to Mr. Neil Piper for drafting the figures and to Ms. Linda Hoffnung for typing the manuscript. Figure 12 was developed by Dr. Lawrence Raphael and Dr. Michael Dorman and I would like to express my thanks to them for allowing me to use this diagram. Figure 13 is reproduced from Delattre, Liberman, and Cooper (1955) and Figure 18 is reproduced from Richards (1973). Appreciation for allowing me to reproduce these diagrams is gratefully acknowledged. Preparation of this chapter was supported, in part, by Public Health Service Grant No. 09252 from the National Institute of Neurological and Communicative Disorders and Stroke.

REFERENCES

Beranek, L. L. 1954. Acoustics. McGraw-Hill Book Company, New York.
Bolinger, D. L. 1958. A theory of pitch accent. Word 14:109–149.
Bolinger, D. L. 1963. Length, vowel, juncture. Linguistics 1. Mouton & Co., The Hague.
Bronstein, A. J. 1960. The Pronunciation of American English. Appleton-Century-Crofts, New York.
Bronstein, A. J., and B. Jacoby. 1967. Your Speech and Voice. Random House, New York.
Cooper, F. S., P. C. Delattre, A. M. Liberman, J. M. Borst, and L. J. Gerstman. 1952. Some experiments on the perception of synthetic speech sounds. J. Acoust. Soc. Am. 24:597–606.
Cooper, W. E. 1976. Syntactic Control of Speech Timing. Unpublished Ph.D. thesis, Massachusetts Institute of Technology, Cambridge, Mass.
Corliss, E. L. R. 1963. Resolution limits of analyzers and oscillatory systems. J. Res. Natl. Bur. Stand. Phys. Chem. 67A:461–474.
Curtis, J. F. 1970. The acoustics of nasalized speech. Cleft Palate J. 7:380–396.
Delattre, P. C., A. M. Liberman, and F. S. Cooper. 1955. Acoustic loci and transitional cues for consonants. J. Acoust. Soc. Am. 27:769–773.
Denes, P., and E. N. Pinson. 1963. The Speech Chain: The Physics and Biology of Spoken Language. The Williams & Wilkins Company, Baltimore.
Fant, G. 1960. Acoustic Theory of Speech Production. Mouton & Co., The Hague.
Flanagan, J. L. 1972. Speech Analysis Synthesis and Perception, 2nd Ed. Springer-Verlag, New York.
Fletcher, H. 1953. Speech and Hearing in Communication. D. Van Nostrand Company Inc., Princeton, N.J.
Gabor, D. 1946. Theory of communication. J. Inst. Electr. Eng. 93(III):429–457.
Gimson, A. C. 1952. An Introduction to the Pronunciation of English. Edward Arnold, Publishers, Ltd., London.
Goldman-Eisler, F. 1968. Psycholinguistics: Experiments in Spontaneous Speech. Academic Press, New York.
Halle, M., G. W. Hughes, and J. P. A. Radley. 1957. Acoustic properties of stop consonants. J. Acoust. Soc. Am. 29:107–116.

Haycock, G. S. 1933. The Teaching of Speech, Hill and Ainsworth, Stoke-on-Trent, England. [Reprinted in United States by The Volta Bureau.]

House, A. S., and G. Fairbanks. 1953. The influence of consonant environment upon the secondary acoustical characteristics of vowels. J. Acoust. Soc. Am. 25:105–113.

House, A. S. 1961. On vowel duration in English. J. Acoust. Soc. Am. 33:1174–1178.

Huggins, A. W. F. 1972. Just-noticeable differences for segment duration in natural speech. J. Acoust. Soc. Am. 51:1270–1278.

Huggins, A. W. F. 1976. Timing and speech intelligibility. Presented at the A. G. Bell Association National Convention, Boston, June 1976. Attention and Performance 7. In press.

Hughes, G. W., and M. Halle. 1956. Spectral properties of fricative consonants. J. Acoust. Soc. Am. 28:303–310.

Kharkevich, A. A. 1960. Spectra and Analysis. Consultants Bureau, New York. [Original Russian Version published in 1957 by the State Press for Technical and Theoretical Literature, Moscow.]

Kingdon, R. 1958. The Groundwork of English Intonation, Longmans Green & Co. Ltd., London.

Klatt, D. H. 1975. Vowel lengthening is syntactically determined in connected discourse. J. Phon. 3:129–140.

Klatt, D. H. 1976. Linguistic uses of segmental duration in English: Acoustic and perceptual evidence. J. Acous. Soc. Am. 59:1208–1221.

Koenig, W. 1949. A new frequency scale for acoustic measurements. Bell Lab. Rec. 27:299–301.

Kozhevnikov, V. A., and L. A. Chistovich. 1965. Speech: Articulation and Perception. Leningrad. English translation: JPRS 30:5–43.

Kryter, K. 1970. The Effects of Noise on Man. Academic Press, New York.

Ladefoged, P. 1975. A course in Phonetics. Harcourt Brace Jovanovich, Inc., New York.

Lane, H. and B. Tranel. 1971. The Lombard sign and the role of hearing in speech. J. Speech Hear. Res. 14:677–709.

Lehiste, I. (ed.) 1967. Readings in Acoustic Phonetics. The MIT Press, Cambridge, Mass.

Lehiste, I. 1973. Rhythmic units and syntactic units in production and perception. J. Acoust. Soc. Am. 54:1228–1234.

Liberman, P. 1967. Intonation perception, and language. MIT Research Monogr. 38. The MIT Press, Cambridge, Mass.

Liberman, A. M., F. S. Cooper, D. P. Shankweiler, and M. Studdert-Kennedy. 1967. Perception of the speech code. Psychol. Rev. 74.

Lindblom, B. 1963. Spectrographic study of vowel reduction. J. Acoust. Soc. Am. 35:1773–1781.

Ling, D. 1976. Speech and the Hearing-Impaired Child: Theory and Practice. The Alexander Graham Bell Association for the Deaf, Washington, D. C.

Lisker, L. and A. S. Abramson. 1975. Distinctive features and laryngeal control. Language 47:767–785.

Malecot, A. 1956. Acoustic cues for nasal consonants. Language 32:274–284.

McDavid, R. I., Jr. 1958. The Dialects of American English. In: W. N. Francis (ed.), The Structure of American English. The Ronald Press Company, New York.

Minifie, F. D., T. J. Hixon, and F. Williams. 1973. Normal Aspects of Speech, Hearing, and Language. Prentice-Hall, Inc., Englewood Cliffs, N.J.

O'Connor, J. D. and G. F. Arnold. 1963. Intonation of Colloquial English: A Practical Handbook. Longmans, Green & Co. Ltd., London.

Ohman, S. 1966. Coarticulation in VCV utterances, spectrographic measurements. J. Acoust. Soc. Am. 39:151–168.

Pearsons, K. S., R. L. Bennet, and S. Fidell. 1976. Speech levels in various environments. BBN Report No. 3281. Bolt Beranek and Newman, Inc., Los Angeles.

Peterson, G. E., and H. L. Barney. 1952. Control methods used in a study of the vowels. J. Acoust. Soc. Am. 24:175–184.

Peterson, G. E., and I. Lehiste. 1960. Duration of syllable nuclei in English. J. Acoust. Soc. Am. 32:693–703.

Pike, K. L. 1946. The Intonation of American English. The University of Michigan Press, Ann Arbor.

Raphael, L. J. 1972. Preceding vowel duration as a cue to the perception of the voicing characteristic of word final consonants in American English. J. Acoust. Soc. Am. 51:1296–1303.

Richards, D. L. 1964. Statistical properties of speech signals. Proc. Inst. Electr. Eng. 111:941–949.

Richards, D. L. 1973. Telecommunication by Speech: The Transmission Performance of Telephone Networks. John Wiley & Sons, Inc., New York.

Stevens, K. N., and A. House. 1955. Development of a quantitative-description of vowel articulation. J. Acoust. Soc. Am. 27:484–493.

Stevens, K. N., and A. S. House. 1961. An acoustical theory of vowel production and some of its implications. J. Speech Hear. Res. 4:303–320.

Stevens, S. S., and H. Davis. 1938. Hearing. John Wiley & Sons, Inc., New York.

Studdert-Kennedy, M. 1974. The perception of speech. In: T. A. Sebeok (ed.), Current Trends in Linguistics, Part 10, pp. 2349–2386. Mouton & Co., The Hague.

CHAPTER 4

SPEECH PERCEPTION AND SENSORINEURAL HEARING LOSS

Arthur Boothroyd

CONTENTS

The term "speech perception" properly applies to the whole of the receptive component of verbal communication. In practice, however, it is mostly used to describe that part of the process by which the motor/acoustic patterns of speech become linguistic structures in the listener's mind. An understanding of this process has been sought by the designers of telephone communication systems and by researchers wishing to build speech recognition and speech synthesis devices. Although we do not yet have a complete description of speech perception, there is now available an impressive amount of information that should be of value to educators of the deaf.

    In this chapter we explore the nature of the acoustic cues to feature and phoneme recognition, the way these cues are incorporated into the perceptual process, and the effects on speech perception of sensorineural hearing loss.

INTENSITY/TIME DOMAIN

Dynamic Intensity Range

The acoustic speech signal covers a wide range of intensity. At any given moment the intensity is different at different frequencies, and at any given frequency the intensity changes from moment to moment. On average, the lower frequencies are more intense than the higher frequencies. The highest intensity is in the region of the first vocal tract formant (approximately 500 Hz) and, at higher frequencies, the spectral density (in decibels per cycle) falls at the rate of approximately 9 dB/octave (Dunn and White, 1940).

The size of the intensity variations within any frequency band depends on the integration time used for measurement. This is essentially the length of time over which sound energy is collected before a measurement is made. Very short integration times (e.g., a few milliseconds) give a very wide range between the silences in stop consonants and the energy peaks during stressed vowels. Somewhat longer integration times (e.g., 0.1 sec) reveal a range of 30–35 dB between strong and weak speech sounds. Combining these variations with the differences attributable to frequency, we see that there is a range of some 40–45 dB between the high intensity low frequency signals and the low intensity high frequency signals.

For the purposes of the present discussion, it is not so important to know the intensity variations in the physical stimulus. What is important is a knowledge of the intensity range over which information of relevance to speech perception is found. The results of various psychoacoustic studies indicate that, from a practical point of view, the dynamic intensity range of speech is roughly 30 dB.

If, for example, the speech signal is lowered in intensity until the weak fricative [θ] becomes unidentifiable, a further reduction of approximately 30 dB is needed before the strong vowel [ɔ] becomes unidentifiable, (Fletcher, 1953, Chapter 4). Similarly, if a white noise masking signal is increased in intensity until it begins to affect phoneme recognition, another 30 dB increase is necessary before phoneme recognition approaches zero (Miller, 1947). And in filtering experiments carried out by French and Steinberg (1947), it has been found that there is a difference of roughly 30 dB between the intensity at which a frequency band begins to contribute to phoneme recognition and the intensity at which its contribution reaches a maximum. Audiologists are familiar with this 30-dB dynamic range as the

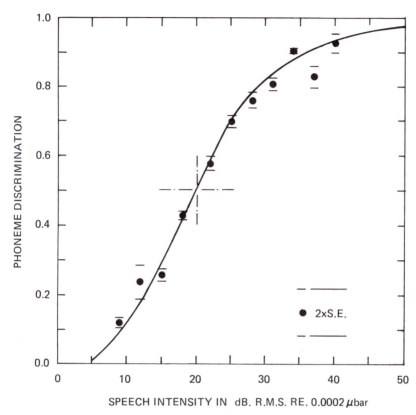

Figure 1. A "normal" articulation function showing the percent recognition of phonemes in (CVC) monosyllabic words as a function of intensity. It will be seen that there is a spread of roughly 30 dB between the intensity at which recognition first begins and the intensity at which it reaches an asymptote. Taken from Boothroyd (1968).

intensity range of the normal articulation function that underlies clinical speech audiometry (see Figure 1).

There are several factors that may increase the dynamic intensity range of speech in practical situations. Variations of stress, speaking effort and distance are obvious ones. Less obvious, but of particular relevance to the hearing aid user, is the orientation of the talker. The radiation characteristics of speech and the diffraction effects of the head are different for high and low frequency sounds. If, for example, the talker faces away from the listener, so that the sound is picked up behind the talker's head, the high frequencies may be attenuated by as much as 15 dB more than the low frequencies, thus increasing the difference of intensity between the weak fricatives and the strong vowels (see Figure 2).

Various experiments have been carried out on the effects of artificially reducing the dynamic range of speech. The simplest technique is "peak clipping," a process by which the amplitude of the speech signal is held to a fixed maximum level. It has been found that large reductions of dynamic range can be accomplished in this way with only small effects on speech recognition. Licklider (1946), for example, found that reducing the peaks by 24 dB (giving a dynamic range of approximately 6 dB) still provided 95% word recognition, and even infinite peak clipping (dynamic range 0 dB), provided 70% word recognition (equivalent to approximately 90% phoneme recognition).

A more sophisticated technique for reduction of dynamic range is syllabic compression. This involves moment-to-moment change of the gain of an amplifier in inverse proportion to the intensity of the input. This type of fast acting compression, unlike peak clipping, can be accomplished without the introduction of harmonic and intermodulation distortion. It does, however, distort the intensity/time patterns of speech and it is not yet clear that it offers significant advantages over peak clipping in terms of speech perception by the hearing impaired. (For a full discussion, see Lippman et al., 1977, and Villchur, Chapter 7).

Audibility

There are a few examples of the direct role of intensity as a cue to phoneme recognition. Stop consonants, for example, are characterized by a sudden rise of intensity after a period of silence, and the difference between nasal consonants and vowels may be perceived partly on the basis of intensity differences. So also may the fricatives [s] and [ʃ] be distinguished from [f] and [θ], and voiceless fricatives from voiced fricatives on the basis of the intensity of high frequency noise.

The main role of intensity, however, lies in the area of audibility. The intensity of the acoustic speech signal should be such, in relation to threshold or ambient noise levels, as to render the significant cues detectable to the listener. In normal conversational speech at 5 or 6 feet from the talker, the acoustic cues for the weak fricatives are some 30 dB above the normal theshold of hearing. Consequently, a postlingually acquired hearing loss of up to 30 dB does not interfere significantly with conversational speech perception. Nor does noise whose high frequency content is less that 30-dB hearing level (HL) (approximately 40-dB sound pressure level (SPL)). The problem of

a)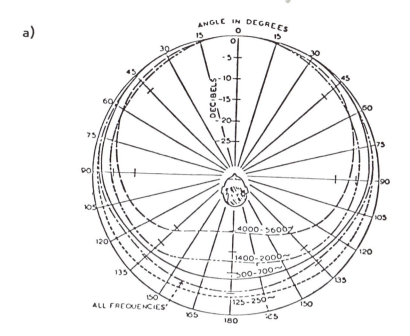

b)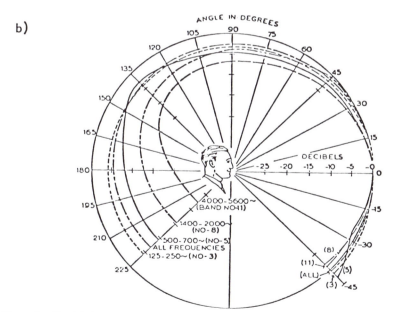

Figure 2. Spatial distribution of pressures in certain frequency bands of speech (*a*) in a horizontal plane through the lips of the speaker; (*b*) in a vertical plane through the lips of the speaker (after Dunn and Farnsworth, 1939). Reproduced by permission of author and American Institute of Physics.

providing audibility of speech cues for the severely and profoundly deaf is discussed later.

FREQUENCY/TIME DOMAIN

Frequency Dependence of Phoneme Recognition

The frequency range of speech includes the lowest fundamentals of voiced sounds and the highest components of fricative noise, perhaps 70–10,000 Hz. As with intensity, it has been found that dramatic reductions of this range can be made without seriously affecting the recognition of phonemes. This was a matter of considerable relevance to the commercial development of the telephone, and it was in this connection that the basic research on frequency dependence of speech perception was done. It is reviewed in a classic paper by French and Steinberg (1947) and in Fletcher's (1953) book on speech and hearing in communication.

The basic procedure used in this research was to measure the recognition of phonemes in nonsense syllables as increasing amounts of high frequency information, and then low frequency information, were removed. The results are usually shown as a pair of curves relating recognition probability to the cutoff frequency of high or low pass filtering. Figures 3 and 4 show the data reported by French and Steinberg, together with similar measurements made by the author with adult and child listeners (Boothroyd, 1968).

The most significant finding of this research, and perhaps the least generally understood, was that under certain circumstances, the acoustic spectrum can be regarded as a series of frequency bands, each contributing independently to the probability of phoneme recognition (see appendix to this chapter). This made possible the development of a procedure by which the efficiency of any transmission system could be predicted from the extent to which it rendered audible each one of a series of 20 frequency bands. The boundaries of these bands were chosen empirically so that each made an equal contribution to phoneme recognition, as shown in Table 1.

From a function showing the relative importance of different parts of the acoustic spectrum we can obtain measures of central tendency and of dispersion; analogous to the parameters used to describe statistical distributions. For example, the "median" frequency as determined from French and Steinberg's data is 1900 Hz. This is the frequency that divides the spectrum into two parts, each contributing equally to phoneme recognition. Despite the use of widely

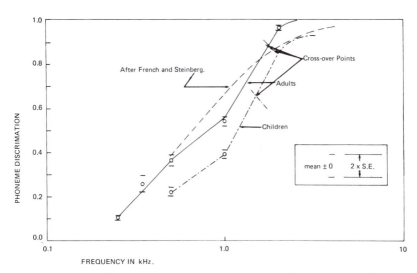

Figure 3.   Relationship between filter cutoff frequency and discrimination for low pass filtering in normal hearing adults and children. The data of French and Steinberg are shown for comparison. Also shown are the crossover points of the low pass and high pass curves. Taken from Boothroyd (1968).

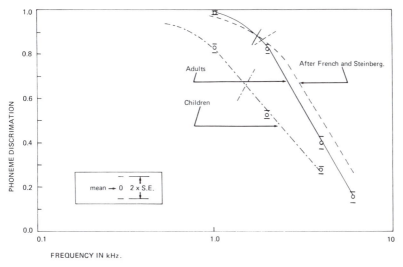

Figure 4.   Relationship between filter cutoff frequency and discrimination for high pass filtering in normal hearing adults and children. The data of French and Steinberg are shown for comparison. Also shown are the crossover points of the low pass and high pass curves. Taken from Boothroyd (1968).

Table 1.   Boundaries and bandwidths of 20 bands of equal importance to recognition of speech sounds

Band	Boundaries (Hz)	Bandwidth (Hz)	Bandwidth (dB)
	250		
1		125	1.76
	375		
2		130	1.29
	505		
3		140	1.06
	645		
4		150	0.91
	795		
5		160	0.80
	955		
6		175	0.73
	1130		
7		185	0.66
	1315		
8		200	0.61
	1515		
9		205	0.55
	1720		
10		210	0.50
	1930		
11		210	0.45
	2140		
12		215	0.42
	2355		
13		245	0.43
	2600		
14		300	0.47
	2900		
15		355	0.50
	3255		
16		425	0.53
	3680		
17		520	0.57
	4200		
18		660	0.63
	4860		
19		860	0.71
	5720		
20		1280	0.88
	7000		

Taken from French and Steinberg (1947).

differing experimental procedures, other researchers have found surprisingly similar values for this frequency. Hirsh et al. (1954), for example, obtained a value of 1700 Hz; Miller and Nicely (1955), 1550 Hz; and the author measured 1700 Hz for adult listeners and 1550 Hz for the children (Boothroyd, 1968).

The "interquartile" frequency range encompasses the center half of the information contributing to phoneme recognition. According to the French and Steinberg data this range is 955–3255 Hz. This is very similar to the frequency range of the second vocal tract formant. The interquartile ranges found by the author were narrower than this— 1200–2600 Hz for adult listeners and 1200–2300 Hz for children— perhaps because only a single talker was used.

It should be stressed at this point that "half the information" does not mean 50% phoneme recognition. For normal listeners, whose phoneme recognition probability is close to 100% under ideal conditions, the removal of half the acoustic information causes only a small increase in the probability of error. For example, in the French and Steinberg study, the effect was to lower phoneme recognition by 10.9 percentage points from 98.5% to 87.6%. This point is further illustrated in Table 2, and is also dealt with in the appendix to this chapter.

Table 2.   Relationship between frequency bandwidth and phoneme recognition probability[a]

Bandwidth (Hz)	Number of contributing bands (X)	Percentage of available information	Phoneme recognition probability (%) ($P_{X/20}$)
250–7000	20	100	98.5
375–5720	18	90	97.7
505–4860	16	80	96.5
645–4200	14	70	94.7
795–3680	12	60	92.0
955–3255[b]	10	50	87.8
1130–2900	8	40	81.4
1315–2600	6	30	71.6
1515–2355	4	20	56.8
1720–2140	2	10	34.3

[a] These data are based on French and Steinberg's 20 bands of equal importance. The value of phoneme recognition probability when all 20 bands are present (P_f) is taken from their data. The remaining values are calculated from the equation:

$$P_{X/20} = 1 = (1 = P_f)^{X/20}$$

where X is the number of contributing bands.

[b] Analogous to an interquartile range.

So far we have discussed the recognition of phonemes as if they were an undifferentiated group, but this is obviously not so. Fletcher (1953, Chapter 18), presented some information on the recognition of individual phonemes as a function of high and low pass filtering. It is difficult to summarize these data, but the following points are of importance:

1. Some phonemes are inherently more easily recognized than others. For example, under the best listening conditions the consonants [f] and [θ] were misinterpreted on 12.7% and 17.3% of occasions, respectively, whereas the consonant [1] and the diphthong [ai] were misinterpreted on only 0.2% of occasions.

2. Phonemes differ considerably in terms of median frequency. For example, the median frequencies for all vowels (except [i]) were between 1000 and 1500 Hz, whereas the median frequencies for many consonants were above 2000 Hz.

3. Phonemes also differ in terms of interquartile range.[1] For many sounds, the critical information for recognition was concentrated over a narrow frequency range, but others were recognizable from information over a broad frequency range. For example, the interquartile range for [α] was 1000–1500 Hz, whereas for [t] it was 500–3700 Hz.

Frequency Dependence of Feature Recognition

It has long been popular to describe the phoneme set of a given language in terms of a smaller number of subphonemic features such as voicing, nasality, and place of articulation. This approach has much more to recommend it than descriptive convenience. The developing child, for example, may acquire mastery over these features at differing rates and it seems that they can function independently at a perceptual level (Menyuk, 1968). It is therefore appropriate to ask about the frequency dependence of the cues to feature recognition.

This question was examined by Miller and Nicely (1955), using an approach similar to that of French and Steinberg, but preserving information on errors of consonant recognition. By application of probability theory to the data presented by Miller and Nicely, due allowance being made for random guessing, it is possible to calculate interquartile frequency ranges for feature perception in addition to the

---

[1] As with the Miller and Nicely data presented later, these interquartile ranges were determined by application of probability theory to the published data. An explanation of the procedure is in the appendix to this chapter.

median frequencies quoted by the writers. The results are shown in Table 3 for three of the subphonemic features. An explanation of the mathematical treatment is in the appendix to this chapter.

It is clear from Miller and Nicely's work that there are marked differences in the frequency distributions of information about the different features. In particular, the information about place of articulation is predominantly high frequency, whereas information on voicing and manner of articulation is available over a wide frequency range, extending into the low frequencies. What is particularly striking is the similarity between the interquartile range for place of articulation obtained from the Miller and Nicely data and that for overall phoneme recognition obtained from the French and Steinberg data. Again, it should be pointed out that these ranges correspond closely with the range of the second vocal tract formant.

This writer is not aware of similar work having been done on the suprasegmental speech features. When listening to filtered speech, however, it quickly becomes obvious that information on rhythm and intonation is, like manner and voicing information, diffusely spread across the acoustic spectrum.

Nature of Acoustic Cues to Phoneme and Feature Recognition

Thanks mainly to work on speech synthesis, we now have a lot of information on the specific nature of the acoustic cues to phoneme and feature recognition. A full description would be beyond the scope of the present chapter and, in any case, it is not clear that a detailed knowledge of this topic is important for work on speech perception in the deaf. The interested reader is referred to Stevens and House (1972) for an up-to-date account. The following discussion will concern only the more salient points.

Much of the information that serves to differentiate vowels from consonants and to differentiate consonants on the basis of voicing and manner of articulation is to be found in the time/intensity patterns of

Table 3. Median and interquartile frequencies for three subphonemic features

Feature	Median frequency (Hz)	Interquartile range (Hz)	Bandwidth (octaves)
Voicing	500	200–1550	3.0
Manner of articulation	750	335–2000	2.6
Place of articulation	1900	880–2650	1.6

Derived from the data of Miller and Nicely (1955).

speech or in the relative times of occurrence of different events. This information is not restricted to any specific frequency range. Initial stops, for example, are characterized by a period of silence (or very low intensity) followed by a sharp increase of intensity, perhaps accompanied by fricative noise of short duration, whereas voiced and voiceless stops may be differentiated on the basis of the intensity of the fricative noise and the time interval between plosive release and the onset of voicing (the voise onset time).

By contrast, much of the information that serves to define place of articulation is to be found in the frequency/time domain. This information is encoded in the resonant frequencies, or formants, and is therefore restricted to specific frequency ranges. The relative values of the first and second formants serve to differentiate all the vowels; the second and higher formants help to determine place of articulation of consonants. The most useful single formant is the second, because its frequency is governed primarily by the shape and size of the cavity in front of the tongue and therefore provides cues to tongue position. We thus have an explanation for the similarity between the frequency range of the second formant and the interquartile range for phoneme recognition and place of articulation identification mentioned earlier.

In connected speech, the movements associated with specific phonemes overlap each other in time. Consequently, some of the acoustic cues to the identity of a given phoneme can often be found in adjacent phonemes. It is now well known, for example, that the identity of a plosive consonant can be determined both by the formants in the plosive burst and by the formant transitions in the following vowel. In the case of the nasal consonants, differentiation may be possible only from formant transitions in neighboring vowels because the resonances of the nasals themselves are very similar.

Not only frequency effects, but also time effects, may be found in adjacent sounds. In English, for example, a voiced final consonant is frequently accompanied by increased duration of the preceding vowel (compare, for example, *eyes* and *ice*). This temporal cue may be more important to recognition than any cues in the consonant itself (Denes, 1955).

One of the most significant findings of research on the cues to phoneme recognition concerns the adaptability of the listener. It seems that many of the cues are not evaluated in terms of their absolute properties, but rather in terms of their properties in relation to the complete repertoire of the talker. It is as though the listener establishes a frame of reference as he samples the speech of the talker and uses this as a basis for evaluation of specific cues. Perhaps the most elegant example comes from the work of Broadbent and Ladefoged (1960), who were able to control the perception of the vowel in the final word of a sentence by manipulation of the vowel formants in the preceding words. This adaptive behavior on the part of the listener has plagued researchers on speech synthesis who find themselves being taught to understand synthetic speech by their machines, just as it has plagued teachers of the deaf who are taught to understand "deaf speech" by their students. It is a component of the speech perception process that is difficult to incorporate into an automatic speech recognition device.

CONTEXTUAL AND LINGUISTIC FACTORS

Throughout most of the foregoing discussion we have dealt with the information in the acoustic signal without considering how this information is used in the perceptual process. The exception was in the last paragraph where the active participation of the listener began to intrude. We were, I hope, reminded that the acoustic speech signal is simply physical evidence that the listener "consults" in the process of deciding what the talker said.

This view of perception as a synthetic, creative activity on the part of the perceiver is widely accepted. On the basis of perceptual experience of the environment and motoric interaction with it, we categorize sensory information and construct an internal conceptual model of our world. When confronted with new sensory information we make and test hypotheses as to its origins. However, although the sensory data act on us from outside, the hypotheses we make and the criteria we use to accept or reject them are generated from our internal model.

So it is with speech perception. We receive auditory data from the acoustic patterns of speech, possibly supplemented by visual data from speechreading. From our own knowledge of the world, of the talker, of the situational context and of the language context, we generate hypotheses about the linguistic content of the utterance. We test these against the sensory data and accept or reject them, using criteria based on estimates of the a priori probability of being correct and of the consequence of error. Particular circumstances will dictate whether, at a given moment, the hypothesis being tested concerns a sentence, a phrase, a word, a syllable or a speech sound. It is quite likely that we deal with the largest units possible, only descending to smaller units to resolve particular ambiguities. It is also quite likely that in order to maximize the two criteria for efficient perception—

accuracy and speed—we ignore a large part of the acoustic information with which the previous sections were concerned. So predictable
is normal conversation that the informational load on the acoustic
signal is generally very light.

It must be stressed that the foregoing comment applies to the
listener with normal language and world models. Such a person is
himself a generator of speech. He is familiar with the phoneme set of
his language as well as with phoneme occurrence and phoneme
sequence probabilities. He has a large lexicon and is familiar with
word occurrence probabilities. He knows the syntax of his language
and is therefore familiar with word sequence probabilities, and he has
a broad knowledge of the world in which he lives, acquired partly
through spoken communication with others. Moreover, he is skilled in
making hypotheses rapidly and in accepting them on the basis of
minimal sensory data, while maintaining a low probability of error.
Clearly these are not characteristics of the developing child or of the
prelingually deaf. Such people do not have the internal knowledge or
perceptual skills of the normal hearing adult and are therefore more
dependent on accurate recognition of acoustic information.

One way of looking at language competence, world knowledge,
situational context, and language context is as additional channels of
information. We have already seen how different parts of the frequency spectrum can contribute independently to phoneme recognition. Now we must add channels that have nothing to do with the
acoustic spectrum. Communication scientists have borrowed the term
"redundancy" to describe the availability of multiple independent
information sources. This is perhaps an unfortunate choice because it
might be taken to imply "unnecessary" or "useless." However, redundancy in this context is far from unnecessary. It is the means by which
the probability of perceptual error can be kept to an acceptably low
value despite the physical and physiologic imperfections of the real
world.

A single example should suffice to illustrate the way redundancy
operates in verbal communication. Consider the statement *I bought
some new shoes*, and the perception of the final phoneme.

1. The listener heard this with two ears. One would have sufficed
    (physiologic redundancy).
2. He heard the complete acoustic spectrum. A small portion would
    have sufficed (acoustic redundancy).
3. Clues to the final consonant were to be found in the consonant
    itself and in the formant transitions and duration of the preceding
    vowel (phonetic redundancy).

4. [z] is one of the few phonemes that can be added to [ʃuː] and still make a meaningful word (lexical redundancy).
5. The word "some" implies that the last word will be a plural (syntactic redundancy).
6. "World knowledge" tells us that shoes come in pairs (semantic redundancy).

To the extent that these different sources of information are independent, they can be incorporated into the general mathematical model developed in the appendix to this chapter.

Quantitative evidence of the effects of context on word perception has been presented by Miller et al. (1951). In one experiment, context was controlled by presenting listeners with a list from which test words were chosen. The signal-to-noise ratio for 50% recognition (corrected for random guessing) varied from −14 dB when the list was two words long, to −4 dB when it was 256 words long. Extrapolation of the data indicated that an open set situation is equivalent to a list of 30,000 words. Also compared in the Miller et al. data were recognition probabilities for words in isolation and the same words in sentences. The results suggest that the effect of linguistic context is approximately equivalent to doubling the acoustic information, as shown in the appendix to this chapter.

Rosenzweig and Postman (1958) have reviewed some data that show the effect of frequency of usage on the perception of words. They showed that the signal-to-noise ratio for 50% recognition changes by approximately 4 dB for every tenfold increase in frequency of usage. It has been suggested by Broadbent (1967) that this type of result can be explained as a bias of acceptance criterion in favor of more probable hypotheses.

EFFECTS OF SENSORINEURAL HEARING LOSS

The most obvious effect of sensorineural deafness is a loss of audibility of acoustic cues. This problem can partly be overcome by amplification. There is, however, a practical limit of approximately 60 dB to the gain of wearable hearing aids, set by the problem of acoustic feedback. It will be recalled that the weakest acoustic cues in conversational speech are at about 30 dB above the normal threshold of hearing. Consequently, the goal of making all significant speech cues audible via a wearable hearing aid can only be realized for hearing losses up to 90 dB (the 30-dB HL of the weak fricatives plus the 60-dB limit of gain).

We can, of course, increase speech intensity by reducing distance from the talker. If the sound is picked up only a few inches from the talker's lips, the intensity of the weak fricatives may be increased to 60 dB HL. Thus, by using group amplifiers or auditory training units, full audibility is theoretically possible for losses up to 120 dB.

There are, unfortunately, several factors that deprive the hearing-impaired listener of acoustic cues, even when amplification is available. One of these is intrastimulus masking. It is a well known consequence of the traveling wave pattern on the basilar membrane that sounds have a masking effect on other sounds of higher frequency. This has been demonstrated for the masking of tones by tones (Fletcher, 1953, Chapter 10); of speech by low frequency bands of noise (Miller, 1947); and of second formant transitions by first formants in synthetic syllables (Danaher et al., 1973; Danaher and Pickett, 1975). It is an inevitable consequence of cochlear mechanics that this "upward spread of masking" becomes relatively more pronounced at higher levels of cochlear stimulation. Thus the hearing-impaired listener may be denied information in the high frequency bands of speech because of masking by lower frequency bands, simply because he is constrained to listen at high intensity levels. An additional problem is that of temporal masking, which may result in a loud sound masking a quiet sound that occurs immediately afterwards, or even immediately before (backward masking). Although none of these intrastimulus masking effects has been adequately researched in hearing-impaired subjects, there is sufficient evidence to indicate their potential importance.

Yet another problem affecting speech perception by the hearing impaired is that of tolerance. It is a characteristic of cochlear deafness that the range of intensities from threshold of audibility to threshold of discomfort is narrower than normal. Very frequently it is less than the dynamic intensity range of speech. If a hearing aid is capable of generating outputs in excess of the user's threshold of discomfort, audibility will be sacrificed in order to avoid pain. (Either the gain will be lowered, or the aid will be removed.) This problem can be overcome by limiting maximum power output, thus giving the user the opportunity to increase gain and render the weaker sounds of speech audible without experiencing discomfort from the loud sounds. Unless the aid employs syllabic compression, this will result in peak clipping with ensuing nonlinearity. There is, however, ample evidence to show that any deleterious effects of harmonic and intermodulation distortion are, in many cases, more than offset by the benefits of dynamic range reduction, especially if the low frequencies are attenuated before clipping (e.g., Thomas and Sparks, 1971).

The problems of speech perception by persons with sensorineural hearing loss cannot, of course, be treated only in terms of audibility. There is also a loss of frequency resolution, and possibly of temporal resolution, which interferes with the discriminability of phonemes and features. From the results of the many research studies on this topic, the following general conclusions may be drawn:

1. Persons with sensorineural hearing losses use the same acoustic cues to speech perception as do persons with normal hearing. If they are denied any of these cues, there are no acoustic substitutes (see, for example, Pickett et al., 1972).

2. When speech recognition abilities are examined in relation to pure tone hearing loss, the highest statistical correlations are found with pure tone thresholds around 2000 Hz (Mullins and Bangs, 1957; Kryter et al., 1962; Young and Gibbons, 1962; Boothroyd 1968, 1972). This is to be expected from what we know of the frequency dependence of phoneme recognition (see Table 1).

3. Place of articulation is the phonetic feature most susceptible to the effects of sensorineural hearing loss (Pickett et al., 1972; Boothroyd, 1976; Risberg, 1976). This is, of course, the feature that is most dependent on frequency information. Research data indicate that it is virtually imperceptible to persons with hearing losses in excess of 90 dB.

4. Perception of voicing, manner of articulation, intonation and rhythm is possible for persons with hearing losses well in excess of 90 dB (Boothroyd, 1976; Risberg, 1976). Most of these features are encoded in the time/intensity patterns of speech. The exception is intonation, but the acoustic cues to intonation are more robust and more widely dispersed than those to place of articulation.

5. Sensorineural hearing loss usually results in increased reliance on low frequency acoustic cues. This seems to be due to a combination of two factors: a) the greater loss of sensitivity to high frequencies usually accompanying sensorineural loss; b) the fact that the more subtle acoustic cues are concentrated in the high frequencies, whereas the more robust time/intensity cues are spread over a broad frequency range, including the low frequencies (see Table 3).

The suggestion made above that there are no acoustic cues that can be substituted for those made unavailable by sensorineural deafness requires some explanation, especially because it runs counter to the opinions expressed by several authorities on this subject and also to statements made previously by the present writer.

Some years ago, I attempted to do for severely deaf children what French and Steinberg had done for normal hearing adults. That is, to determine the relative contributions of different parts of the acoustic spectrum to phoneme recognition (Boothroyd, 1967; 1968). Twenty-five students attending a British school for the partially hearing were used as subjects. Their three frequency average hearing losses ranged from 45–95 dB (ISO). The experimental procedure consisted of measuring correct recognition of speech sounds in lists of (CVC) monosyllabic words presented under various conditions of high and low pass filtering.

When comparing the results of normal and hearing-impaired subjects, three possible outcomes might have been predicted, as illustrated in Fig. 5:

1. Sensorineural deafness results in a reduced contribution of all frequencies to phoneme recognition, but their relative contributions follow the normal pattern.
2. Sensorineural deafness causes a reduced contribution from some frequencies but leaves other frequencies unaffected.
3. Sensorineural deafness causes a reduced contribution from some frequencies but a compensatory increase in contribution from other frequencies.

Twenty-three of the twenty-five subjects gave results that fell into the first two categories. Those with "flat" audiograms generally showed a uniform reduction of contribution across frequencies. Those with sloping audiograms showed a loss of contribution from the high frequencies but often gave normal results in the low frequencies. The two remaining subjects gave results that seemed to show a greater use of low frequencies than was found in normals. The effect was a small one, however, and occurred only in two subjects with steeply falling audiograms. Their hearing losses had given them years of practice in listening to low pass filtered speech, whereas the normal subjects with whom they were compared were tested without training. It is quite possible that only a few hours of listening experience for the normal subjects would have been sufficient to eliminate the difference between them and the two hearing-impaired subjects. In the absence of more convincing evidence to the contrary, it seems reasonable to conclude that, for the subjects used in this study, the contribution of any frequency band to phoneme recognition was either normal, or was reduced.

What then are the goals of auditory training, if not to focus attention on auditory cues that are unused by persons with normal hearing?

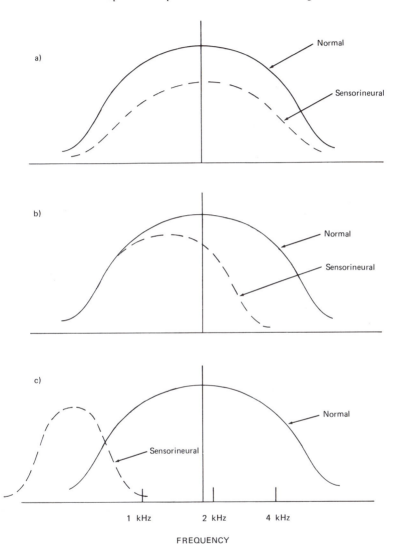

CONTRIBUTION TO PHONEME RECOGNITION

a)

Normal

Sensorineural

b)

Normal

Sensorineural

c)

Normal

Sensorineural

1 kHz   2 kHz   4 kHz

FREQUENCY

Figure 5. Three hypothetical effects of sensorineural hearing loss on the frequency dependence of phoneme recognition. In *a*, the loss of information is uniform across frequencies; in *b*, the loss of information is confined to the high frequencies; in *c*, the loss of high frequency information is compensated by a gain of low frequency information. There is experimental evidence for the occurrence of the first two conditions but not for the third.

They are twofold. One is to make full use of those auditory cues that are still available despite the sensorineural damage. The other is to gain facility with the perception of connected language so that strategies can be learned that make maximum use of situational, contextual, and linguistic redundancy.

Of relevance to this last conclusion are the results of a study carried out recently at the Clarke School for the Deaf (Nittrouer et al., 1976). A group of preteenage hearing-impaired children who seemed to be making insufficient use of their residual hearing spent one period a day functioning by hearing alone. Over a period of several weeks they showed marked improvement in their auditory skills. On formal testing it was shown that this improvement was not to be found in a greater ability to extract cues from the acoustic signal but in the more effective use of these cues in material with internal linguistic redundancy.

Although there may be no untapped sources of acoustic information in speech, there is a largely untapped source of visual information i.e., speechreading. Not only does speechreading provide information, but it does so about the very feature that is most susceptible to the effects of sensorineural damage: place of articulation. Thus vision and hearing can play complementary roles in speech perception for the hearing impaired, giving almost perfect phoneme recognition for losses below 90 dB (Hudgins, 1954; Erber, 1972).

We have been discussing the direct effect of sensorineural hearing loss: the limited availability of auditory information. The individual who becomes deaf after the development of language skills must learn how to perceive speech in spite of this limitation. He must discover how to make and test hypotheses with insufficient evidence. He must be prepared to lower his acceptance criteria and accept a higher probability of error. The goals of aural rehabilitation for such an individual are twofold. One is to bring his attention to bear on the limited acoustic and visual cues still available to him, the other is to provide a comfortable environment in which the new perceptual strategies can be learned. Methods of teaching speechreading have been labeled "analytic" and "synthetic" according to their relative emphasis on these two components.

Prelingual deafness has, of course, more far-reaching effects. The defective input channel impedes the development of the internal knowledge and skills that are an integral part of the speech perception process. The prelingually deaf child typically lacks an intimate knowledge of phoneme probabilities, phoneme sequence probabilities, word probabilities, and syntax. Moreover, his deafness may deprive him of the chance to acquire the "world knowledge" that would permit him to bring appropriate semantic constraints to bear on perceptual decisions.

It has been suggested at various times that alternative input media can be used to establish the necessary internal knowledge and skills. Examples are the written word, sign language, and fingerspelling. At the present time, however, there are no data to indicate that the primacy of audition for the establishment of basic language skills can be usurped. Moreover, there is ample evidence to show that, despite profound, prelingual, sensorineural hearing loss, the auditory channel can continue to play its primary role for a large percentage of the deaf population (Whetnall and Fry, 1964; Griffiths, 1967; Wedenberg, 1967; Pollack, 1970). The prerequisites for this seem to be sufficient residual hearing, supportive and well motivated parents, early identification, appropriate amplification, and the consistent application of an auditory approach.

SUMMARY AND CONCLUSIONS

The acoustic cues to speech perception are contained in the intensity/frequency/time patterns of a given language. Much of the information on prosody and on voicing and manner of articulation is found in the intensity/time patterns and is distributed across a broad spectrum, including the low frequencies. Much of the information on place of articulation is found in the frequency/time patterns and is concentrated in the higher frequencies. These cues are used in the perceptual process as sensory evidence on which decisions are made about internally generated linguistic hypotheses.

Sensorineural deafness limits the availability of acoustic cues by a combination of audibility, tolerance, masking, and discrimination problems. To the extent that auditory information is preserved, the deaf use the same cues to speech perception as do the normal hearing. There are no other acoustic "invariants" to which they can turn. They can, however, use speechreading information, which largely complements limited hearing by providing cues to place of articulation.

The postlingually deaf child must learn new perceptual strategies to cope with reduced sensory data. The prelingually deaf child must also do this, but his situation is further complicated by the fact that his deafness interferes with the development of the internal knowledge and skills that are an integral part of the perceptual process. Although audition alone will not be enough, the indications are that the primacy of audition as a medium for the establishment of basic language skills can often be preserved despite profound sensorineural hearing loss.

In recent years the term "auditory approach" has gained popularity among educators of the deaf, in preference to "auditory training." It is a term that suggests the use of audition as a means to an end rather than as an end in itself. In the opinion of this writer, recognition of the fact that hearing can play its normal role in the acquisition of basic language skills for large numbers of hearing-impaired children has been one of the few developments of major significance in education of the deaf since its inception. Its full implications are yet to be realized.

APPENDIX

SPEECH PERCEPTION AND PROBABILITY THEORY

Application of Theorem of Independent Probabilities

Consider several independent sources of speech information: 1, 2, 3, . . ., n.

Let the probability of recognition of a speech element (sound, syllable, word, etc.) attributable to information in the ith source be P_i. Then the probability of nonrecognition using information from the ith source is $(1 - P_i)$, and the probability of nonrecognition when all sources act together is given by:

$$(1 - P_f) = (1 - P_1)(1 - P_2) \ldots (1 - P_i) \ldots (1 - P_n)$$

or:

$$(1 - P_f) = \prod_{i=n}^{i=1} (1 - P_i) \tag{1}$$

Thus the probability of recognition when all sources act together is:

$$P_f = 1 - \prod_{i-n}^{i-1} (1 - P_i) \tag{2}$$

The condition of independence should be noted. This requires that P_i is unaffected by the presence of information from other sources. This condition is not satisfied:

1. When one source interferes with another, thus lowering P_i (e.g., upward spread of masking, or distractions);
2. When two sources provide identical information, so that the probability of recognition when both act together is the same as the probability when either acts alone;

3. When the two sources interact with each other to provide new information not present in either alone.

It should also be noted that none of the probabilities can equal 1, although they may approach it. That is, there is always a finite probability of error in the recognition of speech elements.

Median Frequencies

Consider the acoustic spectrum divided into two halves, each providing the same independent probability of phoneme recognition, $P_{1/2}$. This probability is then related to the full band probability P_f, by the equation:

$$(1 - P_f) = (1 - P_{1/2})^2 \qquad (3)$$

or

$$P_{1/2} = 1 - (1 - P_f)^{1/2} \qquad (4)$$

The value of P_f given by French and Steinberg was 0.985. Substituting this in Equation 4 gives $P_{1/2} = 0.878$. This agrees very closely with the experimental value of 0.876 at the crossover point of the high and low pass filtering curves.

Quartile Frequencies

Extending the foregoing analysis to four bands, each contributing independently to the probability of phoneme recognition, we have:

$$P_{1/4} = 1 - (1 - P_f)^{1/4} \qquad (5)$$

This equation was applied to Fletcher's data to estimate the interquartile frequency ranges for individual phonemes.

20-Band Data

Consider the acoustic spectrum divided in 20 bands, each contributing equally to the probability of phoneme recognition. The probability associated with a combination of X bands is given by:

$$P_{X/20} = 1 - (1 - P_f)^{X/20} \qquad (6)$$

This equation was used in the preparation of Table 3.

Multiple Choice Tests

In closed set recognition tasks with forced choice responses, there is always a finite probability of correct recognition from random guessing. This is given by:

$$P_g = 1/r \qquad (7)$$

where r is the number of response alternatives. This factor can be included in an additional multiplicative term when calculating error probabilities from independent information sources. For example, in reworking the data of Miller and Nicely in order to calculate interquartile frequencies, the following equations were used:

$$(1 - P_m) = (1 - P_s)(1 - P_g) \tag{8}$$

where P_m = full band probability including effects of guessing and P_s = full band probability excluding effects of guessing;

$$(1 - P_s) = (1 - P_{s/4})^4 \tag{9}$$

where $P_{s/4}$ = quarter band probability excluding effects of guessing and

$$(1 - P_{1/4}) = (1 - P_{s/4})(1 - P_g) \tag{10}$$

where $P_{1/4}$ = quarter band probability incuding effects of guessing.

Figure 11 illustrates the application of these equations to the place of articulation data of Miller and Nicely.

Contextual Information

Verbal language consists of sequences of elements whose probabilities of recognition are anything but independent. Each element has its own intrinsic probability of recognition, but it also has a probability of recognition from information contained in elements that come before or after. The presence of this information will depend, of course, on whether the other elements are

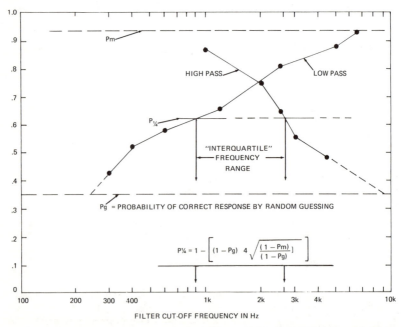

Figure 11. Example of treatment of the Miller and Nicely (1955) data to derive an "interquartile" frequency range encompassing half of the available information on place of articulation.

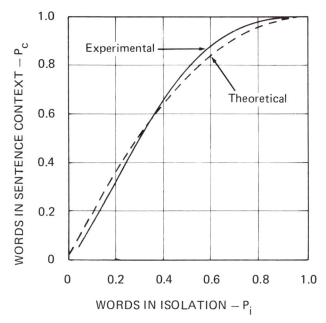

Figure 12.   Relationship between the probabilities of recognition of words in isolation and of the same words in sentences. The full line shows experimental data taken from Miller et al. (1951). The broken line is derived from the equation: $P_c = 1 - (1 - P_i)^2$. In the Miller et al. study, recognition probabilities were controlled by varying signal-to-noise ratio.

Table A1.   Probabilities of recognition of words in isolation and in sentences from Miller et al. (1951)

Word recognition probability		Context factor
In isolation P_i	In sentences P_c	$c = \log (1 - P_c)/ \log (1 - P_i)$
0.1	0.15[a]	1.54
0.2	0.32	1.73
0.3	0.50	1.94
0.4	0.65	2.06
0.5	0.77	2.12
0.6	0.88	2.31
0.7	0.95	2.49
0.8	0.98	2.43

[a] These values were obtained by visual inspection of a graph presented in the Miller et al. paper, and must be considered approximate.

themselves recognized. This effect can be included in the probability equation as a power factor c as follows:

$$(1 - P_c) = (1 - P_i)^c \qquad (11)$$

where P_i is the intrinsic probability of recognition of an element and P_c is its probability of recognition when contextual factors are present. When $c = 1$, context provides no information; when $c = 2$, context provides as much information as do intrinsic factors; when $c = 3$, context provides twice as much information as do intrinsic factors, etc.

In their 1951 paper, Miller et al. provide data on isolated word recognition and recognition of the same words in sentences as functions of signal to noise ratio. Table 11 gives the two sets of probabilities, together with the calculated values of c. Figure 12 shows the relationship between these two sets of probabilities, together with that predicted by substituting $c = 2$ in Equation 11. Although the agreement is not perfect, it can be seen that contextual cues provided about as much information as did intrinsic cues in the Miller et al. study. A closer empirical fit to the Miller et al. data is obtained with:

$$P_c = 1 - (1 - P_i)^{1.5(1 + P_i)} \qquad (12)$$

REFERENCES

Boothroyd, A. 1967. Discrimination by partially hearing children of frequency distorted speech. Audiology 6:136–145.

Boothroyd, A. 1968. Selection of hearing aids for children. Unpublished doctoral thesis, University of Manchester, England.

Boothroyd, A. 1972. Auditory arousal in severely and profoundly deaf children and the effect of stereophonic amplification. The Clarke School for the Deaf, Sensory Aids Research Project, Report # 8. Northampton, Mass.

Boothroyd, A. 1976. Influence of residual hearing on speech perception and speech production by hearing impaired children. The Clarke School for the Deaf, Sensory Aids Research Project, Report #26. Northampton, Mass.

Broadbent, D. E. 1967. Word frequency effect and response bias. Psychol. Rev. 74:1–15.

Broadbent, D. E., and P. Ladefoged. 1960. Vowel judgments and adaptation level. Proc. Royal Soc. 151:384–399.

Danaher, E. M., M. J. Osberger and J. M. Pickett. 1973. Discrimination of formant frequency transitions in synthetic vowels. J. Speech Hear. Res. 16:439–451.

Danaher, E. M., and J. M. Pickett. 1975. Some masking effects produced by low frequency vowel formants in persons with sensorineural hearing loss. J. Speech Hear. Res. 18:261–271.

Denes, P. 1955. Effect of duration on the perception of voicing. J. Acoust. Soc. Am. 27:761–764.

Dunn, H. K., and D. W. Farnsworth. 1939. Exploration of pressure field around human head during speech. J. Acoust. Soc. Am. 10:184–199.

Dunn, H. K., and S. D. White. 1940. Statistical measurements on conversational speech. J. Acoust. Soc. Am. 11:278–288.

Erber, N. P. 1972. Auditory, visual, and auditory-visual recognition of consonants by children with normal and impaired hearing. J. Speech Hear. Res. 15(2):413–422.

Fletcher, H. 1953. Speech and Hearing in Communication. D. Van Nostrand Company, New York.

French, N. R., and J. C. Steinberg. 1947. Factors governing the intelligibility of speech sounds. J. Acoust. Soc. Am. 19:90–119.

Griffiths, C. 1967. Conquering childhood deafness. Exposition Press, New York.

Hirsh, I. J., E. R. Reynolds, and M. Joseph. 1954. Intelligibility of different speech materials. J. Acoust. Soc. Am. 26:530–538.

Hudgins, C. V. 1954. Auditory training: its possibilities and limitations. Volta Rev. 56:339–349.

Kryter, K. D., C. Williams, and D. M. Green. 1962. Auditory acuity and the perception of speech. J. Acoust. Soc. Am. 34:1217–1223.

Licklider, J. C. R. 1946. Effects of amplitude distortion upon the intelligibility of speech. J. Acoust. Soc. Am. 18:429–434.

Lippmann, R. P., L. D. Braida, and N. I. Durlach. 1977. Matching speech to residual auditory function, II. Review of previous research on amplitude compression. Unpublished report, Research Laboratory of Electronics, The M.I.T. Press, Cambridge, Mass.

Menyuk, P. 1968. The role of distinctive features in children's acquisition of phonology. J. Speech Hear. Res. 11:138–146.

Miller, G. A. 1947. The masking of speech. Psychol. Bull. 44:105–129.

Miller, G. A., C. A. Heise, and D. Lichten. 1951. Intelligibility of speech as a function of the context of the test material. J. Exp. Psychol. 41:329–335.

Miller, G. A., and P. E. Nicely. 1955. An analysis of perceptual confusions among some English consonants. J. Acoust. Soc. Am. 27:338–352.

Mullins, C. J., and J. L. Bangs. 1957. Relationships between speech discrimination and other audiometric data: Acta Otol. 47:149–157.

Nittrouer, S., M. A. Devan, and A. Boothroyd. 1976. It's never too late: An auditory approach with hearing impaired pre-teenagers: The Clarke School for the Deaf, Sensory Aids Research Project, Report #24. Northampton, Mass.

Pickett, J. M., E. S. Martin, D. Johnson, S. Brandsmith, Z. Daniel, D. Willis, and W. Otis. 1972. On patterns of speech feature reception by deaf listeners. In: G. Fant (ed.), Proceedings of the International Symposium on Speech Communication Ability and Profound Deafness, pp. 119–133. A. G. Bell Association for the Deaf, Washington, D.C.

Pollack, D. 1970. Educational audiology for the limited hearing infant. Charles C Thomas, Publisher, Springfield, Ill.

Risberg, A. 1976. Diagnostic rhyme test for speech audiometry with severely hard of hearing and profoundly deaf children. Speech Trans. Lab. Q. Prog. Status Rep. 2–3:40–58. Stockholm.

Rosenzweig, M. R., and L. Postman, 1958. Frequency of usage and the perception of words. Science 127:263–266.

Stevens, K. N., and A. S. House. 1972. Speech perception. In: J. V. Tobias (ed.), Foundation of Modern Auditory Theory, pp. 1–62. Academic Press, New York.

Thomas, I. B., and D. W. Sparks. 1971. Discrimination of filtered-clipped speech by hearing impaired subjects. J. Acoust. Soc. Am. 49:1881–1887.

Wedenberg, E. 1967. Experience from thirty years, auditory training. Volta Rev. 69:588–594.

Whetnall, E., and D. Fry. 1964. The Deaf Child. Charles C Thomas, Publisher, Springfield, Ill.

Young, M. A., and E. W. Gibbons. 1962. Speech discrimination scores and threshold measurements in a non-normal hearing population. J. Audiol. Res. 2:21–33.

CHAPTER 5

CLASSROOM ACOUSTICS

Knud Børrild

CONTENTS

HISTORICAL BACKGROUND

The acoustic climate or environment, as a concept in buildings, is of relatively recent origin. Formerly, conditions were accepted as provided by the architects and builders, necessitating resigning oneself to the fact that staying in some building was agreeable while in others it was less comfortable. In some it was pleasant to talk and to listen, in others it was not, and in a few it was almost impossible.

To intervene actively with the acoustic climate was scarcely considered. An exception would seem to have been some of the old European church builders, who, as early as the 1100s, attempted to interfere actively with the acoustic conditions in the churches by installing resonators in the ceiling and walls. Beranek (1959) believes that the resonators were acoustically ineffective, and that nothing

145

more was involved than empty wine bottles and refuse from luncheons, which the bricklayers tried to get rid of in the easiest possible manner, by bricking them into the wall. Discoveries in old Danish churches, however, tend to disprove this otherwise down-to-earth and cozy theory, the resonators undoubtedly having been installed for the purpose of regulating the acoustics, even though the effect was presumably modest. The skill seems to have been forgotten in the course of the Middle Ages, and it was not brought back to life until the second half of the nineteeth century through the experimental and theoretical works of scientists such as Helmholz, and somewhat later, Rayleigh and W. C. Sabine, who provided most of the theoretical foundation that acoustics employs today. These pioneer efforts, however, remained of only limited significance to architectural acoustics during the first decades of the twentieth century (McCroskey and Devens, 1974). The measuring devices were still rather primitive and the interest was limited in the beginning to buildings such as concert halls and radio studios exclusively, where the importance of good acoustic conditions was obvious.

It was well after World War II before the acoustic conditions in schools began to interest anyone other than teachers and students. The interest in the acoustic climate in schools for those with impaired hearing came at about the same time. The improved technique of hearing aids had the result that even small hearing remnants could be used, provided that the useful sounds could be distinguished from the noise. Early in the 1950s the problems relating to the acoustics in schools for the hearing impaired were taken up for study at the University of Manchester, England. Since that time it has been increasingly recognized that the demands made with respect to the acoustic environment of the hearing impaired must not only be equally as strict as those applying to persons of normal hearing, but that the demands must indeed be made considerably more severe if persons using hearing aids are to have reasonable listening conditions.

As everybody is by now aware, a good acoustic environment is important to normal hearing listeners (Beranek, 1959; Brandt, 1958; Brock, 1971). However, to those with impaired hearing who use a hearing aid, even small improvement, which is perhaps not even registered as significant by normal hearing persons, may mean the difference between hearing nothing and hearing everything, or between getting through a working day in a good physical condition and with surplus energy for active leisure, or reaching closing hours with only one desire: no contact again with other people until it is absolutely essential.

This has been a brief historical resume; now let us look at what we are actually talking about when we use terms such as acoustic environment or acoustic climate.

PARAMETERS OF THE ACOUSTIC CLIMATE

Origins and Definitions

The acoustic environment or climate may be defined as that mixture of background noise and useful sounds in which we continually find ourselves. A good acoustic environment may be defined as that situation in which the noise that is irrelevant to us is suppressed as far as possible, while the useful sounds, those that interest us, stand out clearly, and are truly and easily distinguishable (Børrild, 1959).

The acoustic climate in a room of normal shape and size, such as a room traditionally used in teaching, is determined essentially by three factors:

1. Noise transmitted from other rooms, or from the outside
2. Noise produced in the room itself
3. The reverberation time of the room

In cases in which the configuration of the classroom is different from the usual one—which happens occasionally in modern schools—the shape of the room is a factor that must not be ignored, because it might have serious and decisive influence on the acoustic conditions. Also, where larger rooms are concerned, the geometric design of the room is an important factor, because problems of sound distribution may arise.

We can look at each of the factors mentioned above individually, but first let us determine what we mean by noise. Noise is a sound we are not interested in hearing, useful sounds are all sounds we like to hear. This may be illustrated by an example.

If we invite some good friends for dinner in a restaurant in order to have a pleasant conversation with them, any background music will be noise to us. If we subsequently attend a concert and our friends continue the conversation, the talking will be noise, because now it is the music we wish to hear.

External Noise

The first factor, noise, which is transmitted from other rooms or from the outside, can be attacked in many ways, some of which will be quite costly, others simply requiring thought.

When beginning the projection of a new school, the acoustic planning should be started simultaneously with the selection of the location (Knudsen and Harris, 1950). It is a great deal easier to arrive at a good acoustic climate in a school situated on a large lot in a quiet district than one placed on a narrow strip near a freeway and in continuation of the runway of an airport. Schools, especially those for the hearing impaired, should never be placed in the latter location.

The planning of every school should start with asking the acoustician, who should be associated with the school project as closely as the architect, to perform a long range registration of the noise level at the contemplated site. If this turns out to be high, an attempt should be made to find a more appropriate location. The acoustician is not a person who looks over the completed drawings before the contractor sets to work or—still worse, but not unusual—a lifesaver who is called in when it turns out that the school has an unsuitable or unpleasant acoustic climate. In the latter capacity the acoustician may be very useful in connection with older schools, but where new ones are concerned he ought to take part from the very first day. This will produce a better result and will usually save much money.

In the above example the most common source of outside noise was mentioned: traffic noise. As a matter of course, schools are not placed so close to industrial plants or power stations, that industrial noise can become a problem, but a few other outside sources of noise are frequently overlooked, namely, playgrounds and sports grounds, which may be found at every school. The foundation may be laid for a good acoustic climate in the classrooms by ensuring that they do not directly face upon, and are a reasonable distance from, the sports fields and playgrounds. If necessary, noise-abating plantings or noise banks could be installed. The acoustician can contribute suggestions that improve the possibilities of obtaining a good acoustic climate at a reasonable cost. It is expedient, for example, to place rooms in which the lowest possible noise level is of less significance, such as gymnasiums, swimming pools, and other areas in which high levels of noise are produced, facing the strongest outdoor source of noise, thus protecting rooms in which a low noise level is essential. A good acoustic climate may be made possible by concentrating noise-producing rooms in one group, and rooms with a low noise level in another, without close contact between the groups.

It has gradually become the rule that schools—and especially schools for the hearing impaired—are built in one level, and it is likewise common today for the floors to be covered with carpets.

Therefore one may practically ignore steps on a floor partition as a source of noise.

Internal Noise

Noise produced in the room itself is decidedly a function of the teacher's personality where classrooms and other rooms for instruction are concerned; but the acoustician can contribute a great deal to control the level. The most important means in that direction is presumably regulation of the reverberation time—which is discussed later—but other possibilities should also be used.

The students, of course, must be permitted to breathe and move around on their chairs, just as occasionally it may be necessary to turn the leaves in a book. In an ordinary classroom with about 30 students, this will result in a noise level of 45–50 dB(A).[1] In classes for the hearing impaired, where the average class size is much smaller (in Denmark, four to five students) 35–40 dB(A) have been measured. The conditions for maintaining these average levels are that the reverberation time is low, and that the floor is carpeted so that noise from the shuffling of feet and chairs is reduced. If the table tops are covered, for example, with rubber, this will also contribute to a low noise level.

Reverberation Time

The reverberation time is presumably the most important one of the three factors that enter into the description of the acoustic climate in classrooms.

The reverberation time in a room is defined as the period of time, in seconds, that elapses from the moment a sound source is stopped until the sound level has dropped 60 dB. It is normally frequency dependent and should therefore be measured selectively so that the result is presented as a reverberation curve.

The reverberation time occurs because the surfaces in a room will not normally absorb all of the sound energy hitting them, but throw back a certain part of it. The harder and denser the surfaces, the greater will be that part of the sound energy reflected, and the longer it will take until, because of absorption, it is weakened so much that it is no longer audible. Because the reflected sound has longer to travel before it reaches the ear than does direct sound, it will arive later. The

---

[1] For a definition of the dB and dB(A) concepts, see ISO recommendations R 131 and R 357, and IEC Publication 123.

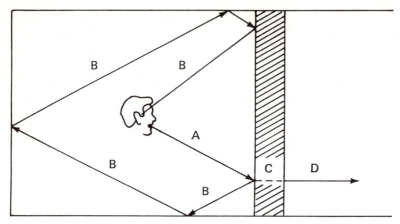

Figure 1. Sound reverberation. *A*, direct sound; *B*, reflected sound; *C*, absorbed sound; *D*, transmitted sound.

more times it hits the limiting surfaces, the later it will reach the ear, and the more it will have weakened. The ear will accordingly perceive a sound that gradually dies away (see Figure 1).

EXAMPLES OF METHODS FOR MEASURING A ROOM'S ACOUSTIC PARAMETERS

Although the acoustic phenomena of a room have presumably been known since man was crawling about in a cave, it is only in fairly recent times that we have been capable of measuring the parameters of the acoustic climate and also, to a certain extent, able to compute them on the basis of drawings and descriptions of a building. How such computations are performed is outside the scope of this chapter, but it would perhaps serve the purpose to give a few examples of the manner in which the measurements may be made.

Noise Measurements

Sound levels can be measured by a sound level meter, some examples of which are shown in Figure 2. If it is desired to register the level over a period of time, a level recorder may be connected of the type, for example, shown in Figure 3. The result of such a registration may be seen in Figure 4. The level is plotted along the *vertical axis*, the time toward the right along the *horizontal axis*.

The same instrument may be used in simple measurements of sound distribution, the level being measured by placing the sound level meter at various locations within the room.

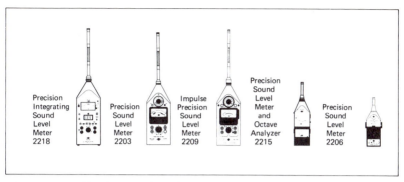

Figure 2.   Sound level meters. Reproduced with permission of Brüel and Kjaer, Naerum, Denmark.

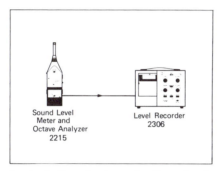

Figure 3.   Noise level meter feeding a level recorder. Reproduced with permission of Brüel and Kjaer, Naerum, Denmark.

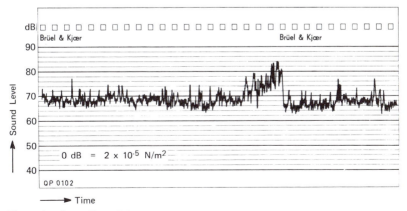

Figure 4.   Recording of the noise level in workshop. Reproduced with permission of Brüel and Kjaer, Naerum, Denmark.

The sound level meter, which is a relatively inexpensive and simple measuring instrument, can also be used for simple measurements of the sound-insulating ability of partitions, i.e., the airborne sound insulation. As a rule, this is frequency dependent, and if a complete curve for the airborne sound insulation is desired, the sound level meter must be combined with a one-octave or one-third-octave filter. A sound source is placed in one of the rooms (the transmitter room), and the sound level is measured first in this room, then in the other room (the receiver room). The difference between the two levels is corrected for the difference in reverberation time between the receiver room and a reference room.[2]

Sound insulation can be measured in a much more refined manner and more quickly if the necessary apparatus is available. See Figure 5, for example. The arrangement is presented in the figure. The result, recorded by the 2307 Level Recorder, may be seen in the *upper left* corner. The difference between the levels in the two rooms may be read directly as the difference between the upper and lower curve for each frequency. Here, too, a correction must be made for the receiver room's reverberation time.

This correction is not necessary in the arrangement in Figure 6, in which the receiver room's data have been coded into the computer in advance, which is then provided with a noise analysis made successively in the transmitter and receiver room. The sound insulation may then be printed by a printer, partly in decibels for each individual measuring frequency, and partly in the form of an insulation curve, if so desired.

In the few cases in which it is not possible to ignore the impact sound transmission through floor partitions, the measurements can be performed with the aid of a sound level meter with filter, and a tapping machine as shown in Figure 7. The measurements can also be performed in a slightly more refined and rapid manner as shown in Figure 8, in which the result in the form of an octave spectrogram printed by the level recorder is shown in the *upper right corner*.[3]

Reverberation Measurements

The reverberation time in a room can be measured in several ways (Brock, 1971; Heckl and Muller, 1975). They all have in common that a sound source is permitted to build up a sound field in a room, and

---

[2] For details of the methods, see ISO Recommendation R 140.

[3] ISO Recommendation R 140 also furnishes definitions and methods where such measurements are concerned.

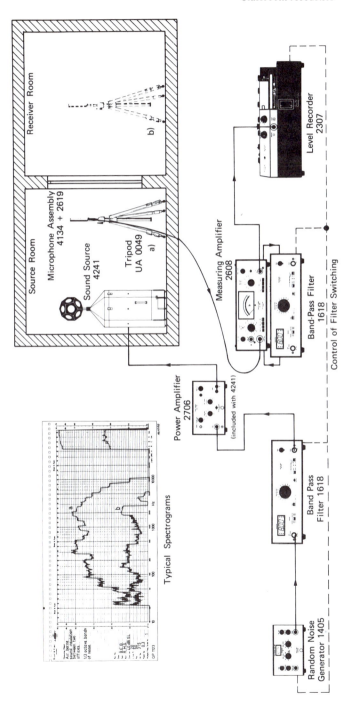

Figure 5.   Set-up for the measurement of air-borne sound insulation. Reproduced with permission of Brüel and Kjaer, Naerum, Denmark.

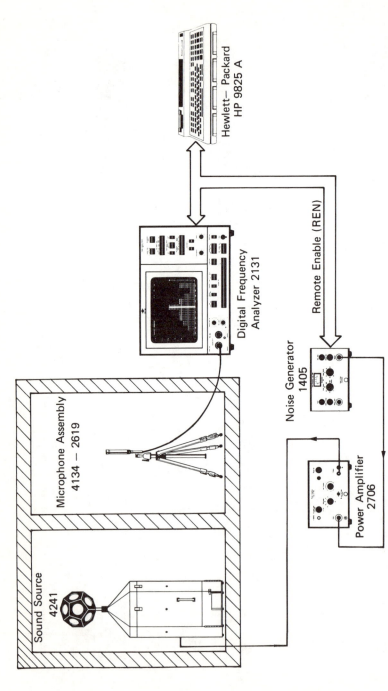

Figure 6. Set-up for the measurement of air-borne sound transmission, using a computer. Reproduced with permission of Brüel and Kjaer, Nærrum, Denmark.

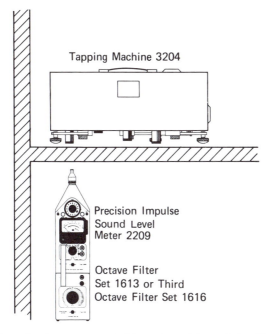

Figure 7.   Set-up for the measurement of impact sound transmission. Reproduced with permission of Brüel and Kjaer, Naerum, Denmark.

upon sudden interruption of the source, the number of seconds it takes for the level to decrease 60 dB is measured. The simplest method is seen in Figure 9. The sound source here is a gun, usually of a special construction. The sound of a gunshot contains a wide frequency spectrum, and with the aid of a spectrometer or a frequency analyzer it is possible to examine the reverberation time within the desired frequency ranges, generally from about 125–4000 Hz. The results can be taken down by a level recorder. Examples are shown on the *right side* of Figure 9. The slope of the curve can be directly converted into reverberation time through the use of a special protractor. If in cases of field measurements one wishes to avoid transporting heavy measuring equipment, the sound of the shots may be recorded on a tape recorder, and the result later analyzed in the laboratory.

The gunshot method is practical and still in use, but because a shot is not entirely well defined as a source of sound, another measuring method is frequently used, as shown in Figure 10. The sound field is developed by a noise generator or a frequency-modulated tone from a sine generator. The generator is suddenly interrupted, and the measurement is then performed as previously described.

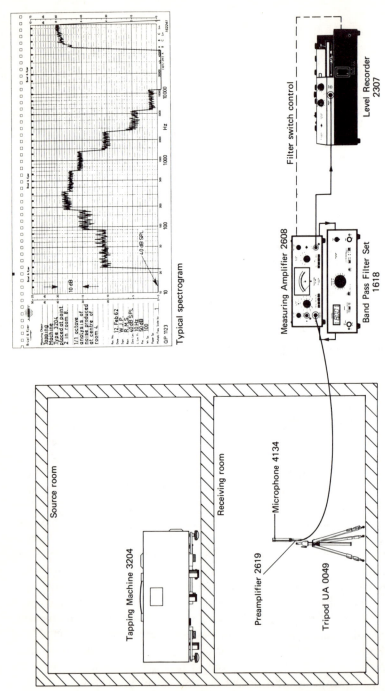

Typical spectrogram

Figure 8.   Set-up for the measurement of impact sound transmission. Reproduced with permission of Brüel and Kjaer, Naerum, Denmark.

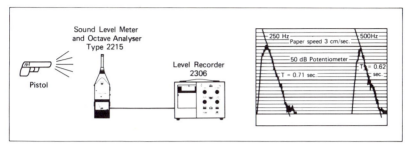

Figure 9.   The gunshot method for the measurement of reverberation time. Reproduced with permission of Brüel and Kjaer, Naerum, Denmark.

Several other possibilities for measuring reverberation time exist. Figure 11 shows one of the newest and quickest methods. It is referred to as the "method of integrated tone bursts." On the special "reverberation processor" it is possible to read directly the reverberation time or, more correctly, early decay time (EDT), which is the reverberation time calculated on the basis of the first 10–15 dB of the decay curve.

ACOUSTIC DEMANDS FOR CLASSROOMS

The Danish building regulations (1977), which, with few limitations, must be followed for every public or private building project in Denmark, also contain requirements with respect to the acoustics in buildings for various purposes, including normal schools and schools for special education of the handicapped.

It would be an unnecessary digression to discuss here all of the regulations relating to schools, but some examples may be given of the requirements for classrooms.

The building regulations use concepts such as I_a, airborne sound insulation index, and I_i, impact sound insulation index.[4] Between classrooms, a minimum horizontal airborne sound insulation of $I_a = 48$ dB is required, and a vertical minimum of $I_a = 51$ dB. Between classrooms used for particularly noisy activities, and other classrooms, it is required that $I_a \geq 60$ dB.

Floor partitions and floors on the ground must be constructed so that the impact sound level does not exceed $I_i = 68$ dB. Under classrooms for noisy activities, the floor separation must be so constructed that the impact sound level in adjacent rooms does not exceed $I_i = 58$ dB.

---

[4] For these definitions and their application see ISO Recommendation R 717.

158   Børrild

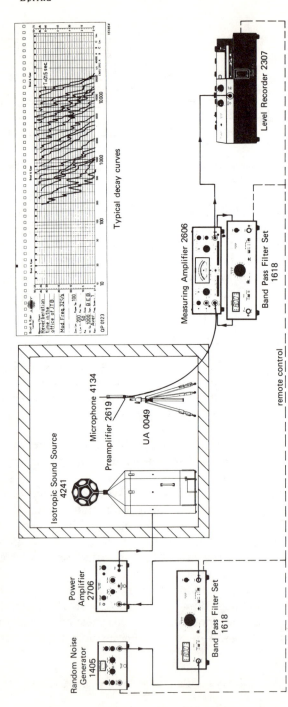

Figure 10.   Set-up for the measurement of reverberation time using a random noise generator with a loudspeaker as the sound source. Reproduced with permission of Brüel and Kjaer, Naerum, Denmark.

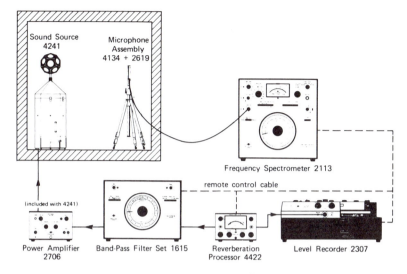

Figure 11. Set-up for the measurement of early decay time. (This method is not generally used, and the Processor 4422 is no longer available.) Reproduced with permission of Brüel and Kjaer, Naerum, Denmark.

The reverberation time in regular classrooms, in the frequency range 125–2000 Hz, must have an average that lies between 0.6 and 0.9 sec, and deviations from the average may not exceed 0.2 sec.

The average reveration time in classrooms for teaching the hearing impaired must not exceed 0.6 sec, and deviations from the average must be less than 0.2 sec (in practice, this rule is interpreted to aim at an average of 0.5 sec, with maximum deviation within the area of 125–4000 Hz, amounting to ±0.1 sec).

The noise level from technical installations may not exceed 35 dB(A). (This provision is also interpreted somewhat more strictly where classrooms for the hearing impaired are involved, a maximum of 25 dB(A) being prescribed). As a supplement to the building code, the Swedish *Acoustical Standards for Schools for the Hearing-Impaired* (Johansson, 1968) are applied in the layout of classes for the hearing impaired.

In Norway, building regulations similar to those in Denmark exist. The requirements with respect to room insulation, noise level, and reverberation time are close to those in Denmark, but the regulations do not contain specific directives for classrooms used in teaching the hearing impaired. In the layout of these special classrooms—just as, of course, in Sweden—the Swedish *Acoustical Standards for Schools for the Hearing-Impaired* are used. These standards have been prepared by the Karolinska Institutet, Technical Audiology (Johansson, 1968).

These standards establish the permissible noise level in classrooms based on the level and dynamics of speech, considering that the weakest phonemes in Swedish speech lie about 45-dB sound pressure level (SPL). Based upon the desire for a signal-to-noise ratio of not less than 10 dB, the maximum permissible noise level is set at 35-dB SPL, or frequency balanced in octave bands:

Hz	125	250	500	1000	2000	4000
Maximum dB level	30	30	30	30	25	20

The reverberation time is determined under the same standards at maximum:

Hz	125	250	500	1000	2000	4000
Sec	0.6	0.5	0.5	0.5	0.5	0.6

The Swedish standards are a voluminous work which, contrary to the Danish and Norwegian regulations, makes much out of explaining the background for the requirements imposed. The acoustic environment that is attained by following such regulations or standards should be verified as follows.

The noise level is measured on the site selected, and with construction data for windows and walls, etc., the reverberation curve and noise level in the classroom is computed. Then a corresponding computation is made, based upon the activity that would normally exist in the adjacent rooms. These two levels are added in accordance with the formula:

$$L = L_2 + \Delta L,$$

where L is the sum of the two levels, L_2 is the greater of them, and ΔL is derived from the curve in Figure 12 by entering the *horizontal axis* with $L_2 - L_1$ and finding ΔL on the *vertical axis*. The sum L is now compared with the higher of the two levels:

1. Noise arising from general activities in the classroom (breathing, shuffling of feet, rustling of paper, etc.)
2. The input sound level on the microphone, equivalent to the internal noise of a good hearing aid

If the noise level resulting from external noise is at least 15 dB below the maximum of levels 1 or 2, it will not in practice act as a disturbance. The internal noise level of the hearing aids of today is so

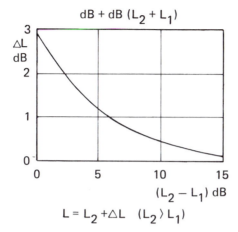

Figure 12.   Decibel addition chart.

low that the first factor will dominate. If we set it at 40 dB(A) in a class with six to eight students, we accordingly have to get down to 25 dB(A) as a total for all other sources of noise combined. This is the ideal requirement, and frequently—especially for schools in larger cities—it is necessary to compromise in order not to run into unreasonable building costs. However, it would do no harm to keep the ideal requirement in mind, and to try to approach it as closely as economically justifiable.

In the United States today, no official body has published acoustic standards pertaining to classrooms in which hearing-impaired children are educated. Under these circumstances, determining what is ideal or even acceptable is very difficult. Applying standards recommended for normal hearing youngsters, Crum and Matkin (1976) found that only one out of 11 classrooms for the hearing impaired could be classified as acoustically acceptable. The problems were produced by noise generated by activities and sound sources adjacent to the classroom, by noise generated within the classroom, and by excessive reverberation because of limited acoustic treatment of the room surfaces. As the authors point out, if this situation were obtained in a middle and upper middle class suburban school district, then the conditions in classrooms in other parts of the country are probably equally poor. If we are unable to begin planning at the time of site selection, then, as is discussed below, we can still take a number of steps to improve the situation.

SOUND TREATMENT AND SOUND INSULATION

What, then, are the available means to attain the desired acoustic environment in a classroom? Generally speaking, there are three: reduction of noise at the source, sound treatment, and sound insulation.

Reduction of Noise at Source

Reduction of noise at the source may be involved, for example, in connection with noise from technical installations. These may be air conditioning systems, heating and water installations, fluorescent lamps, and apparatus being used such as typewriters, tape recorders, and video recorders. Other sources of noise may be produced by the students and instructors shuffling their feet, clattering with pencils on the table tops, etc. It is essential to apply the experience gained over many years with respect to which structures and what methods of installation are most advantageous as seen from the standpoint of noise, and, as previously mentioned, to use suitable surfaces on tables and floors.

One example: fluorescent lamps used to be a problem because the ballast could cause an extremely annoying background noise. It was then necessary to move the ballast outside the classroom, which required a complicated and costly installation. Today, armatures exist that produce very little noise—far below the permissible level—but the noisy types are still being sold, and it is necessary to be careful when buying lighting fixtures for a classroom.

It should be borne in mind when teaching the hearing impaired that hearing aids and radio receivers are sensitive to noises other than the acoustic one. Magnetic noise, perhaps from transformers, and radio noise such as from the thyristor adjustment of lighting, must be reduced at the source so that they do not, through the equipment, cause an acoustic noise whose equivalent input sound level on the microphone of the hearing aid exceeds the background noise level, which we have chosen as the permissible maximum, minus 15 dB.

Sound Insulation and Treatment

Sound insulation and sound treatment are related in that noise originating from the classroom or from the outside results in a lower noise level in a room with a shorter reverberation time. It would therefore be reasonable to continue estimating how much sound-absorbing material should be placed within the confines of the room, and how strongly absorbent it should be; in other words, how great a coefficient of sound absorption it should have. The coefficient of sound absorption is a frequency-dependent constant that indicates for each frequency how great a percentage of the sound energy hitting the material is not reflected. It is determined through laboratory measurements on samples of the materials.

The reverberation time of the room may be determined by means of Sabine's formula:

$$t_{sab} = \frac{0.16\ V}{\sum \alpha_n S_n}\ \text{sec}$$

where t_{sab} is the reverberation time, V is the room's volume in m³, and S_n is the number of square meters that have been used of the material with the absorption coefficient α_n. S_n is multiplied by α_n, for each of the materials that enter into the room's confines, and then added to arrive at the denominator.

This formula exists in several modifications, but Sabine's original formula is reasonably accurate for a room involved with acoustic data, such as a classroom. The reverberation time is computed for a number of frequencies because, as mentioned, α is frequency dependent and the reverberation curve can then be drawn with the frequency as abscissa and the reverberation time as ordinate. Today, such a great selection of materials exists that are suitable for sound treatment, for which laboratory measurements of absorption coefficients have been performed, that it is ordinarily an easy task for the acoustician to arrive at the desired reverberation curve with an aesthetically satisfactory result (Niemoeller, 1968).

At this juncture it should perhaps be mentioned that the reverberation time of corridors and halls should be held as low as possible, because these strongly noise-producing areas may otherwise result in the use of disproportionately heavy—and therefore costly—wall and door constructions.

Based on the criterion established for how loud a noise level may be permitted in the classroom as a result of noise coming from the outside, it can now be computed which constructions may be used in walls, windows, ceilings, floors, and doors. The work here is usually based on laboratory measurements of the constructions' transmission loss, which is a frequency-dependent constant for the structure.

It should be remembered that the transmission loss measured in the laboratory usually indicates a somewhat higher sound-insulating ability than may be actually found through control measurements in the completed building because of, among other reasons, the imperfect execution of the construction plans. In making the computations, a suitable safety margin should therefore be used.

Impact noise is not ordinarily a serious problem with modern one-story schools. When having to place classrooms above each other on several floors, it will generally be an advantage—at times a necessity—to execute the floor construction as a "floating" floor, i.e., in such a manner that the actual floor is without a fixed connection with the remaining building structure, embedded, for example, in resilient material, neoprene, or silicone rubber.

It should perhaps be mentioned that in the construction of one-story schools it will often be possible to get by with a relatively light ceiling construction if the site has been suitably chosen, and if the partitions have been brought all the way up to the underside of the roofing and tightened against it. Unfortunately, it is such a common mistake as to be almost the rule to see light ceiling constructions used without bringing the partitions to the roof. In this case, the ceiling space causes the spreading and mixing of noise from the classrooms, and it is not possible to obtain a satisfactory acoustic environment.

In certain cases—especially in older schools—it is costly and difficult to realize even modest demands with respect to the acoustic environment; for this reason, some schools are totally unsuited for the instruction of the hearing impaired. We have to realize that all of our efforts with respect to sound insulation, sound treatment, and reduction of sources of noise have had one purpose: ensuring a reasonable signal-to-noise ratio. We can also provide this to students who use hearing aids or other amplifying equipment in a different manner, by making the useful sounds stronger than the noise, perhaps by using a very short microphone distance from the useful sounds. The negative effect of a poor acoustic situation can thus be averted or minimized by proper microphone technique.

It is always an advantage to use a short microphone distance (Ross, 1977), so that the equipment referred to below should also be used in schools in which the acoustic environment is good. The appropriate use of classroom amplification equipment will be a powerful educational tool in all educational environments.

CLASSROOM AMPLIFICATION SYSTEMS

Audio Loops

Audio loops have been known and used for a great number of years (Børrild, 1964). An audio loop is constructed as shown in Figure 13. It

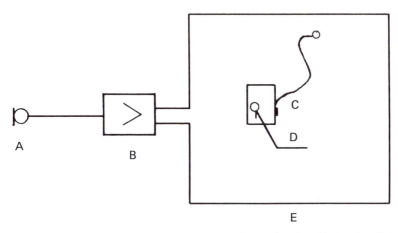

Figure 13.   Audio loop. *A*, microphone; *B*, amplifier; *C*, hearing aid; *D*, telecoil; *E*, audio loop.

consists of a microphone for the instructor, an amplifier, and a loop that circles the area where it is desired to hear the signal. Normally the loop is placed around the walls of the classroom. Through the loop runs a current that varies in strength. The variations are synchronous with the acoustic effects upon the microphone. This current gives rise to the formation of a magnetic field, which likewise varies in strength synchronously with the acoustical effects upon the microphone.

If a hearing aid with telecoil is placed in the magnetic field, a voltage is produced through induction between the poles of the telecoil, varying synchronously with the variation in field strength, and therefore with the acoustic signal on the microphone. We can then use the telecoil in place of, or parallel with, the hearing aid's microphone, and we will have an effect approximately corresponding to the instructor talking directly into each individual student's hearing aid microphone at a distance of 20–30 cm.

Because it is awkward for the teacher to drag the microphone cable behind her, it is customary to replace the microphone plus cable with a wireless microphone and an FM receiver, connected to the input socket of the loop amplifier.

Thousands of loops have been installed in schools for the hearing impaired, and a very substantial number of them do not operate as intended because of less suitable amplifiers or faulty installation. Ordinary amplifiers with voltage feedback may be used, but special current feedback amplifiers are preferable. The cross-sectional area of the loop wire must be adequate. It is a common mistake to use a loop with a large cross-section in order to save amplifier output power. This results in a lowering of the upper limiting frequency so that the signal is transmitted severely limited in frequency. In an ordinary classroom, a cross-sectional loop wire of between 0.5 and 1.0 mm^2 is suitable.

The loop is often placed in such a manner that it has the same horizontal height as the hearing aid of a seated person. This is done because it results in the strongest possible field on a horizontal plane through the hearing aid for a given amplifier output power. However, the loop should be placed slightly out of plane with the hearing aid. This, to be sure, is not as advantageous as seen from an economic standpoint, but it provides a more even field strength distribution on the "listening level," which is especially important in modern instruction where the students are no longer as tied to their seats as earlier.

In Scandinavia we have for many years adjusted our loops in accordance with an unofficial Nordic standard, which states that the field intensity at the intersection between the room's diagonals should be 80 mA/m. This unofficial adoption will presumably be replaced by an amendment to IEC Publication 118. This will probably establish a slightly greater field strength as standard, and determine a frequency range so that it will no longer be possible to save amplifier output power by using loop cross-sections that are too large.

A correctly dimensioned and installed audio loop is an inexpensive and efficient arrangement, but it has the essential disadvantage that the signal cannot be held within the room for which it is intended, but spreads in all directions. The field strength diminishes so slowly that a distance is required of at least 10 m between two audio loops, and this unquestionably limits the possibilities of application in a school. Attempts have been made for many years to solve the overspill problem, but without much luck, and today it may be concluded that it will hardly be possible to solve it satisfactorily.

Radio Transmitting and Receiving Systems

The difficulties caused by the overspill problem in a specialized school led to the Fredericia School in Denmark experimenting as early as the 1950s with other methods of signal transmission. In 1959, the school placed its first radio transmission and receiving system into use. Its construction was basically similar to that of the audio loop system and the teacher still had her wireless microphone, but instead of the amplifier an AM transmitter with six channels was used, corresponding to the microphone transmitters in six different classes. The transmission antenna was a closed loop, placed around the entire school building. Any of the six programs could be received anywhere within the building, the students carrying a small selective AM receiver, electrically coupled to the hearing aid. The system was developed a few years later to cover 12 programs. It has now been retired from service and replaced by simpler and cheaper systems that in recent years have become commercially available. The use of a mixed AM/ FM system must today be considered as obsolete, and the newer systems are all purely FM systems. They can be divided into two principal groups: FM systems with freely radiating antennas, which generally work on frequency bands about 30–42 MHz (Europe) or 70– 80 MHz (United States), and a few on bands above 100 MHz; and 100-kHz systems with closed loops as antennas (FM loop).

The latter system is the simplest and the cheapest. The receiver is very small, and it can easily be built into an ordinary body-worn hearing aid. The transmitter is rather bulky, and because it must be firmly connected to the loop it cannot be made portable. The instructor therefore uses a wireless microphone to transmit to the 100-kHz transmitter. The system operates excellently. There are no overspill problems, even though the same frequency is used in all classes of a school. The receiver is constructed in such a manner that it is automatically locked onto the strongest carrier wave. With correct adjustment of the field intensity in all rooms, it is therefore possible to walk with a receiver from room to room and only hear the program from the class one is visiting at the moment, without disturbances from the adjacent classes.

Wireless FM Systems

The system mentioned above is tied to the classrooms. The FM systems with freely radiating antennas, however, are not. They can also be used outdoors, for example, because no firmly installed apparatus exists. The instructor uses the usual wireless microphone. The receivers exist in two main types: in one type, the receiver and amplifier are built together into one unit that replaces the usual hearing aid, and which is generally somewhat larger than the latter. In the outer type the receiver is an attachment, smaller than or equal in size to a hearing aid, which is galvanically or inductively coupled to the student's regular hearing aid.

Based on my experience, the system in which the usual hearing aid is used as the last link in a transmission chain should be preferred, but something is still lacking before we have the ideal FM system with free radiation. In the ideal system, the coupling between receiver and hearing aid must be electrical. Inductive coupling can be used only in buildings where audio loops are not simultaneously being used. Furthermore, the power amplifier must be the student's own hearing aid, that is, a hearing aid that has been selected because it suits the student, and not one that has been chosen because it suits the radio receiver. The receiver must be made so small that it can be clipped to the outside of the hearing aid without the combination becoming too bulky. In practice, this will probably mean that, for the present, a receiver may not be more than half the size of a normal body-worn hearing aid.

It is probably not realistic at this time to expect such small dimensions on the receivers that they can be placed directly in or on behind-the-ear aids or spectacle hearing aids. It will probably be necessary to accept attachment of the receiver somewhere on the person, and a wire connection to the hearing aid. Body-worn hearing aids, as well as ear-level aids, must be prepared for the installation of the necessary socket and fastening device, and it must be possible to buy extra accessories for the modification of the hearing aids. An international standardization of plug sockets and fastening devices will be required, as will the level and impedance on the hearing aid's input point for the radio frequency signal.

It is possible that the hearing aid manufacturers will not approve of the development as described, but in the long run we cannot be satisfied with the apparatus in use today. There must be a possibility of selecting freely between radio receivers and hearing aids, and to combine them without restriction until we reach a point where a radio receiver is a tiny standard gadget that can be placed into a space provided for that purpose in any hearing aid, regardless of type and manufacture.

The free radiating FM-systems have one inconvenience that—in a sizable special school for the hearing impaired—might turn out to be a serious problem: Each transmitter has to work on a separate frequency, different from that of any other transmitter in the surroundings.

However, the number of frequencies available are limited and the subject of national and international allocation and restrictions. For that reason it might be difficult in most countries to get permission to use the number of frequencies really needed for this purpose.

In Australia, Burgess (1976) has described a free radiating radio system called "Induction Field Telephony," which is remarkable for the important quality that an almost unlimited number of transmitters can work simultaneously rather close to each other, using the same frequency without bringing about any disturbances, because of the fact that the receivers will only pick up the signal from the transmitter that is closest to them.

This "faculty of discrimination" is achieved by using a transmitter designed in such a way that the radiated field strength from the antenna will decrease very fast and steep. In addition, the receivers are provided with "squelch" and with a sensitivity control calibrated in meters. Signals received from a distance outside the radius for which the sensitivity control is set are suppressed, and only transmitters inside the circle with the chosen radius are heard.

Infrared Light Systems

Yet another possibility of signal transmission should be mentioned: transmission via infrared "light." With this method of transmission, the teacher also uses her regular microphone with built-in FM transmitter and an FM receiver as attachment to the infrared transmitter for the purpose of being relieved of the microphone cable. The system is outlined in Figure 14. *A* is the instructor's microphone with FM transmitter, *B*, the FM receiver, and *C* is the infrared transmitter. In *C*, the signal received from *B* is modulated (FM) onto a carrier wave, generally in the area 75–270 kHz, and this signal is

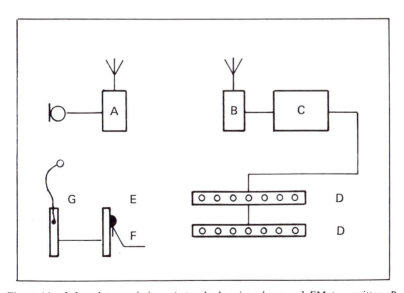

Figure 14.   Infrared transmission. *A*, teacher's microphone and FM transmitter; *B*, FM receiver; *C*, infrared transmitter; *D*, radiators; *E*, infrared receiver, *F*, receiving diode with special optics; *G*, hearing aid.

again modulated onto the infrared light, which is emitted from the radiators, *D*.

An appropriate number of these radiators are installed in the classroom, often one radiator in each corner, so that the entire area is covered without shadows. The modulated infrared light is picked up by the receiving diode, *F*, equipped with special optics, and in the receiver, *E*, the signal is demodulated before it enters into the hearing aid, *G*, in place of or parallel with the hearing aid's microphone signal. The system gives an exceedingly good transmission quality with a large frequency range, because one may allow oneself a large frequency deviation (often 60–100 kHz) without having to worry about adjacent channels.

It would be ideal if *A* and *B* could be eliminated, and *C* and *D* build together into one unit, which the instructor could carry instead of the usual wireless microphone. It can be done, but it is not practical inasmuch as the energy consumption of *C* and *D* is rather large, so large that operation by means of batteries would be costly, and cumbersome with the aid of rechargeable cells. Experiments performed at the Fredericia School further show that a single radiator of the construction now in use cannot with certainty cover a classroom of normal size. The same experiments have shown that sunlight, which also contains infrared rays, can result in noise. Windows in classes in which an infrared system is used should therefore either be provided with a sun filter or adjustable outside venetian blinds, or alternatively with some other form of sun screening, assuming of course they are facing in such a direction that they can be exposed to direct sunlight. The experiments have also shown that a greater assurance of covering the entire classroom is obtained at a lower energy consumption if walls, ceilings, and floors are light than if they are dark, and furthermore that the electrical lighting in the classrooms does not interfere at the levels ordinarily used, i.e., less than 600–800 lux.

Stereophonic Transmission

Of the systems described, the RF system (radio frequency) with freely radiating antennas and the IR system (infrared) can be constructed to transmit stereophonic signals. This involves a doubling of the number of all essential components, and therefore of the price also. Because what is to be transmitted is ordinarily speech from a single speaker that uses a microphone distance of not more than 30 cm, and because to my knowledge it has never been demonstrated that a hearing-impaired person who receives such a signal via two independent channels has a better chance of discrimination than the person who receives the signal—perhaps binaurally—via a single transmission channel, I fail to see any compelling reasons to use the systems in a stereo version.

Child-To-Child Reception

The flaw in all of the systems described is that even though the students hear the instructor at a good signal-to-noise ratio, and themselves at an equally good one via the hearing aid's microphone, they hear their fellow students at a poorer ratio inasmuch as the microphone distance may become considerably larger, perhaps up to 2 or 3 m. It is possible to arrange the systems—and this applies to all systems—in such a manner that the students' speech is also transmitted via audio loop, RF system, FM loop, or freely radiating FM or IR. The students must then be provided each with his own microphone transmitter. Unfortunately, it is only possible to transmit from one microphone at a time without complicating and increasing the costs of the systems in a totally unreasonable manner. The transmitter must therefore be equipped with a switch, and the teacher must interrupt her transmitter when a student wishes to contribute to the discussion, just as the students must remember to switch on the transmitter if they wish to speak, and to turn it off again as soon as they have spoken. Practice shows that the system operates awkwardly and harmonizes poorly with modern children's spontaneity and with modern free teaching methods. We lack a speech-controlled system that produces an equally good signal-to-noise ratio regardless of who is speaking. It should be possible to make it a sort of multiplex with the application of modern digital techniques. Unfortunately, such a system is not presently available. (See Ling, Chapter 6 for additional comments regarding classroom amplification systems.)

RELATIONSHIP BETWEEN ACOUSTIC ENVIRONMENT OF CLASSROOM AND INTELLIGIBILITY OF SPEECH

Let us now look at the part played by the acoustic environment in the intelligibility of speech obtained by persons with normal hearing. It is known that even a modest noise level affects the intelligibility in a negative direction.

The reverberation time has a significant influence upon intelligibility as seen in Figure 15, which shows the relationship between discrimination score and reverberation time in a room the size of a medium auditorium (Ingerslev, 1949). It is noted that there is a small plateau near the optimum reverberation time, where the intelligibility is only slightly affected by small changes in reverberation time. It might be interesting to investigate whether a corresponding plateau

Percent

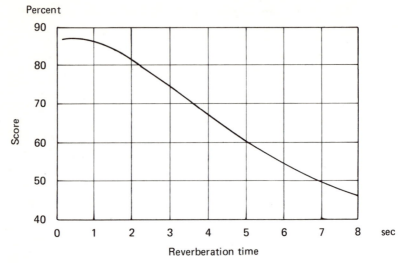

Figure 15.   Score versus reverberation time, normal hearing listeners. (From Ingerslev, 1949. Reprinted with permission.)

may be detected on the intelligibility curve from the hearing impaired with hearing aids.

An extract of the results from a study made at the Fredericia School approximately 20 years ago is shown below. The reverberation curves were smooth, and the times stated are averages of the values for 250, 500, 1000, and 2000 kHz. Scores are average scores for the experimental group which consisted of a number of the school's students in the 10–14 year age bracket. The microphone distance was large: 3 m.

Room	A	B	C	D
Reverberation time (sec)	2.2	1.1	0.6	0.2
Mean score (%)	34	43	59	68

The scores, as may be seen, gradually increase toward lower reverberation times, and the figures seem to indicate that no plateau exists for hearing aid wearers, or that it is located at such low values for the reverberation time that it is not economically or practically feasible to attain it.

At the Kendall Demonstration School, Gallaudet College, a special classroom was established early in the 1970s, where noise level as well as reverberation time could be controlled. The reverberation time could be varied between the limits of 0.3 and 0.7 sec, i.e., within the interval recommended for use in classrooms for the hearing impaired.

In this classroom, a number of researchers performed tests in connection with the acoustic environment's influence upon the discrimination ability of the hearing impaired. The project resulted in a number of internal reports, of which only a few have been published, to my knowledge.

Several of the results obtained confirmed earlier experiments and assumptions, but one of them was quite surprising, because it indicated that there was no significant difference in discrimination scores at 0.3 and 0.7 sec reverberation time. Repeated experiments with different research techniques confirmed the observation that, for the hearing impaired with modern hearing aids, as well as for those with normal hearing, an area seems to exist near an optimum reverberation time where small variations in reverberation time have no significant influence upon the discrimination score.

The key to the understanding of the difference between the result from the Fredericia School and that from the Kendall Demonstration School may presumably be found in the words "modern hearing aids." The investigation at the Fredericia School was made with hearing aids of the 1959 model. It is conceivable that modern hearing aids with improved frequency curves, lower harmonic distortion, and lower intermodulation would produce a different result. In order to check this hypothesis, we repeated some of the measurements from 1959. The measurements in room *B* could not be repeated because it no longer exists, but the remaining ones could be repeated with the persons involved in the experiments now using the 1976 model hearing aids.

The results are as follows:

Room	A	C	D
Reverberation time (sec)	2.2	0.6	0.2
Mean score (%)	38	57	56

It should be borne in mind that the experimental group differs from the original one, and that therefore the levels are not directly comparable.

The result is in close harmony with that of the Kendall Demonstration School, thus supporting the hypothesis that the acoustic environment's influence upon the discrimination score is minimized by modern hearing aids. Further research is required to develop this point, however, because some contrary evidence does exist. For example, Nabelek and Pickett (1974) found that discrimination scores in the 0.3-sec reverberation time were higher than for the 0.6-sec reverberation time across a number of signal-to-noise conditions.

SPECIAL PROBLEMS AND ARRANGEMENTS IN CLASSROOMS OF DIFFERENT TYPES

In classrooms for students of normal hearing, the acoustical environment will not normally result in problems, provided arrangements have been made for a reasonable noise level and a reasonable reverberation time, as described above.

For a number of years, however, there has been a tendency to make the classrooms continuously larger, and also a tendency to increase the average size of the class, and this has in certain cases caused problems with sound distribution, because the level of the instructor's voice can easily become too low in the rear of the classroom. A contributory cause of these problems has also been that it is no longer "in" for the instructor to sit at a rostrum, elevated 20–25 cm above the students' level. I presume it is considered to be more democratic for the instructor to "be on a level" with the students, but with respect to the sound distribution it has had the unfortunate effect that the direct sound from the instructor must now pass above and between several rows of students before it reaches those in the rear. Hair and clothes are excellent sound absorbing materials, and the sound level is consequently reduced in the back of the classroom.

The unfortunate sound distribution can be improved if an inclined reflector is placed on the wall behind the instructor, or on the wall opposite the instructor. The distribution of sound absorbing materials on ceilings and walls can also be changed so that the center area of the ceiling is kept clear and reflecting.

It has become continuously more customary even for severely hearing-impaired students to be given the opportunity of trying to get along in an ordinary school, and as the only student with impaired hearing in a class. If this is to succeed without placing an entirely unreasonable burden upon the hearing-impaired student, various supporting arrangements will have to be made. I shall not consider the educational ones in this context, only the technology that can support the "integrated" or "mainstreamed" student in many ways.

With respect to the acoustic environment, the classroom should meet the demands placed on a classroom for the hearing impaired.

The average size of the class should be slightly fewer than a class without hearing-impaired students. The placing of the teacher should be more fixed than is ordinary in modern teaching, and in such a manner that her face is well exposed to the light. As an example, therefore, she should not place herself with her back toward the window. The hearing-impaired student will have to place himself rather close to the instructor, with his back or side toward the light, and in such a position that it will not be necessary for him to distort himself in order to be able to lipread his classmates. An RF system consisting of a wireless microphone for the instructor and a receiver coupled to the student's hearing aid will be absolutely essential, and for this purpose the type with freely radiating antenna is preferable.

In Denmark it has become customary to concentrate hearing-impaired students in special classes in larger public schools, the so-called special education centers. This involves a compromise between integration in a normal class and going to a school for the deaf. There is nothing, however, at least insofar as the acoustic and technical requirements are concerned, that should distinguish such center classes from a class in a school for the deaf.

The center classes may have certain advantages, including a shorter distance to the students' homes, although in other areas they are handicapped in comparison with the schools for the deaf. In the latter, for example, the acoustics in all rooms are designed for persons with hearing aids, and the concentration of technical equipment makes possible adequate and immediate service thereof by available, specially trained technicians. It is also possible to have a wide selection of experts for complete audiometric examinations and for instructing the teaching staff in the use of the technical equipment. As seen from the viewpoint of the technician, the acoustician, and the audiologist, the school for the deaf is the best place for teaching the hearing impaired affected by profound hearing handicaps. Parents, educators, psychologists, and politicians are welcome to have a different opinion.

Modern instruction requires space and the opportunity for constant variation. Nothing must become set or formalized, not even the physical frames of teaching. This—and perhaps a certain influence from the office environment—has given rise to a new fashion in school construction, the open space schools.

In its extreme form, the open space school is a large room in which all activities take place, except for the more noisy ones, such as physical education and music. If all possibilities of an open space school were to be used, this would require a total reorganization of the school's work, and for the instructor, a thoroughly new thinking on education. Such a new thinking and reorganization requires a considerably longer period of time than it does to build a school, presumably a teacher generation or two. Therefore most of the open space schools I have seen are used almost as traditional schools with walls between the classrooms. Each teacher sits somewhere on the large floor with his little crowd, trying to create some manner of privacy by means of screens and bookcases between his group and the neighboring groups. Where students of normal hearing are concerned, this can be accomplished successfully if the reverberation time is held very low, as low as economically and practically feasible. A steady background noise level of about 45–50 dB is a help in not hearing what the neighboring groups are doing. This can be accomplished, for example, with "acoustic perfume" such as the music used in office complexes and supermarkets, or one might omit doing too much about reducing the noise from the air conditioning system.

Where students with hearing aids are concerned, the open space school is a serious matter. For the reasons previously discussed, a high background noise level cannot be accepted. The only possibility that remains to create acceptable acoustic conditions is to increase the area per student so that there will be room for greater distance between the groups, or to make the ground plan irregular with many nooks and corners, and with passages between the instruction areas suitable for the creation of sound traps. Furthermore, areas must be established that are acoustically separated from the rest of the room and that are used for especially noisy activities, as well as for those activities that require optimum listening conditions.

In the open space school, RF systems are necessary. The IR systems cannot be used, and audio loops and FM-loop systems are not practical because they are tied to one place and therefore limit the mobility. Only RF systems with freely radiating antenna harmonize with the open space school.

The problems will presumably be alleviated when the adaptation of teaching methods to the open space school has been accomplished. Among others, this would perhaps result in a far more individualized instruction, and more self-study and project-oriented work, which can take place individually or in small groups, all provided the open space school survives the span of years the adaptation will require.

ENVIRONMENTAL ACOUSTICS

The title of this chapter is "Classroom Acoustics." However, concerning the first half of the title, it must be remembered that even hearing-impaired children spend only a limited part of their lives in class-rooms. Home, working place, different means of transportation, shopping centers, and church are other sides of life, and in those sur-roundings it is also of importance for the hearing impaired to be able to function without being given an extra handicap by poor acoustic conditions.

It is—broadly speaking—possible to transfer the results of the investigations made and the experience collected in the classroom to other surroundings, and fortunately an acoustic environment suiting the hearing impaired will also be agreeable and attractive to normal hearing persons. Anyway, who did decide that department stores, shopping centers, bus stations, and airports must have the impossible acoustic climate that most of them have today?

We would all benefit from having something done to the acoustic climate in places like that.

Even for a person with completely normal hearing it is often impossible to understand the announcements given via the public address systems in the above mentioned places. I see no reason why we should accept the miserable conditions, especially as it is not really difficult to improve them considerably. Why not equip the places where public address systems are used with audio loops to make it possible for the hearing impaired to receive at least the announce-ments with a minimum of distortion?

It would be a rather inexpensive arrangement and would certainly help a lot, particularly if a sign were put on the door telling that there is a loop. Audio loops might not be the best solution in the long run, but until we have a better and internationally standardized system, audio loops are quite feasible.

Most homes have a reduced reverberation time because of carpets, curtains, and furniture. In some homes, the noise level caused by traffic, radio, TV, phonograph, air conditioner, etc., is a problem. It is possible to muffle or avoid most of the noises sources in a home, if attention is just payed to the fact that they represent a nuisance for the hearing impaired.

Just two examples: if the traffic noise is very disturbing, it is sometimes possible (but somewhat expensive) to reduce it indoors by replacing the windows by new and tight sheets of "Thermoglass." Of course, an air conditioner will then be necessary, and it is recommend-able to look for a type that is as silent as possible.

The sound from radio and TV must not pour out overwhelmingly from the loudspeakers if one or more members of the family would rather do something else than join the audience. Those who want to listen can use headphones. The newest and most elegant solution to the problem, however, is for the radio or TV set to be equipped with a small infrared transmitter, which can be received by normal hearing persons as well as the hearing impaired.

Some new TV sets are made with built-in infrared transmitters. Neither the IR transmitter nor the receiver is too expensive, as the price for one transmitter and two to three receivers will usually be less than the price paid for a decent hearing aid.

Ordinarily, it is desirable for the hearing impaired to use the personal hearing aid for the amplification of the signal. In that case, the connection between the IR receiver and the hearing aid is easily arranged either via induction and the telecoil in the aid or via direct electrical input. To make it possible to use the last mentioned method of coupling, it will be necessary—in most cases—to have a small modification mode on the aid for the necessary input socket, but a few of the newest aids on the market—both body-worn and ear-level aids— are delivered from the factories with input sockets for audio signals from a receiver of some sort.

Last but not least, it should not be forgotten that the radio systems with free radiating antennas are fit for use any place indoors and outdoors, if it is profitable—and it almost always is—to have the acoustic contact with the hearing impaired influenced as little as possible by changing distance from the speaker and the acoustic environment as a whole.

The task must be in any situation to deliver the useful sound to the hearing aid as pure, clear, and undistorted as possible, and with any kind of noise suppressed as much as possible.

The second half of the title is "acoustics," but that should not lure us into the mistake that the environment is perfect for the hearing impaired, even if the acoustic environment is. For most hearing impaired it is very important to be able to lipread, and in order to watch facial expressions and body movements and to get the most out of visual cues, good and correct lighting is a necessity (Erber, 1974a,b). However, as Kipling said, that is quite another story.

REFERENCES

Anon. 1977. Bygningsreglement. Boligministeriet København (Ministry of Housing), Denmark.

Beranek, L. L. 1959. Acoustic Measurements. John Wiley & Sons Inc., New York.

Børrild, K. 1959. The Acoustic Environment in Schools for the Deaf, Fredericiaskolen. The State School for the Deaf, Fredericia, Denmark.

Børrild, K. 1964. The Problems of Induction Loops and a Way to Solve Them, Fredericiaskolen. The State School for the Deaf, Fredericia, Denmark.

Brandt, O. 1958. Akustisk Planering, Statens Namnd for Byggnadsforskning, Stockholm.

Brock, J. 1971. Acoustic Noise Measurements. Brüel and Kjaer, Copenhagen.

Burgess, V. R. 1976. The Induction-Field Wireless Hearing Aid, National Measurement Laboratory, Chippendale, Australia.

Crum, M. A., and N. D. Matkin. 1976. Room acoustics: The forgotten variable? Lang. Speech Hear. Serv. Schools 7:106–110.

Erber, N. P. 1974a. Visual perception of speech and deaf children. Recent developments and continuing needs. J. Speech Hear. Disord. 39:179–185.

Erber, N. P. 1974b. Effects of angle, distance and illumination on visual reception of speech by profoundly deaf children. J. Speech Hear. Res. 17:99–112.

Heckl, M., and H. A. Muller. 1975. Taschenbuch der Technischen Akustik, Springer-Verlag OHG, Heidelberg.

Ingerslev, F. 1949. Akustik. Teknisk Forlag, Copenhagen.

Johansson, B. 1968. Akustiska kvalitetsnormer for skolar for horsel-skadads. Karolinska Institutet, Teknisk Audiologi, Stockholm.

Knudsen, V. O., and C. M. Harris. 1950. Acoustical Designing in Architecture. John Wiley & Sons Inc., New York.

McCroskey, R. L., and J. S. Devens. 1974. Acoustic characteristics of public school classrooms, constructed between 1890 and 1960. Paper presented at the convention of the American Speech and Hearing Association. Las Vegas.

Nabelek, A. K., and J. M. Pickett. 1974. Monaural and binaural speech perception through hearing aids under noise and reverberation with normal and hearing-impaired listeners. J. Speech Hear. Res. 17:724–739.

Niemoeller, A. F. 1968. Acoustical design of classrooms for the deaf. Am. Ann. Deaf. 113:1040–1045.

Ross, M. 1977. Classroom amplification. In: Hodgson and Skinner (eds.), Hearing Aid Assessment and Use in Audiologic Habilitation, The Williams & Wilkins Company, Baltimore.

CHAPTER 6

AUDITORY CODING AND RECODING
An Analysis of Auditory Training Procedures for Hearing-Impaired Children

Daniel Ling

CONTENTS

There's more to hearing than meets the ear. The ears function to receive and analyze sounds, but recognition, identification, and comprehension of the elements of spoken language demand higher level activities—those involving the brain (see Fry, Chapter 2). Of particular importance in speech reception are memory processes that allow us to hold items in short and long term store, and cognitive processes that direct an active search for stimuli and their meaning. The active (as opposed to passive) use of our senses has been stressed by J. J. Gibson (1966) who points out that we not only hear, we listen; we not only touch, we feel; we not only see, we look. Some hearing-impaired children may need to use either the eyes, the skin, or both as alternative or supplementary modalities. However, the ears are the most natural channel for speech reception and hence their use is emphasized in this chapter.

Hearing impairment is not an all-or-none condition. In some cases it may be so slight as to cause no handicap, and in others, no vestige of hearing may remain. Most hearing-impaired children have at least a residue of audition that can be used for speech reception when appropriate hearing aids are provided (Boothroyd, 1970; Ling, 1964; Watson, 1961). For certain children, use of a hearing aid from early infancy and adequate exposure to normal patterns of speech afford sufficient experience to promote spoken language skills (Whetnall and Fry, 1971). For others, specific auditory training procedures must be provided if meaningful use is to be made of residual hearing (Wedenberg, 1951). In general, the greater the hearing impairment, the more frequent individualized and structured auditory training sessions probably need to be.

Although a distinction between auditory experience and auditory training was made in the above paragraph, it is by no means clear how these terms should be defined. Fry (see Chapter 2) addresses himself to the essentials of auditory experience, but a consensus of which (and how) skills should be taught through auditory training has not yet been reached. This is probably because no comprehensive theoretical framework for auditory training has been proposed. The literature relating to the topic (to be referenced later) reveals that auditory training has been widely regarded as an isolated subject to be taught, rather than as a supplement to auditory experience and an integral part of speech and language processing. Few experimental studies of auditory skill acquisition have been carried out and most accounts of auditory training boil down to discussion of the hearing levels, the acoustic properties of speech, the characteristics of amplification systems, and statements of faith and philosophy. Those that describe sequences of skills to be taught tend to focus upon arbitrarily derived discrimination exercises, which progress from gross (nonverbal) to fine (verbal) differences along an assumed continuum.

PROCESSES INVOLVED IN SPEECH RECEPTION

To provide a suitable framework for discussion of the processes involved in the auditory (and visual or tactile) encoding of speech, reference will be made throughout this chapter to the model presented as Figure 1. In this model, speech reception is depicted as a process involving selective information flow through four stages, from the ears, eyes, or skin into long term memory. Active search and selection of material at each stage, directed by central processes, is indicated by the four *arrows* to the left of the diagram. *Arrows* to the right of the model indicate how these stages relate to detection, discrimination, identification, and comprehension. Of course, the model is somewhat speculative and certainly an oversimplification, but an effective model has to be less complex than the system it is designed to represent. No attempt has been made in this model to differentiate structures and functions. Certainly the ears, eyes, and skin are structures and the different types of memory depicted may have specific physical bases (Squire, 1975), but a mechanistic interpretation of the model is to be avoided.

Speech sequences take time to produce and their duration varies according to the number of subphonemic features, phonemes, words, or sentences they contain. They also take time to process. It is because the early parts of a sequence can be stored and meaning abstracted while later parts of the message are also being received that spoken language can be understood. Thus speech reception can be viewed as a task involving both serial and parallel processing. One can deal simultaneously with speaker characteristics, suprasegmental patterns, phonemes, syllables, words, and syntactic structures. This is not to say that conscious attention is directed routinely or even equally to all levels of a message. Rather, one seems to direct such attention to whatever levels meet one's needs, usually those that yield the most meaningful interpretation of the speaker's intent, in short, to the semantic properties of what is said. Because meaning does not usually reside in suprasegmental patterns, in subphonemic units (distinctive features), in phonemes or even in syllables, higher level linguistic units tend to be the listener's main concern. However, lower level units serve to differentiate between meaningful items, and normal listeners can recover them from the speech stream when they wish or need to attend to them.

When a listener is hearing impaired, several features, phonemes, or syllables may be inaudible to him, yet a message containing these elements may be understood. Such is the case if either the missing elements can be supplied through vision or touch or if the listener already has sufficient lexical, syntactic, or semantic knowledge to extract sufficient information from the partial patterns available to him to effect closure. Thus it is impossible to overemphasize the role of previously

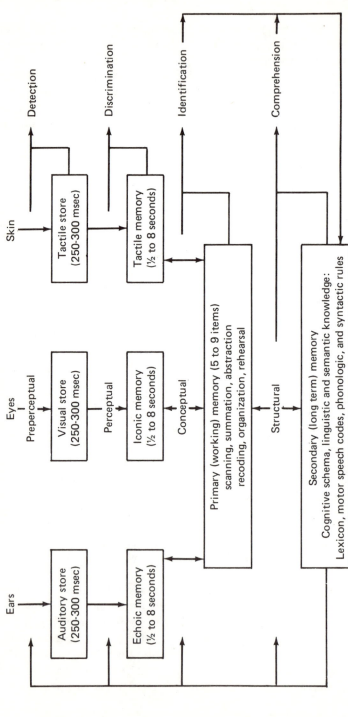

Figure 1.   Possible paths of information flow in speech reception by hearing-impaired children.

acquired knowledge in speech reception. The extent to which speech can be segmented, decoded, and transformed into perceptual, conceptual, and structural units is dependent upon information that has already been stored in an enduring form (see *bottom box* of Figure 1).

Knowledge of linguistic rules facilitates speech reception; so, too, does the listener's ability to speak. Motor speech codes, when available, provide a listener with a matrix of possibilities against which incoming information can be compared. Normal hearing listeners may be able to interpret speech without reference to motor speech codes and, indeed, Lenneberg (1962) has described a case in which elementary receptive language skills had developed in a child who could not speak. However, other workers (e.g., Shvachkin, 1973; Garnica, 1973) have demonstrated that speech perception skills in normal hearing listeners can be positively influenced by speech production. Among hearing-impaired listeners, who can not receive a complete range of acoustic information, ability to produce speech may be considerably more important. In short, effective training of auditory skills in children should not only encompass the presentation of stimuli for detection, discrimination, identification, and comprehension, but emphasize meaningful, memorable, auditory experience within a framework of language acquisition and motor speech development.

A variety of models for auditory speech reception have been proposed, several of which are described in a text edited by Wathen-Dunn (1967). Some are also discussed by Sanders (1977). New models are frequently proposed as more data are gathered or as a new purpose for explanation of the speech reception process emerges (Massaro, 1975; Pisoni, 1975). Models cannot be regarded as adequate or final explanations of the speech reception process; merely as organizational structures representing current state-of-the-art thinking.

The model proposed in this chapter is no exception. It suggests that information detected by the ears (on eyes or skin) is retained in sensory storage for 250–300 msec, a sufficient duration for primary reception of speech units having syllabic length (Massaro, 1972). Information then apparently passes through an echoic stage, which may last several seconds (Cole, Coltheart, and Allard, 1974) during which items in the sound stream are categorized and synthesized into linguistic units. The contents of this store may be considered as being that portion of continuous speech that the listener is "hearing out" as the speaker talks. Units that are meaningful then pass into primary (working or short term) memory, which usually has a capacity of five to nine chunks of information (Miller, 1956). Unlike items in echoic store, the chunks of information contained in primary memory are not necessarily auditory. When conscious rehearsal is not involved, they are likely to be more abstract; more conceptual than perceptual (Belleza and Walker, 1974). In Figure 1, all senses are shown as providing input to this stage at which summation and recoding takes place. It has long been known that hearing-impaired children tend to have marked primary memory deficits for verbal material and less marked problems for visual-nonverbal recall (see Ling, 1974 for a review).

Deficits in speech reception can, of course, be present in one or more of the four major stages depicted in Figure 1. Thus severe peripheral hearing impairment, because it prevents detection of some elements of the spoken message, may also inhibit discrimination, aural encoding in primary and secondary memory, identification of verbal items, and the comprehension of a spoken message. Children with peripheral hearing loss are not alone in having deficits affecting the auditory system. Some children with normal hearing levels cannot detect the sequential order of brief stimuli (Tallal, 1976). Others may have higher order language learning difficulties (Rees, 1973). It is reasonable to assume that yet others have such disorders coupled with peripheral hearing impairment. However, adequate tests to specify the nature of such problems in the presence of hearing impairment, which can pervasively affect all levels of speech reception, remain to be devised. Currently, one can only assume such additional defects to be present if a hearing-impaired child fails to respond to auditory training provided under optimal conditions.

Identification of the order in which the organism receives stimuli is, of course, essential to adequate speech reception. Basic work in this area (Hirsh, 1976; Sherrick, 1976) suggests that as more sense modalities are used, longer intervals between stimuli are required for successful identification of temporal order. Such findings may indicate that multisensory speech reception, as depicted in the first two stages of the model shown as Figure 1, may be fundamentally more difficult than the use of audition alone. It is recognized that visual input (speechreading) can usefully supplement audition for most hearing-impaired subjects (see Erber, 1974 for a review) but it is by no means certain that strong concentration on visual speech reception in early childhood does not further impair children's ability to make the most of their residual hearing. Further research is required to determine the extent to which vision and touch can help or hinder the various processes involved in receiving spoken language.

TYPES OF AMPLIFICATION USED IN AUDITORY TRAINING[1]

Before electronic hearing aids became generally available, auditory training of hearing-impaired children was often carried out through the use of speaking tubes. The use of simple tubing to carry sound from the teacher's mouth to the child's ear prevented the usual drop in intensity (about 6 dB/doubling of distance) that characteristically occurs in open, nonreflective areas. The use of tubing for both group and individual auditory training could be seen in certain schools as recently as the 1930s (Guilder and Hopkins, 1935).

During the 1940s, electronic group aids came into general use, and auditory training, if provided at all, tended to be in the form of group lessons. Because personal, portable electronic hearing aids were not generally available, or too heavy to be worn at that time, children given auditory training were expected to develop listening skills only in class and were usually only given the opportunity to do so once or twice a week. It was demonstrated that even such limited training improved speech and academic skills (Hudgins, 1954; Clarke, 1957).

Hard Wire Systems

Group and speech training hearing aids of the type referred to above are still in use. They employ high quality microphones, desk-mounted amplifiers and headphones, and are usually excellent quality speech transmission systems. Because the size of the components employed in these systems does not have to be considered, they can be selected solely on the basis of their performance. Thus the best of these "hard wire" systems can deliver as much gain as any child might need, their output can be controlled by attenuators, their frequency range may extend from under 100 Hz to over 7000 Hz and their distortion levels are low. Because the microphone(s) feeding these systems can be placed at a distance from the headphones (preferably close to the speaker's mouth) feedback can be completely avoided even when very high intensity levels are required and high signal-to-noise ratios can be maintained. Such hard wire systems may be considered as superior to any other form of amplification for severely and profoundly hearing-impaired children. Their superiority over individual aids is easily demonstrated (see Miller and Niemoeller, 1967). Hard wire systems are not generally popular with either teachers or children mainly because they tether a child to a desk. Group aids have therefore been

[1] See also Chapter 5.

largely replaced by induction loop systems, radio systems, or the exclusive use of individual hearing aids.

Induction Loop Amplification

Induction loop systems became popular as soon as small, easy-to-wear individual hearing aids were developed (from the 1950s). Coils incorporated in such aids permit the speech signal, radiated from a loop of wire installed around the teaching area, to be received by magnetic induction. Loop induction systems offer equivalent signal-to-noise condition to hard wire systems but have one advantage over them: they permit the child to move freely within the looped area. However, they have some disadvantages. The speech signal can be received over a certain range outside the looped area (a condition known as "overspill"). Hence loops cannot be used in adjacent classrooms. Because loop induction systems involve the use of individual aids, their weaknesses include poorer frequency range, higher levels of distortion, and frequent breakdown of individual aid components (cords, receivers, batteries). Unless the impedance of the loop is carefully matched to the output impedance of the amplifier used to drive the system, additional distortion may be produced. Loop induction remains a viable system for young children at home, where overspill is of no consequence and can be helpful in certain situations in schools. For example, if the sound system of a film projector is used to drive a loop, the sound track can be heard and the mechanical noise of the projector excluded while watching movies. The numerous possibilities offered by loop induction have been described by the writer (Ling, 1966, 1967). Unless carefully installed and maintained, such systems tend to be unreliable (Ross, 1969; Matkin and Olsen, 1970; Huntington, 1976) but properly designed and cared for, they may be strongly recommended for a certain range of applications at home and at school.

Radio Systems

Radio hearing aid systems are currently popular both for group and individual work. Their use has recently increased largely because speaking into a radio microphone permits signal-to-noise ratios comparable to those obtained with hard wire or loop systems and because the use of different broadcasting frequencies allows their use in adjacent classrooms without overspill. In general, they provide amplification that is inferior to that obtained from hard wire systems but their many advantages, which include speech contact over substantial distances indoors or outside, render them acceptable even though they may not provide optimal amplification for certain children.

Individual Hearing Aids

Individual hearing aids have undergone considerable change since they came into general use by hearing-impaired children in the 1950s (Berger, 1970). They have certainly become smaller but their decrease in size has not been matched by increases in fidelity and reliability (Zink, 1972). Most of what was said in a review article on hearing aids (body-worn and head-worn instruments) by the writer some years ago (Ling, 1971) still remains true. Trends in fitting have, however, emerged since then, the main one being towards more widespread use of ear-level instruments.

Ear-level hearing aids can, by and large, provide as much gain, as much output, and as wide a frequency range as body-worn instruments. They can also offer equivalent fidelity. The advantages of binaural ear-level hearing aids include freedom from clothes-rub (a problem that causes considerable masking in body-worn instruments) and better potential for localization of sound. Their most positive advantage is that they are small and hence cosmetically more acceptable. Their main disadvantage is that they are more prone than body-worn aids to acoustic feedback because the microphone is closer to the receiver. Thus earmolds that do not afford a perfect seal prevent the effective use of ear-level hearing aids at high power. Imperfectly fitting earmolds are less likely to cause feedback with body-worn instruments, where the microphone is separated from the receiver by at least 10 inches. With young children, whose ears are growing, it is virtually impossible, even with the most advanced earmold technology, to ensure a consistently good earmold seal for more than a few weeks at a time. Thus children who need high power hearing aids (aids with output levels of 120 dB or more) are likely to be able to obtain optimal amplification only sporadically from ear-level instruments. Of course one should seek to fit ear-level hearing aids in preference to body-worn hearing aids, but only if their characteristics are optimal for the child and if the required power can be delivered consistently.

There has long been discussion of the possible effects of a child using more than one system of conventional amplification in the course of his schooling. Some workers consider that it may be confusing for a child to hear one pattern through his individual aids and another through a hard wire system and recommend that only individual aids should be worn to ensure consistency of input. This concern seems to be without foundation on either practical or theoretical grounds. Consistency of speech input is at best an illusion, because it varies with distance from the speaker, with the level of ambient noise and from speaker to speaker. Furthermore, because individual aids are generally inferior to hard wire systems, sounds (such as [s], for example) may only be detectable by certain children if a hard wire system is used. As indicated by the model shown as Figure 1, knowledge of sounds gained through such training and entered in long term store should help the child receive speech when listening to the inferior patterns provided by his individual hearing aids.

Frequency Transposition

Work on frequency-transposing (coding) hearing aids has continued since a new impetus was given to the topic by Johansson (1966). So far it has met with little success. Except for limited purposes such as [s-ʃ] detection and discrimination (Guttman, Levitt, and Bellefleur, 1970) devices that operate in real time (transpose instantaneously as the speaker is talking) have not been shown to help speech reception significantly more than conventional amplifiers (Ling, 1968, 1969; Ling and Doehring, 1969; Ling and Maretic, 1971). Frequency-shifted time-compressed speech, which requires recording and playback, has been slightly more successful (Beasley, Mosher and Orchik, 1976) but speech processed in such a way cannot be presented simultaneously with a speechread pattern. It is possible that there may be genuine advantages to real time frequency transposition, and that these have been obscured by subjects' previous experience with nontransposed speech (see Velmans, 1975). There would, however, be severe ethical problems posed in fitting young children with frequency transposing aids unless one had strong evidence that they could yield results superior to those obtainable with conventional amplifiers. There is no such evidence available at present.

In-depth discussion of design trends in group and individual hearing aids and frequency transposing amplifiers is outside the scope of this chapter. More details in this regard are provided by Hirsh in this text (see Chapter 8).

DETECTION

The acoustic properties of particular speech patterns—suprasegmental (intonation, stress, etc.) and segmental (vowels, diphthongs, and consonants)—have been fairly clearly defined. Although there is much more to learn about the acoustics of running speech, the variant and invariant energy that provide the cues that allow us to differentiate sounds in relatively simple contexts can now be specified. Our current knowledge in this regard has recently been described by this writer (Ling, 1976) and is also discussed by Levitt in this book (see Chapter 3). It is essential for those working with hearing-impaired children to know how suprasegmental information is carried, the relative intensity and frequency of vowel formants, the characteristic acoustic cues that provide information on the manner, place, and voicing of consonants, and the ways in which the acoustic properties of consonants are changed when they are blended in speech. Only with such knowledge can one predict what a child can detect with unaided hearing or select and adjust hearing aids that permit the child to detect the fullest possible range of speech components. Because data on the acoustics of speech are already available in the literature, it is assumed throughout this chapter that the reader is familiar with them.

Figure 1 indicates that speech reception capabilities cannot be assumed even if a wide range of speech sounds can be detected. It also indicates that the experienced listener does not have to receive all speech components in order to understand a message. However, inexperienced listeners, such as hearing-impaired children, must be able to detect most, if not all, aspects of speech if they are to learn mainly or exclusively through audition. In short, a child needs to have better speech detection capability than an adult if he is eventually to make the utmost use of his hearing. The situation is akin to that of the skilled reader who can decipher a partly obliterated text as compared with a child who would find it difficult or impossible to make sense of incomplete written patterns.

Detection is necessary but insufficient for learning speech reception skills. Failure to appreciate that the speech detection needs of children differ from those of adults has led to the widespread use of hearing aids that are unsuitable for young children because they reproduce too little of speech in the low and mid frequency range.

Detection and Hearing Aid Selection: The Five-Sound Test

Detection of Low, Mid, and High Frequency Speech Components Most hearing-impaired children are better able to detect low frequency energy than high frequency energy. Low frequency energy in speech carries less information on both consonants and vowels than does high frequency energy. On the other hand, most of the suprasegmental and paralinguistic information in speech (pitch, intonation, intensity, stress, rhythm, speaker indentity, and speaker's mood, etc.) is carried by low frequency energy. Some important segmental cues also exist in the low end of the speech spectrum, for example, the vowels /i/ as in *tee* and /u/ as in *too,* have first formant energy around 300 Hz and certain consonant manner distinctions are detectable under 500 Hz (e.g., /m/ versus /b/). Similarly, certain consonant voicing distinctions (e.g., /p/ versus /b/ or /s/ versus /z/) may be more readily discerned by hearing-impaired children when some low frequency energy is present, particularly where these distinctions depend on durational cues relating to vowel length.

It is particularly important for the child to be able to detect all vowels, because vowels differentiate words such as *bid* and *bed,* carry suprasegmental structure, and vary systematically with adjacent consonants. Such variant energy cues contained in the vowel-to-consonant and consonant-to-vowel transitions are frequently more salient to the hearing-impaired child than the invariant energy associated with the consonants themselves. Thus many children who cannot hear the burst energy of, say, the /p/ or /t/, can hear the difference between the words *hit* and *hip* because the vowel is predictably modified by the two consonants. The reader can verify this by asking a listener to identify the two words when they are spoken without releasing the final /t/ or /p/. Most vowel cues on the identity of adjacent consonants are carried by second formant transition, although some cues on manner and place of production are carried by first formant transitions. It is, therefore, imperative that the child's hearing aid be selected (or adjusted) in such a way that the second formant energy of all vowels falling within the child's range of hearing is rendered audible. If the second formant energy of the front vowels (which lies above 2000 Hz) cannot be rendered detectable then their first formant energy (which lies under 500 Hz) must, if possible, be made so.

A great deal of low frequency amplification is not required to render first formant features detectable (and discriminable) to most severely hearing-impaired children (Ling, 1963; Leckie and Ling, 1968). If the amount of gain provided at 200–300 Hz is at least 30–40 dB less than that provided at 2000–3000 Hz, it is unlikely to cause significant spread of masking (see Ling, 1963). Significant masking will, however, occur if there is too little differential between low and high frequency gain. To provide no gain whatever at 200–300 Hz is to block the use of any low frequency hearing the child may possess, for none of these low components can then enter the child's auditory system either via the hearing aid, or via the ear, because the canal will be effectively sealed by the earmold.

Effects of Peak Energy in the Mid Frequency Range upon Detection   Too much gain at, or just above, 1000 Hz tends to affect speech reception through upward spread of masking more adversely than a small amount of gain below 300 Hz. This is because the greatest amount of masking occurs in the frequency range just above the masking sound. Because the crucial information on place of consonant production is carried principally in the range of 1800–3200 Hz, peaks of gain just below this range, which serve only to emphasize the relatively strong second formant energy of central vowels, are particularly noxious. They may also cause mid frequency sounds to surpass the child's threshold of tolerance. As a result, the child may turn down the gain of the aid to avoid discomfort and thus reduce the amplification actually required for the detection of sounds higher or lower in frequency.

Underfitting and Overfitting   Although it is common for some hearing aids to be underfitted (to provide too little gain for the detection of certain frequencies), it is not unusual for others to be overfitted (to provide too much output). Underfitting most frequently results from the misconception that the "speech range" lies between 500 and 2000 Hz, and that sounds outside this range are unimportant. In fact, the speech frequency range is about 80–8000 Hz, which encompasses the fundamental of a male bass voice and the highest components of /s/. Underfitting should not occur if the implications of the above discussion have been understood. Overfitting most frequently results from failure to establish the child's threshold of tolerance for sound at various points across the full frequency range of speech and subsequent recommendation of hearing aids with output levels that exceed a child's tolerance levels. It is, of course, possible for a child to be underfitted in the low and high frequency ranges and overfitted in the mid frequency range. An example of such fitting has been given above. It is not always possible to establish tolerance thresholds with accuracy and, in any case, they may change as training proceeds. The teacher/therapist and parents should therefore be alert to any sign that sharp, sudden noises or particular speech sounds cause the child discomfort. Hearing aids with a lower output ceiling or with some form of automatic gain control that limits output to within the child's limits of tolerance can usually be fitted without sacrificing gain requirements (D. Ling, 1975).

Tolerance problems are often wrongly assumed to be present when an older child keeps his aid switched off or turns down the gain to a minimum (and inadequate) level. Turning the aid down or off may, in itself, be more of an indication that the child regards the use of hearing as unimportant than evidence of a tolerance problem. It occurs most often among children who receive too little auditory stimulation and who are not consistently expected to listen. In such cases the remedy lies with the teacher/therapist and his work rather than with the audiologist and the hearing aid. Factors such as the relative gain of an aid at various frequencies and the child's attitude toward amplification render it difficult to accept the child's preferred setting as equivalent to his best listening level (see Gengel and Foust, 1975; Power, 1968).

Hearing Aid Selection Strategies and Thresholds of Detection The selection of hearing aids for children is, in general, based on pseudoscientific rather than on precise procedures. The selection task is particularly difficult with young children at the prelinguistic level because speech discrimination measures cannot be used. Hence the audiologist who relies on speech discrimination scores in selecting hearing aids has no way of confirming the validity of his choice. The teacher/therapist must, therefore, be prepared to accept the responsibility of modifying the response characteristics of the instruments selected if the child's reactions to speech and other sounds make this need evident in the course of training.

It is not uncommon for a hearing aid to be chosen so that its frequency response curve theoretically falls about half-way between the child's pure tone threshold and his threshold of tolerance. The margin of error in this procedure can be quite large, because the earmold can substantially alter the aid's in-the-ear response characteristics. Furthermore, if the child's threshold for pure tones is obtained using earphones (calibrated with a 6-cc coupler), his threshold of tolerance is established in free field condition, and the response of the aid is measured in a 2-cc coupler, there is considerable risk of spurious calculation. Given that the threshold measures obtained on a young child may also be unreliable, and that assumptions relating to the power of speech that the child will encounter have to be made, one must regard the procedure with strong reservations.

Some workers seek to avoid the problems inherent in a procedure such as that described above by using a master hearing aid. Even if master hearing aid testing is carried out with microphone placement comparable to that encountered in actual hearing aid use and even if the system incorporates the child's personal earmolds, there is room for several types of error. First, master hearing aids incorporate but a small number of possible characteristics. Selection of aids is therefore both dictated and limited by the type and range of characteristics included, which are usually chosen quite arbitrarily. None of them may be optimum for a particular child. Take, for example, a master hearing aid designed to provide various degrees of attenuation of frequencies below 1000 Hz, a major peak in response at or just above 1000 Hz, and no significant amplification beyond 3000 Hz. Such an instrument would lead to inadequate hearing aid fittings because peaks at or about 1000 Hz are undesirable (see above) and because sounds above 3000 Hz (if audible) can contribute greatly to speech intelligibility and can be reproduced by personal hearing aids. Second, the procedure demands the production and fitting of personal aids that match the characteristics selected on the master hearing aid in respect to all parameters. Such a match is feasible but improbable. Third, the adequacy of a particular selection rests upon the validity of a) the stimuli chosen, b) the child's responses to them, and c) the examiner's procedures. The reader may wish to speculate on these aspects of master hearing aid test validity and to formulate a description of stimuli, responses, and procedures that could be considered entirely satisfactory in testing young children. Nobody has published such a description to date.

The Five-Sound Test Whatever theoretical bases are used to select a hearing aid for a child, a practical check to determine whether the aid permits optimum detection of speech components is essential. To make such a check is a simple matter. We use the five speech sounds /u/, /a/, /i/, /ʃ/, and /s/ as stimuli. With the baby, one can determine whether these sounds can be detected through the aid at levels normally met in conversational speech by means of conditioned orientation reflex audiometry. The older child can merely be asked to raise a finger or clap his hands when he hears the stimulus. All children with measurable residual hearing up to 1000 Hz should be able to hear the three vowel sounds spoken in a quiet voice at a distance of at least 5 yards. Children with measurable hearing up to 2000 Hz should be equally well able to hear the /ʃ/. Children with hearing up to 4000 Hz should detect the /s/, those with thresholds for this frequency at 100 dB, at about 1 or 2 yards, and those with better thresholds, at greater distances. The test, used in the presence of noise also allows one to determine whether upward spread of masking occurs, for the high consonants will not be heard as well in noise as in quiet if such is the case.

The child's ability to detect all five of the sounds discussed above demonstrates his ability to detect all aspects of speech, because these five sounds encompass the frequency range of all phonemes and the voiced sounds contain sufficient harmonics to convey suprasegmental information. Ability to hear the /ʃ/ predicates ability to hear /i/ and to differentiate /i/ and /u/, because the second formant of /i/ falls in the same frequency range as /ʃ/. Ability to hear /u/ but not /i/ indicates poor high frequency hearing and inadequate gain for the low (200–300 Hz) frequencies, because /u/ and /i/ have similar first formant values. Ability to hear /a/ but not /u/ indicates insufficient gain below 1000 Hz, because the first formant of /a/ and the second formant of /u/ both fall in the range 750–1000 Hz. Inability to hear the /ʃ/ indicates either absence of hearing or inadequate amplification in the range 2000–2500 Hz. Inability to hear the /s/ similarly indicates either absence of hearing around 4000 Hz or insufficient gain for the high frequencies.

The "five-sound test" described above is a particularly useful guide in adjusting the response curve of the hearing aid to provide optimum detection of vowels and their formant transitions. If the test reveals that the /a/ is audible to a child with hearing up to 3000 Hz at a distance of several yards but /i/ is not, then gain at 2000–3000 Hz should be increased relative to gain at 1000–1500 Hz. If /a/ is audible when whispered, yet /u/ and /i/ can be heard by such a child only when spoken, then gain at 1000–1500 Hz should be reduced relative to that above and below this frequency band to avoid upward spread of masking and tolerance problems resulting from over amplification of mid frequency sounds. If the child has no hearing above 1000 Hz, and only /a/ is audible, then frequencies below 300 Hz should be increased so the first formants of /u/ and /i/ can be heard and suprasegmental information can be made available. Low frequency sounds should never be emphasized, nor should they ever be cut to the point that components of certain vowels become inaudible.

The five-sound test can also be used by the professional worker as a direct check on the frequency responses of the hearing aid. If one says these five sounds while listening to a hearing aid, each should be amplified without significant distortion. As a rule, all three vowels should be about equally audible and the consonants should be clearly reproduced. If /ʃ/ sounds unnaturally high or low, then an unwanted peak in the 2000–3000 Hz range is indicated. If /s/ is not audible to the normal hearing listener through the hearing aid, then it will be inaudible to the hearing-impaired child. To listen to an aid in this fashion can, with experience, become the practitioner's or parents' most efficient check, equal to a Brüel and Kjaer analysis. To test a hearing aid simply by turning it on to see if it produces feedback is not enough.

Detection of Partial or Degraded Speech Patterns

Most hearing-impaired children are unable to detect all components of speech. The majority, those with severe high tone loss, find it particularly difficult to hear the invariant energy of high frequency fricatives and the variant energy that offers cues on place of consonant production. These components may be inaudible or distorted even when amplification is optimum.

Severe hearing loss causes detection problems somewhat analogous to those that can be heard when listening to acoustically filtered speech. Indeed, Owens, Talbott, and Schubert (1968) and Sher and Owens (1974), among others, have shown that normal hearing subjects listening to speech low pass filtered at 2000 Hz tend to respond somewhat like listeners with comparable high frequency hearing loss. Bilger and Wang (1976) recently confirmed that auditory perceptual confusions are systematically related to audiometric configurations, but also showed that the number of errors and the type of errors subjects made reflect relatively independent aspects of auditory function. It would seem that types of errors made relate closely to subjects inability to detect sounds, and quantity of errors made relates to the integrity of the residual hearing present. Types of error are thus largely predictable from an audiogram (or filter setting) whereas quantity of errors is idiosyncratic.

Normal hearing children usually detect all speech sounds with ease. However, hearing-impaired children may have to be trained to detect sounds that lie close to their thresholds of hearing, and it may be a year or so before a reliable threshold for even the detection of pure tones can be established (Hine and Furness, 1975). Early failure to respond to a pure tone at a high intensity level does not, therefore, necessarily signify complete deafness for that particular frequency. Similarly, improvement in early audiograms may reflect improvement of listening (and hence improvement in detection) rather than a true amelioration of hearing level.

Normal listeners rarely seek to detect sounds at or near threshold levels, and speech is usually received well above threshold. Hearing-impaired children also need to receive speech at suprathreshold levels if they are to discriminate between the sounds that they can detect. The less severely hearing impaired the child, the higher above threshold effective listening levels are likely to be. For example, children with mild hearing losses averaging about 30–40 dB may find that speech is most intelligible when presented 50 dB above threshold of detection, whereas the most effective listening level for children with hearing loss averaging 80 dB may be threshold of detection plus only 20 dB.

It is important to determine detection thresholds not only for particular sounds, but for components of these sounds. Thus a child with severe hearing impairment that is more marked for high than for low frequencies may be able to detect the first formant of the vowel [i] as in *heed,* which falls around 300 Hz for many speakers, yet not be able to detect the second formant of this vowel, which lies over 2000 Hz. In such a case, the [i] will sound rather like [u]. Indeed, children who can detect the second formant of [i] and will correctly repeat the vowel when it is presented at, say a distance of a yard, may not detect this formant at 2 or 3 yards and will respond with [u] when [i] is presented at this greater distance. Such a phenomenon is not limited to vowels. It can occur with several other sounds and transitions from one sound to another. Thus detection is closely related to discrimination ability, and often in quite subtle ways.

Suprasegmental Patterns   Most hearing-impaired children, adequately aided, can detect voice and hence the suprasegmental patterns of speech (intensity, duration, pitch, and rate variations), because they are carried by low frequency energy. Children taught in effective auditory-oral programs rarely, therefore, develop the abnormally flat, arhythmic voice patterns that were typically found among those taught by more traditional visual-oral methods. To detect suprasegmental patterns optimally, the lower harmonics should be made audible. For most children, this requires that their hearing aids reproduce frequencies below 300 Hz. It is important to note that suprasegmental information, particularly intonation, is not readily conveyed by vision or touch, the alternative sense avenues in speech reception (see Figure 1). Even presence or absence of voice cannot be reliably detected in speechreading (Risberg, 1974) and, because the skin is relatively insensitive to frequency, pitch information cannot be transmitted through a single channel vibratory aid. So far as the detection of suprasegmentals is concerned, there is no good substitute for optimum use of residual hearing.

Vowels   All vowels can be detected by children whose hearing extends up to 1000 Hz, because first formants of all vowels fall below this frequency. Nevertheless, as mentioned earlier, second formant energy, which carries much of the information on place of consonant production, may be inaudible to many children unless amplified to a considerably greater extent than the lower components.

Unless second formant energy is detectable, auditory confusions among vowels will predictably occur (Owens, Talbott, and Schubert, 1968). Inability to detect second formant energy is not an insuperable barrier to vowel reception in English if lipreading is used to supplement audition. This is because lip shape and tongue position are related in English. As the lips are rounded, so is the tongue raised and retracted. As the lips spread, so is the tongue raised and brought forward. Once this relationship is understood by the child, the vowels can be easily identified (Ling and Bennett, 1975). Nevertheless, if hearing is not fully exploited and first formant information is not being detected, the hearing-impaired child will tend to make errors in vowel production. Tongue position is visually masked by the lips in [u] and by the teech in [i]. Unless the child can detect the low frequency formants associated with these sounds, therefore, his tongue will tend to assume (or remain in) a neutral position and an abnormal vowel will result. Neutralization of tongue position when the lips are correctly rounded for [u] or spread for [i] results in a first formant that is pitched higher than it should be, and the skilled teacher/therapist can simply, by hearing such an abnormality, determine that child is not detecting first formant energy adequately in vowel reception and vowel reproduction.

Consonants   Cues on manner of consonant production are present from below 500 Hz to over 2000 Hz. However, children with hearing only for low frequency sounds can be expected to differentiate nasals, semivowels, plosives, and liquids on the basis of cues that exist well below 750 Hz if the hearing aids selected allow their detection (see D. Ling, 1976, pp. 261–265). Manner cues are not readily seen in lipreading, hence profoundly hearing-impaired children who have been trained visually and do not use their residual hearing typically confuse [m] and [b]. Such confusions reflects poor (nonauditory) teaching strategies or inadequate hearing aids more frequently than poor hearing potential, because the cues differentiating these manner distinctions are perceptually salient if rendered detectable through audition (Aston, 1972).

Cues of place of consonant production cannot be detected unless residual hearing extends well above 1500 Hz. Most such cues fall between 1800 and 3200 Hz (see D. Ling, 1976, pp. 267–273). Children without hearing in this frequency range cannot, therefore, be expected to detect the cues that allow them to differentiate [p], [t], and [k], for example. Not surprisingly, it has been found that unisensory (auditory only) training is less effective with such children than with those whose hearing extends across the high frequencies (Stewart, 1965). Fortunately, cues on place of consonant production are relatively easy to lipread.

Voicing distinctions in consonant production are cued either by vocal cord vibration, the relative durations of the consonant and the vowel (or nasal) proceding it, or by both (Raphael, 1972; Raphael, Dorman, Tobin, and Freeman, 1974). Unless both the vowel and the consonant are detectable, therefore, voicing confusions are likely to occur. Cues on the voicing of consonants cannot be detected visually, hence confusions on voicing suggest that auditory information is not being used. Failure to detect voiced/voiceless distinctions is as often caused by inadequately fitted hearing aids or too much attention to visual speech reception, as to insufficient hearing potential. This was indicated by work carried out by Bennett who, through auditory training, taught some of the most visually oriented, profoundly hearing-impaired children in a school for the deaf to detect, discriminate, and produce voiced/voiceless distinctions (Bennett, and Ling, 1973). Because detection of fine differences in the sequential timing of acoustic events is involved in making voiced/voiceless distinctions, it may be assumed that the difficulties experienced by some children in this regard may be attributable to problems relating to the first two stages of sensory processing depicted in Figure 1 (also see Aaronson, 1968).

Selective Attention   Selective attention is the process by which the organism "gates" stimuli in such a way that signals significant to it are accepted and competing input (noise) is rejected (Solley and Murphy, 1960). According to Neisser (1967, p. 88) selective attention involves treating stimuli that we search for in a different, more sophisticated way than other stimuli. Furthermore, he suggests that this process occurs at a very early stage in auditory processing (as information is "read out" from the sensory store shown as the first stage in Figure 1). Thus selective attention allows the organism to establish figure-ground relationships, to perceive signals embedded in noise.

To detect signals that are embedded in noise is a particularly difficult task for the hearing-impaired person, because only partial or degraded patterns may be available to him. Hence signal-to-noise ratios tend to be intrinsically greater for a person with hearing impairment than for the normal hearing listener. Extraneous noise therefore tends to affect the hearing-impaired person's speech reception to a greater than normal extent (Carhart and Tillman, 1970).

We know, then, that the hearing-impaired child inevitably must experience great difficulty in detecting certain speech components in noise, and that his ability to detect significant components of the speech signal will depend heavily upon his knowing what to search for. It therefore seems reasonable to suggest that initial auditory training should be provided under optimum acoustic conditions (high signal-to-noise ratio) and that early attention should be given to spoken language skills so that he is more clearly aware of the nature of the signals that are significant. In brief, there are good arguments for initial training with amplification (such as hard wire, loop, and radio) systems that can provide better signal-to-noise ratios than individual hearing aids. There are also grounds for planning work that relates speech and language very specifically to auditory training (Grammatico, 1975, Lorenz, 1961). As the child's skills develop, of course, the speech and language knowledge accumulated in long term store (see Figure 1) will guide his selective attention, and optimum signal-to-noise conditions will then be less important to him (see Boothroyd, 1967).

Some hearing-impaired children—those with a limited frequency range of audition—must, of course, be able to attend selectively to more than one sensory channel in order to detect essential features of speech. What type of training most effectively leads to optimum detection of components in multisensory speech reception and how individual differences affect multisensory processing of speech are topics that have yet to be studied.

DISCRIMINATION

Measures of Discrimination

The term "discrimination" as employed in this chapter refers simply to the listener's ability to differentiate one sound or series of sound patterns from another. The sound(s) may or may not be meaningful, and ability to discriminate sound patterns does not imply ability to recognize or identify them except in the very limited context in which they are presented. They can be held in echoic or primary store (see Figure 1) and are not necessarily retained for more than brief intervals of time.

There are several basic forms of discrimination task. The most commonly met are outlined below. The simplest is that in which the subject is called upon to say whether two sequentially presented patterns were the same or different. The *AB, X* procedure is slightly more complex. Two different patterns (*A* and *B*) are presented followed by a third (*X*), which is identical to either *A* or *B*, and the subject is asked to say which. Another variety of discrimination task involves matching to a sample. This may be labeled as an *X, ABC* procedure, in which the sample, as "anchor" unit (*X*) is presented and then followed by three patterns (*A, B,* and *C*) one of which matches the sample (*X*). There are, of course, many variations possible and the set *AB* can be extended to include a relatively large number of items. The larger the number of items in a set and the longer the interval between them, the further one moves towards identification or recognition processes. In teaching hearing-impaired children, discrimination tasks are rarely undertaken using audition alone. Usually, the set is specified visually using models, pictures, or the written form and the child is asked to point to or in some other way indicate which member of the set was presented.

Training Methods

Discrimination training readily lends itself to programmed instruction, because sets of stimuli can be specified visually and the response act— such as pressing a window or button—can initiate logic circuitry that automatically signals correct or incorrect responses. Such a device was used by Doehring and Ling (1971) to train severely hearing-impaired children in the discrimination of vowels in words such as *bell, ball,* and *bill.* The training resulted in steady increases in correct responses. However, there was no transfer of the learned discrimination to a word recognition task incorporating some of the same words used in training. Similar inability to generalize from discrimination training to more complex tasks was also shown by Baldwin (1973). However, when the writer has required spoken rather than nonverbal responses in studies with hearing-impaired children, e.g., Ling and Maretic (1971), some ability to generalize has usually resulted. It may be that spoken responses are more likely to lead to improved storage of the features differentiating the stimuli used, a result predicted by the model presented as Figure 1.

Speech and Nonspeech There is no consensus as to whether training with nonverbal stimuli lead to improved ability to discriminate speech. Alos (1972) and Perdoncini and Barbera (1972) suggest that training hearing-impaired children to discriminate between increasingly fine differences in the frequency, intensity, and duration of tonal stimuli will result in better speech reception skills. However, Stritzver (1958) found wide variations among hearing-impaired children's pitch discrimination (difference limen) and speech reception scores. Although confirming findings by Hopkins and Hudgins (1953) that speech perception was superior among those whose hearing extended over the high frequencies, Stritzver found no correlation between speech perception scores and frequency discrimination at 1000 and 2000 Hz, although there was such a correlation at 500 Hz. Certainly, hearing-impaired children's frequency discrimination for low frequency sounds can be improved with practice (Gengel, 1969) but so, too, can it be improved among normal hearing children who have relatively poor frequency discrimination yet have no problems in speech reception (Soderquist and Moore, 1970).

There are marked differences in the way that speech and nonspeech stimuli (other than music) are discriminated, both by normal hearing and hearing-impaired listeners. It has been suggested that this is because we have specialized capacity for perceiving speech and language stimuli (Liberman, Cooper, Shankweiler, and Studdert-Kennedy, 1967). Ability to discriminate the sequential order of related sounds such as speech is certainly better than ability to discriminate the order of unrelated nonspeech stimuli both among normal hearing listeners (Warren, Obusek, Farmer, and Warren, 1969) and among hearing impaired children (A. H. Ling, 1975).

Most auditory training programs for hearing-impaired children described in the literature include the discrimination of nonverbal sounds (Bangs, 1954; Clarke School for the Deaf, 1971, Hogan, 1961; Pollack, 1970, Sanders, 1971). Furthermore, most articles on the topic imply, if they do not explicitly state, that training discrimination between sounds such as those produced by bells, drums, whistles, and car horns leads to better speech discrimination (Asals and Ruthven, 1956; Anselmini and Wallin, 1959; Beck, 1968; Johnson and Seigenthaler, 1951; Rollins, 1972). This notion cannot be supported. Knowledge of environmental sounds is important in its own right (Withrow, 1974). However, little or no amelioration of speech discrimination can be expected to result from training with gross nonverbal sounds. Their acoustic characteristics are too different, they are likely to be processed in different hemispheres of the brain, and perceptual and memory strategies appropriate for one type of sound are inappropriate for the other (see A. H. Ling, 1976).

Discrimination of Phonetic and Phonologic Level Material   The idea that auditory training should begin with discrimination of gross differences and proceed to increasingly finer differences has been a central theme throughout the history of auditory training (see Watson, 1961, 1962; Watts, 1969). It has been stressed for over 50 years in the

United States (Ballenger and Patterson, 1935; Goldstein, 1939; McKenzie, 1919). Programs that accord with the idea can, however, be readily structured using speech. Suprasegmental patterns can be grossly different from each other, are more grossly different than vowels that in turn are more difficult to discriminate than differences in manner of consonant production and so on. However, recent work stemming from studies by Eimas, Siquel and Jusczyk and Vigoretto (1971) and Eimas (1974) among others, brings into question whether such structure is, in fact, desirable. Their work indicates that normal hearing infants can make very fine discriminations—even categorical distinctions (Miller and Morse, 1976)—among consonants in syllabic context as readily as gross discriminations among suprasegmental patterns. Furthermore, Kuhl and Miller (1975) have found that vowels are more attended to by (are more salient for) young infants than pitch contour; the reverse of what would be assumed in a gross-to-fine auditory training program.

It seems then, that discrimination of at least some segmental sounds is commonplace in very early infancy, well before speech can be produced. This is not to say that discrimination skills are complete in normal hearing infants during the 1st year. Edwards (1974), Garnica (1973), Shvachkin (1973), and Waterson (1971) have shown that in phonologic development, discrimination skill increases with age and speech production skill, even into a child's 4th year. It also seems that discriminations between sounds learned at the phonetic level in early infancy have to be relearned at the phonologic level, that is, when they are used meaningfully.

On the basis of findings relating to discrimination at the phonetic and phonologic levels in normal children, one may speculate 1) that in auditory training we should, from the beginning, test and teach a wide range of suprasegmental and segmental discriminations, using non-meaningful as well as meaningful speech sounds and speech sequences as a preparatory step to ensure later linguistic development; 2) that training at the phonetic (nonmeaningful) level should be related to the development and differentiation of the child's motor speech patterns, and 3) that one can not expect discriminations mastered at the phonetic level to be spontaneously applied at the phonologic level. Discriminations may have to be relearned when they are used in the broader context of meaningful speech.

Hearing impairment is rarely total. Some potential for auditory speech discrimination is therefore present in most hearing-impaired children and development of discrimination skill may be expected within the frequency range of the child's residual hearing. Detection of the sounds to be used for discrimination training is, of course, a prerequisite. It is possible to teach some children to discriminate between phonetic level pairs such as [ʃa-sa] even when the [s] is inaudible, for they may do so on the basis of classifying the [ʃa] as noise + vowel and the [sa] as silence + vowel. Learning such a discrimination is unlikely to be helpful in phonologic speech. Similarly, if all components of three words (A, B, C) presented for discrimination are not detectable, then A and B may be discriminated as categorically different from each other, yet C may be discriminated, not through reference to its own acoustic features, but as "neither A nor B."

Finally, discrimination is a half-way house between detection and identification. We have seen that young children might take some time before they respond reliably to tests measuring thresholds of detection. We may expect that it will take considerably more exposure to spoken language patterns before a child's potential for discrimination can be achieved. Verbal discriminations can only be learned if the stimuli are presented consistently and frequently (Berkowitz, 1968). Only if speech sequences can be discriminated categorically can they be identified and processed at optimum speaking rates. Thus every effort should be made to ensure abundant duration and quality of exposure to normal patterns of speech through both specific training and everyday experience.

IDENTIFICATION

To be able to identify sounds or sound sequences one must, clearly, have had previous experience of them. Because the extent of one's previous experience with anything may vary, the depth or certainty of identification may also vary. One may simply recognize that sound sequences presented have been experienced previously, much as one might, in the street, recognize persons to whom one has been introduced without remembering who they are. Alternatively, one may be able to identify sounds or sound sequences previously encountered as meaningful items, much as one can identify people with whom one is thoroughly familiar under a variety of social conditions. In the first case, most characteristics of the sound sequences (or persons) were stored only in primary memory (Figure 1, Stage 3) and in the second, they were stored in secondary memory through enduring associations with other experience. Thus identification is not an all-or-none affair, but rather, a continuum bridging discrimination and comprehension.

Auditory identification of speech sounds or sequences, then, requires that the listener is provided with an adequate quantity of experience. Sufficient quality of experience is also essential. If the characteristics of given speech sounds or sequences are not clearly discriminable from one another, then no amount of exposure will be adequate to permit their absolute identification. Not to recognize this fact will lead to many hearing-impaired children being unable to learn spoken language skills. It is not enough to "talk, talk, talk" if the child is "deaf, deaf, deaf."

Sensory Interaction in Identification

If the characteristics of speech sounds or sound sequences are not sufficiently discriminable to permit a child to identify them through audition alone, then the use of other sense modalities should be considered. Material processed in primary memory may be sense related (one can readily recall voice patterns). It need not, however, be specifically stored in the form of auditory, visual, or tactile imagery. At this stage it can be an encoded representation of the input received in any or all sense modalities (see Figure 1). Thus in multisensory speech reception, identification may involve scanning the spoken message for differentiating characteristics that are heard, seen, or felt.

Because training in speech identification demands encoding in primary memory, such training necessarily calls for the child to adopt particular encoding strategies. If the strategies adopted are compatible with those required in everyday speech reception, then the likelihood of the child generalizing the identification skills learned in training to everyday situations will be enhanced. If, on the other hand, the training is such that the child is taught to identify speech sounds or sequences on the basis of cues that will not be generally available in real life situations, then effective carry-over from training cannot be expected. Examples of cues provided in training that inhibit generalization include the persistent use of contexts (e.g., closed sets) that confine the child to discrimination tasks, and thus make little demand on his primary memory, and exaggerated auditory or visual patterns such as unduly slow speech accompanied by jaw, lip, or facial gestures that are rarely met outside the training situation.

Encoding and Rehearsal

Identification requires an interaction between material stored in secondary memory and the incoming message. It is therefore a conceptual rather than a perceptual task. If the materials to be identified are speech sounds, then ability to produce these speech sounds and to use imagery based on speech production skills is rehearsing them in primary memory will be advantageous. If the materials to be identified are linguistic rather than phonetic, then knowledge of semantic, lexical, and syntactic rules and constraints will help the child in the identification task. If some cues on part of the message are missing (as with hearing impairment they are likely to be), then such reference to data in secondary memory will allow the identification of the whole, and the "chunking" of information, which will allow it to be held in primary store (Miller, 1956).

As with discrimination, identification is improved when the population of alternatives is reduced (Miller, Heise, and Lichten, 1951). Identification is also improved for the normal listener when the semantic content of the message is anticipated (Bruce, 1958; Leiberman, 1963). The need to be able to hold information in primary store so that identification can be assisted by syntactic knowledge has been very well demonstrated by Clark and Begun (1968) and Levelt (1970). If communication by spoken language is to be fostered, then primary emphasis should be given to helping the child learn language through appropriate auditory/articulatory or multisensory speech encoding strategies. Concentration on the written form may help a child learn language (which is necessary for speech reception), but it may also establish abnormal encoding processes that relate to semantic content (Moulton and Beasley, 1975) or writing (Conrad, 1970) rather than speech, even to the point where vocalizing hinders rather than helps the understanding of language (Conrad, 1971).

Training to Develop Speech Identification Skills

There is very little in the literature on auditory training that relates to the development of speech identification skills. Identification seems to occupy a no man's land situated between discrimination exercises and training procedures to develop spoken language comprehension. That the child must develop appropriate auditory/articulatory encoding processes in primary memory is, however, good reason for teachers to concentrate at least some of their efforts on work involving speech identification. Training the child to imitate speech sounds and longer and longer speech sequences with less and less contextual support seems to be one viable means of teaching identification skills. However, though imitation may be appropriate in training discrimination and identification skills, its benefits in promoting comprehension of spoken language are in some doubt (see Prutting and Connolly, 1976; Ling, 1976, p. 385).

COMPREHENSION

As with discrimination and identification of speech, comprehension of speech can occur at a multitude of levels. A child can be said to comprehend speech if he obeys an order (e.g., "Don't touch!") the meaning of which is conveyed by tone of voice. He may also be said to comprehend speech if he reacts appropriately to a spoken message that is accompanied by abundant nonverbal cues. Such comprehension is a far cry from understanding a lecture on an unfamiliar subject that is presented without any supporting visual materials. The fact that there are many levels at which spoken language may be comprehended, suggests that teacher/therapists can design carefully graded programs through which they and parents can promote the development of speech reception from the earliest stages of infancy.

Comprehension implies the derivation of meaning. The situations that are most meaningful to the child are most likely to promote comprehension of the speech patterns presented in these situations and to provide motivation and reinforcement required for learning. Ideally, the child's growing comprehension of speech, fostered by gradual increase in the complexity of the language provided and reduction in the redundancy afforded by contextual cues, should parallel the child's cognitive growth (Menyuk, 1976). It should also parallel his acquisition of motor speech codes (Figure 1, Stage 4).

Influences of Technological Advances

As hearing aids became portable the need to tether children to hard wire amplification systems in order to provide them with auditory experience diminished. The advent of wearable hearing aids led not only to children wearing them in and out of school, but to the initiation of an auditory approach with hearing-impaired children in early infancy. Techniques for extending training in spoken language comprehension through the use of individual aids have been suggested in a great many publications over the past 25 years. Among those of particular interest are Bollbach (1958), Ewing and Ewing (1971), Griffiths (1964), Horton and McConnell (1970), Huizing (1951), Ingall (1963), Northcott (1975). Pollack (1964), Scott (1948), Simmons-Martin (1972), Wedenberg (1951), and Whetnall and Fry (1971). Detailed discussion of these and the many other books and articles on the topic is outside the scope of this chapter.

Comprehension and Environment

There has been a growing awareness that the quality of auditory experience required for the comprehension of spoken language is not easy to provide in special schools for the hearing impaired. Normal patterns of speech and behavior and a stimulating range of life experience are an essential basis for optimum development of spoken language skills. There has therefore been a trend towards the integration of hearing-impaired children into regular schools, a trend which the improved spoken language achievements of children trained from early infancy in parent-infant programs has helped to encourage (Ling, Ling and Pflaster, 1977). Among those who have advocated programs leading to parent involvement and regular school placement are many of the workers mentioned in the preceding paragraph. Others include Anselmini (1959), Berg (1971), Berg and Fletcher (1970), Bloom (1974), Buchli (1964), and Stone, Feidler and Fine (1961).

Comprehension involves the synthesis of incoming information and stored experience, both cognitive and linguistic. Comprehension, then, demands detection, discrimination, and identification skills, and a history of meaningful experience. This has to be borne in mind when working to develop comprehension in children whether at home, in regular schools, or in special schools and classes. Thus hearing aids have to permit optimum detection of speech and the acoustic properties of the home or classroom must be such that the speech signal is not masked by ambient noise or reverberation (Niemoeller, 1968; Ross and Giolas, 1971). Those working with the child, parents or professionals, must be able to assess and teach the necessary discrimination and identification skills (or have someone available to help them do it) through criterion referenced training (Glaser, 1963). They must also be able to design and exploit speech and language learning experiences according to the individual child's needs and interests (Ling, 1976).

CONCLUDING REMARKS

Although some form of auditory training has been provided for hearing-impaired children in certain programs for many years, optimally effective use of residual hearing seems to remain the exception rather than the rule. In relatively recent years, technology has provided instrumentation that, although far from perfect, could render at least some speech sounds audible and intelligible to the majority of hearing-impaired children. Ability to exploit residual hearing has, however, lagged behind technological growth, not merely because inertia is a potent force in education, but because the research necessary to give workers a clear sense of direction remains to be carried out.

Numerous problems limit the application of effective auditory training. Four of the most important are specified below. First, results are generally superior if children begin to use their residual hearing in early infancy, yet early identification of hearing impairment is the exception rather than the rule. Second, selection of hearing aids for young children, particularly those at a prelinguistic stage of development, involve inexact, arbitrary procedures. Thus many children are fitted with hearing aids that do not permit optimum detection of speech. Third, there is a shortage of skilled teacher/therapists capable of carrying out ongoing assessment and training of young children. Fourth, educational provision has not yet become sufficiently diversified. Thus many children capable of obtaining more benefit from auditory-oral education are consigned to schools or classes where visual-oral, multisensory-oral, or "total communication" approaches more suitable for other hearing-impaired children are used (see Ling, Ling, and Pflaster, 1977).

Existing problem should not be allowed to obscure present and future possibilities for the better and more widespread use of residual hearing. Problems such as those mentioned above can be overcome through research, more appropriate training of personnel, and strong professional and parental insistence that individualized instruction be provided in accordance with the spirit of United States Public Law 94-142. Furthermore, current knowledge, diligently applied, can lead to the acquisition of fluent spoken language skills by most hearing-impaired children.

The material presented in the body of this chapter and the writer's experience suggest that tentative conclusions relating to auditory training may be drawn as follows:

1. Auditory training may be considered as a series of structured, progressively ordered exercises in the detection, discrimination, identification, and comprehension of speech.
2. Auditory training should be closely related to cognitive and linguistic growth and to motor speech development.
3. Auditory training should be geared toward meeting the needs of individual children. Because cognitive, linguistic, and speech skills vary from one child to another and as hearing impairment may range from slight to total deafness, the notion of an "auditory training syllabus" that could be applicable to all hearing-impaired children is untenable.
4. Auditory training is distinct from auditory experience. Auditory experience, exposure to an abundance of meaningful speech and

sound, may be sufficient for one child to master spoken language skills, but insufficient for another. Auditory training should be provided prescriptively as a supplement when particular auditory skills cannot be acquired simply through auditory experience.

5. Auditory training may include the detection, discrimination, identification, comprehension, and enjoyment of nonverbal sounds, but it may not be assumed that speech reception skills will be fostered by such training.

6. Both auditory training and auditory experience should be provided, so far as possible, under optimum acoustic conditions. It is particularly important for the child to receive speech at high signal-to-noise ratios initially so that he can most readily acquire the phonologic, linguistic, and semantic rules and the vocabulary that can enhance his speech reception under less ideal acoustic conditions.

7. Hearing aids that allow the child to detect, discriminate, identify and comprehend the fullest possible range of speech sounds are a prerequisite in the auditory training of a hearing-impaired child. Because severely and profoundly hearing-impaired children cannot hear sufficiently well with individual aids under certain conditions, hard wire, induction loop, or radio systems remain useful adjunctive means of amplification.

8. Binaural ear-level hearing aids are preferable to any other fitting only if they can provide consistently adequate gain without acoustic feedback and providing that detection, discrimination, identification, and comprehension of speech with such aids is equivalent or superior to that achieved with body-worn instruments. Significantly poorer speech reception with binaural aids should be demonstrated before a monaural fitting is considered.

9. Because many hearing-impaired children have to learn how to listen, results of early hearing tests with pure tones or speech are not necessarily valid. Hearing aids for children should be selected and adjusted by the child's teacher/therapist in the course of ongoing training rather than on the basis of preliminary audiologic tests. It follows that teacher/therapists should be well trained in the necessary audiologic techniques.

10. Auditory experience and auditory training by themselves cannot provide all children with adequate speech reception skills. Some children, particularly those with severe or profound impairment whose hearing loss extends over a limited frequency range, need to use vision, and possibly touch, as supplementary or alternative sense modalities for effective speech reception.

212 Ling

11. Auditory skills develop most readily if experience and training are provided from early infancy. If one begins late in childhood one not only has to overcome the problems associated with the hearing impairment, but those that derive from early sensory deprivation.

12. Professionals alone can not provide all the auditory experience and training that most hearing-impaired children require in order to master spoken language skills. Thus parents (or those in loco parentis) should be informed and helped to give their children the necessary experience and training at each successive stage of development.

REFERENCES

Aaronson, D. 1968. Temporal course of perception in an immediate recall task. J. Exp. Psychol. 76:129–140.

Alos, J. G. 1972. El metodo auditivo del Dr. Perdoncini (Methods of auditory training of Dr. Perdoncini). Fono Audiol. 13:8–21.

Anselmini, A. A. 1959. Auditory training: Design for growth. Basic considerations. Volta Rev. 61:322–323, 342.

Anselmini, A. A., and M. K. Wallin. 1959. Auditory training: Design for growth. Instructional techniques. Volta Rev. 61:461–466, 486.

Asals, F. B., and H. C. Ruthven. 1956. Auditory training for the primary grades. Volta Rev. 58:205–207.

Aston, C. H. 1972. Hearing-impaired children's discrimination of filtered speech. J. Audiol. Res. 12:162–167.

Baldwin, R. L. 1973. An investigation of generalization in the vowel discrimination learning of hearing impaired children. Unpublished Ph.D. dissertation, University of Kansas.

Ballenger, H. C., and B. A. Patterson. 1935. "Aural" or "acoustic" method of treating deafness. Arch. Otolaryngol. 22:410–415.

Bangs, T. E. 1954. Methodology in auditory training. Volta Rev. 56:159–164.

Beasley, D. S., N. L. Mosher, and D. J. Orchik. 1976. Use of frequency-shifted/time-compressed speech with hearing-impaired children. Audiology 15:395–406.

Beck, G. B. 1968. A developmental programme of auditory training. Austr. Teach. Deaf 9:88–100.

Belleza, F. S., and J. Walker. 1974. Storage-coding trade-off in short term store. J. Exp. Psychol. 102:629–633.

Bennett, C. W., and D. Ling. 1973. Discrimination of the voiced-voiceless distinction by severely hearing-impaired children. J. Audit. Res. 13:271–279.

Berg, F. S. 1971. Breakthrough for the hard of hearing child. EAR publication, Smithfield, Utah.

Berg, F. S., and S. G. Fletcher. 1970. The Hard of Hearing Child: Clinical and Educational Management. Grune & Stratton, Inc., New York.

Berger, K. W. 1970. The Hearing Aid, Its Operation and Development. National Hearing Aid Society, Detroit.

Berkowitz, J. 1968. Verbal discrimination learning as a function of experimental frequency. Psychon. Sci. 13:97–98.

Bilger, R. C., and M. D. Wong. 1976. Consonant confusions in patients with sensorineural hearing loss. J. Speech Hear. Res. 19:718–748.

Bloom, F. 1974. Auditory training. Hearing 29:318–321.

Bollbach, B. L. 1958. Enriching deaf children's experience through auditory training. Volta Rev. 60: 411–413.

Boothroyd, A. 1967. Theoretical Aspects of Auditory Training. In: Proceedings of the International Conference on Oral Education of the Deaf, pp. 705–728, Vol. 1. A. G. Bell Association, Washington, D.C.

Boothroyd, A. 1970. Distribution of hearing levels in the student population of the Clarke School for the Deaf. Clarke School for the Deaf, Sensory Aids Research Project, Report #3. Northampton, Massachusetts.

Bruce, D. J. 1958. The effect of listeners' anticipations on the intelligibility of heard speech. Lang. Speech. 1:79–97.

Buchli, M. C. J. 1964. Home-education of very young deaf children. Voix Silence, 8:26–32.

Carhart, R., and T. W. Tillman. 1970. Interaction of competing speech signals with hearing losses. Arch. Otolaryngol. 91:273–279.

Clark, H. H., and J. S. Begun. 1968. The use of syntax in understanding sentences. Br. J. Psychol. 59:219–229.

Clarke, B. R. 1957. Use of a group hearing aid by profoundly deaf children. In: A. W. G. Ewing (ed.), Educational Guidance and the Deaf Child, pp. 128–159. Manchester University Press, Manchester, England.

Clarke School for the Deaf 1971. Auditory Training. Clarke School for the Deaf, Northampton, Mass.

Cole, R., M. Coltheart. and F. Allard. 1974. Memory of a speaker's voice: Reaction time to same or different voiced letters. Q. J. Exp. Psychol. 26:1–7.

Conrad, R. 1970. Short-term memory processes in the deaf. Br. J. Psych. 61:179–195.

Conrad, R. 1971. The effect of vocalizing on comprehension in the profoundly deaf. Br. J. Psych. 62:147–150.

Doehring, D. G., and D. Ling. 1971. Programmed instruction of hearing-impaired children in the auditory discrimination of vowels. J. Speech Hear. Res. 14:746–754.

Edwards, M. L. 1974. Perception and production in child phonology: The testing of four hypotheses. J. Child Lang. 1:205–219.

Eimas, P. D. 1974. Auditory and linguistic processing of cues for place of articulation by infants. Percept. Psychophys. 16:513–521.

Eimas, P. D., E. R. Siqueland, P. Jusczyk, and J. Vigorito. 1971. Speech Perception in infants. Science 171:303–306.

Erber, N. P. 1974. Visual perception of speech by deaf children: Recent developments and continuing needs. J. Speech Hear. Disord. 39:178–185.

Ewing, A., and E. C. Ewing. 1971. Hearing-impaired children under five. A guide for parents and teachers. Manchester University Press, Manchester, England.

Garnica, O. 1973. The development of phonemic speech perception. In: T. Moore (ed.), Cognitive Development and the Acquisition of Language. pp. 215–222. Academic Press, New York.

Gengel, R. W. 1969. Practice effects in frequency discrimination by hearing impaired children. J. Speech Hear. Res. 12:847–856.

Gengel, R. W., and K. O. Foust. 1975. Some implications of listening level for speech reception by sensorineural hearing impaired children. Lang. Speech Hear. Serv. Schools 6:14–20.

Gibson, J. J. 1966. The Senses Considered As Perceptual Systems. Houghton Mifflin Company, Boston.

Glaser, R. 1963. Instructional technology and the measurement of learning outcomes: Some questions. Am. Psychol. 18:519–521.

Goldstein, M. A. 1939. The Acoustic Method for the Training of the Deaf and Hard-of-Hearing Child. The Laryngoscope Press, St. Louis.

Grammatico, L. F. 1975. The development of listening skills. Volta Rev. 77:303–308.

Griffiths, C. 1964. The auditory approach for preschool deaf children. Volta Rev. 66:387–397.

Guilder, R. P., and A. Hopkins. 1935. Program for the testing and training of auditory function in the small deaf child during preschool years. Volta Rev. 37:5–11, 79–84.

Guttman, N., H. Levitt, and P. A. Bellefleur. 1970. Articulatory training of the deaf using low frequency surrogate fricatives. J. Speech Hear. Res. 13:19–29.

Hine, W. D., and H. J. S. Furness. 1975. Does wearing a hearing aid damage residual hearing? Teach. Deaf 73:261–271.

Hirsh, I. J. 1976. Order of events in three sensory modalities. In: S. K. Hirsh, D. H. Eldrege, I. J. Hirsh, and S. R. Silverman (eds.), Hearing and Davis: Essays Honoring Hollowell Davis. Washington University Press, St. Louis.

Hogan, Sister J. L. 1961. The ABC of Auditory Training. St. Joseph Institute for Deaf, St. Louis.

Hopkins, L., and C. V. Hudgins. 1953. The relationship between degree of deafness and response to acoustic training. Volta Rev. 55:32–35.

Horton, K. B., and F. McConnell. 1970. Early intervention for the young deaf child through parent training. In: Proceedings of the International Congress on Education of the Deaf, pp. 291–296. Vol. 1. A. G. Bell Association for the Deaf, Washington, D.C.

Hudgins, C. V. 1954. Auditory training—its possibilities and limitations. Volta Rev. 56:339–349.

Huizing, H. 1951. Auditory training. Acta Otolaryngol. 100(suppl.):158–163.

Huntington, A. 1976. Tests on induction loops in current use in schools for the deaf. Teach. Deaf, 74:7–18.

Ingall, B. I. 1963. An address . . . Teach. Deaf 61:24–36.

Johansson, B. 1966. The use of the transposer for the management of the deaf child. J. Int. Audiol. 5:362–372.

Johnson, A. F., and B. M. Siegenthaler. 1951. A clinical auditory training program. J. Speech Hear. Disord. 16:35–39.

Kuhl, P. K., and J. D. Miller. 1975. Speech perception in early infancy: discrimination of speech sound categories. J. Acoust. Soc. Am. 58(suppl.1) (abstr.):S56.

Leckie, D., and D. Ling. 1968. Audibility with hearing aids having low frequency characteristics. Volta Rev. 70:83–86.

Leiberman, P. 1963. Some effects of semantic and grammatical context on the production and perception of speech. Lang. Speech 6:172-187.

Lenneberg, E. H. 1962. Understanding language without ability to speak. J. Abnorm. Soc. Psychol. 65:419-425.

Levelt, W. J. M. 1970. Hierarchical chunking in sentence processing. Percept. Psychophysics 8:99-103.

Liberman, A. M., F. S. Cooper, D. P. Shankweiler, and M. Studdert-Kennedy. 1967. Perception of the speech code. Psychol. Rev. 74:431-461.

Ling, A. H. 1974. Sequential processing in hearing-impaired children. In: C. Griffiths (ed.), Auditory Techniques, pp. 97-106. Charles C Thomas, Publisher, Springfield, Ill.

Ling, A. H. 1975. Memory for verbal and nonverbal auditory sequences in hearing-impaired and normal-hearing children. J. Am. Audiol. Soc. 1:37-45.

Ling, A. H. 1976. The training of auditory memory in hearing impaired children: Some problems of generalization. J. Am. Audiol. Soc. 1:150-157.

Ling, D. 1963. The use of hearing and the teaching of speech. Teach. Deaf 61:59-68.

Ling, D. 1964. An auditory approach to the education of deaf children. Audecibel, 13, 96-101, 1964.

Ling, D. 1966. Loop induction for auditory training of deaf children. Maico Audiological Library, Series 5, No. 2.

Ling, D. 1967. Installation and operation of loop induction systems in real-life situations. Audecibel. 16:61-70.

Ling, D. 1968. Three experiments on frequency transposition. Am. Ann. Deaf 113:283-294.

Ling, D. 1969. Speech discrimination by profoundly deaf children using linear and coding amplifiers. IEEE Trans. Audio Electroacoustics AV-17(4):298-303.

Ling, D. 1971. Conventional hearing aids: An overview. Volta Rev. 73:343-352.

Ling, D. 1975. Amplification for Speech. In: D. R. Calvert and S. R. Silverman (eds.), Speech and Deafness, pp. 64-88. A. G. Bell Association Washington, D.C.

Ling, D. 1976. Speech and the Hearing-Impaired Child: Theory and Practice. A. G. Bell Association Washington, D.C.

Ling, D., and C. W. Bennett. 1975. Training severely hearing impaired children in vowel imitation. Hum. Commun. 3:5-18.

Ling, D., and D. G. Doehring. 1969. Hearing limits of deaf children for coded speech. J. Speech Hear. Res. 12:83-94.

Ling, D., A. H. Ling, and G. Pflaster. 1977. Individualized educational provision for hearing impaired children. Volta Rev. 79:204-230.

Ling, D., and H. Maretic. 1971. Frequency transposition in the teaching of speech to the deaf child. J. Speech Hear. Res. 14:37-46.

Lorenz, M. L. 1961. Speech and Auditory Training. St. Joseph Institute for Deaf, St. Louis.

Massaro, D. W. 1972. Preperceptual images, processing time and perceptual units in auditory perception. Psychol. Rev. 79:124-145.

Massaro, D. W. (ed.). 1975. Understanding Language. Academic Press, New York.

Matkin, N. D., and W. O. Olsen. 1970. Induction loop amplification systems: classroom performances. Asha 12: 239–244.

McKenzie, L. B. 1919. Stimulating the language centers through auditory channels. Volta Rev. 21:725–732.

Menyuk, P. 1976. Cognition and language. Volta Rev. 78: 250–257.

Miller, C. L., and P. A. Morse. 1976. The "heart" of categorical speech perception in young infants. J. Speech Hear. Res. 19:578–589.

Miller, G. A. 1956. The magical number seven, plus or minus two: Some limits on our capacity for processing information. Psychol. Rev. 63:81–97.

Miller, G. A., G. A. Heise, and W. Lichten. 1951. The intelligibility of speech as a function of the context of the test materials. J. Exp. Psychol. 41:329–335.

Miller, J. D., and A. F. Niemoeller. 1967. Hearing aid design and evaluation for a patient with severe discrimination loss for speech. J. Speech Hear. Res. 10:367–372.

Moulton, R. D., and D. S. Beasley. 1975. Verbal coding strategies used by hearing-impaired individuals. J. Speech Hear. Res. 18:559–570.

Neisser, U. 1967. Cognitive Psychology. Appleton-Century-Crofts, New York.

Niemoeller, A. F. 1968. Acoustical design of classrooms for the deaf. Am. Ann. Deaf 113:1040–1045.

Northcott, W. H. 1975. Normalization of the preschool child with hearing impairment. Otolaryngol. Clin. N. Am. 8:159–186.

Owens, E., C. B. Talbott, and E. Schubert. 1968. Vowel discrimination of hearing impaired listeners. J. Speech Hear. Res. 11:648–655.

Perdoncini, G., and M. Barbera. 1972. Bases physiologiques de la rééducation auditive de l'enfant sourd. J. Franc. otorhinlaryngol. 21:909–910.

Pisoni, D. B. 1975. Information processing and speech perception. In: G. Fant (ed.), Speech Communication. Vol. 3, pp. 331–337. John Wiley & Sons, Inc., New York.

Pollack, D. 1964. Acoupedics: A uni-sensory approach to auditory training. Volta Rev. 66:400–409.

Pollack, D. 1970. Educational Audiology for the Limited Hearing Infant. Charles C Thomas, Publisher, Springfield, Ill.

Power, D. J. 1968. The setting of listening levels in auditory training. Australian Teach. Deaf 9:123–128.

Prutting, C. A., and J. E. Connolly. 1976. Imitation: A closer look. J. Speech Hear. Disord. 41:412–422.

Raphael, L. J. 1972. Preceding vowel duration as a cue to the perception of the voicing characteristic of word-final consonants in American English. J. Acoust. Soc. Am. 51:1296–1303.

Raphael, L. J., M. F. Dorman, C. Tobin, and F. Freeman. 1974. Vowel and nasal durations in vowel-nasal-consonant sequences in American English. Haskins Laboratories. Status report on speech research SR-37/38, pp. 255–261.

Rees, N. 1973. Auditory processing factors in language disorders: The view from Procrustes' bed. J. Speech Hear. Disord. 18:304–315.

Risberg, A. 1974. The importance of prosodic speech elements for the lipreader. In: H. B. Nielson and E. Kamp (eds.), Visual and Audiovisual Perception of Speech, pp. 153–164. Scandanavian Audiology, Suppl. 4. Almqvist & Wiksell Periodical Co., Stockholm.

Rollins, J. C. 1972. "I heard that." Auditory training at home. Volta Rev. 74:426–431.

Ross, M. 1969. Loop auditory training systems for pre-school hearing impaired children. Volta Rev. 71:289–295.

Ross, M., and T. G. Giolas. 1971. Effects of three classroom listening conditions on speech intelligibility. Am. Ann. Deaf 116:580–584.

Sanders, D. 1971. Aural Rehabilitation. Prentice-Hall Inc., Englewood Cliffs, N.J.

Sanders, D. 1977. Auditory Perception of Speech. Prentice-Hall Inc., Englewood Cliffs, N.J.

Scott, E. 1948. Auditory training cannot begin too early. Volta Rev. 50:423–425.

Sherrick, C. E. 1976. The antagonisms of hearing and touch. In: S. K. Hirsh, D. H. Eldredge, I. J. Hirsh, and S. R. Silverman (eds.), Hearing and Davis: Essays Honoring Hallowell Davis. Washington University Press, St. Louis.

Shvachkin, N. K. 1973. The development of phonemic speech in early childhood. In: C. Ferguson and D. Slobin (eds.), Studies of Child Language Development, pp. 91–127. Holt, Rinehart and Winston, New York.

Simmons-Martin, A. 1972. The oral/aural approach: Theoretical basis and rationale. Volta Rev. 74:540–551.

Soderquist, D. R., and M. J. Moore. 1970. Effects of training in frequency discrimination in primary school children. J. Aud. Res. 10:185–192.

Solley, C. M., and P. Murphy. 1960. Development of the Perceptual World. Basic Books Inc., New York.

Squire, L. R. 1975. Short-term memory as a biological entity. In: D. Deutsch and J. A. Deutsch (eds.), Short Term Memory. Academic Press, New York.

Stewart, J. L. 1965. Effectiveness of Educational Audiology on the Language Development of Hearing Handicapped Children. Final Report. Office of Education (DHEW), Washington, D.C.

Stone, L. J., M. F. Fiedler, and C. G. Fine. 1961. Preschool education of deaf children. J. Speech Hear. Disord. 26:45–60.

Strizver, G. L. 1958. Frequency discrimination of deaf children and its relationship to their achievement in auditory training. Volta Rev. 60:304–306.

Tallal, P. 1976. Rapid auditory processing in normal and disordered language development. J. Speech Hear. Res. 19:561–571.

Velmans, M. 1975. Effects of frequency "recoding" on the articulation learning of perceptively deaf children. Lang. Speech 18:180–194.

Warren, R. M., C. J. Obusek, R. M. Farmer, and R. P. Warren. 1969. Auditory sequence: Confusion of patterns other than speech or music. Science 164:586–587.

Waterson, N. 1971. Child phonology: A prosodic view. J. Linguistics 7:170–221.

Wathen-Dunn, W. (ed.). 1967. Models for the Perception of Speech and Visual Form. The M.I.T. Press, Cambridge, Mass.

Watson, T. J. 1961. The use of residual hearing in the education of deaf children. Volta Rev. 63:328–334; Volta Rev. 64:31–38.

Watts, W. J. 1969. Auditory training. Teach. Deaf 67:4–18.

Wedenberg, E. 1951. Auditory training of deaf and hearing children. Acta Otolaryngol. 94:1–129.

Whetnall, E., and D. B. Fry. 1971. The Deaf Child. Charles C Thomas, Publisher, Springfield, Ill.

Withrow, F. B. 1974. The fine art of auditory training, or is anyone listening? Volta Rev. 76:415–419.

Zink, G. D. 1972. Hearing aids children wear: A longitudinal study of performance. Volta Rev. 74:41–51.

CHAPTER 7

SIGNAL PROCESSING

Edgar Villchur

CONTENTS

PURPOSE OF SIGNAL PROCESSING

Signal processing in hearing aids introduces changes into the speech signal, over and above amplification, that are designed to make the signal better suited to the distorted perception of a hearing-impaired listener. The changes themselves constitute a distortion of the original signal, but a useful one, like the optical distortion of corrective eyeglass lenses. These changes are normally introduced electrically, but changes related to frequency response can also be introduced acoustically, in the earmold and associated tubing.

    Successful signal processing would restore or partially restore acoustic speech cues that are significant to meaning, that have been lost because of perceptive omissions and distortions in the patient's residual hearing. Where restoration is not possible, experimental processing has attempted to substitute new acoustic cues that the listener must learn as part of a new speech code.

TYPES OF PERCEPTIVE
DISTORTION AFFECTING RECOGNITION OF SPEECH

Persons suffering from nonconductive hearing impairment are likely to be plagued by a number of perceptive distortions in addition to the loss of hearing acuity. The most familiar of these distortions is the frequency-selective nature of the hearing loss. In the most common type of impairment, hearing loss increases with frequency, and high frequency consonant information is reduced or lost. When the increase of hearing loss at high frequencies is both precipitous and great, the loss is sometimes referred to as the "ski slope" type.

The loss of hearing sensitivity is often accompanied by recruitment, that is, by a recovery of hearing sensitivity as the sound intensity increases above threshold. The patient's loudness response becomes progressively closer to normal at higher levels, implying an abnormally fast growth of loudness with intensity and a reduction of the dynamic range of hearing. Complete recruitment, in which sound at some high intensity level is heard at normal loudness, is common. The discomfort levels of those patients with recruitment who do not have an accompanying conductive impairment are likely to be within the range of normal discomfort levels.

A person with impaired hearing may be subject to abnormal masking effects. Masking may be greater than normal when the masker is of a different frequency than the masked sound (increased spread of masking), or when the masker occurs at a different time than the masked sound (increased forward or backward masking).

Another perceptive distortion, likely to be found in cases of profound deafness, is the loss of frequency selectivity and discrimination.[1] The patient's ability to extract frequency information from speech—to use speech-formant cues and to hear the frequency-intonation patterns of words and sentences—is reduced or destroyed.

Although this list of perceptive distortions is not complete, it includes those distortions to which signal processing has so far been addressed. It is important to realize that a person with impaired hearing is likely to suffer from a multiplicity of simultaneous distortions, and that any one of these distortions may be sufficient to erode or destroy intelligibility. The designer of signal-processing experiments must therefore take into consideration the possibility that a particular

---

[1] Frequency selectivity is the ability to distinguish frequency components that occur simultaneously in a complex sound. Frequency discrimination is the ability to distinguish the difference in frequency between successive signals (Evans, 1977).

processing scheme is a necessary but insufficient measure for improving speech reception for a particular subject.

SIGNAL PROCESSING IN CURRENT HEARING AIDS

Low Frequency Rolloff

Parker (1953) reported that a sharp low frequency rolloff at 670 Hz improved, by about one-fourth, the average of PB word scores for eight of his ten subjects with sensorineural hearing impairment. Parker attributed the improvement primarily to a relief of the forward-masking effect of low frequency, high intensity vowel sounds on succeeding high frequency, low intensity consonants. It is significant that two of Parker's subjects showed a large reduction in word list scores when the low frequency rolloff was introduced: from 46% to 28%, and from 66% to 12%.

Low frequency rolloff may also be beneficial to some patients for reasons other than the relief of forward masking. It may improve their perception of higher frequency vowel formants and formant transitions, either by reducing the effect of an abnormal spread of masking from lower frequency formants (Danaher and Pickett, 1975), or by reducing amplification in a frequency region where the patient has reduced hearing loss.

The Veterans Administration yearly publication *Hearing Aid Performance Measurement Data and Hearing Aid Selection Procedures* shows that most current hearing aids provide a low frequency rolloff of 12–18 dB/octave below a transition frequency in the region of 700 Hz to 1 kHz, while a few provide flat response between 250 Hz and 1 kHz.[2] The rolloff can be expected to benefit most patients and to be bad for a few.

Low frequency attenuation can also be introduced by a vented or open earmold. An open mold allows sound in the frequency range below approximately 1 kHz to enter the ear unamplified. An open mold can be used with the microphone on the same side of the head as the receiver when the gain required is not very large. The Contralateral Routing of Signals (CROS) configuration, which places the microphone on the opposite side of the head from the receiver, allows a combination of open earmold and higher gain.

No rigorous studies exist that make it possible to predict when a patient will benefit from flat response below 1 kHz. Ling (1964)

---

[2] The Veterans Administration curves are of coupler measurements, but in the frequency range below 1 kHz such measurements are good representations of real-ear response.

showed benefits from extended (but still sloping) low frequency amplification for profoundly deaf subjects. Such subjects are likely to have
useful residual hearing at low frequencies only, and it stands to reason
that such a patient cannot afford to lose low frequency speech
information in the amplified signal. The two Parker subjects whose
intelligibility scores were reduced by the 670-Hz cutoff were the ones
with the most severe high frequency losses, which is consistent with
Ling's results.

Although some hearing aids have an electrical adjustment for the
low frequency rolloff, the control provided is usually over only a small
range.

High Frequency Emphasis

Many current hearing aids have coupler-measured response curves
that show some degree of high frequency emphasis relative to 1 kHz.
The amount of emphasis, with a few exceptions, is limited to a total of
5–10 dB. Control of high frequency emphasis is sometimes provided,
but such control is typically over a small range.

This high frequency emphasis is for the purpose of compensating
for the common increase of hearing loss with frequency above 1 kHz.
However, as will be seen in the discussion of inadvertent hearing aid
processing, the frequency response recorded in a coupler measurement
is quite different from the effective response of the hearing aid when it
is in place on a real ear. A response measurement that compares aided
to unaided hearing sensitivity directly will show that the high frequency emphasis of the coupler measurement is exaggerated, and may
not exist at all.

The control of high frequency response in fitting a hearing aid
today is for the most part accomplished by choosing among different
models, a very coarse method of control. It can also be accomplished
by manipulation of the earmold bore and tubing, as described by
Killion (1976).

Limiting

Limiting prevents the hearing aid from producing sound beyond a
given sound pressure level (SPL). It protects the user against
amplified high intensity sounds that might otherwise become painfully
loud. It allows the user to set his hearing aid volume control for the
best level for speech, without having to provide himself with a protec-
tive margin against occasional high intensity sounds in the environment.

The simplest form of limiting is in allowing the output transistor
to reach saturation at the signal-output protection level. This mode of

operation creates high distortion. A more sophisticated form of limiting, called compression limiting, uses an amplitude compressor with a high compression ratio (the ratio, expressed arithmetically, of input level change in decibels to output level change), in which the threshold of compression (the input level at which compression begins to operate) is set so that compression does not begin to operate until just below the maximum sound pressure level that is intended to reach the patient. For example, if compression is first engaged when the output reaches 123 dB SPL, and the compression ratio is 10:1, a 20-dB increase of gain or of input level will increase the output by only 2 dB, to 125 dB SPL. This protection is achieved without the high distortion of the transistor-saturation system.

When the limiting circuit is placed after the volume control (as is usually done), so that the signal level cannot be varied after limiting, the system is referred to as output limiting. When the limiting circuit is placed before the volume control, allowing variation of the level of the limited signal, the system is called input limiting.

Slow-Acting, Full Range Amplitude Compression

Slow amplitude compression refers to compression with relatively long attack and release times. The compression threshold is made low enough so that the compressor operates over all or most of the dynamic range of speech, but the response of the compressor is sluggish, so that it cannot reduce the differences in level among speech elements that succeed one another rapidly. This type of compression is designed to reduce the amount of variation in long-term average speech levels. It can, for example, reduce the intensity differences between stressed and unstressed words in a sentence, or among the voices of talkers at different distances from the listener, but it cannot act on the intensity difference between a vowel and an adjacent consonant in the same syllable. Slow compression is sometimes referred to as automatic volume control or AVC.

Fast, Full Range Amplitude Compression

Fast compression is also designed to operate over most or all of the dynamic range of speech, and the attack and release times are short enough so that the compressor can reduce the differences in level between high intensity and low intensity elements of the same syllable. An attack time of the order of 1 msec and a release time of the order of 20 msec is about right for this purpose (Villchur, 1973), although doubling these values is likely to be tolerable. Instantaneous release would allow compressor action to follow the instantaneous amplitude of individual wave forms, an operating mode that would create severe distortion in a conventional compression system.

Fast compression is intended to compensate for recruitment, which creates an exaggerated contrast of loudness relationships within the same syllable as well as among different syllables and words in a sentence, and which can reduce intelligibility severely. In speech perception marred by recruitment, weak consonants are likely to drop below hearing threshold even after the speech has been amplified as much as the patient will tolerate, that is, to any level that keeps high amplitude speech elements below discomfort levels.

The compressors in current hearing aids are of the single-channel type, which means that one compressor is assigned to the entire frequency spectrum. It follows that a) the instantaneous gain of the compressor over the entire frequency spectrum is controlled by whatever input signal element has the highest intensity at a given moment, and b) the compression ratio, which determines the degree to which signal level contrasts at the input are reduced in the output, must be the same at all frequencies. Thus the intensity relationships between two simultaneous signals cannot be changed: a high level, low frequency noise will reduce the gain of the hearing aid for high frequency consonants occurring at the same time, although the opposite effect is needed. Furthermore, the common need for higher compression ratios at higher frequencies, to compensate for the typical decrease of the dynamic range of hearing at higher frequencies, cannot be met.

Figure 1 shows the relationship between the signal output and signal input in a full range compressor and in a compression limiter.

Inadvertent Signal Processing by Hearing Aids: Adding to the Effects of Perceptive Distortion

Hearing aids have been improved greatly over the past decades, but they have failed to provide proper compensation for recruitment and for accentuated high frequency loss. Ironically, in some ways they have contributed to making these perceptive distortions less tolerable.

The pinna and the ear canal have significant effects on the frequency distribution of received signals (Shaw, 1974), and the conventional modern hearing aid bypasses these effects. An insert earmold raises the resonance frequency of the ear canal to a frequency that is typically above the band useful to the hearing aid user, except when the canal is left open. A hearing aid that measures flat in a coupler really has a broad dip, centered at 2.5–3 kHz, if we compare its response in the coupler with that in actual use, or with the response of

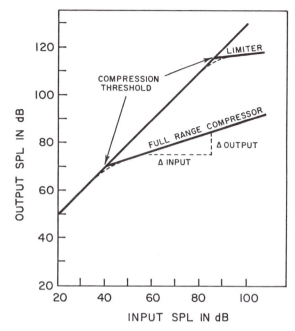

Figure 1.   Relationship between signal input and signal output in compression amplification. The 45° diagonal represents linear amplification with 30 dB of gain. The compression ratio (Δ input/Δ output) of the full range compressor is 3: The compression ratio of the limiter is 10. The output of the full range compressor would normally be subject to further amplification.

good over-the-ear earphones. This is a point that has been emphasized in recent years by Pascoe (1975), by Dalsgaard and Jensen, (1976), and by the introduction of the KEMAR manikin, described by Burkhard and Sachs (1975).

The differences between the coupler-measured frequency response of a hearing aid and its effective response relative to unaided listening vary with the individual user and with the location of the receiving microphone. Dalsgaard and Jensen have made probe-tube measurements of these differences on a group of subjects for three types of microphone mounting (as worn in a body aid, in an ear-level aid with a front-facing microphone, and in an ear-level aid with a bottom microphone). Pascoe has made aided versus unaided threshold measurements with the hearing aid microphone in eyeglass frames. The Dalsgaard-Jensen measurements for an ear-level aid with a front-facing microphone are shown in Figure 2. The differences between coupler and probe-tube measurements in Figure 2 would have been greater if it were

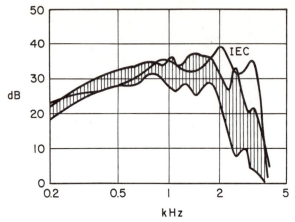

Figure 2.   Frequency-response measurements of an ear-level hearing aid with front-facing microphone. *Solid line:* 2-cc coupler measurement. *Shaded area:* Range of functional response of the aid, under the conditions that the earmold seals the ear canal and the listener faces the sound source, for five subjects. Measurements were made with a probe-tube microphone. (From Dalsgaard and Jensen, 1976; reprinted with permission.)

not for the fact that a 2-cc coupler understates real-ear receiver response above 800 Hz by almost 4 dB/octave (Sachs and Burkhard, 1972).

The most accurate way to assess what Pascoe calls the functional frequency response of a hearing aid is to compare aided with unaided thresholds, or aided with unaided ear canal SPLs measured with a probe microphone, for the individual subject listening in the free field. Another method is to measure the hearing aid response on KEMAR. The cheapest and the easiest method is to use coupler measurements and to extrapolate them to real-ear, free field measurements with correction curves derived from KEMAR measurements or from the averages of measurements such as those in Figure 2, chosen for a particular type of microphone mounting. The last two methods do not take individual patient differences into account, but they are much more valid than using coupler measurements directly to represent the effective frequency response of a hearing aid.

A sharp peak in hearing aid response will increase the problems of recruitment. A large part of the limited dynamic range available to the patient may be used up by the narrow peak, and he will be prevented from using enough amplification for the rest of the frequency band, which contains most of the speech information. The more limited the dynamic hearing range of the patient, the more crucial it is to give him a hearing aid with smooth response. The patient's adjustment of hearing aid gain may be more a function of peak-frequency signal level (which he must keep below discomfort) than of the overall level of the speech. For the profoundly deaf, a single sharp response peak can reduce by more than half the dynamic range of input signal available to the patient, as illustrated in Figure 3.

Smooth frequency response in a hearing aid is possible through proper management of the earmold and tubing. The principles of this management are discussed by Lybarger (1972), and Killion (1976) has developed and described an effective method of adjusting tubing/earmold characteristics. In the Killion design, damping plugs suitable to the cross-section and length of the tubing are inserted at proper points of the acoustical path from receiver to the inner tip of the earmold, and the cross-sectional area of this path is made progressively larger as it approaches the ear canal. These design procedures result in a very substantial improvement in the smoothness of the overall frequency response of the hearing aid.

Current hearing aids, with only a few exceptions, have little or no useful response above 3.5 or 4 kHz. The attendant loss of high fre-

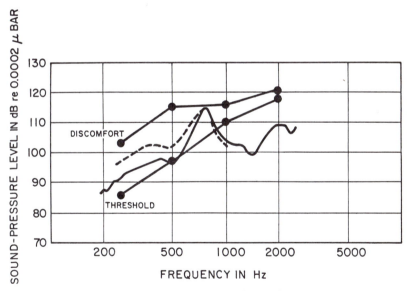

Figure 3.   Effect of peaked hearing aid response. The threshold and discomfort curves outline the average dynamic range of hearing of a group of profoundly deaf children at the Clarke School for the Deaf. The *irregular solid line* is the frequency response of a commercial hearing aid, as reported by the Veterans Administration in 1973. The *dashed line* shows maximum speech levels over the frequency spectrum that can be produced by this aid without exceeding patient discomfort at the frequency of the peak, making allowances for the frequency distribution of speech energy.

quency speech information would not be very significant to normal listeners, but the loss may be more important to persons with sensorineural deafness, who do not have access to as large a reserve of redundant speech cues as normal listeners do. Ross (1975) has summarized a group of experimental studies that reported the advantage to the hearing impaired of extending the upper frequency range of hearing aids beyond the current norm. Killion's design for hearing aid "plumbing," in addition to reducing the irregularity of frequency response, is capable of extending high frequency response significantly.

In some cases of sensorineural deafness the dynamic range of hearing between threshold and discomfort becomes very small at high frequencies. When this condition exists, a high frequency cutoff in the hearing aid may be beneficial; it protects the ear from high frequency speech energy that seems to do more harm than good. Piminow (1963) has reported that high frequency suppression can be useful for the severely deaf, and one of the subjects represented in Figure 5 (Villchur, 1973), who had a dynamic range of hearing at 4 kHz of only a few decibels, required a sharp rolloff in amplifier response above 3.5 kHz for the best speech reception.

EXPERIMENTAL SIGNAL PROCESSING

Amplitude Compression

The early history of amplitude-compression processing consisted of various experimenters in the field presenting well thought-out hypotheses as to why compression *should* work. The first reasoned proposal for using compression as compensation for recruitment, that I am aware of, was made by Steinberg and Gardner (1937). They wrote: "owing to the expanding action of this type of loss [they were referring to recruitment] it would be necessary to introduce a corresponding compression in the amplifier. . . ."

Caraway and Carhart (1967) reported an experiment with 36 hearing-impaired subjects that cast a pall of gloom on hopes that compression would prove useful in hearing aids. They reported that their subjects were unable to take significant advantage of the increased speech information that compression was capable of providing.

More recent experimental work on compression has been reported by Villchur (1973, 1974), Barfod (1976), and Yanick (1976). A common denominator of the methods used by these experimenters

is that signal processing is based on an analysis of the hearing characteristics of the subject: an attempt is made to present the signal to the
individual subject in a form most suitable to his abnormal dynamic
span of hearing, as this span varies over the frequency spectrum.

All of the above experimenters use a two- or multichannel
approach. They do not compress the speech band as a whole, but
divide it into separate frequency bands and compress each band
separately, according to the requirements of the subject's residual
dynamic range of hearing in that band. Thus, elements of the speech
signal or of noise in one frequency band do not provide inappropriate
control of speech-signal elements in another frequency band. The
compression ratios for each channel are chosen on the basis of the
relationship between the abnormal and the normal hearing span in the
frequency band of that channel, and postcompression frequency-selective amplification is used, either by amplifying the channels selectively
or by applying frequency-selective amplification to the summed
output of all channels.

Another characteristic that these compression systems have in
common is the choice of compression thresholds, at levels low enough
that the weak elements of speech receive the increased relative amplification provided by compression, and high enough so that noise that
is below speech levels can fall away as rapidly as possible.

Finally, all of the compressors used in the later experimental
studies were able to perform their tasks with many times less wave-
form distortion than was accepted a decade ago.

The use of complex circuitry to compensate for recruitment can
only be justified if there is good evidence that recruitment deteriorates
speech intelligibility significantly. Two types of models have been used
to demonstrate the effects of recruitment on intelligibility (Villchur,
1973, 1974). One model consisted of a bank of amplitude expanders
followed by a filter,[3] and the other used normal listeners subjected to
masking by frequency-shaped noise.[4] Either the expanders or the
masking produced thresholds and equal-loudness contours in normals
similar to those of hearing-impaired subjects with recruitment, and
either the simulated or the induced recruitment was sufficient to
reduce intelligibility severely at the listener's preferred level. In each
case intelligibility was restored by a combination of compression and

---

[3] An amplitude expander performs a function opposite to that of a compressor: The
gain increases rather than decreases with input level, and this increasing gain can be
used to stimulate the accelerated loudness growth of recruitment.

[4] The temporary hearing loss created by masking is accompanied by recruitment,
as pointed out by Steinberg and Gardner (1937).

frequency-selective amplification, indicating that it was indeed the artificially accelerated loudness growth that had been responsible for the loss of intelligibility.

Figure 4 shows the relationship between the frequency/amplitude characteristics of conversational speech and the frequency/amplitude characteristics of the hearing of a normal listener. The speech was measured by Dunn and White (1940) in ½-octave bands and ⅛-sec intervals at 30 cm from the talker. The highest amplitude elements of short term speech levels fall close to the ISO 74-phon equal-loudness contour, a little past the middle of the threshold-discomfort dynamic range. It should be noted that there is a generous amount of headroom between the highest speech levels and discomfort levels, and that the low amplitude elements of speech lie well above normal threshold.

Figure 5 shows the corresponding relationship between the frequency/amplitude characteristics of speech and the hearing characteristics of a hearing-impaired subject. The threshold levels and equal-loudness contour represent average measured values for six subjects with moderate-to-severe sensorineural deafness. The 1-kHz reference levels for each equal-loudness measurement were determined by the

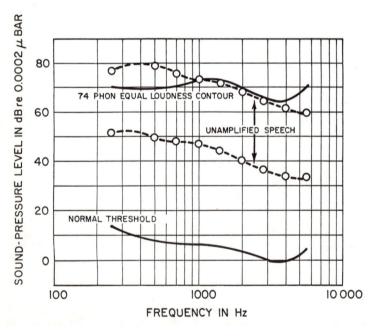

Figure 4. Proportionate positions of conversational speech levels (as measured by Dunn and White, 1940) relative to amplitude range between normal thresholds and the ISO 74-phon equal loudness contour (Villchur, 1973).

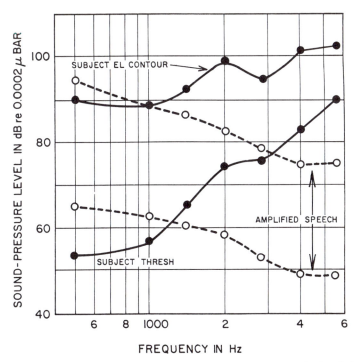

Figure 5.   Levels of amplified speech (at subject's preferred all-pass level) relative to amplitude range between thresholds and equal-loudness contour of hearing-impaired subjects (From Villchur, 1974; reprinted with permission.)

subject's preferred all-pass level for listening to amplified speech. Thus the relationship between this deaf-subject equal-loudness contour and the amplified speech at preferred listening level is analogous to the relationship shown in Figure 5 between the 74-phon normal equal-loudness contour and unamplified speech at conversational level.[5]

It is evident from Figure 5 that a large and significant part of the speech will be inaudible to the subject represented, even after he uses the amount of amplification that he prefers. Much of the acoustic information identifying consonants appears at levels below his threshold. More gain would lift some of the low amplitude speech elements above his threshold, but would invoke the danger of amplifying high amplitude sound past his discomfort level.

---

[5] The 30-cm distance used in the Dunn-White measurements makes for speech levels higher than the levels of most conversational speech. An equal-loudness contour lower than the 74-phon contour might have been more representative of everyday conditions.

Compression processing reduces the dynamic range of the input signal to fit a reduced dynamic range of hearing. The normal dynamic range of hearing that includes conversational speech—shown in Figure 4 as the distance between threshold and the 74-phon equal loudness contour—is about 66 dB at all frequencies from 1–4 kHz. The corresponding abnormal hearing span shown in Figure 5, relative to speech amplified to the subject's preferred level, is 32 dB at 1 kHz and 19 dB at 4 kHz. Following the method of calculation that I used (Villchur, 1973), the relationship between normal and abnormal hearing spans calls for a compression ratio of 2:1 at 1 kHz and 3.5:1 at 4 kHz. Furthermore, if the higher frequency elements of the compressed speech are to be brought within the hearing span of the subject represented in Figure 5, equalization in the form of high frequency emphasis relative to 1 kHz is required.

It is of interest that when the six subjects of Figure 5 were allowed to make their own processing adjustments for intelligibility, they chose to reduce high band compression ratios to an average of 2.8:1, and to reduce the calculated high frequency emphasis in the range above 3 kHz.

Figure 6 shows the ideal compression/equalization processing calculated for one of the six subjects of Figure 5. The actual processing, which used two-band compression combined with frequency shaping, produced only an approximation of the processed-speech band shown. The dynamic range of the speech was first reduced by compression (using a higher compression ratio for the high frequency band, which extended down to 1.5 kHz), to make it possible for the processed speech to fit between the subject's thresholds and his preferred-speech-level equal-loudness contour. High frequency emphasis (calculated in terms of functional gain) was then applied, which tilted the compressed speech band so that it would, at the subject's preferred overall level, be amplified to its proper relative levels over the frequency spectrum. If compression had been used without frequency equalization for this subject, the levels of some critical high frequency elements of speech would only have been lifted from well below his threshold to just below his threshold. However, the subject performed better with an equalization curve that provided no further high frequency emphasis above 4 kHz.

Encouraging results have been reported in improving speech intelligibility for subjects with recruitment by the use of compression/ equalization processing, but these results must be considered experimental only. Further laboratory and field experiments are required.

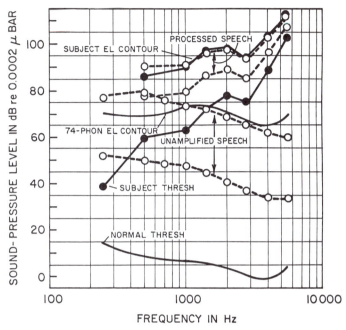

Figure 6.   Ideal compression/equalization processing for a subject with recruitment and accentuated high frequency loss. The processed speech levels have the same relative position in the abnormal dynamic span of hearing as the unamplified speech levels have in the normal span (From Villchur, 1973; reprinted with permission.)

Frequency Equalization

Pascoe (1975) was able to improve speech intelligibility for subjects with moderate sensorineural impairment by the use of frequency equalization alone. He used high frequency emphasis, which he described in terms of functional gain rather than in terms of coupler measurements, designing the equalization to match the individual subject's mildly sloping loss at threshold. Barfod (1976) was also able to improve intelligibility significantly by equalization alone. Barfod used equalization that was designed to compensate the subject's equal loudness contour near the amplified peak speech levels, rather than to compensate the threshold curve. The Barfod subjects had worse high frequency impairment than the Pascoe subjects, and Barfod's equalization approach is consistent with this increased loss. Like Pascoe, Barfod calculated his equalization in terms of functional gain.

A common factor in these two experiments was the relatively moderate nature of the hearing losses of the subjects. When a subject

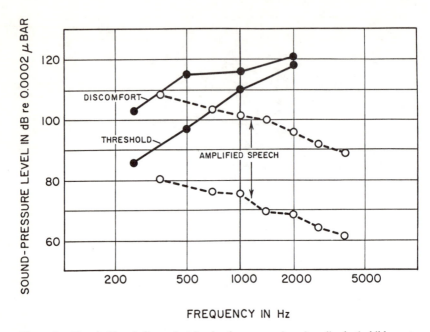

Figure 7.   Threshold and discomfort levels of a group of profoundly deaf children at the Clarke School for the Deaf. Speech is shown amplified as much as discomfort levels will allow. (From Villchur, 1977; reprinted with permission.)

is only moderately deaf, a large amount of headroom remains between the levels at which he chooses to listen to speech and his discomfort levels. When such a subject is using an amplifying system without compression, the loudness relationships that he hears between individual speech elements may not be the same as for normal listeners, but by making the sacrifice of using more amplification than is most comfortable for the vowels, he can bring the weak consonants to a sensation level high enough that he can identify them. A hearing-impaired person who does not have a large amount of headroom above his threshold cannot use this stratagem because high amplitude elements of speech and of other environmental sounds will occasionally reach his discomfort levels.

Even in moderate losses, the use of an appreciable amount of high frequency emphasis in a wearable hearing aid is risky unless compression or limiting is also used. The ringing of a telephone or the clatter of silverware contains high frequency energy that may be amplified to a painful level.

SIGNAL PROCESSING
FOR THE PROFOUNDLY DEAF: SPEECH-ENCODING AIDS

In profound deafness the patient's useful residual hearing is commonly limited to low frequencies, below 1 kHz or even below 500 Hz. Experimental attempts have been made to move high frequency speech information into this low frequency range by arithmetic frequency shifting, by geometric frequency division, or by vocoder systems. These experiments have been reviewed by Pickett (1972). Although some experimenters have reported initially encouraging results, none of the systems has shown consistent success.

One reason that has been used to explain the lack of success of speech-encoding systems is the difficulty of learning a new, unnatural acoustic code for speech recognition. There is, however, another serious difficulty: a profoundly deaf person is likely to suffer from many severe perceptive distortions, any one of which destroys intelligibility, and uncompensated distortions may still be operative in listening to the new speech code. Two potentially disabling perceptive distortions that are not affected by frequency-lowering systems are the loss of frequency resolution (reduction of the ability to differentiate among signal elements on the basis of frequency), and a decrease of the range between threshold and discomfort to very small values.

Franklin (1975) reported that when low and high frequency bands of speech were separated and presented dichotically to subjects with sensorineural hearing impairment, there was an improvement in speech recognition attributable to a release from peripheral masking by the low band. It is possible (Villchur, 1977) that dichotic presentation may also be a useful device in compensating for the lack of frequency resolution.

A severe reduction of the dynamic range of hearing is illustrated in Figure 7, which shows the average threshold and discomfort-level curves of a group of profoundly deaf children at the Clarke School for the Deaf, data reported by Boothroyd (1974). The frequency/amplitude band of conversational speech, amplified to the maximum level allowed by the discomfort-level curve, is plotted against the dynamic hearing range. Even with ideal frequency equalization, which would allow higher frequency portions of the speech to be amplified into the subject's dynamic hearing range, there is good evidence that all elements of speech will frequently drop simultaneously below all thresholds, creating intermittent periods of silence and a broken-up quality that destroys intelligibility (Villchur, 1977). This hypothesis implies that attempts to process speech for the profoundly deaf, as a first order of business, must compensate for their typically narrow dynamic range of hearing. A multichannel compression/equalization system would provide such compensation, and previous processing attempts for this population may have been compromised by the lack of compression. A key to signal-processing experiments is the fact that a particular processing system may be necessary but insufficient for restoring speech intelligibility.

REFERENCES

Barfod, J. 1976. Multi Channel Compression Hearing Aids. Report No. 11, The Acoustics Laboratory, Technical University of Denmark.

Boothroyd, A. 1974. Sensory capabilities in normal and hearing-impaired children. In: R. E. Stark (ed.), Sensory Capabilities of Hearing-Impaired Children. University Park Press, Baltimore.

Boothroyd, A. Private communication.

Braida, L. D., N. I. Durlach, B. L. Hicks, R. P. Lippmann, W. M. Rabinowitz, and C. M. Reed. 1976. Matching speech to residual auditory function. I. Review of previous research on the frequency-gain characteristics for linear amplification systems. II. Review of previous research on amplitude compression. III. Review of previous research on frequency lowering. Report of Research Laboratory of Electronics, Massachusetts Institute of Technology. [For copies write MIT, Rm. 36-709, Cambridge, Mass. 02139.]

Burkhard, M. D., and R. M. Sachs. 1975. Anthropometric manikin for acoustic research. J. Acoust. Soc. Am. 58:214–222.

Caraway, B. J., and R. Carhart. 1967. Influence of compressor action on speech intelligibility. J. Acoust. Soc. Am. 41:1424–1433.

Dalsgaard, S. C., and O. D. Jensen. 1976. "Measurement of the insertion gain of hearing aids" J. Audiol. Tech. 15:170–183.

Danaher, E. M., and J. M. Pickett. 1975. Some masking effects produced by low-frequency vowel formants in persons with sensorineural hearing loss. J. Speech Hear. Res. 18:261–271.

Dunn, H. K., and S. D. White. 1940. Statistical measurements on conversational speech. J. Acoust. Soc. Am. 11:278–288.

Evans, E. F. 1977. Peripheral auditory processing in normal and pathological ears. Eighth Danavox Symposium, Sensorineural Hearing Impairment and Hearing Aids. Scand. Audiol. Suppl. 6.

Franklin, B. 1975. The effect of combining low- and high-frequency passbands on consonant recognition in the hearing impaired. J. Speech Hear. Res. 18:719–727.

Killion, M. C. 1976. Earmold plumbing for wide-band hearing aids. J. Acoust. Soc. Am. 59(Suppl. 1):S62(A). [Full report available from Industrial Research Products, Inc., a Knowles Co., 321 Bond Street, Elk Grove Village, Ill. 60007.]

Ling, D. 1964. Implications of hearing aid amplification below 300 cps. Volta Rev. 66:723–729.

Lybarger, S. F. 1972. Ear molds. In: J. Katz (ed.), Handbook of Clinical Audiology, Chap. 32. The Williams and Wilkins Company, Baltimore.

Parker, C. 1953. The effects of the reduction of "short time fatigue" on speech intelligibility for "perceptively" deafened individuals. Ph.D. thesis, State University of Iowa.

Pascoe, D. P. 1975. Frequency responses of hearing aids and their effects on the speech perception of hearing-impaired subjects. Ann. Otol. Rhinol. Laryngol. 84:(Suppl. 23).

Pickett, J. M. 1972. Status of speech-analyzing communication aids for the deaf. IEEE Trans. Aud. Electroacoust. V. AU-20. 1:3–8.

Piminow, L. 1963. The application of synthetic speech to aural rehabilitation. J. Audiol. Res. 3:73–82.

Ross, M. 1975. Hearing aid selection for pre-verbal hearing-impaired children. In: M. Pollack (ed.), Amplification for the Hearing Impaired. Grune & Stratton, Inc., New York.

Sachs, R. M., and M. D. Burkhard. 1972. Zwislocki Coupler Evaluation with Insert Earphones. Report No. 20022-1, Industrial Research Products, Inc., Elk Grove Village, Ill.

Shaw, E. A. G. 1974. The external ear. In: W. D. Keidel and W. D. Neff (ed.) Handbook of Sensory Physiology, Vol. V/1, Auditory Systems. Springer-Verlag, New York.

Steinberg, J. C., and M. B. Gardner. 1937. The dependence of hearing impairment on sound intensity. J. Acoust. Soc. Am. 9:11–23.

Veterans Administration (Annual). Hearing Aid Performance Measurement Data and Hearing Aid Selection Procedures (U.S. Government Printing Office, Washington, D.C.

Villchur, E. 1973. Signal processing to improve speech intelligibility in perceptive deafness. J. Acoust. Soc. Am. 53:1646–1657.

Villchur, E. 1974. Simulation of the effect of recruitment on loudness relationships in speech. J. Acoust. Soc. Am., 56:1601–1611.

Villchur, E. 1977. Electronic models to simulate the effect of sensory distortions on speech perception by the deaf. J. Acoust. Soc. Am. 62:

Yanick, P. 1976. Effects of signal processing on intelligibility of speech in noise for persons with sensorineural hearing loss. J. Am. Audiol. Soc. 1:229–239.

CHAPTER 8

COMPENSATORY ELECTROACOUSTIC PROCESSING OF SPEECH

Ira J. Hirsh

CONTENTS

All children with hearing impairment are faced with a number of problems affecting their biologic, emotional, and cognitive well-being. If the hearing impairment is moderate to severe, and precedes language development, then language learning is difficult. The development of language in humans seems to depend on the child's capacity to hear both his own vocalizations and those of others around him. If the hearing impairment is sustained in school years, after language development has progressed with normal hearing, the most direct effects are on reception of the speech of others and the relation between such speech (whether in the form of teaching, tape-recorded programs or talks, etc.) and the school learning that uses spoken information. In all stages of development and with all degrees of hearing impairment, there is a complex interplay between hearing, language learning, production, and cognitive development.

Thus, when a child's hearing impairment is treated successfully, many other aspects of development and learning are also treated. No matter what the degree of severity of a child's hearing impairment, his communication skills and other products of learning stand to benefit from medical treatment (where possible), special teaching and learning opportunities, and some form of hearing aid or other prosthetic device. The focus of this chapter is those devices: their function, the kind of information that they provide, the listening tasks for which they are helpful, and the ages and degrees of hearing loss for which different kinds are most useful.

The rationale that demands our consideration of prosthetic devices is the following. The audiogram of a hearing-impaired child shows us the degree of hearing loss at the different frequencies tested. Unless medical or surgical treatment can restore that impaired hearing system to normal or nearly normal sensitivity, we must modify the signals that come in so as to compensate for what cannot be heard. For example, if the audiogram shows that there is loss only at the high frequencies, then a hearing aid that emphasizes those same frequencies may be sufficient for almost total rehabilitation. If, on the other hand, the loss is moderate to severe, and involves all frequencies, then a hearing aid alone, even though it is selected carefully to optimize the residual hearing particularly for speech, may not suffice, and the child may need complementary therapy in the form of special teaching for lipreading, speech production, and rules of language, which do not come easily when the input from others is restricted. Finally, if a severe or profound loss shows that there is sensitivity only for the low frequencies (a sensitivity that may be mediated by the skin's tactile system rather than the auditory system), then a hearing aid can provide only cues for that low-frequency region where information regarding the melody, stress pattern, and durations of speech is transmitted. In order for such a child to distinguish among the majority of individual speech sounds, reception by other than auditory means, whether by lipreading or the output of more complicated prosthetic devices for the skin or the eye, will be required. These "compensatory" devices are discussed below.

Now we wish to examine the several ways in which the acoustic representation of speech may be processed or transformed so as to provide a hearing-impaired child with information regarding speech sounds that is as nearly equivalent as possible to that available to a normal hearing child. In discussing the possibilities for various kinds of processing, we need to attend to at least three categories of children with hearing loss: moderately hearing impaired, severely hearing impaired, and profoundly deaf. In addition, we must consider whether the device is to contribute to initial learning, or whether some language learning has already taken place. Another consideration is the kind of listening task in which the suitability or efficacy of a device or system might be demonstrated.

SPEECH-SIGNAL PROCESSING

Because the traditional way of describing a hearing impairment has been the loss of sensitivity or elevation of threshold in decibels, it is natural that the earliest systems for compensating for a hearing loss attempted to reverse the loss in decibels by applying to the speech signal a gain in decibels. The earliest devices were purely mechanical or acoustic, and involved reducing the volume into which speech would be radiated to a mouthpiece and tube. This ensured that all of the energy was contained in a relatively small volume and could thus produce larger pressure changes in the ear canal. Although this reduction of radiation volume into a resonant tube also resulted in bandwidth compression so that what gain was available (about 20 dB) was restricted to a relatively narrow band, fortunately this narrow band was in the region of frequencies important for speech perception (see Goldstein, 1939). The development of the telephone by A. G. Bell also contributed to the development of electrical hearing aids over about a quarter of a century. Then the vacuum tube began a half-century of development of amplifiers that could convert the electrical output of microphones into relatively large electrical signals for earphones. The enormous change was a broadening of bandwidth and increases in gain to 60 dB and more. After that half-century, the vacuum tube was replaced by the transistor, which is used in much the same way but makes possible instruments that are smaller and less demanding of external electrical energy.

The electrical form of speech, such as that produced by a microphone, has in more recent times been subjected to other kinds of processing than mere amplification. Analysis into frequency bands and transformation into pulse codes have been developed for a variety of applications. These schemes have also found their way into the engineering of devices for assisting the hearing impaired. What follows is a brief review of some of the principles involved (see Pickett, 1968).

Acoustic Amplification

Hearing-aid amplification has already been considered by Villchur (Chapter 7). The transduction of acoustic to electrical energy and the subsequent amplification of electrical signals carries certain costs, such as frequency distortion, amplitude distortion, various products of modulation, and the introduction of system noise. All of these factors have been studied in the more general context of telephone and radio transmission. Their effects on speech intelligibility have been reviewed by Fletcher (1950), Miller (1951), and Licklider and Miller (1951).

Most of those results concern normal listeners, however, and the effects of these transmission factors on hard-of-hearing listeners is known less well. The systematic approach of the laboratory with controlled degrees of frequency distortion, of amplitude distortion, and of similar factors has not often been used with hard-of-hearing subjects. What information we have is based largely, with only a few exceptions, on correlative studies that compare the performance in speech intelligibility of individual types or models of hearing aids in circumstances where the investigator either did not or could not specify precisely the value of some of these factors in the aids under study.

Frequency distortion, or modification of bandwidth, is one item to be noted especially. The large bandwidth of the speech signal (200–8000 Hz) had to be sacrificed in the transduction or amplification processes of early hearing aids. Electromechanical microphones and earphones did not transduce equally well at all frequencies. Although the "equalization networks" of radio and telephone transmission were bulky, some of the same compensatory principles were incorporated into subsequent designs in hearing aids. At the same time, it was early observed that because hearing loss did not often occur uniformly at all frequencies, uniform gain was not always the appropriate goal, anyway. This philosophy of tailoring the response of the aid to mirror or compensate for the form of the audiogram held, and still holds to a certain degree, in spite of the Harvard report (Davis et al., 1946) and the British Medical Research Council report (1947), which concluded that uniform response or moderate increase in gain with frequency was suitable for almost all cases. In our own laboratories at The Central Institute for the Deaf (CID) tailoring has again been demonstrated to be effective in a laboratory study aimed at increasing speech intelligibility for older patients (Pascoe, 1975) and for those persons with those sharply discontinuous audiograms associated with noise exposure (Skinner, 1976). These reports concern detailed manipulation of gain as a function of frequency, a manipulation that incorporates not only the audiogram and discomfort thresholds of the patient, but also factors related to the resonance characteristics of the ear canal and the diffraction characteristics of the head (Miller, 1974).

Before turning to other forms of signal processing, we must make one further observation concerning the methods used for evaluating the adequacy of a hearing aid amplification system. The bulk of the clinical literature on this subject refers to intelligibility scores, most often for lists of words delivered in quiet. For older aids, the hope that the addition of a noise background would make hearing aids more distinguishable in terms of intelligibility seemed not to be realized

(Shore, Bilger, and Hirsh, 1960), but with newer types (Pascoe, 1975) the hope revives. As we consider the application of these systems to hearing-impaired children, particularly as used in the youngest years, we shall have to develop other dimensions for evaluation beyond the recognition of items on speech tests. Hearing aids can also be measured in terms of acquisiton of both speech production and listening skills and of language communication over longer segments than words.

Original Acoustic Signal Delivered to Other Senses

The speech signal, either in its original acoustic form or amplified in an electrical form, may of course be directed to senses other than hearing. The original acoustic form with appropriate temporal dynamics is preserved, but the output is applied to an alternative sensory channel. The best known example is provided by Gault (1928), who applied the acoustic speech signal directly to the skin as a vibrotactile stimulus. The results were not outstanding and seem not to be better than those obtained by delivery of the same acoustic energy to the ear canal in acoustic form, where it might be available to either a defective auditory system or the skin. Such direct vibrotactile stimulation with the raw acoustic pattern of speech probably contributes most as a cue supplementary to cues available in lipreading (Erber, 1974). The very rapid changes of speech are not available, partly because of the low-pass characteristic of the vibrotactile receptor system (as used on fingertip or palm), and partly because of the low-pass transducing characteristics of large electromechanical vibrators. Attempts at transducing the same acoustic signal to an electrical output for electrical stimulaton of the skin or for a light output for the eye (for example with a glow-modulator tube or more modern devices) have been almost absent, although Saunders (1974) has tried a one-channel electrocutaneous device and the "voice" bar of Upton's eyeglasses is such an application (Gengel, 1976).

Frequency Analysis with Band Outputs

In radio and telephone transmission, many schemes have been developed to reduce the necessary bandwidth for transmitting speech. Fundamental to some of these systems is the analysis of the original speech signal into contiguous frequency bands. Such analysis has also inspired the development of some alternative schemes for assisting the hearing impaired.

At least two applications have used the electrical output of such bands to drive electroacoustic transducers, that is to render the newly processed speech signal once again into acoustic form. For example, Pimonow (1962) described a device that compresses the reception bandwidth in such a way that the original speech spectrum is squeezed into the frequency region below 300 Hz. In his device the output of each of the analyzing filters was used to modulate a group of more closely spaced low-frequency carriers to synthesize a new kind of acoustic message. Still another scheme, suggested by Johansson (1964), divides the speech spectrum into two parts, and then transmits the low frequencies without change and processes the high frequencies in such a way as to generate low frequencies. A kind of "mirror reflection" around the dividing frequency puts together for the impaired ear the original low frequencies and a new set of low frequencies that correspond in time to high-frequency sounds in the original message. Similar concepts have been reported by Lafon and Perdoncini. Although the history of these developments includes early demonstrations of improved intelligibility, such devices have not been widely accepted.

Speech in electrical form, analyzed into frequency bands, can also be converted to sensory displays other than auditory. Quite a few developments have involved the conversion of such electrical signals to vibratory stimuli, where the output of each band goes to a different place on the skin. Pickett and Pickett (1963) describe one such device, designed in Gunnar Fant's laboratory in Stockholm, in which the outputs of 10 such frequency bands were applied to the 10 fingertips. Some speech sounds and some features could be recognized, but here again the initial successes of the laboratory have not been followed by clinical application. Results seem to be highly dependent on training (Engelmann and Rosov, 1975). More recently, Scott and De Filippo (1976) have described a system that divides the spectrum of speech into two frequency ranges, the low-frequency portion being delivered to the palm surface of the thumb as vibration, and the high-frequency portion to the skin on the back of the thumb as electrocutaneous stimulation. The apparent advantage of this system over earlier tactile ones is that the difference in location on the skin is redundant with a difference in the quality of sensation. Risberg has installed a similar device in some Swedish classrooms. Still further developments along these lines are likely to be made.

The visual analog of such a device might be represented by a row of light sources, each displaying the output of a particular frequency band. But the rapid changes of the speech signal in the outputs of such frequency bands cannot easily be seen by the eye and therefore some translation of both time and intensity into spatial dimensions must be made. In Risberg's "Lucia" visual aid, where amplitude was represented by the length of a vertical column of light, the display essentially formed an acoustic spectrum, which could change quite rapidly for continuous speech. A better known translation is that of "visible speech" (the spectrograph), where time is shown as a left-to-right continuum in space and frequency is represented vertically. The use of the visible-speech direct translator was studied over a rather long period of time and involved research groups at the Bell Telephone Laboratories, a school for the deaf in Ypsilanti, Michigan, and at The Johns Hopkins University (Stark, Cullen, and Chase, 1968). Some intelligibility was realized, and at least a few profoundly deaf individuals have succeeded with purely "visual conversation." The device has not emerged from laboratory studies to classroom use. A similar display has become available recently (Stewart et al., 1976), which is essentially an instantaneous, direct-reading spectrograph. Like the ordinary paper spectrograph, this device is limited to a 2.5-sec segment of speech, and, although apparently quite useful for the teaching of particular items or features of speech production, cannot easily be used for reception of continuous speech.

Following on the model of visible speech, still another device has been designed (Saunders, 1974), which converts the output of frequency bands to electrocutaneous stimulation. Saunders uses one dimension of skin space on the abdomen to represent frequency. Such patterns are like the visible speech patterns on the direct translator, but there is no persistence in time, so that such perception is the analog of viewing visible speech through a narrow vertical slit.

Some systems which have enjoyed extensive use in schools have used a kind of natural frequency analysis. A simple example in the large, electromagnetic vibrator that is held in the hand or the fingertips and which by its very nature imparts to the skin vibratory stimuli for the low frequencies only. Such devices have been described by Børrild (1968), and their efficacy has been demonstrated in a quantitative manner (Erber and Cramer, 1974; Erber, 1974).

Phonetic Coding

The systems for processing speech signals that we have considered so far are characterized by properties of the systems—whether frequency analysis or bandwidth compression—and electrical outputs to either acoustic devices or other transducers. These principles of operation would apply equally well to all kinds of input sounds. Now let us consider the possibility that we could in addition install in an external device some of the properties of the human auditory system that seem to be most relevant for the processing and comprehension of speech sounds. We have acquired much new information over the past several decades about the acoustic characteristics of speech and the particular characteristics or features that are important for the perception of speech. Phonemic feature systems like that of Jakobson, Fant, and Halle (1956), coupled with acoustic analysis and synthesis, have provided a large, although as yet incomplete, catalog of the acoustic features on the basis of which normal listeners discriminate and recognize speech sounds. We know less about the mechanisms of coding and storage that permit comprehension of continuous speech.

In the extreme, we might want a device that "tells" the listener which speech sounds had been presented, without requiring that he make the analysis himself directly from acoustic signals presented to his ears or other kinds of signals presented to other sensory modalities. In short, we speak of a speech-sound recognizer, somewhat like the phonetic typewriter that has been one goal for research programs on automatic speech recognition. This goal is partially realized in the visual feature display of Upton (1968). Upton's eyeglasses contain a small visual display in which distinctive visual signals, vertical or horizontal light bars arranged in a small configuration, indicate the presence of certain phonetic features like voicing, friction, plosivity, etc. The circuitry that recognizes these features is not merely concerned with frequency analysis but also with other features that vary in the time domain. This recognition circuitry is the heart of the device and the visual output is only one of many possibilities that one could think of. Because such a display constitutes, if not a new language, at least a new phonemic feature system within a language, we could infer that a fair amount of learning is involved. Indeed, such seems to be the case in early evaluations (Gengel, 1976).

The basic idea of phonetic coding and the display of different features to different places is not new to practitioners in aural rehabilitation. The combined use of a low-frequency vibrator, a somewhat higher but still low-pass hearing aid and auditory system, and lipreading represents a kind of crude phonetic coding, with voicing and prosody in the low-frequency elements and place of articulation conveyed through lipreading. If we can instrument feature recognizers, then of course their outputs can be addressed to whatever sensory systems are healthy and not otherwise deployed in receiving speech intelligibility. An additional problem, better addressed by other authors in this book, concerns the use of intersound information in coding those individual sounds.

LET THE PROCESSING FIT THE TASK

This brief survey probably presents too much information for the teacher or the audiologist who must decide what sort of signal-processing is most suitable for a particular child. Must we consider hearing aids, vibrators, band-compression systems with outputs for a skin display or for a visual display for all hearing-impaired children? In general, we should remember that the milder the loss and later its onset, the less will be the demand for complex signal processing. A mild hearing loss in an elementary-school child, if it cannot be cleared up by medical treatment, may be largely alleviated by a properly selected hearing aid and some special teaching or rehabilitative procedures. A severe hearing loss in a prelanguage infant will first require amplification at an early age, and later, the learning of good speech production in the nursery, kindergarten, and elementary years may well be aided by some sophisticated visual display that can show the young talker subtle differences that he cannot appreciate by hearing.

The main point of this presentation is to suggest a coordination of the principles underlying development of a given aid, the particular task that the hearing-impaired person is to accomplish, the stage of development when that task is crucially important, and the nature of the impairment. The ideal system could be installed on a very young hearing-impaired baby. It would serve to develop awareness of sound, and would enable the child to infer from the speech of persons around him the rules of his language and its phonologic system, to monitor his own speech so as to provide adequate feedback for correct speech, and to recognize and comprehend speech spoken to him. Such a "super aid" is not likely to be for some time to come.

Several of the contributors to this volume have seen fit to analyze the auditory perceptual function into components: detection, discrimination, identification, and comprehension. The distinctions among these tasks, therefore, need not be repeated here. We should examine, however, how each of the categories of processing outlined above might contribute to these tasks. At the risk of belaboring the obvious, I should point out that the hierarchy that is implied in those four components of auditory perception is not necessarily the order in which those tasks are mastered either in normal development or in the development of the hearing-impaired child (Erber and Hirsh, 1977).

Awareness of Sound

Although not all of the nuances implied by the term "sound awareness" are evident in the writings of experienced teachers of very young deaf children (Whetnall and Fry, 1970; Simmons-Martin, 1976), I am reasonably certain that their use of the term includes detection of sound. However, just as detection can be represented as a discrimination task between signal and no signal, so "awareness of sound" can be represented as the ability to discriminate sound from no sound. This is an important point, which should suggest to us that to be effective, "bathing an infant in sound" should not mean merely constant acoustic stimulation. More important is the contrast between presence and absence of sound. Ramsdell (1960) emphasizes that sounds provide us with information about the ongoing character of life and events around us. This information is conveyed by pulses of sound of different duration and of different repetition rates, which we learn to interpret as signals that a machine started or that a person spoke or that a vehicle went by. (Animals that are raised in light can be functionally as blind as those raised in darkness if the light consists only of a homogeneous, diffuse field without any patterning.) If a hearing aid provided a more or less constant sound consisting of system noise within the aid, clothing noise, uncontrolled environmental noises in the room, etc., it is doubtful that it would serve to enhance sound awareness. In fact, one might argue that it would teach an infant to ignore sound. For some authors (Guberina, 1964; Perdoncini et al., 1966) this possibility is so important that they have withheld hearing aids until the patients have been exposed to rather controlled sounds or vibrations that differ in temporal pattern, in spectrum, and in intensity.

What are the spectral features of these environmental or human sounds of which the infant must become aware? Except for fricative consonants and the output of some steam radiators, these sounds are principally low frequency sounds. Recall that our initial goal is to help the child learn to detect sound, to tell the difference between sound-on and sound-off, and perhaps learn to make more subtle discriminations between long sounds and short sounds, between sounds that recur rapidly and those that recur slowly, etc. Under sound awareness we are not setting as a goal the ability to discriminate among individual sounds, particularly where such discriminations are based on differences in quality or spectrum, fundamental pitch, or loudness. If the teachers of these very young infants really mean that awareness of sound is the first goal to be realized, then the system requirements for this phase of auditory development are not much more complicated than low frequency energy applied directly to the skin as a tactile input. The essential point is that whatever sensory input is used, auditory if possible and tactile if necessary, the stimulus patterns must signal on- and off-characteristics, because, if they can do that, they can also act to signal some basic prosodic features of speech and other sounds: duration, rhythmic stress, number of sound events, etc.

Social Communication

Soon after a normal infant becomes aware of sound, he also comes to appreciate the utility of sound in interacting with others. He quickly learns that his own production of sounds can be followed by satisfactions: smiles, expressions of affection, food, comfort. Real interaction is accompanied by his own reaction to the sounds of others, and in particular to differences in those sounds. Before we require that hearing-impaired infants begin to discriminate the frequency of sound formants or voice-onset time, we should remind ourselves that social communication at an early age does not consist of well formed sentences whose words are drawn from vocabularies of several hundred thousand words. A limited amount of information is transmitted in this early communication, and not many different categories need to be discriminated or remembered. Precision is not the hallmark either of speech production or speech reception in the early stages of development. Even up through the early elementary grades, articulatory habits of young normal hearing children are quite sloppy, not nearly so precise as those of adults (Eguchi and Hirsh, 1969). Later on, as vocabulary increases, as sentences grow longer and more elaborate, social communication draws on a greater repertory of speech sounds and requires greater precision in distinguishing among them. It is my opinion, not based on clear scientific evidence, that the processing of the speech signal aimed at displaying acoustic differences between phonemes would not be used until late stages of language acquisition. I expect to hold this opinion until such a time as the processing devices are small enough and batter-proof enough to warrant installation and everyday use by infants or younger children.

Pattern Discrimination

Much of our new knowledge in acoustic phonetics concerns contrasts between phonemes within phoneme families. It is natural, therefore, that many processing schemes have focused on the cues associated with such contrasts. English vowels differ principally in the location in frequency of first and second formants. The spectrogram and "Lucia" display those formants very well to the eye. Such visual indicators may serve as feedback for vowel production. They are more limited as devices for receiving vowel information, not only because they are large and bulky, but also because the eyes can apparently do better reading lips than reading such visual displays. Even more sophisticated devices, like the computer-derived display of the surface of the tongue, seem more appropriate to instruction in production than in reception. Some contrasts, like /s/ and /sh/, are also based on spectral differences and therefore frequency-band analysis can yield displays helpful for discrimination. Here again, such visual displays, a simple S-light or S-meter, can be useful in speech training.

More sophisticated schemes may be used to encode other phonemes or phonemic features. Without recounting the catalog, we can state the basic principles. If the acoustic characteristics of a feature can be specified, and further can be defined across a variety of talkers, then circuitry can probably be designed to create an output signalling that feature. However, in narrative speech, such features occur in bundles within phones, and the phones follow each other rapidly with sequential pre-effects or posteffects. Two consequences follow. First, instruction on feature combinations for correct production or recognition of speech sounds must be generalized from the isolated example to the context of continuous speech to demonstrate the validity of the instruction. Second, in order to render successfully the stream of speech, features and phones, the display must use dimensions in one or another sense modality to encode time variations.

Prospects for practical engineering of systems for transforming speech signals into displays for the eye and skin are promising indeed. When such displays can portray phoneme targets or phoneme features they will likely find enthusiastic application in instruction. Remember, however, that those who will benefit most from such aids are severely or profoundly deaf children whose reception or monitoring of speech cannot be served by auditory systems alone.

Speech and Language

The ultimate goal of a processing system or sensory aid for the profoundly deaf is to serve as a self-contained communication device, one which is able to provide otherwise unavailable information sufficient to permit conversation, attendance at lectures and church, and the enjoyment of radio, television, motion pictures, and other auditory experiences. There are three problems connected with the design of such a device. Two have already been mentioned: first, there is the technical problem of displaying the processed form of phones or phonemic features when the transitions to and from such phones are missing; second, there is the modality problem, where eye or skin are called on to handle long successions of rapidly changing events. A discussion of alternative processing systems must take note of the compatibility between dimensions of the stimulus pattern and dimensions of perception peculiar to different sensory modalities (Julesz and Hirsh, 1972). There are some aspects of the acoustic form of speech that seem to be inherently characteristic of sound. In particular, I would emphasize the notions of change, rate of change, and rhythmic pattern in the acoustic message. Although sometimes these temporal aspects must be sacrificed when speech is processed for a less temporally sensitive modality, it is probably essential that some temporal features be preserved. On the other hand, if preservation of temporal form requires holding to an acoustic representation of the signal that cannot be heard, then we must yield to some sort of transformation that cannot portray time as time.

The third problem concerns memory, both long-term memory in which phonologic and grammatical rules and semantic knowledge are stored, and short-term memory that allows us to hold incoming chunks of information until relations and patterns among them are established. It may be that the auditory or articulatory form in which verbal material is held in short term memory is a result of years of normal speaking and hearing, but we cannot assume that other forms of sensory input would serve the storage role as well.

OTHER SENSORY MODALITIES

There seem to be four characteristics of the auditory system that make it markedly superior to others for the perception of speech: frequency analysis, handling of rapid temporal changes, immediate and direct monitoring of speech production, and a state of being open at all times and in all directions to acoustic input.

In that frequency range corresponding roughly to periodicity pitch, acoustic stimulation of even severely impaired auditory systems (but not of the profoundly deaf) can provide some frequency discrimination that permits the recognition of the melody or prosodic features of speech and usually of variations in the first formant of vowels. Frequency analysis in the upper range of frequencies will most likely benefit from stimulation to other sensory modalities, although neither the skin nor the eye can resolve high-frequency differences directly. Some sort of transformation must be made into another dimension, such as the vertical axis of the spectrogram, for vision or tactile perception.

For rapidly changing events, periodicities up to about 200 Hz seem to be distinguishable on the skin but not in the eye. Even more rapid changes and continuous transitions among the sounds of speech can be represented, but again the time and frequency domains must be transformed to dimensions of space, certainly for the eye and in many instances for the skin.

The immediacy of feedback from speech production is closely related to the fact that the ears are always open. With normal hearing, one cannot escape monitoring his own speech. Displays that attempt to portray speech features must be accompanied by training that is long enough to establish a habitual association between the display and the articulatory and phonatory gestures, analogous to that formed between speech and hearing from the earliest months of sound-making in the crib.

SUMMARY

Some principles have been reviewed of actual or possible systems for processing the acoustic form of speech in such a way as to provide speech information for persons with impaired hearing. At this time, it seems that either acoustic amplification or transformation to a direct vibrotactile stimulus will permit the first stages of sound awareness and may even, when combined with lipreading, allow gross discriminations among a small set of sounds needed for early stages of social communication.

More subtle differences between speech sounds can also be displayed by sophisticated electronic circuits that produce outputs corresponding either to major acoustic dimensions or to coded phonetic dimensions. So far, such displays for the skin or for the eye, because they are focused on particular phonemic dimensions, seem to be most usable in situations in which those phonemic dimensions themselves are a subject of instruction, such as in speech training. A combination of such displays, which could be used by severely or profoundly hearing-impaired persons to receive continuous speech, remains a hope that is not yet realized.

Further analysis of how the normal auditory system perceives speech may suggest new techniques for translating speech into other sensory forms. We should then be able to apply such techniques in helping the hearing-impaired individual make use of his healthy sensory systems for speech communication.

REFERENCES

Børrild, K. 1968. Experience with the design and use of technical aids for the training of deaf and hard of hearing children. Am. Ann. Deaf 113:168–177.

Davis, H., C. W. Hudgins, R. J. Marquis, R. H. Nichols, G. E. Peterson, D. A. Ross, and S. S. Stevens. 1946. The selection of hearing aids. Laryngoscope 56:135–163.

Eguchi, S., and I. J. Hirsh. 1969. Development of speech sounds in children. Acta Otolaryngol. Suppl. 257.

Engelmann, S., and R. Rosov. 1975. Tactual hearing experiment with deaf and hearing subjects. Except. Child. 41:243–253.

Erber, N. P. 1974. Auditory-visual perception of speech: A survey. In: H. B. Nielsen and E. Kampp (eds.), Visual and Audio-Visual Perception of Speech, pp. 12–30. Almqvist & Wiksell Periodical Company, Stockholm.

Erber, N. P., and K. D. Cramer. 1974. Vibrotactile recognition of sentences. Am. Ann. Deaf 119:716–720.

Erber, N. P., and I. J. Hirsh. 1977. Auditory training. In: H. Davis and S. R. Silverman (eds.), Hearing and Deafness. 4th Ed. Holt, Rinehart and Winston, Inc., New York.

Fletcher, H. 1950. Speech and Hearing in Communication. van Nostrand, New York.

Gault, R. H. 1928. On the extension of the use of the sense of touch in relation to the training and education of the deaf. Am. Ann. Deaf 73:134–146.

Gengel, R. W. 1976. Upton's wearable eyeglass speechreading aid: History and current status. In: S. K. Hirsh et al. (eds.), Hearing and Davis, pp. 291–299. Washington University Press, St. Louis.

Goldstein, M. 1939. The Acoustic Method. Laryngoscope Press, St. Louis.

Guberina, P. 1964. Verbo-tonal method and its application to the deaf. Proceedings of the International Congress for the Deaf, Gallaudet College, Washington, D.C.

Jakobson, R., Fant, G., and Halle, M. 1956. Preliminaries to Speech Analysis. The MIT Press, Cambridge, Mass.

Johansson, B. 1964. New coding amplifier system for the deaf. Proceedings of the 3rd International Congress on Acoustics, pp. 655–657. Elsevier, Amsterdam.

Julesz, B., and I. J. Hirsh. 1972. Visual and auditory perception—An essay of comparison. In: E. E. Davis and P. B. Denes (eds.), Human Communication: A Unified View, pp. 283–340. McGraw-Hill Book Company, New York.

Lafon, J. C. 1966. Appareil amplificateur à compensation pour la surdité profonde. Int. Audiol. 6:343–345.

Licklider, J. C. R., and G. A. Miller. 1951. The perception of speech. In: S. S. Stevens (ed.), Handbook of Experimental Psychology, Ch. 26. John Wiley & Sons Inc., New York.

Medical Research Council 1947. Committee on Electro-Acoustics. Hearing

Aids and Audiometers. MRC Special Report Series No. 261, HM Stat. Off. London.

Miller, G. A. 1951. Language and Communication. McGraw-Hill Book Company, New York.

Miller, J. D. 1974. Possible importance of head-diffraction and ear canal resonance for speech perception and hearing-aid design. J. Acoust. Soc. Am. 55:462(A).

Pascoe, D. P. 1975. Frequency responses of hearing aids and their effects on the speech perception of hearing-impaired subjects. Ann. Otol. Rhinol. Laryngol. 84(suppl. 23):1–40.

Perdoncini, G., E. Jucker, and A. Lehmann. 1966. Nouvelles protheses auditives. Int. Audiol. 6:346–349.

Pickett, J. M. (ed.). 1968. Conference on speech-analyzing aids for the deaf. Am. Ann. Deaf 113:116–326.

Pickett, J. M., and B. H. Pickett. 1963. Tactual communication of speech sounds by a tactual vocoder. J. Speech Hear. Res. 6:207–222.

Pimonow, L. 1962. Vibrations en Régime Transitoire. Dunod, Paris.

Ramsdell, D. A. 1960. Psychology of the hard-of-hearing and deafened adult. In: H. Davis and S. R. Silverman (eds.), Hearing and Deafness. Revised Ed. Holt, Rinehart, and Winston, Inc., New York.

Risberg, A. 1968. Visual aids for speech correction. Am. Ann. Deaf 113:178–194.

Saunders, F. A. 1974. Electrocutaneous displays. In: F. A. Geldard (ed.), Conference on Vibrotactile Communication. The Psychonomic Society, Austin, Tex.

Scott, B. L., and C. L. De Filippo. 1976. Evaluating a two-channel lipreading aid. J. Acoust. Soc. Am. 60:S124–S125(A).

Shore, I., R. C. Bilger, and I. J. Hirsh. 1960. Hearing aid evaluation: Reliability of repeated measurements. J. Speech Hear. Disord. 25:152–170.

Simmons-Martin, A. 1976. Facilitating positive parent-child interactions. In: D. L. Lillie and P. L. Trohanis with K. W. Goin (eds.), Teaching Parents to Teach. pp. 75–85. Walker and Company, New York.

Skinner, M. W. 1976. Speech intelligibility in noise-induced hearing loss: The effect of high-frequency compensation. Ph.D. dissertation, Washington University, St. Louis.

Stark, R. E., J. K. Cullen, and R. A. Chase. 1968. Preliminary work with the new Bell Telephone visible speech translator. Am. Ann. Deaf 113:205–214.

Stewart, L. C., W. D. Larkin, and R. A. Houde. 1976. Real-time speech spectrographic display (SSD). J. Acoust. Soc. Am. 59(Suppl. 1):S69.

Upton, H. W. 1968. Wearable eyeglass speechreading. Am. Ann. Deaf 113:222–229.

Villchur, E. 1973. Signal processing to improve speech intelligibility in perceptive deafness. J. Acoust. Soc. Am. 53:1646–1657.

Whetnall, E., and D. B. Fry. 1970. Learning to Hear. Wm. Heinemann, Ltd. London.

CHAPTER 9

ISSUES AND EXPOSITION

Mark Ross and Thomas G. Giolas

CONTENTS

Presented and discussed in this chapter are those issues and topics relating to the auditory management of children not covered previously in this book. Some areas relevant to this document's purpose either did not fit or were omitted from the preceding chapters, and it is our intention now to fill in these remaining information gaps.

Each of the "issues" presented could well be the subject of a complete chapter by itself, but although this would be a worthy effort, it is beyond the scope of the present document. We have chosen not to follow strictly a review of the literature format in our presentation, but rather to attempt to extract those generalizations permitted by the research, presenting our own viewpoint when the research is ambiguous or contradictory. We prefer this approach to the common practice followed by many who simply abstract research articles, presenting the conclusions, but not critically evaluating them or attempting to integrate the findings with previous and possibly contradictory work. It is hoped that in the following pages, we will not be susceptible to this same criticism.

EFFECT OF HEARING AID
AMPLIFICATION UPON RESIDUAL HEARING

The possible adverse effect upon residual hearing of wearing hearing aids is a frequently expressed clinical concern. There is a straightforward analogy between the known adverse effect upon hearing acuity of high level environmental noise exposure and the use of hearing aids. According to this analogy, if prolonged exposure to high intensity sounds will damage and continue to damage a previously normal ear, why would not continued exposure to high level hearing aid amplified sounds damage the user's ear? The answer to this is that it can and probably has, and that it is a possibility no clinician should ever ignore. Having said this, however, and as we review the evidence, we shall see that no child need be deprived of effective amplification because of the fear of this occurrence.

Early Studies

From the first published study in the English language literature (Kinney, 1953), there have been approximately 20 published articles dealing with the topic. Those appearing before 1970 were reviewed in detail by Markides in 1971. The general impression one is left with after reviewing this literature is one of uncertainty. The variables involved in large scale studies of this type make it a difficult area to research. These variables involve many aspects of subject selection, audiometric calibration, and what has been impossible to ascertain in any study, knowledge of the actual sound pressure levels in the ear canal of a subject over specified periods of time. The results of these large scale studies before 1970 tend to show that a minority of subjects apparently exhibit a further decrement in hearing acuity attributable to hearing aid usage.

There have been four reports that have documented the effects of hearing aid amplification for a given individual (Harford and Markle, 1955; Sataloff, 1961; Ross and Truex, 1965; Jerger and Lewis, 1975). In these instances, the use of the hearing aid was associated with a shift in auditory thresholds in the aided ear; when the hearing aid was switched to the previously unused ear, the thresholds in the formerly aided ear recovered somewhat, while the currently aided ear demonstrated a threshold shift. The same course of events could be shown a number of times for the same subject: a drop in hearing actuity in the aided ear and a recovery when the aid was removed. These impressions were supported by three experimental studies that demonstrated that exposure to high level amplified sounds produced temporary threshold shifts in small groups of hearing-impaired children (Lockett and Ling, 1964; Macrae, 1967, 1968).

As we have reviewed the literature thus far, the situation seems far from promising. The use of hearing aids seems to be associated with a further decrement in hearing acuity for an unknown proportion of children wearing hearing aids. This possibility has led to the suggestion that great caution be exercised in recommending binaural hearing aids for children, because the effect of overamplification cannot be separated from that possibly intrinsic to the pathology intself (Jerger and Lewis, 1975). In other words if threshold shifts occur in both ears, one cannot ascribe the shifts either to the hearing aids or to the underlying pathology. In this reasoning, a monaural aid, shifted from ear to ear, would permit the distinction to be made. Fortunately, the recent evidence is not nearly as pessimistic as this formulation would suggest. Furthermore, the recent research has profited by the excellent critique in this area provided by Markides (1971), and thus has minimized (but not eliminated) the many confounding variables.

Recent Studies

Hine and Furness (1975) examined the annual audiograms of 21 children in a school for the partially hearing. For most of the subjects, four audiograms made in four successive years were available for examination, with the authors examining three main effects: differences among frequencies, ears, and years. Their results indicated no cases of statistically significant deterioration in hearing acuity in any of the children. On the other hand, they reported that over one-third of the children showed a slight improvement in measured thresholds in the aided ears. They attributed this finding to an enhanced ability to respond to auditory signals fostered by school program that emphasized the use of residual hearing.

Darbyshire (1976) evaluated the audiograms of 100 hearing-impaired children over a period of 2 years 9 months during which the children wore "high gain and/or high output hearing aids." The author evaluated possible changes in hearing acuity over this period in the better amplified ear (in binaural cases), and in all aided and unaided ears. Additionally, the subjects were grouped by type of audiogram configuration. He reports that there was no evidence that the wearing of a hearing aid caused deterioration of hearing. On the contrary, he found a slight improvement in the aided ears as opposed to a slight decrement in the unaided ears (except for 4000, Hz for which no improvement occurred in the aided ears, although a decrement did occur in the unaided condition). In the author's judgment, sustained amplification with properly fitted hearing aids enabled children to give better responses to pure-tone stimuli; he did not feel that this was simply a function of maturation and improved listening skills, because the slight improvement occurred only in one (aided) and not in the other (unaided) ear. His findings and impressions support those of Hine and Furness (1975).

The last, and perhaps most carefully controlled study on this topic to date, was completed by Markides in 1976. He used four groups of children, 30 in each of the first three groups, and 10 in the last one. The children in group A were fitted monaurally with hearing aids whose maximum output ranged from 130–136 dB sound pressure level (SPL); the children in group B were fitted monaurally with aids whose maximum output ranged from 116–128 dB SPL; the children in group C were not using hearing aids at all; and the children in group D used binaural aids similar to those used by the children in group B. All the children in all groups had congenital, bilateral, sensorineural hearing impairments. Their hearing was tested at 6-month intervals over a 3-year period by the same audiologic team, at the frequencies 500, 1000, 2000, and 4000 Hz. His results showed a tendency for improved sensitivity in all aided ears at all tested frequencies, with the greatest degree of improvement manifested 6 months after the aids were first used. Children wearing the more powerful aids showed the same positive tendency as children wearing the less powerful aids (including both ears of the binaural users). On the other hand, all the unaided ears, including both ears (unaided) of the children in group C, showed a slight decrement in hearing acuity during the course of the investigation. The author (Markides, 1976) interprets his results to support the contention that the use of a hearing aid, far from diminishing peripheral hearing acuity, enables an individual to improve his responsiveness to auditory stimuli (although probably not "improving" the threshold function as such). In this he agrees with the interpretations of both Hine and Furness (1975) and Darbyshire (1976).

Some Speculative Discussion

It is tempting to ascribe the results of these last three studies to our advances in selecting and supervising the use of hearing aids with children. Not only did they not find a diminishment in hearing acuity in an aided ear—a possibility that has been worrying clinicians for years—but they report that the amplified sound may actually enable the children to use their hearing more effectively. What, then, is different now than in previous years? We would like to speculate that, at least in the institutions from which these investigators drew their subjects, we have learned to fit hearing aids to children more appropriately, at an earlier age, and have been able to make the auditory experience a pleasant one and an integral part of their lives. Perhaps in these institutions they do not provide children with hearing aids whose maximum outputs are far in excess of what they need or can tolerate. It used to be that manufacturer's would point with pride to instruments that could deliver outputs in excess of 146 dB; apparently it gave a competitive advantage in dealing with the unsophisticated purchaser if they could point to the increased amplification possible with their instrument as compared to their competitors. To some extent this still occurs, and children are still exposed to unnecessarily high, and probably traumatizing, levels of amplified sound. However, this is probably not the entire explanation of the results in the three above studies.

If our surmise is correct, that the children in the above studies were beneficiaries of the trend in recent years toward earlier and earlier amplification, then it is possible that the circumvention of the adverse effects of auditory sensory deprivation could have played a significant role in the above results. We know, at least with rats and mice, that early auditory deprivation increases the latency of auditory neural responses at the inferior colliculus by a factor of 2 to 3 (Clopton and Silverman, 1976), and that this sound deprivation (either surgically or environmentally) produces morphologic changes in the brain stem auditory nuclei (Webster and Webster, 1977). We suspect (although we cannot prove) that these physiologically based changes in function, attributable to early sound deprivation, may very well increase the susceptibility of the auditory system to the traumatic effects of high levels of sound.

Another factor that we cannot prove, but which has appealing logic, is the possible relationship between one's attitude toward perceived auditory stimuli, and susceptibility to acoustic trauma.

Lipscomb (1976) has pointed out that viewing noise damage to the ear as a monotonic function of noise exposure may be a gross oversimplification of what actually occurs. He reports that "noise can be regarded as a bionegative stimulus which serves to occlude the capillaries of the inner ear and thus reduce blood flow just at the moment the ear requires all the oxygen and other nutrients it can possibly receive." Positive subjective responses and attitudes toward loud sound diminishes the stress reactions in the body, thus obviating the bionegative effects in the inner ear. In other words, according to this formulation, if the high level sound stimuli is subjectively desirable, the vasoconstriction of the capillaries in the inner ear will not occur, and the flow of nutrients will not be impeded at the moment they are most needed. Therefore, one's attitudes toward the incoming auditory stimuli is important. If a child has been fitted late with a hearing aid, which sometimes works but more often does not, if he experiences uncomfortably loud sound stimuli at frequent intervals, or if his use of residual hearing is de-emphasized in his training and as a basis for communication, then the child may very well view amplified sound negatively and thus demonstrate the bionegative effects in the inner ear discussed by Lipscomb (1976). It would follow then, that early, appropriate, and meaningful sound amplification may well serve to protect a hearing-impaired child from further damage to his residual hearing. Admittedly, this is hardly the kind of formulation that can be conclusively proved at this time, but it does fit the facts and reinforces our efforts to intelligently exploit the presence of residual hearing at an early age.

Just about all the studies published on this topic have used children as the experimental populations. Considering all the data available in many centers on adults, and that problems are more likely to be communicated than their absence, we suggest that these data probably do not support the presence of significant threshold shifts related to hearing aid amplification for the overwhelming majority the adult clients. Furthermore, one might speculate that the same reasons apply for adults as did for the children in the preceding three studies. Most hearing-impaired adults using hearing aids like and desire the amplified sounds; they want to improve their communication ability. The fact that they wear hearing aids at all attests to this fact. If the amplified sound produced more negative than positive experiences for them, one can hardly prevent an adult from simply discarding the instrument, and indeed many do. We can assume, therefore, that the adults who consistently wear hearing aids are more positively than negatively oriented to the amplified signals. If the preceding hypothesis is correct, the positive attitude of these adults helps protect them from the potentially negative effect of high levels of sound in the ear, as it does with children who have similar positive orientations to amplified auditory signals.

BINAURAL AMPLIFICATION

For reasons for which we are not really aware, the topic of binaural versus monaural amplification is a controversial issue in our field. Although "common sense" seems to be a disreputable notion in some quarters, still the idea that two ears can somehow provide auditory advantages that one ear cannot seems to be a pretty valid common sense supposition. In spite of this, the concept has generated a great deal of research, not to say argument, and has absorbed a great deal of professional time and energy. In our estimation, the manner in which the question has usually been formulated has been a time-consuming belaboring of the obvious: of course two ears are better than one; they can provide auditory experiences not possible with one ear. For clincial populations, we should not be asking this general question at all, but rather, for what specific subjects does a monaural aid serve as well or better than a binaural hearing aid? This question is formulated so that the normal aided situation is considered to be binaural, with exceptions made in specific instances where it can be demonstrated that binaural offers no advantages over that possible with a monaural hearing aid. As most clinicians will recognize, this way of formulating the question is completely out of phase with the manner in which it is usually posed, which is, would a second hearing aid somehow offer advantages that a single one would not? We do not consider this to be subtle distinction at all, but one that may have serious implications for a hearing-impaired child. We return to this point at the conclusion of this essay; for now, let us examine the evidence regarding binaural versus monaural amplification.

Defining the Problem

There is a vast amount of literature on this topic, which we attempt to distill in a few pages. The interested reader is referred to a more extensive review just recently completed (Ross, 1977a). In order to reduce the verbiage while communicating the essence of the topic, we shall have to make a few restrictive decisions. First, we shall ignore any research that used normal hearing individuals as subjects. Although we believe that such research is applicable to an impaired population, it is also reasonable to assume that the normal binaural superiority is disrupted in the presence of an otic pathology. Second, we shall not attend to any research that did not process the stimuli through hearing aids before presentation to the hearing-impaired subjects. There is evidence to suggest that processing speech through hearing aids has a more detrimental effect upon hearing-impaired than normal hearing listeners (Finitzo-Hieber, 1975) and it is conceivable that such processing may obviate any possible binaural advantage for the hearing-impaired subjects. In other words, advantages may be apparent in the earphone situation that do not appear in the aided listening situation. Our goal is to focus this review on studies with the greatest face validity; namely, studies in which hearing aids were used by hearing-impaired subjects.

One final point before proceeding: although this book deals with children, most of the research we shall be referring to used adults as subjects. The reason for this, of course, is that there has been relatively little research on this topic with hearing-impaired children; what there is has usually used rating scales, by parents or teachers, as the means to evaluate binaural compared to monaural hearing aid functioning. Hearing-impaired children, who ordinarily demonstrate speech and language deviations, are simply not good candidates for the usual experimental paradigm, which employs speech discrimination tests of one type or another. In our judgment, however, results obtained with hearing-impaired adults can be generalized to hearing-impaired children. We have no reason to believe that the auditory factors underlying binaural/monaural functioning with adults are any different than with congenitally hearing-impaired children, although this applies most strongly, and maybe only as is seen below, to children who have experienced binaural amplification at an early age.

Speech Discrimination Studies

In the review referred to above (Ross, 1977a), 17 studies were examined that compared the speech discrimination scores obtained with binaural and monaural hearing aids for hearing-impaired subjects. Fourteen of these showed binaural superiority and three showed binaural/monaural parity.

Interestingly enough, in none of these studies was the experimental situation designed to maximize face validity. The most frequent listening condition facing a hearing-impaired person would be where the signal emanates from a point straight ahead, with noise issuing from any or all locations around the subject. In contrast, the usual geometry of the loudspeakers in these studies was to have the primary and secondary speakers 45–60 degrees to the right and left of a subject, in spite of the fact that we try to teach our clients to face the person speaking. In a few of the studies, only a primary loudspeaker was used, located directly in front, from which the signal emanated, with or without the presence of a competing signal transmitted through the same loudspeaker. Some studies used an artificial head to pick up the test stimuli for later transmitting to a subject via earphones, thus precluding the minimal head movements on which much of the binaural advantage presumably rests. No study we have been able to find maximized the face validity of the test situation in that 1) hearing-impaired rather than normal hearing subjects were tested, 2) who used hearing aids instead of earphones, 3) with the primary speaker located directly in front, 4) and secondary speakers presenting competing noncorrelated signals all around the subject (from both sides and rear), 5) with real sentences as test stimuli that included key words of low and high contextual predictability (Kalikow, Stevens, and Elliot, 1977).

The differences in discrimination scores in the above studies that prove, statistically, binaural superiority rarely seem very impressive on an absolute basis. The difference may be 4 or 8%, perhaps less than the error of measurement, and clinicians easily dismiss such differences as being nonsignificant in a clinical sense. If so, we suggest that the following points be kept in mind: a statistically significant difference means that something, on a group basis, is going on in one condition not true in the other condition. We should not dismiss significant differences, no matter how small, as being meaningless. We do not know what the subjective correlate is of a few percentage points in discrimination scores. How important is this real difference in understanding speech to the individual involved? Does this difference move the person from barely not understanding in a given situation to just about getting the gist of the conversation? Is the effort involved in understanding speech substantially reduced in the binaural situation, although the difference in actual discrimination scores may seem minimal? What we are saying here is that clinicians should not be so enamored of "objective" evidence, that they ignore what patients have been trying to tell us for years regarding their experiences with binaural aids. It sometimes seems that if we cannot or do not measure a dimension, it does not exist. If a patient states that there is a better appreciation of auditory space with binaural hearing aids, or that his responses are quicker and his communicative confidence greater in the binaural condition, then we should not too quickly dismiss their impressions as purely wishful thinking. It may be, and we must keep this possibility in mind, but we should also show them a little more respect and not arbitrarily dismiss their judgments.

Localization and Loudness Summation

Five studies (see Ross, 1977a) evaluated localization ability with and without binaural hearing aids, and all demonstrated binaural superiority. This was most manifest at lower sensation levels. At higher sensation levels, for the monaural condition, the isolation of the nonaided ear is not perfect and, as has been shown, is able to participate in the listening experience (MacKeith and Coles, 1971). One study compared loudness summation function curves with monaural and binaural hearing aids for hearing-impaired subjects, and found results comparable to those obtained with normal hearing subjects under monaural and binaural listening conditions. These results demonstrated that with the use of binaural hearing aids, hearing-impaired subjects could obtain the same loudness sensation they experienced in the monaural condition with 5-6 dB less SPL. What this finding means, of course, is that we thereby reduce the likelihood of threshold shifts occurring, and furthermore, possibly reduce the extent of spread of masking effects ordinarily occurring with high level SPL inputs to the ear (Danaher and Pickett, 1975).

Variability of Results

A common theme to many of these studies is the great variability found within a group of hearing-impaired individuals; although group trends undeniably demonstrate binaural superiority, some individuals in the group may not manifest the same superiority. Part of the reason for these atypical results may be ascribed to the need for training or experience with a binaural signal before the benefits could be manifested (Fisher, 1964; Bergman et al., 1965; Nabelek and Pickett, 1974). Another possibility is the lack of experimental rigor in the procedures. For example, live voice presentation of the stimuli, or accepting talk-back responses in a sound field, particularly in the presence of competing noise, is hardly conducive to reliable results. That reliability in the test administration is possible was amply demonstrated by Olsen and Carhart (1967) in a study that evaluated test-retest correlation coefficients for binaural and monaural conditions, in quiet and in noise. Finally, however, the fact remains that some individuals with hearing losses do not indeed perform better with binaural hearing aids, although we have rarely seen one who performed poorer with binaural as opposed to a monaural hearing aid.

This is really the key question, as we noted above, that must be addressed: that is, what factors characterize the individual who is not a binaural hearing aid candidate? We shall return to this question later.

Binaural/Monaural Comparisons with Children

In regards to hearing-impaired children, all the studies we were able to locate showed superior functioning with binaural hearing aids. Four of these studies used speech discrimination measures to differentiate binaural/monaural hearing aid functioning (Liden and Nordlund, 1960; Fisher, 1964; Lankford and Faires, 1973; 1975) and one used localization ability (Kuyper and deBoer, 1969). From a research point of view, none of these studies is very satisfactory, basically because of a factor none of the investigators could control. They were dealing with children who simply did not make the best subjects for this kind of research. In an effort to circumvent the measurement problem, a number of investigators have interviewed parents and teachers of hearing-impaired children or employed rating scales to distinguish monaural/binaural hearing aid functioning (Bender and Wiig, 1960; Lewis and Green, 1962; Luterman, 1969; Ross et al., 1974). In all of these reports, teachers and parents noted that the binaural condition was associated with superior binaural functioning.

Binaural Candidacy

The evidence clearly demonstrates the general superiority of binaural functioning for most hearing-impaired individuals. We cannot assert that all hearing-impaired persons are binaural candidates; what we must consider are those personal and audiometric variables that negate its value for specific individuals. Other than the person who has no residual hearing in one ear, we can offer little information in this respect. Asymmetry of threshold configurations or suprathreshold functions in the two ears do not, per se, contraindicate binaural amplification. The ability of the normal auditory system to fuse two disparate signals is a long established technique in central auditory testing. The hearing-impaired person with a peripheral, as opposed to a central, site of lesion should be able to employ his central auditory system in a similar fashion. This was a suggestion made by Rosenthal, Lang, and Levitt (1975), based on the results of their study, in which they showed that it was possible to improve consonant intelligibility by presenting a low frequency band to one ear and a high band to the other ear, compared to just the high band intelligibility score in one ear. Rand (1974) found similar results using synthetic formants, in that he was able to increase the effectiveness of the second and third formants as speech cues by simultaneously presenting the first formant to one ear and the higher formants to the opposite ear. Using a hearing-impaired population, Franklin (1975) showed an improvement in their speech discrimination scores when a low (240–480 Hz) and a high band (1020–2040 Hz) were passed to opposite ears rather than the same ear. The concept of a "split band" binaural hearing aid, to circumvent possible spread of masking effects in a broad band presentation, implies that threshold symmetry is not a prerequisite for binaural superiority. As it happens, approximately 40% of hearing-impaired children display asymmetrical configurations in both ears, and thus a condition in which each ear can provide different, and possibly complementary, information to the brain (Byrne and Dermody, 1974).

Early Versus Later Binaural Amplification

An unknown and univestigated variable pertaining to binaural hearing aid candidacy, or the degree and dimensions of improvement that can be expected, is time. Are children who are fitted with their first binaural hearing aid at an early age able to derive more benefit, or realize the actualization of different binaural dimensions, than the children so fitted at a later age? We do not really know, although we can make some educated guesses. In respect to early amplification per se, it is now widely believed and practiced that it is necessary for maximum development of speech and language through an auditory approach. One reason for early management is that a delay in stimulating the auditory pathways may produce auditory sensory deprivation effects, with a consequent reduction in the speech and language development mediated auditorily. It is reasonable to believe that the same logic holds regarding binaural amplification: the more delay, that is, the longer the central nervous system is deprived of patterned, binaural auditory input, the less likely it is that the maximum potential of the binaural system will be realized. A recurring, but unresearched, clinical observation is the patient who presents bilaterally similar threshold configurations with greatly superior speech intelligibility scores in the monaurally aided ear. One can argue that this indeed is the reason why the one ear was selected for amplification in the first place, but it is difficult to hold to this opinion when the person was fitted with the hearing aid preverbally. This example not only serves to illustrate the observations of Tees (1967) Patchett (1977), Clopton and Silverman (1976), and Webster and Webster (1977) regarding the behavioral, physiologic, and morphologic consequences of auditory deprivation in general, but it also has special implications for binaural functioning. Silverman and Clopton (1976) observed that units in the inferior colliculus are activated by clicks delivered to the contralateral ear. Working with rats, they report, as an indication of binaural interaction, the suppression of this activation by ipsilateral clicks. When the animals were monaurally auditorially deprived shortly after birth for a period of 3–5 months, the ipsilateral clicks could no longer suppress contralateral activity and thus abolished this evidence of binaural interactions. They point out, at least in the rat, the time-locked nature of this observation; deprivation occurring later either had no or just minimal effects.

We need no reminder that rats are not children and that one should generalize such results with caution. Furthermore, Silverman and Clopton (1976) only studied one phenomenon at only one level in the auditory system. What relation this information has regarding the binaural behavior of hearing-impaired children is simply not known. It seems to us, however, that in the interests of children, the presumption should be in their favor. There is more likelihood that a delay in binaural amplification (as well as in sound amplification in general) would limit their ultimate binaural behavior than that it would have no effect. We simply cannot wait for all the evidence to come in before we make clinical decisions; we see children every day in our clinics and we must make our decisions on the basis of the best evidence we have to date. And this is that auditory sensory deprivation in general, and binaural deprivation specifically, is a real danger that we can preclude with early binaural amplification. We would make this suggestion even if one were certain that the two ears of a young child displayed widely divergent threshold configurations. We would ascribe many of the failures we have had with such children to the lengthy delay before binaural fittings were tried, that is, to the irreversible sensory deprivation effects that may have ensued. This is not to say that placing a binaural instrument on an older child would be of no value and should not be attempted. First, as was pointed out earlier, the advantages may not be apparent until after a fairly lengthy trial. Second, there are binaural advantages that do not depend upon binaural interaction as such, but simply relate to the favorable location of a hearing aid in reference to a talker. Third, we may not be dealing with an all-or-nothing situation; some gains are better than none, and some interaction dimensions, such as loudness, may be possible whereas others, such as localization, may be absent. Finally a clinician should always test his recommendations against the results;

beginning with the presumption that the normal situation is binaural, he should continually observe the child, formally and informally, to validate and, if necessary, to modify his recommendations.

DIRECTIONAL HEARING AIDS

When directional aids first appeared on the market, they seemed able to remedy an auditory problem in schools not possible with auditory trainers. These latter devices require that the speaker intend that his utterances be heard by the child or the children he is talking to, whether he is addressing an entire class of hearing-impaired children, or a class of normal hearing children in which one or several hearing-impaired children are also included. The teacher does not intend that children to whom she is not talking receive her speech as loud and clearly as when she is directly addressing them. This is exactly what occurs with auditory trainers in many regular classrooms in which one form or another of individualized instruction is taking place. In these situations, the teacher is circulating around the classroom, checking work and other individual activities; if she is wearing an open microphone around her neck, the mainstreamed hearing-impaired child or children are the recipients of many irrelevent (for them) utterances, which tend to interfere with their reception of messages directed to them by other children or teachers. This is not what happens with normal hearing children in the same situation; for them, the intensity of the teacher's speech drops with increasing distance, an event that does not occur with an auditory trainer. To use an auditory trainer effectively in a mainstream environment requires that the teacher or the child deactivate her transmission when the speech is not directed to the child in question, and activate when it is. This sounds simple, but in the atmosphere of the average classroom, with so many competing demands and concerns, it is a very difficult practice to master. Directional hearing aids seemed to be the answer to this problem.

With directional aids, the intensity of an acoustic signal arriving from a 0- or 45-degree azimuth is greater than signals arriving from other locations. The microphone, in other words, is designed to favor signals arriving from some directions and deemphasize signals arriving from other directions. For the listener, this means that by facing a speaker, his speech will be louder relative to competing sounds emanating from other points of the compass. The logic regarding the use of such instruments in a classroom in which much individual instruction is taking place seems obvious: the child simply faces the person who is talking to him, thus perceiving this speech in a relatively favorable signal-to-noise ratio. This will not occur with an omnidirectional aid, because the microphone is equally sensitive to signals arriving from any direction. Yet, in spite of this appealing rationale and apparent logic, the research designed to substantiate the theoretical expectations seems to have uncovered more relevant questions than it has answered. The presumed advantages of directional hearing aids for hearing-impaired youngsters in regular classrooms is one of the questions that remains open.

Primary and Secondary Speaker Locations

A number of topographic arrangements of loudspeakers have been used in this area of research, to both capitalize on the directionality aspect and to increase the face validity of the test situation. The usual location of the primary speaker has been directly to the front or to a 45-degree angle from the hearing aid. The location of the secondary speakers delivering the competing signals has been more variable, ranging from a single speaker at 180 degrees or suspended over the listeners head, to a battery of five speakers arranged at 60-degree intervals around the subject (with the primary speaker at 0 degrees). With few exceptions (Lentz, 1972a; Kelley and Miller, 1975), all the studies comparing intelligibility scores with and without a directional hearing aid has shown the superiority of the directional aids (Lentz, 1972b; Frank and Gooden, 1973; Lentz, 1973; McFarland and Moss, 1973; Nielsen, 1973; Lentz, 1974; Sung, Sung, and Angelelli, 1975; Mueller and Johnson, 1976). This superiority was manifest only when a competing noise was present; in quiet, no difference was obtained between the directional and omnidirectional hearing aids. Several of the studies located the primary and secondary speakers in a manner to maximize the face validity of the test situation, that is the primary speaker was directly in front of the listener with the secondary speakers ranged around the subject (Lentz, 1973; Nielsen, 1973). Generally, this aspect of the research has supported the concept of directional hearing aids as a potentially useful device in noisy situations. However, several troublesome and possibly confounding variables do remain.

Degree of Directionality

One common variable in considering research with directional versus omnidirectional aids is the degree of directionality as a function of frequency, both that intentional in the design and that resulting from poor quality control. Generally, with competing signals emanating from the rear, the more directionality in the microphone, the higher the discrimination scores (Sung, Sung, and Angelelli, 1975; Mueller and Johnson, 1976). This generalization must be qualified by several factors: one is the variations of directionality across frequency observed with different directional aids (which may occur even though the average front-back intensity ratio differs little). It has been shown that at some frequencies some directional aids evidently favor signals arriving from a rearward azimuth, and thus provide more amplification for competing noise signals at these same frequencies than for speech signals arriving from the front of a listener (Sung, Sung, and Angelelli, 1975). The other is the effect of the acoustical environment upon the directional characteristics of a hearing aid. In a very carefully instrumented and controlled study, Formby and Studebaker (1976) demonstrated the variations in directional characteristics of three directional aids in an anechoic chamber, a sound-treated audiometric booth, a typical living room, a clinical classroom, and a church lecture/classroom. Different aids showed different directional characteristics in the same environment, and the same aid displayed markedly different directional characteristics in different environments. The more reverberant the listening environment, the less the measured directionality in a directional hearing aid, with some directional aids becoming virtually nondirectional in the more reverberant environments. According to Formby and Studebaker, the poorest environment for measuring the characteristics of a directional microphone is the conventional sound-treated audiometric test booth, because of large standing wave patterns that occur. They also report that, although present, this is less of a problem with omnidirectional aids.

Unfortunately, most of us are simply unable to measure the directional characteristics of directional hearing aids in our clinics, not to mention the interacting effect of different room acoustics. Ironically, after many years of agitation, and after the need was long since apparent, our commercial colleagues have finally provided us with relatively low cost instrumentation to assess the electroacoustic characteristics of conventional hearing aids and auditory trainer receivers. Now we are faced with a situation with directional hearing aids in which not only can we not measure the directional characteristics of a directional hearing aid, but the measurements of any of the other electroacoustic characteristics are of suspect validity. We have tried to standardize the position of directional hearing aids in our sound box, with uncertain results. We dislike depending entirely upon manufacturer's specifications in the hearing aids we dispense; given

optimal quality control when an aid leaves the factory, which is prob-
lematical, we know that hearing aids change their characteristics over
time, particularly with children, and we prefer to keep a much tighter
control on the aids we put on children. Knowledge of the complete
electroacoustical performance of a hearing aid is not a luxury, but a
necessity. Recently, an apparently valid method of assessing the directional and other electroacoustic characteristics of hearing aids in a
sound-treated audiometric test suite has been described (Brey,
Caustin, and McPherson, 1977). The procedure uses the standard
Brüel and Kjaer (B & K) measuring instrumentation in a fairly traditional manner, except that the measuring microphone and coupler (to
which the hearing aid is attached) and the reference microphone (to
control the SPL of the input sounds at the face of the hearing aid
microphone) is placed in the test suite; the remainder of the instrumentation can either be in the test room, or the signals patched
through outside of the room. The authors have shown that with the
proper placement of the reference microphone, the standing wave
effect in an audiometric test-suite can be eliminated. Although
ingenious, the procedure requires pre-empting the test room from
scheduled audiologic evaluations while the directional aids are being
assessed, or makes the electroacoustic instrumentation unavailable
during audiologic evaluations. In either case, clinical efficiency is
likely to be impaired, and we do not see this procedure being adopted
into the clinical routine. This is unfortunate, because potentially
valuable information regarding the performance characteristics of
directional hearing aids cannot now be ascertained in the average
clinic.

Reverberant Environments

The presently unpredictable effect of reverberant environments upon
the reception of speech through a directional hearing aid has serious
implications for the mainstreamed hearing-impaired child. Classrooms are reverberant places, as Børrild has discussed in this volume.
The advantages of directional microphones as measured in an
anechoic chamber or a sound-treated audiometric test room may not
hold in the environment the children normally wear amplification.
Formby and Studebaker (1976) have pointed out how these environments may obscure the directional capacity of a microphone because
of the reflection pattern of sounds; simply put, sounds that have their
primary source behind such a hearing aid may, through reflection,
also impinge upon the microphone in a frontward direction. Indeed,
Nielson (1973) comments that the directional effect is reduced when

the distance from the desired signal is increased beyond 1 or 2 m. Lentz (1972a) compared speech discrimination scores with a directional and omnidirectional hearing aid in a reverberant room and found no difference between the hearing aids. This latter study is the only one we have found that directly investigated the effect upon speech discrimination of a reverberant room on directional hearing aids. Certainly, considering the significance of this topic for hearing-impaired individuals in general, it is a subject worthy of more intensive examination than it has heretofore received.

The Binaural Effect

Only two of the studies investigating speech discrimination with directional hearing aids have employed a binaural condition (Lentz, 1973; Nielson, 1973). In both studies, the primary signal was directly in front, and the secondary speakers, delivering the competing signals, were arranged around the subject. The results showed the binaural directional aid superior to the binaural omnidirectional, but only under the more adverse listening conditions. The test environment for both studies was a sound-treated audiometric test booth, and thus a possible reverberant effect was minimized. We do not know if the binaural condition with directional hearing aids would demonstrate superior speech discrimination scores in a reverberant situation compared to binaural omnidirectional aids, although, as indicated above, Lentz (1972a) did not find such a superiority in the monaural comparison.

Our viewpoint in clinical research is that the conditions should be arranged so as to maximize face validity. In keeping with this orientation, it is apparent that we have not yet asked the most appropriate research question on this topic, insofar as the mainstreamed hearing-impaired child is concerned. What we would like to know is if binaural directional hearing aids can provide improved speech comprehension compared to binaural omnidirectional aids under the conditions faced by a hearing-impaired child in a noisy, reverberant classroom. Lacking such information, we can only speculate, which we shall now proceed to do.

Binaural listening with hearing aids differs from monaural listening in that interactions of the two central auditory pathways are now possible, a situation less likely in a monaural presentation. The precedence effect states that the binaural system operates on the first arriving acoustic pulses carrying specific information, and suppresses later arriving, reflected pulses of the same sound (except those arriving within about 30 msec of the initial event, which then add loudness and timbre to the listening experience). Thus, normal hearing individuals can localize the source of a sound in a highly reverberant environment or focus upon a desired signal in a welter of competing acoustic events. We can hypothesize a somewhat similar occurrence when binaural directional aids are compared to binaural omnidirectional aids in a reverberant room. The initial acoustic pulses seen by both types of aids should be similar, other electroacoustic dimensions being the same. For the directional aids, however, the reflected pulses that arrive at the microphones from other than a frontal location are attenuated additionally by the activity of the microphones. Not only should this enhance the signal-to-noise ratio at the eardrum, compared to binaural omnidirectional aids, but more signal information is provided the central auditory system for its contribution to the auditory process. Thus we would expect superior performance with the binaural directional aids. This same superiority would not necessarily hold, or be of the same magnitude, when a monaural directional aid is compared to a monaural omnidirectional aid in a reverberant situation. Though we would expect some improvement in the signal-to-noise ratio at the eardrum for the directional aid, the degree of reverberation, the distance from the sound source, and whether the listener is in the near or far field will probably heavily influence the results, with no contribution possible in the monaural condition from the interaction of the two central auditory pathways. Although the study by Formby and Studebaker (1976) clearly indicates that, from an electroacoustic point of view, directionality is reduced or absent in reverberant environments, yet the time course of acoustic events upon the microphones was not investigated, and thus the possible contribution of the binaurally mediated precedence effect acting upon these events could not be predicted from this study. We can best learn whether binaural directional aids supply advantages for listening under reverberation compared to any other condition by making this a topic for some well controlled specific studies. We have barely scratched the surface on this entire field of important questions.

The Subjective Effect

In our clinical/educational responsibilities, we do not have the luxury of deferring an entire topic because we lack hard experimental data. The children are there and demand that we make the best choices we can, given the information we do have available. It may, and probably will be, sometime before the experimental situation regarding directional hearing aids becomes clear, with all variables under control and valid generalizations possible from the evidence on hand. Under these circumstances, we should not discount individual and group subjective reports. Furthermore, we can obtain insights with these reports not possible with experimental studies, simply because studies do not evaluate all the dimensions of personal experience recounted by people wearing hearing aids. We should not make the error of believing that because we have not or are unable to measure a dimension, it is either not there or it is insignificant for the person involved.

In a mail questionnaire, Lentz (1974) found an overwhelming preference for directional aids among those subjects who had experienced both types. The primary reason for this strong preference was that listening in noisy environments was much easier, resulting in more comfortable listening, less personal irritability, and longer wearing time. No problems were reported in this study which related to directional aids specifically as opposed to problems common to both directional and omnidirectional aids.

In the Nielson (1973) study, far fewer subjects were used but they were examined both objectively, with speech discrimination scores, and subjectively under several conditions. The subjects wore each type of aid at home for a period of 3 weeks. Both types of aids were indistinguishable visually (the directional feature was removed for the omnidirectional condition), and neither the subjects nor the project leaders knew which aids were directional and which were not. Thus a double-blind condition obtained. The subjects were also asked their preference in a simulated group discussion, when trying both types of aids. The simulated group discussion consisted of noise from a rear speaker, a girl's and a woman's voice from the two side speakers, and a male voice issuing from the front speaker (to which the subjects presumably had to attend, although this was not specified). In the simulated group discussion, the majority of subjects (15 to 5) preferred the directional aid. However, this preference did not follow through in the home trial, in which there was no significant difference between the directional and omnidirectional aids. Some of the subjects stated that they preferred the directional aid for hearing, but found that disturbing "rubbing" sounds vitiated the advantages of the instrument. This rubbing sound occurred when hair touched the surface of the aid, or when they had to set the controls. Because all the subjects wore one model of hearing aid, the problem could be unique to this model instrument, rather than general to all directional aids. This is similar, however, to complaints that one hears moderately frequently about directional hearing aids, plus the inconvenience, for some, of not being able to hear sounds well from the rear and the side.

The possible advantages of directional aids merit their consideration for the child whose educational program does not lend itself to the use of an FM auditory trainer. We suspect that many audiologists have made some elementary errors in logic, by generalizing some bad feed-back regarding directional aids to encompass all directional aids and all potential candidates. First, as we have seen, directional aids differ among themselves and modify their characteristics to some extent depending upon the environment in which they are being used; no clinician would conclude that a bad experience with a bad hearing aid therefore precludes hearing aid candidacy for a particular individual, and this same reasoning should hold true for a poor directional aid. Second, bad feedback from some does not inform us of the proportion of individuals who are and who are not candidates for directional hearing aids (not to mention what factors underlie auditory and nonauditory candidacy for such an instrument). We are, it seems, much more likely to be the recipients of complaints than compliments and although they should not be ignored, they should be put into an overall perspective.

The point here, as we work with our clients and most specifically children, we should not find ourselves committed too early to a specific recommendation. Trial periods of 30 days will soon be required for all hearing aid clients by federal regulations; such a trial is a mockery if there is no mechanism for evaluating the results of our recommendations. For children, we can make trial recommendations, and then visit the schools to observe the child and talk to the teachers and the parents. Perhaps, given audiologist with access to classrooms and budgetary support for their visits, the children can actually be given a comparative hearing aid evaluation in one of the classrooms in which he is required to hear in order to learn. Certainly the possible benefits for some children merit some creative clinical activity on our part.

EFFECT OF LISTENING CONDITIONS UPON
SPEECH RECEPTION ABILITY OF THE HEARING IMPAIRED

Børrild has already commented (Chapter 5) upon the negative effect of poor classroom acoustics upon speech intelligibility, and the likelihood that these same conditions would have an even greater effect upon hearing-impaired persons. Ling (Chapter 6) also refers to the increased sensitivity of the hearing impaired to poor listening conditions. The fact that many hearing-impaired individuals demonstrate greater relative shifts in discrimination score than normal hearing people, under the same sensation level conditions of noise and speech, was documented by the author more than 15 years ago (Ross et al., 1965). This was not the first such study to make this observation. We view this concept as a crucially important one for all involved in educating hearing-impaired children to understand; thus we shall take this opportunity to review and expand upon it in some detail.

Normal hearing people are likely to use the evidence of their own ears in judging the suitability of a listening environment. If the conditions are such that they can comprehend speech with a minimum of difficulty, then they may well assume that the conditions are also suitable for the hearing-impaired listener. Their judgments are likely to be accurate only in the extreme cases of excellent or horrendous listening conditions. Noise seems to be an inevitable concomitant of our western civilization and few listening environments will demonstrate excellent acoustic qualities. We are more likely to find horrendous acoustic situations, but in this case their inappropriateness is apparent. For the most part, the usual listening condition would fall somewhere between the superior and the deplorable. It is under these more frequent conditions that normal hearing individuals will consider the evidence of their own ears in deciding whether the acoustic climate is also appropriate for hearing-impaired persons. These are precisely the situations, in which the listening environment is just mildly disruptive, if at all, for normal hearing people, that serious consequences for understanding speech occur for hearing-impaired subjects. Let us consider the evidence.

A dramatic example of the relative effect of noise upon the speech intelligibility scores of normal and hearing-impaired listeners was given by Tillman, Carhart, and Olsen in 1970. They found a 30-dB spread between the signal-to-noise (s/n) ratios with which normal and hearing-impaired listeners could achieve a 40% discrimination score. The normal listeners could obtain this score with a -12 dB s/n, whereas it took a $+18$ dB s/n for the hearing-impaired subjects to achieve the same score. This finding cannot be dismissed as an accidental artefact unique to the conditions obtaining in one study. At least three other studies found that hearing-impaired listeners require a higher s/n ratio than normal listeners in order to reach their maximum word discrimination score. Gengel (1971) reported that many hearing-impaired listeners would discard their hearing aids rather than listen to speech with s/n level less than $+10$ dB; he recommended that the signal-to-noise levels should always exceed 15 dB. Similar recommendations were made by Erber (1971). Nabelek and Pickett (1974) measured discrimination scores under various conditions of noise and reverberation. They report that a s/n of plus 10 dB "is the lowest ratio that should be considered for hearing-impaired listeners wearing hearing aids in reverberant rooms." A number of studies have showed that the actual s/n ratio existing in classrooms is much poorer than this (reviewed in Ross, 1972). The same situation undoubtedly pertains in many other environmental situations.

In an impressive dissertation completed at Northwestern University, Finitzo-Hieber (1975) studied the interacting effects of noise, reverberation, and hearing aid usage upon the speech discrimination scores of both normal and hard-of-hearing children. Because her results support and extend the findings of a much previous work, we shall examine them in some detail. The experimental conditions chosen in her study reflect fairly accurately the actual listening conditions confronting hearing-impaired children in real life; thus moderately valid generalizations can be made. Her results are summarized in Table 1.

Let us first consider the optimal condition: no reverberation or noise and listening through high fidelity speakers. We see from Table 1 that the normal hearing children achieve a score of 95% while the hard of hearing children achieve a score of 88%. As the noise level increases in the O.O sec reverberation time condition, the scores of the normal hearing children drop by 35% (from 95–60%) while the scores of the hard-of-hearing children drop by 46% (from 88–42%).

Table 1.   Speech intelligibility scores for normal hearing, unaided hard-of-hearing, and aided hard-of-hearing children under different reverberation times and signal to noise ratios

Reverberation time (sec)	Signal-to-noise ratio (dB)	Normal hearing	Unaided hard-of-hearing	Aided hard-of-hearing
0.0	Quiet	95	88	83
	+12	89	78	70
	+6	78	66	60
	0	60	42	39
0.4	Quiet	93	79	74
	+12	83	69	60
	+6	71	55	52
	0	48	29	28
1.2	Quiet	77	62	45
	+12	69	50	41
	+6	54	40	27
	0	30	15	11

Data from Finitze-Hieber, (1975).

We see here one of the main effects of noise upon discrimination score. Not only did the hearing-impaired group achieve lower scores in the optimal condition, but the effects of increasing noise was relatively greater for them than for the normal hearing group. As can be seen in the far right column of scores, the drop in scores is slightly increased when the speech is processed through a hearing aid before being delivered to the impaired listeners. With no reverberation at all, the hearing-impaired listeners obtained a score of 39% under the 0 s/n ratio. Unfortunately, this is not an unusual situation in many classrooms (Sanders, 1965).

The same pattern can be found in the 0.4 sec reverberation time. The normal listeners achieve a 93% score in quiet, whereas the hard-of-hearing youngsters obtain a score of 79%. The difference of 14% is greater than in the previous condition and reflects the increased sensitivity of the hearing-impaired listeners to increased reverberation. As the noise increased, the scores for the normal hearing children dropped from 93–48%, or a difference of 45%. Under the same condition, the scores for the hearing-impaired dropped from 79–29%, or a difference of 50%. The greater relative effect of noise can again be seen. Again, the scores are still slightly poorer in the aided condition.

Finally, in the 1.2 sec reverberation time condition, a not uncommon situation in many rooms, the combined effects of noise, reverberation, and aided listening are mostly clearly apparent. We see here the relatively greater effects that reverberation per se produces upon the discrimination ability of the hard-of-hearing children: the greater relative effect that noise per se produces; and finally, the additional effect of listening to the speech through wearable hearing aids. The 11% score in the bottom right corner of the table indicates the kind of speech understanding a hearing-impaired youngster can obtain under conditions obtaining in many current listening environments.

In a very ingenious study, Setliff (1975) demonstrated how the acoustical environment can affect the intelligibility of the language sample received by hearing-impaired children in a regular (and noisy) nursery. The teacher's voice was simultaneously recorded via FM telemetry from one microphone around her neck and another microphone on a hearing-impaired child's chest. Thus, the same speech signal could be recorded on a two-track tape recorder, one from the teacher's microphone and one from the child's microphone. The teacher's transmission represented good microphone technique; the close distance between the teacher's mouth and the microphone reduced the negative effect of the acoustic situation (See Børrild, Chapter 5). The transmission from the child's microphone represented the usual listening condition, one in which the teacher and a child using hearing aids were some distance apart during a speaking situation. In one condition, the negative effect of the acoustic environment could be averted; in the other, it could not. Transcribers, with a good command of the English language and of the situational constraints obtaining in the classroom, understood 26% fewer of the words transmitted from the child's microphone than the teacher's microphone.

The difference represents more than a significant difference in comprehension scores; recall that the scores were achieved by normal hearing adults. Children attempting to use the distorted auditory signal for the processing and learning of language and speech skills are being deprived of potentially available acoustic information. The inability to consistently or adequately relate the acoustical events to ongoing experiences not only diminishes their dependence upon audition, but forces them to become primarily visual communicators (Ross and Giolas, 1971). The normal hearing children in the same environment, listening to speech with their two good ears rather than through an electroacoustic device delivering an imperfect signal to an impaired ear, seem able to function quite well in circumstances so detrimental to the hearing-impaired children.

Every person dealing with hearing-impaired children must understand the concepts developed in this section if they are to appropriately manage the listening conditions for the maximal exploitation of residual hearing. It is not sufficient for the children to have perfectly operating and adjusted hearing aids; the acoustic situation in which they listen can negate all of our other efforts if its effect is not carefully considered.

THE LAST LINK

In this volume, we have provided the reader with the rationale and a great deal of information bearing upon the auditory management of hearing-impaired children. We may acknowledge the potential for natural speech and language development inherent in the impaired auditory system; we may have identified the acoustic correlates in the speech signal underlying the most salient speech perceptual cues; we may have provided the most effective amplification of the speech signal possible in an optimum acoustic environment; and we may have freely drawn upon the normal processes of speech perception in our expectations and training procedures for the child; yet all this activity, information, and good intentions will be voided by a broken cord or a dead battery in the child's hearing aid/auditory trainer. In this sense, the hearing aid/auditory trainer is the last link in our educational chain. As we shall see, it is probably the weakest link as well.

An auditory approach has one overriding rationale: and that is that the child must perceive an auditory signal, with the most effective auditory approach implying that the speech signal perceived by the child is optimally packaged into his residual hearing range. If the auditory signal the child perceives is distorted, intermittent, or frequently absent, if there is a random quality about the auditory sensations—now they are here and now they are not—and the child cannot depend upon their predictable occurrence, then the child is not likely to realize his auditory potential. He may, on the contrary, develop negative associations to the hearing aid and what it implies, and consciously or unconsciously focus his energies on the modality he can depend upon: vision.

In our view, it is better not to provide a child with a hearing aid/auditory trainer at all than to give him one that sometimes works and sometimes does not, and when it does, works poorly. If the child is not wearing such an instrument, then we cannot engage in the self-deceptive assurance that we are "doing all we can" in exploiting the auditory modality. Our deficiencies are then apparent. The problem is much more insidious when the children are wearing their hearing aids/auditory trainers at all times, for then it seems that we are providing appropriately amplified sounds, when in reality all we may be doing is giving them a pain in the ear. There is no way that we can take the continued operation and optimum performance of a hearing aid/auditory trainer for granted; these instruments, particularly as worn by children, exemplify a perfect instance of Murphy's Law: if anything can go wrong, it will.

The fact that children's hearing aids frequently either do not work or work poorly should come as no surprise to anyone who has ever dealt with them in more than a cursory manner. The first documentation of this well known clinical observation, however, was not made until 1966 when Gaeth and Lounsbury evaluated the hearing aids of 134 children and found that, by the most lenient criteria, only one-half the children's hearing aids could be considered adequate. Since then, a fairly large number of similar studies have been completed, documenting the same deplorable situation: at best, only about one-third to one-half of children's hearing aids could be considered functioning adequately in any given day (Coleman, 1972; Northern et al., 1972; Zink, 1972; Findlay and Winchester, 1973; Porter, 1973;

Skalka and Moore, 1973; Hanners and Sitton, 1974; Coleman, 1975; Schell, 1975; Bess, 1976). Although the reasons include just about anything that can possibly go wrong with a hearing aid, many of the problems should never have occurred, but once apparent, could have been corrected with a minimum of skill and effort. In the next essay we shall enumerate some of the more common problems and suggest some monitoring procedures designed to disclose them.

The situation of auditory training systems is similar, but in some respects even worse. They are more complicated, and thus there are more opportunities for things to go wrong (Matkin and Olsen, 1970a, b; Sung and Hodgson, 1971; Hodgson and Sung, 1972; Wilson, Hoversten, and Thies, 1972; Matkin and Olsen, 1973; Sung et al., 1973; Sung, Sung, and Hodgson, 1974). Considering just the RF systems, which is the most likely kind of unit for our "mainstreamed" child, there is the teacher's microphone/transmitter to be considered as well as the conventional hearing aid component. As one brief example, we once received four RF units and found that only one was operating properly at the time of delivery. The RF or the audio gain for two was inadequate, and one could not detect the teacher's transmission through the RF transmission. Several of these units, as well as others, went back for repairs a number of times before the problems were finally corrected. In the meantime, of course, the children were being deprived of an effective classroom amplification system.

It is at this very practical level that our theoretical intentions and our current practices diverge the most. We have looked at the accomplishments of many of our hard-of-hearing children and concluded that, in view of their speech, language, and academic deficiencies, a substitute educational approach was necessary. After all, this reasoning goes, the children are the beneficiaries of the best audio media (hearing aids/auditory trainers) available, yet they still exhibit many horrendous problems. We have no doubt that most hard-of-hearing children require extra assistance, but this should supplement effective auditory management and not substitute for it. The children are not receiving effective auditory management when their hearing aids/ auditory trainers do not operate properly or at all. No educational program for these children can be considered even adequate if this prime precondition is not met. Every such setting, every classroom that has such a child enrolled, must institute a daily hearing aid/auditory trainer monitoring and troubleshooting program. Otherwise we may be inadvertently depriving or limiting the child of his most effective means of learning and communicating.

MONITORING AND TROUBLESHOOTING

The classroom teacher and the parents bear the major responsibility for ensuring that the hearing aids and auditory trainers operate at all times in the classroom. The older children of elementary school age can be taught to share this responsibility, with middle and high school age children taking this task upon themselves. Monitoring the performance of the hearing aids need not be complicated or a time-consuming affair; done in a systematic manner, we have evidence that the incidence of hearing aid malfunctions can be reduced (Hanners and Sitton, 1974).

We shall here describe only the general principles of a monitoring and troubleshooting program, rather than go into the specific details, for several reasons. One is that this information is already available and can be consulted (Downs, 1971; Hanners, and Sitton, 1974; Ross, 1977c), and second no detailed list of potential problems and their remedies can ever reflect the myriad of unique events that occur when children and hearing aids meet. We prefer to communicate the general principles, with the expectations that they can be applied in all specific instances.

Each morning, hearing aids and auditory trainers should be examined visually and auditorially. The visual evidence of physical abuse often signals a concomittant auditory problem. The examiner observes the earmold, to determine if it is clean, intact, and unoccluded by cerumen. Once inserted in the child's ear, he observes whether it fits properly and that it does not result in acoustic feedback or discomfort. Cords are examined for fraying and poor or incomplete juncture with the receiver or the aid; tubing is examined for cracks, crimping, and inflexibility. The controls on the hearing aid/auditory trainers are checked to ensure that they are as recommended. The battery compartment is examined for proper contacts and the battery voltage is read on a battery tester. The teacher/parent then listens to the aid with either his own earmold, or a specially purchased hearing aid stethescope. This latter device permits listening to external receivers via a snap-on ring, or right through the earmold of either a body or an ear level aid, via flexible connector. After some practice, the examiner is able to determine if the device sounds differently than it had, that is, if it is producing excessive distortion, noise, intermittent sounds, or inadequate amplification. This is a difficult experience for someone with normal hearing, because it requires listening to high level sounds (distortions may be apparent only at high output levels and not low). However, a moderate compromise can be made without permanently traumatizing the listener's ears. At any time during the day, the teacher/parent should be prepared to check the instruments once again, if it seems that the child's auditory responsiveness or general behavior has changed.

These daily visual/listening tasks must be supplemented by frequent electroacoustic evaluations of the hearing aids/auditory trainers. Relatively low cost devices are now available in many audiology programs to accomplish this task. We suggest that an electroacoustic evaluation be conducted at least two or three times a year, with extra evaluations when the visual/listening monitoring suggests the presence of a problem. At these times, we measure the four basic electroacoustic dimensions of the instrument (gain, output, frequency response, and frequency range), the noise floor (the amount of noise measured in the instrument with no acoustic input), and the harmonic distortion. We want to ensure that the gain and output is sufficient but not excessive, that the frequency response does not display marked peaks and valleys, and that the frequency range encompasses the desired frequencies.

The receiver portion of an RF auditory trainer can be checked the same way as hearing aids. It is only a little more difficult to check the RF microphone/transmitter; it must be turned on, and while one person is talking into it, another individual listens to the receiver at a suitable distance. We suggest that the talker rotate his orientation to the listener and that the listener do the same. The point of this step, and the other listening checks described above, is to try to experience the auditory situation from the child's perspective. Frequently, problems will be apparent to the ear (such as an excessively noisy classroom or stray FM transmissions) that are not evident to the eye.

Most of the defects uncovered in a monitoring and trouble-shooting program can be taken care of right on site. Batteries can be changed, new tubing ·or cords supplied, controls reset where they belong, and new earmolds or earmold impressions made. Defects dealing with the electroacoustic performance of the hearing aids require factory repairs. In all the years we have dealt with this requirement, we have never seen a perfectly satisfactory repair performance. As Zink (1972) found, aids sent back for repair often come back unrepaired, or display an entirely unique set of problems. Possibly the most efficacious solution, practiced by a number of programs, is to have a number of perfectly operating back-up units on hand, of the type that went back for repairs. We do not subscribe to the practice of supplying either inadequately performing loaner hearing aids or changing the system of amplification (from an RF auditory trainer to hearing aids, for example) as a "temporary" substitute or as an administrative convenience. Too often, this temporary situation may last for months, with immeasurable harm to the child involved. This "last link" in the acoustic chain must not vitiate or negate all of our preceding enlightened efforts.

THE AUDIOLOGIST AS EDUCATOR

Audiologists are frequently viewed as highly skilled paramedical technicians whose duties center on the administration of an increasingly large number of audiometric tests for purposes of medical diagnosis and treatment (Ross and Giolas, 1977). The unfortunate degree of truth to this assertion, however, obscures the unique role that well trained audiologists are equipped to fill regarding the habilitation of the hearing-impaired child. The information contained in this volume was not compiled as an academic exercise; on the contrary, correctly applied, it can improve the speech, language, and academic performance of many hearing-impaired children. The key term here is "correctly applied," and this is where the well trained audiologist enters the picture.

Let us consider the average mainstreamed hard-of-hearing child. During the course of the average week, he may have significant contact with five or six regular teachers; one may teach math and science, another reading and social studies, a third may be a remedial reading specialist, while still others will be his art, physical education, music teachers and so on. Usually, nothing in the training and experience of these teachers have equipped them with the specialized knowledge regarding the unique problems this child manifests and the unique remediation measures required to manage him appropriately. Most such personnel we have seen are positively motivated; they are teachers and they want to teach this child too. However, they are not familiar with the implications of different types and degrees of hearing loss, and the measures that must be taken to ensure an optimally amplified signal at all times. A properly trained public school speech pathologist can help fill this void, but not completely. This individual will still require the back-up services of an audiologist, both for direct audiologic services to children and as a specialized informational resource for all the school personnel. For audiologists to provide optimum audiologic services to children in schools, we must consider three factors. The first is their job description. What are we asking them to do in the public schools? The second is their training. This of necessity follows from what we expect of them. The third relates to ensuring their physical presence in the schools, a job location not heretofore considered a major employer of audiologists.

Job Description

The Joint Committee on Audiology and Education of the Deaf has developed *Guidelines for Audiology Programs in Educational Settings for Hearing-Impaired Children* (see Appendix A). With some minor modifications and extensions, the job description outlined in the *Guidelines* is also applicable for audiologists working in the public schools. One widespread modification would be the overall supervision of the hearing conservation program carried out in most public schools. The audiologist can train the personnel who directly conduct the hearing screening, calibrate the equipment, administer complete audiometric tests to the children who fail the screening, make and follow-up on the medical referrals, acquaint school personnel with the potential educational impact of minor or fluctuating hearing losses, and keep the appropriate records. In other words, they would be responsible for implementing the *Guidelines for Identification Audiometry* (see Appendix B).

The actual job description of an audiologist is dictated as much by the number, type, and competencies of the other personnel in the schools as his own. It is vitally important to keep a team perspective in mind, and to work with rather than around other involved professionals. In the real world, some overlap of function almost invariably occurs, particularly in dealing with the speech, language, and educational implications of a hearing loss and the implementing of the most efficacious intervention procedures. However, no such overlap or territorial dispute should occur during consideration of the electroacoustics involved in providing an optional speech signal to the children or for the most part, in functions that deal with the detection, measurement, and definition of potentially handicapping hearing losses.

What we are now seeing is a convergence of audiologists working in schools and a national recognition of the presence of many underserved and poorly managed hard-of-hearing children. These trends are too recent for clearly defined and widely accepted job descriptions of the audiologist to emerge. Audiologists are still in a position where they have to "sell" themselves and their potential contributions to the welfare of hard-of-hearing children to many of their professional colleagues. They have to demonstrate, most convincingly with children, the presence of management vacuums not only unfilled, but of which their colleagues are not even aware. It will not be an easy task.

Audiologists' Training

We do not think that a revision in the standards for clinical competency by the American Speech and Hearing Association is necessary (we are here referring to the standards, or their equivalency, and not membership in ASHA as such). The standards provide sufficient latitude and scope to train educationally oriented audiologists as well as medically oriented ones. We do need to ensure that the specific content of much of our academic material reflect the primary needs of hearing-impaired children, much of which is incorporated in this book. Furthermore, the necessary supervised practicum with children and in schools must be provided during the audiologist's training, for experiential reinforcement of the academic material.

Audiologists must be superbly knowledgeable about hearing aids and auditory trainers, from the care, fitting, and acoustics of earmolds, to electroacoustics of the instruments involved, to the kinds of acoustic and language signals impinging upon the microphone, and finally, to the effect of different listening environments upon the reception of auditory signals. They must be able to relate all of this information to the characteristics of particular losses, but yet recognize that children represent a more complicated entity than a set of ears. A solid grounding in developmental psycholinguistics is required in order to comprehend and be able to communicate the impact of the hearing loss upon speech and language and its reflected impact upon educational achievement. Some exposure to the basics of therapeutic counselling (for parent contacts) and interpersonal communication (for professional contacts) is very desirable. Basically, what we are suggesting is the training of educationally (broadly defined) oriented audiologists whose audiometric tests are primarily conducted for non medical management rather than medical diagnostic purposes.

Time is an important ingredient in this training. In our view, it takes 2 years, after a complete undergraduate program, to train audiologists who can then function in a public school environment. We include some portion of the intervening spring or summer for intensive practicum experiences. It takes this long to present the range of required academic content, the scheduling of sufficiently diverse practicum exposures, and to permit students to begin absorbing and integrating all they have been exposed to.

Presence in Public Schools

As we have already indicated, the information contained in this book is meant to ultimately assist hearing-impaired children. If there is nobody in the schools who can apply this information, then the contributors have been engaged in a futile exercise, and the children will simply continue floundering as they have been. We cannot ask others in the school to accomplish tasks for which they are not trained, and we cannot ask them to take on too many additional duties without the quality of education deteriorating for all the children. We view the teachers, speech pathologists, and the audiologists as all working together to improve services for hearing-impaired children, each contributing and sharing their unique insights. In this perspective, the audiologist is a resource person whose clients are as much the other school personnel as the children themselves.

We are convinced that the usual model of providing audiologic services to hearing-impaired children in regular schools is completely inadequate. In a "good" follow-up program, the children are scheduled for yearly audiologic evaluations (which may include a hearing aid recheck) in a clinic administratively and physically separate from the children's school. At the completion of this evaluation, the audiologist forwards to the school a report of his findings. From this point on, events conspire to completely obliterate or vitiate the services of the evaluation or the recommendations of consequent actions. Reports frequently are not seen by all, or even some, of the individuals concerned with the child's care. They may be filed by the office in locations not usually accessible to the child's current teachers; even when seen by the child's teachers, the language of the reports are often incomprehensible to the nonspecialist without an oral translation by the audiologist. The hearing aids may malfunction soon after the clinic evaluation, with no control over whether any repairs, which may or may not have been needed, modified the response of the instrument in an unacceptable fashion. With little information regarding the child's classroom requirements, the audiologist cannot intelligently recommend an auditory training system. Furthermore, he cannot ensure that it is being used appropriately when recommended. The point of all this is that he must be there; he must be where the action is, where the children are being educated. There is no more powerful tool in education than the knowledge of language, and no better way to learn language than through audition. The audiologist, by his presence in the schools, can increase the hearing-impaired child's opportunities to learn language through the proper exploitation of his residual hearing.

There are a number of effective models through which audiology services can be provided to hearing-impaired children in regular schools. The most efficient model would be for a school system to hire an audiologist and to provide him with a well equipped facility. Such a model is possible only if the school system enrolls about 8000 pupils.

Using an average incidence of hearing screening failures and number of hearing-impaired children in the population, this number of pupils would be enough to keep the audiologist busy with useful endeavors. Consider that about 5–10% of children usually fail hearing screening tests, of which about 3–5% require a complete audiologic evaluation, or about 300–400 such evaluations a year. Fifteen to thirty per one thousand school children will demonstrate some degree of more or less permanent hearing loss, ranging from mild to profound. In a population of 8000 school children, about 100 children will have or require amplification. The selection of appropriate hearing aids or auditory trainers, taking ear impressions, supervising their use, and instructing other personnel in troubleshooting them are other time consuming and vital activities in which such an audiologist can be engaged. There may be one or more resource or self-contained classrooms for some of the more severely hearing-impaired children in such a school system; the audiologist will be intimately involved in this program. Retests of problem children, the younger children, and new children, participation in staffings and parental and agency contacts will guarantee a full day work load for such an audiologist all during the school year.

Without a well equipped facility, the audiologist can still perform many of these functions, and act as a school liason with the testing center for activities that he cannot personally accomplish. It is surprising how many clinic visits can be precluded with the appropriate use of a relatively inexpensive portable audiometer, an impedance bridge, and an electroacoustic analyzer.

The organization of public school collaboratives, in which a number of school systems cooperate in managing the needs of low incidence "special" children, means that rural and smaller districts need not be deprived of the services of an audiologist. As an interim measure, it is quite feasible to contract services with an external facility, ensuring that the audiologist who tests the children in the clinic is given frequent access to the classrooms and personnel in the schools (which requires a budgetary inducement to the audiologist's employer). Mobile vans are another useful technique in rural districts, or even in urban centers. This will permit the clinic to visit the children, and preserve valuable classroom instruction time for the children by eliminating the need for travel.

In short, we are making a case for school-based audiologists, not to increase employment opportunities for these people, although it will have this effect, but to try to bring together a valuable resource for the children and the children themselves. This is really a self-evident point, and one wonders why it is done so rarely and so reluctantly.

REFERENCES

Asha 1975. Guidelines for Identification Audiometry.

Bender, R., and E. Wiig. 1960. Binaural hearing aids in young children. Volta Rev. 62:113–115.

Bergman, M., H. Rusalem, S. V. Malles, H. Cohan, and E. McKay. 1965. Auditory rehabilitation for hearing impaired blind persons. Asha Monogr. 12.

Bess, F. H. 1976. Characteristics of children's hearing aids in public schools. Mimeographed paper, Bill Wilkerson Hearing and Speech Center, Nashville.

Brey, R. H., E. I. Caustin, Jr., and J. H. McPherson. 1977. Comparison of measurements of the characteristics of directional microphone hearing aids in an IAC test room and an anechoic chamber. J. Am. Audiol. Soc. 2:173–181.

Bryne, D., and P. Dermody. 1974. An incidental advantage of binaural hearing aid fittings, the "cross over" effect. Br. J. Audiol. 8:109–112.

Carhart, R., and T. W. Tillman. 1970. Interaction of competing speech signals with hearing losses. Arch. Otolaryngol. 91:273–279.

Clopton, B. M., and M. S. Silverman. 1976. Latency changes for unit responses at rat inferior colliculus after early auditory deprivation. J. Acoust. Soc. Am. 60(suppl. 1):S82.

Coleman, R. F. 1972. Stability of children's hearing aids in an acoustic preschool. Final report, Project 522466 (Grant No. OEG-4-71-0060, U.S. Department of Health, Education, and Welfare), Washington, D.C.

Coleman, R. F. 1975. Is anyone listening? Lang. Speech Hear. Serv. Schools 6:102–105.

Danaher, E., and J. Pickett. 1975. Some masking effects produced by low frequency vowel formants in persons with sensorineural hearing loss. J. Speech Hear. Res. 18:261–271.

Darbyshire, J. O. 1976. A study of the use of high-power hearing aids by children with marked degrees of deafness and the possibility of deteriorations in auditory acuity.

Downs, M. 1971. Maintaining children's hearing aids: The role of the parents. Maico Audiol. Library Ser. 10:Report 1.

Erber, N. P. 1971. Auditory and audiovisual reception of words in low-frequency noise by children with normal hearing and by children with impaired hearing. J. Speech Hear. Res., 14:496–512.

Findlay, R. C., and R. A. Winchester. 1973. Defects in hearing aids worn by preschool and school age children. Presented at the American Speech and Hearing Association Convention, Detroit.

Finitzo Hieber, T. 1975. The influence of reverberation and noise on the speech intelligibility of normal and hard of hearing children in classroom size listening environments. Ph.D. Dissertation, Northwestern University, Evanston, Ill.

Fisher, B. 1964. An investigation of binaural hearing aids. J. Laryngol. Otol. 78:658–668.

Formby, C., and G. A. Studebaker. 1976. The effect of environment upon the directional performances of directional hearing aids. Presented at the American Speech and Hearing Association Convention, Houston.

Frank, T., and R. C. Gooden. 1973. The effect of hearing aid microphone types on speech discrimination scores in a background of multitalker noise. Maico Audiol. Library Ser. 11:Report 5.

Franklin, B. 1975. The effect of combining low and high frequency passbands on consonant recognition in the hearing impaired. J. Speech Hear. Res. 18:719–727.

Gaeth, J. H., and E. Lounsbury. 1966. Hearing aids and children in elementary schools. J. Speech Hear. Disord. 31:283–289.

Gengel, R. W. 1971. Acceptable speech-to-noise ratios for aided speech discrimination by the hearing-impaired. J. Audiol. Res. 11:219–222.

Hanners, B. A., and A. B. Sitton. 1974. Ears to hear: A daily hearing aid monitor program. Volta Rev. 76:530–536.

Harford, E. R., and D. M. Markle. 1955. The atypical effect of a hearing aid on one patient with congenital deafness. Laryngoscope 65:970–972.

Hine, W. D., and H. J. S. Furness. 1975. Does wearing a hearing aid damage residual hearing? Teach. Deaf 73:261–271.

Hodgson, W., and R. Sung. 1972. Comparative performance of hearing aid microphone and induction coil for a sentence intelligibility test. J. Auditory Res. 12:261–264.

Jerger, J. F., and N. Lewis. 1975. Binaural hearing aids: Are they dangerous for children? Arch. Otolaryngol. 101:480–483.

Kalikow, D. N., K. N. Stevens, and L. L. Elliot. 1977. Development of a test of speech intelligibility in noise using sentence materials with controlled word predictability. J. Acoust. Soc. Am. 61:1337–1351.

Kelly, B. R., and B. B. Miller. 1975. A comparison of commercially available directional and non-directional hearing aids. Presented at the American Speech and Hearing Association Convention, Washington, D.C.

Kinney, C. E. 1953. Hearing impairments in children. Laryngoscope 63:220–226.

Kuyper, P., and E. deBoer. 1969. Evaluation of sterophonic fitting of hearing aids to hard-of-hearing children. Int. Audiol. 8:524–528.

Lankford, S. E., and W. L. Faires. 1973. Objective evaluation of monaural vs. binaural amplification for congenitally hard-of-hearing children. J. Audiol. Res. 13:263–267.

Lankford, S. E., and W. L. Faires. 1975. Binaural versus monaural speech discrimination by experienced monaural listeners with congenital hearing loss. Paper delivered to the American Speech and Hearing Convention, Washington, D.C.

Lentz, W. E. 1972a. Assessment of performance using hearing aids with directional nondirectional microphones in a highly reverberant room. Paper presented at the American Speech and Hearing Association Convention, San Francisco.

Lentz, W. E. 1972b. Speech discrimination in the presence of background noise using a hearing aid with a directional sensitive microphone. Maico Audiol. Library Ser. 10:Report 9.

Lentz, W. E. 1973. Speech discrimination using directional hearing aids in the presence of multiple noise sources. Presented at American Speech and Hearing Association Convention, Detroit.

Lentz, W. E. 1974. A survey of individuals who have utilized both directional and omnidirectional hearing aids. Presented at the American Speech and Hearing Association Convention, Las Vegas.

Lewis, D., and R. Green. 1962. Value of binaural hearing aids for hearing impaired children in elementary schools. Volta Rev. 64:537–542.

Liden, G., and B. Nordlund. 1960. Sterophonic or monaural hearing aids. Acta Otolaryngol. 53:361–365.

Lipscomb, D. M. 1976. Ways noise can damage the ear. Hearing Aid J. 29:10, 34.

Lockett, H. I., and D. Ling. 1964. Auditory fatigue and hearing loss. Med. Officer 112:68–72.

Luterman, D. 1969. Binaural hearing aids preschool deaf children. Maico Audiol. Library Ser. 8:Report 3.

MacKeith, N., and R. R. A. Coles, 1971. Binaural advantages in hearing of speech. J. Laryngol. Otol. 85:213–232.

Macrae, J. H. 1967. TTS and recovery from TTS after use of powerful hearing aids. J. Acoust. Soc. Am. 43:1445–1446.

Macrae, J. H. 1968. Recovery from TTS in children with sensorineural deafness. J. Acoust. Soc. Am. 44:1451.

Markides, A. 1971. Do hearing aids damage the user's residual hearing? Sound 5:99–105.

Markides, A. 1976. The effect of hearing aid use on the user's residual hearing. 5:205–212.

Matkin, N., and W. Olsen. 1970a. Response of hearing aids with induction loop amplification systems. Am. Ann. Deaf 115:73–78.

Matkin, N., and W. Olsen. 1970b. Induction loop amplification systems: Classroom performance. Asha 12:239–244.

Matkin, N., and W. Olsen. 1973. An investigation of radio frequency auditory training units. Am. Ann. Deaf 118:25–30.

McFarland, W., and R. Moss. 1973. The effect of a directionally sensitive hearing aid on the aided speech discrimination performance of hearing-impaired individuals. Presented at the American Speech and Hearing Association Convention, Detroit.

Mueller, H. G., and R. M. Johnson. 1976. The effects of various front-to-back ratios on the performance of directional hearing aids. Presented at the American Speech and Hearing Association Convention, Houston.

Nabelek, A. K., and J. M. Pickett. 1974. Monaural and binaural speech perception through hearing aids under noise and reverberation with normal and hearing-impaired listeners. J. Speech Hear. Res. 17:724–739.

Nielsen, H. B. 1973. A comparison between hearing aids with directional microphone and hearing aids with conventional microphone. Scand Audiol. 2:173–176.

Northern, J. L., W. McChord, E. Fisher, and P. Evans. 1972. Hearing services in residential schools for the deaf. Maico Audiol. Library Ser. 11:Report 4.

Olsen, W. O., and R. Carhart. 1967. Development of test procedures for evaluation of binaural hearing aids. Bull. Prosthetics Res. 10(7):22–49.

Patchett, T. A. 1977. Auditory pattern discrimination in albino rats as a function of auditory restriction at different ages. Dev. Psychol. 13:168–169.

Porter, T. A. 1973. Hearing aids in a residential school. Am. Ann. Deaf 118:31–33.

Rand, T. C. 1974. Dichotic release from masking for speech. J. Acoust. Soc. Am. 55:678–680.

Rosenthal, R. D., J. K. Lang, and H. Levitt. 1975. Speech reception with low-frequency speech energy. J. Acoust. Soc. Am. 57:949–955.

Ross, M. 1977a. Binaural versus monaural hearing aid amplification for hearing impaired individuals. In: F. Bess, (ed.), Childhood Deafness, Causation, Assessment, and Management. Grune & Stratton, Inc. New York.

Ross, M. 1977b. Definitions and descriptions. In: J. Davis, (ed.), Our forgotten children: Hard of hearing pupils in the schools. Leadership Training Institute, University of Minnesota, Minneapolis.

Ross, M. 1977c. Hearing aids. In: B. Jaffe (ed.), Hearing Loss in Children, pp. 676–698. University Park Press, Baltimore.

Ross, M. and T. G. Giolas. 1971. Effect of three classroom listening conditions on speech intelligibility. Am. Ann. Deaf. 116:580–584.

Ross, M. and T. G. Giolas. 1977. Audiology at the crossroads (again?). Tejas 3:19–22.

Ross, M., M. F. Hunt, M. Kessler, and M. P. Henniges. 1974. The use of a rating scale to compare binaural and monaural amplification with hearing impaired children. Volta Rev. 76:92–99.

Ross, M., D. A. Huntington, H. A. Newby, and F. G. Dixon. 1965. Speech discrimination of hearing-impaired individuals in noise. J. Audiol. Res. 5:47–72.

Ross, M., and E. H. Truex, Jr. 1965. Protecting residual hearing in hearing aid user. Arch. Otolaryngol. 101:480–483.

Sanders, D. A. 1965. Noise conditions in normal school classrooms. Except. Child. 31:344–353.

Sataloff, J. 1961. Pitfalls in routine hearing testing. Arch. Otolaryngol. 73:717–726.

Schell, Y. 1975. A program for electro-acoustic evaluation of hearing aids. Presented at the American Speech and Hearing Association Convention, Washington, D.C.

Setliff, W. M. 1975. A study of hearing aid intelligibility in an acoustic preschool classroom. Presented at the American Speech and Hearing Association Convention, Washington, D.C.

Silverman, M. S., and B. M. Clopton. 1977. Critical period for the development and maintenance of binaural interaction. J. Acoust. Soc. Am. 60(Suppl. 1):S82.

Skalka, E. C., and J. P. Moore. 1973. A program for daily "troubleshooting" of hearing aids in a day school for the deaf. Presented at the American Speech and Hearing Association Convention, Detroit.

Sung, G. S., R. J. Sung, and R. M. Angelelli. 1975. Directional microphone in hearing aids. Arch. Otolaryngol. 101:316–319.

Sung, G., R. Sung, W. Hodgson, and R. Angelelli. 1973. Intelligibility of speech transduced via classroom-installed FM and conventional audio induction loop amplification systems. Presented at the American Speech and Hearing Association Convention, Detroit.

Sung, R., G. Sung, and W. Hodgson. 1974. A comparative study of physical characteristics of hearing aids on microphone and telecoil inputs. Audiology 13:78-89.

Tees, R. C. 1967. Effects of early auditory restriction in the rat on adult pattern discrimination. J. Comp. Physiol. Psychol. 63:389-393.

Tillman, T. W., R. Carhart, and W. O. Olsen. 1970. Hearing aid efficiency in a competing noise situation. J. Speech Hear. Res. 13:789-811.

Webster, D. B., and M. Webster. 1977. Neonatal sound deprivation affects brain stem auditory nuclei. Arch. Otolaryngol. 103:392-396.

Wilson, M. D., G. H. Hoverston, and T. L. Thies. 1972. Applications of acoustical analysis equipment in maintaining an auditory training system in a program for the deaf and hard of hearing. Presented to the American Speech and Hearing Association Convention, San Francisco.

Zink, G. D. 1972. Hearing aids children wear: A longitudinal study of performance. Volta Rev, 74:41-42.

CHAPTER 10

DISCUSSION SUMMARY

As explained in Chapter 1, the contributors to this book had an opportunity to discuss each other's chapter during a 2-day symposium. The raw transcription of their discussion extended to over 200 pages. Many of the issues raised were later incorporated into the authors' revisions of their chapters. Some interesting and pertinent topics that did not arise, or that were only minimally mentioned, are included in the previous chapter. After this weeding out process, we were left with a great many interchanges between the participants that were stimulating and illuminating and that we felt would provide the reader with provocative "state of the art" insights. We opted not to edit these remaining interchanges into a narrative form, because we would then have lost the personal flavor of the exchanges. We left out more than we would have liked to, and occasionally combined or reorganized several statements because of space limitations. What remains, we hope, has captured the essence of a rewarding 2-day experience with a group of eminent nationally and internationally acclaimed authorities.

SPEECH AND LANGUAGE DEVELOPMENT

Hirsh:

I think that Dennis [Fry] has restated in his paper the widely accepted observation that all peoples of the world learn languages when they can hear and speak. Vision is at best a poor substitute. The visual system is more sluggish, and even for looking at the movements of lips and tongue, there are rapid changes there from which the eye can't get information.

Auditory Basis of Language Development

Fry:

If I may say so, another factor is of course that the actual amount of input is reduced because you have to be seeing the person. All this is part of the set of conditions affecting the learning of language.

Hirsh:

I was only going to argue with the emphasis on auditory in a different context, but having limited our scope to the hard-of-hearing child, then I cannot but agree on the primacy of auditory. What's interesting is that a couple of you earlier used the expressions "auditory management" and "acoustic management" almost interchangeably and I would want to differentiate sharply between those two adjectives. It is really the auditory processing that Dennis holds for and I'm much more enthusiastic about holding for the acoustic in the sense that speech turns up in acoustic form. There are some aspects of speech that are that way because they are acoustical and so, for whatever sensory display we would invent, whether merely amplification or other, the closer you can stay to the acoustical dimensions of the speech signal, the better off you're going to be in getting information transmitted.

Boothroyd:

I would like to support the distinction between auditory and acoustic management. Obviously if you are talking about a totally deaf child you are no longer talking about auditory management, but you may be talking about acoustic management, that is, if you're going to work on visual speech training lessons and so on.

Fry:

I think I might be in a minority. Acoustic to me is the specification of the stimulus and auditory is the processing thereafter. Acoustic management to me then would imply strictly the manipulation of physical factors.

Hirsh:

No, you see, because there are some acoustical dimensions of speech that can be sensed through other modalities than hearing, and they still retain their acoustical properties; like the skin.

Villchur:

I think that none of you would disagree that there are children for whom we have no choice but to make the display other than auditory. None of us, I think, would disagree that when a child has sufficient residual hearing, that's what we should work on. Perhaps this book will throw some light on the dividing line, where we give up on the residual hearing and go to another type of display. I think that there is a tendency to give up too soon. I think that there are capabilities in what we think of as very little residual hearing that have yet to be exploited.

Fry:

Can I just interject a question here? You see, methods are not mutually exclusive and if there is some residual hearing, I believe that it can supply information in many cases where it is in fact disregarded. Take fundamental frequency, for instance, the ability to learn that there are intonation patterns: It seems to me that we don't pay it quite enough attention. In this case we may need to use another mode in addition to the auditory, but I don't believe that these modes should be mutually exclusive.

Villchur:

Certainly there is a transition point where the child uses half of one and half of another. Beyond that point, he uses less and less of his hearing.

Hirsh:

There's another problem that would have to be included to be helpful to people who work with these children, and that's the other side of this coin. There is the child with a moderate hearing loss who, because of the vagaries of educational placement, becomes a profoundly deaf child.

Levitt:

In other words, his performance is equivalent to that of a deaf child.

Hirsh:

Yes, he may be shifted off to a school and taught the sign language at an early age. The question is can some of these expert teachers in the elementary schools do anything about that? Up until what age could they do something about it? Could they recapture a communicating individual, who should communicate on the level that would be predicted on the basis of his hearing level alone? I'm just raising the question. I do not know the answer.

Boothroyd:

You [Fry] are writing about the primacy of the auditory channel in speech and language development, and what you're essentially saying is that audition has that primacy. However, you say speech and language and I think what we are talking about is spoken language development. I personally perceive language itself as being something that is not necessarily tied to the spoken form and that sign language to me carries with it and in it, all the definitions you might impose upon language. I see language as being a product of cognitive development together with its use, motivations, and needs. I guess the question that I'm trying to ask is whether there is a primacy for spoken language for which we agree that audition has a major role to play? Is there something special about the spoken form of language, and about its auditory learning, which makes it special in relation to language?

Fry:

I think what makes it special in relation to language is that all our observations have shown it to be a jolly efficient way of acquiring language. I think I've tried to state in my chapter the conditions in

which some other mode could achieve the same result. So far we
haven't seen much in the way of evidence that would say another
mode is generally equally efficient. Certainly no language is
acquired except through sensory input.

Ling:

I think, if I may address this point, that motivation is really the key
to this: that speech and language do something for us. Now Ira

[Hirsh] has raised the point of the child learning sign language.
Now people who teach a child sign language consider that there is
sufficient motivation that the language that the child can use is a
viable language. There is no question that sign language is a viable
language in its own right. It's not English or spoken language but it
is a language. Accepting this, we have to ask whether signs are sufficient for the child. If they are, then can there be enough motivation to learn speech? I think that the answers have to be that signs
are not sufficient and that there is reason to motivate children to
speak. It's quite clear that written language is parasitic on spoken
language and that a lot of what we're doing in education is in fact
teaching through the written form. We gain a lot through the
written form. Because the written form is parasitic on phonologic
parameters of language and sign language does not contain these,
then it is pretty evident that there is a very good argument in favor
of teaching speech and spoken language and, therefore, it is a good
argument in favor of using an auditory approach. I think that one
has to be fairly clear that there are lots of benefits from learning
spoken language. There's another point that I would like to make
on Dennis's chapter. There are studies (see Shvachkin reference in
Chapter 6), for example, that do show that children perceive
phonologic contrasts better when they're able to produce them.
That is, when they're able to produce the phonologic contrasts then
they're able to recognize these phonologic contrasts in new words.
Thus production would certainly seem to aid reception. There's
confusion of terms here, I think, because when it comes to reception, I'm fairly sure that there is a motor component that may be
particularly important for hearing-impaired children. When we are
listening to a particular message we are using our knowledge of language and of speech in order to understand this message. We're
looking primarily for understanding and probably production has a
tremendous role to play in this.

Fry:

Could I just interject that there's an interaction between production and reception. I think I've spoken here about certain contrasts being solidified and confirmed by the articulatory practice. The only point I'm making, however, is that the starting point must be the perception of some difference, because until you have that, you can't do anything. You don't by accident flip your tongue in a particular way and say, "Oh yes, that sounds so; therefore, these sounds must be different."

Ling:

I'm not sure. The baby often babbles or moves his tongue around and produces a sound which then, in fact, is heard. He does do just what you say he doesn't do, which is to flip his tongue around and then say, "OK. . . ."

Fry:

That's why I thought it worthwhile to talk about this point, because the babbling and linguistic stages are discrete. He manages to make those sounds, but until he perceives them in a language context, he can't even reproduce them. When he comes to the lingual state, he can't do things that he could do when he was babbling. On the basis of your argument, I think he should find the sounds very easy because he used to be able to do them. He doesn't; he finds them very hard. And it is not until he's perceived the difference that he can implement it in articulation (I'm talking here about normal development). It seems to me that this is kind of inescapable.

Ling:

I think that you're following up the notion that there is a discontinuity between babble and language and I'm not sure that discontinuity is as marked as people say. I think that there is probably much more continuity than people have been ready to admit.

Boothroyd:

I have a comment on the same point, this question of perception (reception) and production. When we talk about the child who we say can understand everything said to him, we're actually thinking about perception in terms of internal representations of the message. That internal representation can be at an acoustic, phonetic, phonologic, linguistic, or at a level of meaning. I think that what happens to the developing child is that he can make the jump to the level of meaning before he can make a full internal linguistic representation. The point at which he can make a full linguistic representation is the point at which he can also produce the message. I think that the fact that understanding precedes production is the fact that the child is operating within a limited context and can make a lot of synthetic or global jumps from perception of limited portions of the message. He can figure out what is being said, what is meant, and everything else. So depending on how you define perception, recognition and so on, I'm not sure that reception in that sense precedes production.

Fry:

I would want to comment, by the way, that as far as I'm concerned, the jump is never from the perception to the meaning, but from the meaning to the perception. I really feel that this is the way to look at it. By the word "meaning" here I only want to convey the connection between an event out there and some signal. I use "meaning" in this sense.

Hirsh:

You mean a referent event.

Fry:

Yes! Because some sound is associated with milk, it's the event of having milk to drink that leads him to know that milk sounds in a certain way and he must distinguish it from cake. Now, having gone that way, he won't even be able to attempt to produce his own version of the two things, milk and cake, until he's heard there is a difference in the signals that come in. He knows they're different things because one's liquid and one's solid, but he won't be able to make any attempt at producing signals that are different until he's heard that there is a difference. That's why I've made quite a thing of this expanding system. You make whatever expansions are necessary for your system, nothing more, and then you can expand this and make still further differentiations. I don't want to belabor it too much, but that's why I feel rather that the reception must come first.

Ling:

Can I follow-up something there? You know I think that there are many ways in which you can get this sort of differentiation. As a practicing teacher of the deaf, I find quite often that children with severe high tone loss quite predictably have great difficulty in place discrimination. For example, they may have difficulties in perceiving the difference auditorily between /d/ and /g/. Now in this case they may substitute /d/ for a /g/ or vice versa. I have often found that by teaching children to make (i.e., produce) that distinction and to recognize the associated oral-sensory motor patterns, then they come to recognize that there is an auditory distinction. The auditory distinction in this case isn't necessarily the primary thing. It's secondary. Similarly, if a child is unable to make any auditory distinction, one can teach him first with some sort of visual input and then go back to the auditory channel in which he can then make that distinction.

Fry:

You're absolutely right. I really don't argue with that at all. It's not being superficial to say, though, that the muscular event is a signal received. I think that fits very well. When he spots that as an afferent signal, as it were, then he has the distinction.

Hirsh:

Once you regard the articulatory process as another source of signals for reception, then the argument disappears.

Villchur:

Dan [Ling] how do you explain the jump from the motor sense to being able to make the distinction in sounds?

Ling:

I think that what you're doing is simply showing the child that there is a distinction and that maybe the cues were too weak for him to make this distinction auditorily, but once he realizes that there is a distinction to be made, then a fine tuning occurs. You not only hear, you listen. You're teaching the child that there is something to listen for.

Villchur:

If you were dealing with an adult, you could teach him by showing him spelling, but he still may not be able to hear the distinction. Is there something special in pronouncing it?

Ling:

I think there's something very important in motor speech and the orosensory motor patterns it provides. In various studies that we've carried out, we have had a pointing response, for example, in discrimination between *bill, bell,* and *ball.* The child just punches a particular window with a microswitch behind it, which in turn operates a gadget that reinforces if the child is right and does something else if he's wrong. We found that children learn this sort of thing and do well on it, but have a problem in generalizing. If, however, we use speech as your response, you tend to get very much better generalization. In short, there's something quite distinct about speech.

Fry:

If I may go back to what you just said, Dan is again reinforcing the point that each individual finds his own cues.

Levitt:

I had some comments but most of them have actually come up in various forms. First of all, I found the chapter a very good overview, touching bases on just about everything of importance. I was fascinated as much by what was not said as by what was said. I just wanted to mention three things; two of them have already been raised. One was what you [Fry] said, about the critical time period for the acquisition of language. I think the evidence is very strong that there is a critical time period and that children learn language much more rapidly in the very early years. When that time period ends, one doesn't know exactly. The emphasis on the early years I didn't see strongly stated.

Neural Plasticity

The second issue was plasticity. It was very interesting when you discussed other modalities in the early part of the chapter. The tone as I read it was that it's not practical. It may work but there are technical difficulties. The summary section of your chapter had a much stronger statement, which I happen to agree with, is that there's no evidence, at this point in time, that the visual or any other modality will in fact do much better with language acquisition. I realize it's an open question, but the early part of the chapter had a slightly different tone to the final conclusions. To my view the final conclusions were closer to the truth than the early part. With respect to plasticity, there are some interesting points of view that I've seen expressed elsewhere. There are the ideas of George Sperling, who cites by way of example the Japanese and Chinese hieroglyphic input to children. His argument is that there are some data here in these symbol systems in which there are no rules link-

Rules of Language

ing symbols together. You know you have a symbol for a certain object and a symbol for a certain action. Children learn very rapidly at the beginning, they pick up the vocabulary very quickly, and then hit a saturation point. Other children who are taught written language, in which the rules of language come early, start off much more slowly, but after a while pick up enormous speed and at some point will exceed by far the linguistic skills of those who learn by just the symbol systems that do not have implicit rules. I'm only saying we should perhaps develop a system of symbols that has the rules built into them. The point is that there is a major discussion

Feature Detectors

about whether or not one can use the visual system for acquiring language without auditory input. On that issue at least, the code word in this part of the world is feature detectors. There's a whole issue of whether or not the auditory system is especially built for

language, and whether there are special feature detectors in the
auditory system that are tuned in for language, so to speak, that
don't exist in the visual system. I know there are different points of
view on this, but perhaps the person who's going to be involved
ought to know the conflict or the differences of opinion in the field.

Hirsh:

It's a little like the reception-production issue. Nobody would deny
that there are feature detectors in the auditory system, in the sense
that the term can be used to apply to any specific mechanisms in
any sensory modality that are designed to discriminate between
certain kinds of perceived events. Then you can argue either that
those feature detectors are defined by the properties of human languages from the start, or you can argue that human languages
developed so as to take advantage of the feature detectors that were
installed in the auditory system. That's an interesting theoretical
argument, but I'm not sure the teaching practice would be different
because of it.

Levitt:

If you believe that you could acquire language just as easily through
the visual sense without any auditory input, this might change the
approach you use with young deaf children.

Visual
Language
Development

Hirsh:

I don't think so. That is to say, if you believe that the acquisition of
language means the acquisition of spoken language.

Levitt:

Not necessarily.

Hirsh:

All right, then let's restrict this to spoken language. Acquisition of
spoken language will be encouraged, will be taught, occasions will
be provided in the same way no matter which of those theoretical
positions you use. If the languages were so designed to take
advantage of what feature detectors there are in the auditory
system, then surely it was the way in which the speech mechanism is
used that demands the properties of those feature detectors in its
processing by the listener.

Levitt:

I would like to agree, but I can't in the sense that there are people
who go about saying that the way to learn language is through sign-
ing and there are very distinct differences between sign language
and spoken language, or language that goes through the ear. One
very big difference that occurs with some sign language is that the

word order is very different. It may well be that order is one of the first things a child picks up. You may interfere with that by using sign language as opposed to the purely oral approach.

Hirsh:

If your criterion for language is going to be reading, then it seems to me that most written languages are reflections of phonologic aspects of speech. They're alphabet codes. At least for that set, speech is the way in. In fact, I don't really understand, and you may know, how instructors in signs actually get kids started reading without the alphabet/phonologic code to teach, because presumably there is no phonologic system to begin with. I don't know how that's done.

Fry:

If I may say so, it changes the shape of the learning curve. This is one of the things that Harry [Levitt] was talking about. First of all, I don't believe that there is any visual representation of language that doesn't have syntax, which is what you were suggesting. That, of course, I simply don't believe; but if you have word chunks or word-size chunks, the freedoms are such that every word added is just a word added. You have a very much larger ensemble of signals. It's like when people try to learn to read spectrograms. They are not able to read them as successions of representations of phonemes, but only as word gestalts. You can learn 2000 and it takes just as long to learn the next 2000 and just as long to learn the next 2000, because you are not capitalizing on the restricted inventory. For that reason, getting from sign language to reading is a rather lengthy business. If in this I've not mentioned early diagnosis and treatment, it's the only thing I've ever written in my life on this subject in which I didn't. As to the critical period, there doesn't seem to me much doubt that children learn language best between the ages of 0 and 7. However, where the hearing-impaired child is concerned, I'm sure there's a critical rate of input, but I'm not so sure there's a critical age. Given this qualification, in the natural course of events children do it better when they're young, but given that, what is critical is the amount of input.

Ling:

And the quality of the input.

Fry:

If quality, in fact, refers to the acoustic conditions, I'm with you entirely. I'm sure it's absolutely true.

Ling:

Perceptual Cues

Can I ask Dennis to reply to the feature detection thing that Harry raised? If there are feature detectors in the auditory system and, as

Ira says, we have no doubt that there are, can we consider hearing impairment to be destructive of certain feature detectors, for example, fricative feature detectors, a more or less complete high tone loss?

Fry:

This comes back to the point I was making before. All this is done by the individual ingenuity in learning of the particular child. Short of complete destruction of any auditory processing, I do not believe that certain hearing losses get rid of certain cues. They do not. Cues are not like that. Cues are features that an individual brain has discovered for making a distinction. Of course, it is perfectly true that with certain losses those cues would have to be of a certain kind; the possible range of cues is much restricted. All this is true, but the cue is in the brain and not out there. I do think this is very, very important.

Ross:

You're saying then that the hearing-impaired child would use physically different cues than a normal hearing child, which he himself constructed?

Fry:

We know that they do. I have some observations that show this quite clearly. I have a girl who says, "The sun shone brightly," and everyone would say, "This is a normal speaker." When I test her with a noise band changing the lower cutoff, she's incapable of distinguishing *shirt* from *cert* on the basis of that noise band. She answers randomly. So she's using another cue. That's why I don't feel sympathy with this business about feature detectors.

Villchur:

You mean she's using another cue to pronounce the words?

Fry:

I think the way she does it, Ed, is that she knows what a noise is and then she shapes her articulation so that the vowel formant transition is the appropriate one and this gives you *shirt* in one case, *cert* in the other.

Boothroyd:

Are you suggesting that she learned to make the difference from her auditory input? She wasn't taught how to make the distinction?

Fry:

No, I don't think she was. Again, people work on kids' speech. We know that perfectly well, but what is interesting is her inability to sort *cert* and *shirt* on the basis of noise.

Hirsh:

Dennis doesn't speak against this notion of feature detectors. He says that there's a multiplicity of them. She uses the one that's available.

Fry:

That's right, but it does not say that that available set is common to everybody. I've often used the example of color-blind people, who are necessarily using a different type of visual cue for certain distinctions.

Ross:

If we took a number of normal hearing people and filtered conditions so that the frequencies carrying /s/ and /sh/ were filtered out, could you teach the distinctions to normal hearing people under those filtered conditions? That would support your point.

Boothroyd:

I agree that you might teach the distinctions in perception but not in production. I think it takes a whole range of cues that are available to make a particular distinction or generate a particular group of sounds. You can certainly be selective in the process of perception and learn how to make distinctions on the basis of limited cues. However, in order to reproduce the distinctions properly I think you need information about all significant features.

Fry:

I don't think that's so. In fact, isn't the girl I'm citing an example of that? She can't get the noise cue but she produces the sounds so you wouldn't know it wasn't a normal person.

Boothroyd:

This is why I asked you if someone had told her; if she had had the relevant input through some other modality, as in descriptive training.

Giolas:

You're saying she couldn't learn to say them without help or did she learn them naturally by listening to them?

Boothroyd:

That's what I'm questioning. There are ways to make distinctions, to recognize certain differences in certain sound groups on the basis of only a limited amount of available information or a limited group of available features. I'm suggesting, however, that in order to have reproduced these distinctions in her own speech on the basis of purely auditory input and feedback, she really would have needed access to all the cues that are of importance in our perception. . . .

Guest (B. Wernberg):

Auditory Feature Detectors

I think this is an appropriate point at which to identify or try to define the difference between acoustic correlates or properties and those things that were talked about earlier as features. The words have been used fairly broadly and I'm not sure that I understand how you're using these terms. I think I understand how Harry has used them in a physical sense, but when do these dimensions or properties or correlates become features? It seems to me to be a very critical issue that you would want to grapple with. What do you mean by features? Are you using this synonymously with acoustic dimensions? Not all acoustic dimensions or properties are features.

Hirsh:

When I think of auditory features, I mean the dimensions of hearing that correspond, for example, to phonetic features. If you take the original dozen or so that Jakobsen, Fant, and Halle proposed 20 years ago, the labels that are used for those phonetic features differ as to what aspect of the real world is represented. Grave/acute seems to refer to acoustical matters, whereas there are others that refer to articulatory matters. Finally there are a few that refer to the perceptual correlates, It was a hope, you know, that you'd be able to specify all three levels for all features. I guess that those who are interested in such feature systems are still working on it.

Levitt:

I would be happy to use the term feature in the phonetic sense in defining the feature effect. Strict phonetic feature interpretation. A feature would be something that if changed would change the meaning of what is said. A characteristic is some other correlate of the physical stimulus. An example here is in a change in intonation rather than a change of hoarseness or roughness of the voice. One may be related to harmonic structure, the other has very specific meaning depending upon the shape of the content. I would use feature in that context. In my mind the term feature is linked to a change in the meaning of what he is saying. The other characteristic is in the perceptual domain.

Hirsh:

Your example serves also as a vehicle for a distinction we were wrestling with earlier. Take the suprasegmental features of information in a sentence. Ann Geers has finished a study on intonation patterns in sentences and certain phenomena were observed in connection with whatever the acoustical correlates of intonation pattern are. What was interesting in the same study was that some of those phenomena were also observed in the case of profoundly deaf adults lipreading alone through a video recording of the same spoken sentences with no sound at all. Now there, you see, you still have what I consider to be an acoustic feature, that is, the temporal aspect of the acoustic stream, but now being received by the eye in lipread form. It's clearly duration because I don't think you can see intensity or frequency.

Ling:

I want to ask another question of Dennis. At the beginning, our charge was to relate some of this to certain things in practice. One of them was the regimen of treatment and the success or failure criteria. If your approach is the auditory approach, how do you assess its success or failure and how long do you persist in it? What sort of guidelines do you give to the practitioner in terms of carrying on through this or some other alternative? When do you select alternatives?

Success or Failure Criteria

Fry:

My only comment is that it is a function of the amount of input that is given. Therefore, you don't ask how long do I continue this, but how much have I put into this child? You could say, in half an hour I can pour in so much, but all I'm saying is that it is a function of how much and how continuously and in what conditions this child is receiving speech input that is tightly coupled with events in the external world.

Ling:

What do you do? How do you specify whether a child is in fact getting this stuff auditorily? How do you define whether he is getting enough auditorily? Or that he needs supplementary cue systems, and so on?

Fry:

The only comment I make on that is I believe we should place still more emphasis on measuring reception and be less hypnotized by production. I think you are doing this and I think we need to get more and better methods of measuring how much that child can take in. I think on that basis you could judge. If the child was able to say very little, but took in quite a lot, I say you are being successful.

Ling:

Then what are the actual things that you look for to see whether the kid is taking it in? Now speech is a very indirect measure of what the child is hearing, we know that. What is a more direct measure?

Fry:

You have to accept some other behavioral sign, but you have these tests which involve pointing or pressing a button.

Ling:

I don't think we have. Oral education has most often been measured in terms of academic achievement, which is even more indirect than speech. Really, if you're looking at the measurement of an oral system, then you have to look at speech reception measures, speech production measures, and spoken language measures. These are the three areas you have to concentrate upon. Now speech production measures are relatively simple. Lots of people have gone a fair way with this. Speech reception measures, however, are very poor. With spoken language measures we're getting there. (By spoken language, I mean the rule system. Language as presented in spoken form.) However, I think the actual speech reception area is a very weak one, and I don't think we have good measures for it.

Boothroyd:

One of the dangers is the use of multiple choice procedures, which often permit the subject to give the right answer for the wrong reason, because the cues he's using are not necessarily related at all.

SIGNAL PROCESSING

Villchur:

I would propose to discuss signal processing under two categories: one would be the ways in which the signal is processed in current hearing aids (and it is processed to some extent). The other would be experimental processing. The purpose of the signal processing, of course, is to present speech to people with impaired hearing in a form that is least affected by their perceptive distortions, or indeed may actually compensate for their perceptive distortions. Researchers such as Liberman [*Perception of The Speech Code,* A. M. Liberman, F. S. Cooper, D. P. Shankweiler and M. Studdert-Kennedy, Haskins Laboratories, New York] have emphasized that the relationship between the nature of speech and the nature of the perceptive mechanism is not an accidental one. In the evolutionary process, we have developed speech to have characteristics that are best adapted to the perceptive mechanism (or the other way around.) When the perceptive mechanism is impaired and isn't working right, in a sense what we do when we process speech is to interfere in this evolutionary process and change the nature of the speech, so that it is better matched, it is better adapted, to this perceptive mechanism.

Ross:

When you use multiband compression, do you find that the overlap of the bands produces any kind of perceptual interference pattern?

Villchur:

When I first did the experiment in two-band compression, because I was afraid of interference, I used a special system in which I protected the cross-over region with a sort of umbrella based on extending the sensor bands further on. However, further experiments indicated that it was not necessary and that a reasonable slope between the two channels, perhaps 24 dB or even 18 dB/octave, would be sufficient, and that there was not the interaction that I was afraid of.

Ross:

How far are we from a wearable hearing aid incorporating the multiband compression system?

Villchur:

(At least one company (Dyn-Aura) makes a little chip—well, not a chip, an IC—which is a perfectly good, viable compressor. I don't know of anyone who has combined it and made a two-channel compressor of it.

Hirsh:

We have one in the making, but even if everything works out and even if it sounds great, the problem is that we have only one and a second one will have to be made by hand by the same engineer. I'm not sure how many hearing aid companies will get interested in producing such devices even if they turn out to be valid for a certain number of cases. That's an economic problem.

Villchur:

I think there are very few cases of cochlear loss that would not benefit from compression but, and I think this explains some of Pascoe's results [See Chapters 7 and 8], if the residual dynamic range is reasonably large, there is enough head room between amplified speech levels and discomfort levels so that even if you don't have the ideal matching of the dynamic range of the speech to the dynamic range of hearing, frequency equalization works without it. It is the more severe cases that really require compression. The less severe cases may be able to use it, but you can get away without it. In a case with very little residual hearing at high frequencies, I would hope to restore the speech up to about 800 Hz, nothing more. The little residual hearing at higher frequencies is not useful. The best I would hope to do would be to match the dynamic range of the speech to this section of hearing up to 800 Hz and perhaps add synthetic fricatives at 800 Hz. That would be three processes put in simultaneously: whether that would be enough, I don't know.

Boothroyd:

The third process being the surrogate fricatives?

Villchur:

Yes. One is compression and the other is frequency equalization: you have to bend the compressed speech band to fit the frequency/

amplitude hearing area. The third would be surrogate fricatives. If that doesn't work you keep all three and see what else is needed.

Boothroyd:

There's something implicit in everything you've said, and I'm sure you would be surprised to think that anyone else might not appreciate this point, but in a lot of the work on hearing aid selection people have looked only at the relationship between the audiologic test findings of the individual and the response characteristics of the hearing aid. They have not considered the fact that the hearing aid is acting as an intermediary between the speech signal, ambient noise, and the audiologic characteristics of the user. It frequently happens that the demands of these three variables are incompatible.

Ambient Noise

Villchur:

Noise is a special problem. What I think about noise, or any interference, is that it has a much greater effect on the hearing impaired than it does on normals, not because of any special characteristic of their hearing, but simply because they are working on a minimum of acoustic cues, perhaps just enough for them to hold on with their fingernails. They don't have the vast reserve of redundant cues we do, and so when noise comes along and throws out a few cues that normal listeners can easily afford to lose, they are over the edge and they go. With my subjects, when intelligibility was improved in quiet by processing it was improved at least as much in noise. Another very interesting thing I found was that the compressor systems that I used had a lot of circuit noise, sounding more or less like white noise, and when I listened at the levels at which the subjects were listening, I got worried and asked if the noise bothered them. They said "What noise?" The circuit noise was below their thresholds.

Hirsh:

I'd like to ask a question about the surrogate fricatives, or the transposer. There is one thing that bothers me about that notion, at least from a theoretical point of view (from a practical point of view they may be very good): in order to ensure that you get some discrimination among different high frequency sounds, you put this energy into low frequencies and by so doing you risk throwing away some cues that were already there, mainly the suprasegmental ones; the rhythmic succession of syllables depends on there being silences between sounds. Now in the same frequency region you will introduce some new low frequency sounds that will occur when the high frequency sounds ocurred in the original message and break up that rhythmic pattern, or at least make a different rhythmic pattern.

Surrogate Fricatives

It seems to me that, at least on theoretical grounds, it would bring in one kind of phonetic reception at the cost of throwing away another one.

Ling:

That's precisely what I found when I was doing this work with frequency transposition.

Villchur:

Well, I've never heard the Johansson system so I can't answer for it. I can answer for my system of synthetic fricatives. In my case it's a single ⅓-octave band of noise, which is inserted at the very top of the useful frequency range of hearing of the person. It is amplitude modulated by the high frequency sound above 4 or 5 kHz, and I can tell you that not only is the original pattern and the suprasegmental features of the speech not interrupted, it is improved. You hear sounds like the /s/ and the attack of the /t/ a little bit better, filling in the rhythmic pattern.

Ling:

Would you hear the fricative components of the voiced fricatives like /z/ and so on.

Villchur:

Yes, if they're strong enough. The whole thing's adjustable. You can make it just barely audible or you can make it very audible. The difference is, I think, that the Johansson system introduces transposed sound into the entire range up to 1 Hz. When you play the speech with my synthetic fricatives—I used normals listening through a 500-Hz cutoff at 98 dB/octave—aside from the subjective effect when you do intelligibility testing, there's about 25% improvement.

Ling:

Loudness Discomfort Level

There's another point that I think is rather fascinating. You've Arthur's data on the LDL [loudness discomfort level] and you've regarded it as something of a fixed entity. Silverman at C.I.D. did some work on LDL and he found that LDL's improve slightly with exposure and practice. I can remember talking to Bertil Johansson about this and he said that they had some data from Swedish schools in which the children in fact became more sensitive to loudness, and instead of having tolerance levels set at 110, they came down 105, 100, and so on. It seems to me that when we're talking about this, we're talking as if an LDL is a pretty stable sort of thing. Do you really think that that is so?

Villchur:

No, but the thresholds aren't stable either. I'm simply giving the example of what happens when the dynamic range of hearing is severely restricted. The deaf person hears only the most intense elements of speech, and all other elements drop out. The results produced by an electronic model of this disability were confirmed in two cases in which the subject made an unsolicited comment reflecting the fact that he was perceiving only the peaks of the speech signal. They said, "The speech is all broken up" and "It cuts out."

Ling:

Well, it does, and there are sort of straightforward reasons why you can say this, because of the nature of speech and the amplification curve. You know the vowel /a/ has louder second formants than /i/, loudness in terms of actual subjective loudness, and for many kids at a distance of 3 or 4 yards, /a/ is the only vowel they can hear. This sort of thing is very, very patchy. The sound will come and go and so will the suprasegmentals that are carried by the vowels. One of the things that really fascinated me was your claim or statement that there seems to be a loudness expansion with peaks. There is certainly a tendency to turn down a peaky aid and then reduce the extremes because the peaks poke into the discomfort level. However, it seems to me that if there are peaks in this mid frequency range just about 1000 or so and they are fairly sharp, then far more masking tends to occur in the immediately following range. In other words, place discriminations that are very much over 1500 Hz are more adversely affected when there are peaks of that type. Moreover, virtually every manufacturer of aids puts out a series of curves and they show loads of different low frequency cuts. Some call them slopes, but many of them just peak around 1000. There's no doubt that such peaks are undesirable, but why do they occur at or around 1000, and what can be done to eliminate them since there is no question that they cause a great deal of difficulty?

Villchur:

I'm happy to say that there is an answer. Most of the peaks derive from the characteristics of the receiver; the peaks that occur are likely to be worse than you see in the curves because the receiver plus the plumbing, which is random, makes it even worse; but there is a solution. There are ways of plumbing the hearing aid so that the response is exceedingly smooth and so that the slope of the curve can be adjusted to whatever you like, sloping up, flat, or sloping down. This is done by a combination that consists of boring out the inside of the earmold so that there is a gradual increase in diameter of the path into the ear—it becomes a horn—plus the use of damping plugs in the tubing. [See Killion reference in Chapter 7.]

Ross:

*Coupler
versus
Real
Ear
Responses*

I have a question about this. You've been defining what I think are coupler responses; the real ear response we know is different. Ira was talking about real ear responses in a sound field, aided and unaided, and getting marked improvement in speech discrimination when the aided thresholds paralleled the normal audibility curve. The peaks may not be there in the real ear, or they may be worse or they may be different. In defining peaks observed in the coupler as the problem, we may be defining the wrong problem.

Ling:

It's an interesting sort of thing that this correlates very well with the shape of the audiogram. Many children have a saucer-shaped audiogram with poorer hearing in the mid frequencies than in the high or low. This type of hearing aid (with a 1000-Hz peak) doesn't bug them at all. It fills in; but it bugs the average child who has a straight ski slope.

Boothroyd:

There's another problem that comes up and I think Mark [Ross] was referring to it earlier. Compression reduces the amplification of the stronger, low frequency sounds relative to the high intensity low frequency sounds, but in some cases what the listener needs is an increase of amplification for the weaker sounds.

Villchur:

You're talking about single channel.

Boothroyd:

Well, any kind of compression means you're going to run into the simple problem of amplification once the loss gets about 90 dB. Under normal environmental circumstances with the kind of distances you're talking about in running speech, no amount of tailoring of the frequency response or compression circuitry is going to solve the problem of enough gain.

Villchur:

I think that what you're saying is that when you use the kind of compression plus equalization that I was talking about, the demands on the hearing aid are greater in the sense that we want the hearing aid to do what it really needed to do to begin with. However, I would point out, and I consider this an exceedingly important advantage of the two-channel compression hearing aid, that when my average subject adjusted the intensity of the sound to the most comfortable loudness consistent with maximum intelligibility, he adjusted the processed speech 3 dB lower than he adjusted the unprocessed speech; and I think that's a big advantage. Pickett has shown that one of the sources of perceptive distortion is simply the raw absolute intensity of the sound. When he fed normal subjects sound of the same intensity, they too suffered in intelligibility. If you can cut 3 dB out with compression and perhaps another 3, 4, or 5 dB out with binaural amplification, the reduction of intensity alone is a worthwhile advantage.

Ross

What I was thinking of was that because the average speech input for high frequencies is much less, the gain at the high frequencies would need to be much more in order to get above threshold, and then you're running into feedback problems.

Villchur:

Yes, but you see in terms of the requirements of gain, you use a higher gain amplifier for the high channel. You don't have to have high gain in both channels. Antifeedback measures must, of course, be increased.

Børrild:

How do you (Villchur) control what's coming out of an earmold made as you describe?

Villchur:

In this particular case it was measured on the KEMAR manikin but I believe validated by a probe microphone. Mead Killion is acutely conscious of the difference between coupler response and what Mark called real ear response, what I call orthotelephonic response, and he calls etymotic response. It's the pressure that's actually there at the eardrum, compared to the pressure in comparable free field conditions.

Børrild:

It's very difficult to measure the pressure close to the eardrum.

Villchur:

It can be done. Yes, you can do it by threshold; (Hirsh's suggestion) you can do it by probe, or you can do it by getting the pressure point further back and then using a formula to transpose to the eardrum.

Ross:

I'd just like to bring up something that you mentioned a moment ago: the real ear responses. A lot of the research we've had in the past has looked at the relationship of different distortions and intelligibility. The reason we've had such inconsistent results is because we have looked at coupler defined distortions and frequency responses and compared them to real ear measured discrimination test scores. I think a lot of our inconsistent results occurred because coupler responses do not tell us about a specific real ear response. We don't know if the peaks are still there when they're in the real ear or if some kind of distortion occurs. Is this something you would consider a valid point?

Villchur:

I think that that is very true. In the past, in looking at frequency response, what they've looked at has been something other than what existed.

Ling:

For one thing, transient response has never really been looked at in most of these sorts of studies, whereas other types of distortion have been fairly well measured.

Villchur:

That's true. There are many distortions to look at and I think it would be wrong to follow the more esoteric types of distortion until we have put to rest the obvious. What you do is pursue those effects that are gross and you try to do something about them before you pursue the more exotic difficulties.

Ling:

Frequency Response

There is one thing arising out of this discussion that again goes back to our charge this morning, which is to relate a lot of this to clinical practice. I think we are going to have to face questions such as establishing things like LDL's on children. It happens to be quite a problem. One reads a lot about this bisection of the loudness discomfort level and the threshold of detection, and one arrives at these figures somewhat arbitrarily at times. With children at the prelinguistic level, there are no really good solid measures, objective measures of LDL.

Ross:

Ira was telling me that Margo Skinner [at C.I.D.] has done some things that some manufacturers (Victoreen) and dealers (Wallenfells) have done in bisecting the LDL and the threshold of detection to arrive at an MCL. That still doesn't tell us what the upper limit (LDL) is. For the moderately hearing impaired it's not that urgent, but for the severely impaired it is.

Ling:

I think the weakness of the MCL system is that people talk about it as if it is unchanging with frequency characteristics. You put a hearing aid on someone and you can determine their MCL. Their MCL is going to change according to whether you have most amplification in the high frequencies or the low frequencies, and whether there are peaks; so LDL and MCL are very much determined by the frequency response of the hearing aid.

Ross:

These psychoacoustical functions are also frequency selective, so that the LDL and MCL may both be different at different frequencies. If you built into the response of your instrument that pattern of amplification . . .

Villchur:

That will work, as I said, if you have a lot of head room. If the dynamic range is fairly large to begin with, then the listener can turn the volume up a little louder than he really wants it and he manages to hear the consonants well enough. He hears the high intensity vowels as a little too loud, and he hears the soft consonants as not quite loud enough. It's a compromise, but he has enough head room so he can play with it.

Ling:

It's really interesting to see how head room changes according to the degree of hearing loss. With someone who has a fair amount of hearing you can work 40–50 dB above threshold. A further loss of 10 dB, then it's 30–40 dB above threshold; loss of 20 dB, then it's less, and with the profoundly deaf kid, you may have to work at 10 dB above the threshold or else you're in real trouble.

COMPENSATORY ELECTROACOUSTIC SIGNAL PROCESSING

Ling:

Can I follow up your [Hirsh] statement about the sort of non-specific stimulation being quite adequate in the early or initial stages. I think that exposure to undifferentiated patterns is not going to be very helpful to a young baby and that pattern perception is probably crucial. I remember Hal Davis making a really big point about this at the 1964 Toronto Conference. It was the consensus there that this pattern perception was really a crucial thing.

First Stages of Sound Awareness

Hirsh:

I may have overstated or you may have overinterpreted. I don't mean that the hearing aid system of such a babe turns on the noise and turns it off whenever there's sound in the environment. There's still patterning. In particular there's patterning in time even though it may be in the large low frequency sounds. Beyond that, in communication that takes place, even in a nursery school situation between teacher and child, the vocabulary is so limited that there just isn't much information being transmitted. There doesn't need to be such a wide band system for the transmission of little information. You'll say that that's going to change very quickly and I'd have to agree, because you want to expand on that vocabulary immediately and start building it, you the parent and you the teacher. However, at the very beginning it's sound versus no sound, and then long sound versus short sound, and then loud sound versus weak sound. Children don't know what dimensions of sound to attend to, and we who know something about sound can manipulate those dimensions in early training so that you can reinforce, for example, these systematic discriminations on these different acoustical dimensions. Proponents of this point of view are particularly worried about the influence of environmental noise. If you just slap a hearing aid on, it's very difficult to single out what are the dimensions to be attended to. So if you're going to use an amplifying system, then you're going to have to be sure that the environmental sounds are down to a minimum as you suggest in some of your [Ling] paragraphs, so that the figure stands out from the ground.

Fry:

I'm still not clear on this sound versus no sound concept really, because as far as I can see, no sound is the whole universe of acoustic input that is not linked with some external reference and sound is whatever gets so linked. To this extent, of course, I have no doubt in my mind that the argument is fallacious because the whole business is done after the stuff gets into the brain.

Hirsh:

Dennis, there is a point I think worth pushing further. If you have event A and a sound associated with it and event B and the sound associated with it, it is very important that when A is followed by B, there be no sound in between. That degree of patterning is important because otherwise you'll have kind of a homogeneous background of sound. I recall that animals, not only those raised in darkness but also those raised in light but with ping pong balls sewed over the eyes (undifferentiated light), also lost the use of their eyeball systems; visual systems.

Fry:

But are we talking about the auditory system at that level? I personally was not. I'm talking about upstairs.

Hirsh:

I was talking about the level that you and Edith Whetnall called appreciation of sound: sound awareness.

Fry:

To me it doesn't convey very much quite frankly, except in this very lowest general sense, which you mentioned just now. That is, if the child were in such a condition that sounds make no impression whatever in any condition, one might say that there is an absence of sound awareness. For me personally I don't find the idea so useful, the idea of sound awareness.

Hirsh:

Once you start to differentiate among sounds, then you're pulling away from it.

Ling:

I think Dennis is rather like me feeling that you have to have the best possible pattern right from time zero. Ira mentions a very similar point, which is the one about Upton's eyeglasses. That is, whether you present in the transform of the acoustic signal the sort of raw data from which the child can extract the features, or whether you actually present the results of the extraction. The human being is so structured that the extraction of the thing for himself is of the greatest importance; therefore, the more complex the display, the more chance the child has of extracting the features. This goes along with what Dennis said this morning about the child learning through actually searching. I'm very doubtful in view of the choppy nature of the signal obtained, that a child could learn if we throw a number of distinctive feature extractions at him. They're segmented in time and there's no overall flow as there is with speech. I think it's much better for the child to extract the pattern. A great deal of research would be needed to show things one way or the other, but instinctively I would think that the more complex pattern is going to be superior.

Hirsh:

What I really want to know from those of you who are practitioners is about this old notion that you should retain the same listening system from as early as possible. Don't change it. Don't change from classroom hearing aid to wearable. Don't change from coded to uncoded. How important is that?

*Consistency
Of Amplification*

Ling:

I think the notion of consistency in speech input is an illusion from the start. You have different signal-to-noise ratios. You have different intensities with distance. There is no such thing as consistent speech signals, so to talk about putting a hearing aid on a kid and saying, even though it's inferior to a group hearing aid, it's going to be better because it's going to be consistent is a specious argument in my view. Certainly a good quality group aid is a really good system. If this is the system that provides the best cues for a particular child, then this is what you should use. However, I think there is a difference between high quality conventional amplification and surrogate, transposed, or radically changed speech. I think that here again one has to question whether poor results with tranposed speech are attributable to the fact that you are using quite a different oral encoding system. When I was at the Massachusetts Institute of Technology, I listened to a frequency warped transposition system in which the low frequencies are less radically changed than the highs. I could certainly detect all of the speech sounds. I could discriminate them quite readily. I could even learn to identify most of them, but when I tried to understand running speech I couldn't. On introspection I felt that the reason that I couldn't was that the sounds didn't accord closely enough with those for which I had already developed an encoding system. Whether frequency warp would work with a baby who didn't have an already established system standing in the way, I don't know. We shouldn't, clearly, mix radically changed and conventional amplification, but, I don't see any point in seeking more consistency than that.

Hirsh:

This is the practical matter that leads me to suggest that if a child is sufficiently in need of one of these fancy systems, we can put them on and just use band amplification in the frequency range where he has sensitivity in the earliest years. I'm suggesting that that much may suffice for the low information, reception, and transmission that goes on in those earliest years and that we'll get things refined later on when we have some speech instruction accompanying his career in the schools.

Villchur:

What I heard Ira say was that the first hearing aid worn by the babe is used for following patterns of sound, for detecting patterns of sound, and that fancy processing wasn't needed for that. I don't know whether it's true or not, but I haven't heard anything really to contradict it. I haven't heard anyone say that the first thing the child does is other than get sound patterns.

Hirsh:

He could even listen to 1000 Hz low pass babble of his own production and doesn't that contain a lot of information? Can't we forget about the fancy high pass processing until later on?

Boothroyd:

Auditory-Motor Association

I would like to raise the question of the importance of the auditory-motor association. We discussed this in relation to perception and production earlier. If you're going to have to wait until the child gets into school and starts formal speech work before imposing the transformed patterns, 5 years opportunity to build auditory-motor association will have been lost. For the normal child the actions of speech and the sounds of speech are one and the same thing. One can stand for the other. That's why when he hears speech, he can reproduce it. This provides one argument against the idea of postponing the "fancy" treatment. Another important question is whether one should create a simplified acoustic environment for the hearing-impaired child in order to ease him into the process of auditory perceptual development. The idea of not putting the hearing aid on until the child has reached the ability to respond and be aware of sound is supported by some writers. Others think the child should simply be given the patterns in the hope that he has the normal complement of neurons that are going to permit him to abstract. The same argument appears in relation to the question of consistency in amplification. I agree with you, Dan, that this is a red herring. However, there is a different kind of consistency that is very important. Suppose we have a wearable hearing aid and a group hearing aid, and suppose the wearable hearing aid is no good for the child. It's as though he isn't wearing anything when he puts the hearing aid on. So part of the time the child is functioning nonauditorily and part of the time he's functioning auditorily. That presents the danger of really interfering with his natural process of perceptual development. Even if both instruments are suitable to him, we know that in the real environment with a real wearable hearing aid, there are limits on gain because of the acoustic feedback problem. Many of the children are not going to get a sufficiently intense signal for it to be complete. They're going to hear the louder components, but they're not going to hear the quieter ones. At the same time we know that in the real environment there will be a lot of noise, which will also interfere with the quieter components. Even if we could solve the problem of gain, we couldn't improve the signal-to-noise ratio simply through more amplification. This is where the benefits of the group hearing aid are apparent. It is not that the group aid provides better quality amplification in terms of frequency response, distortion, and everything else. What it does is just improve the signal-to-noise ratio and increase the input signal so that we can provide for audibility of the signal even for the very deaf child. In theory, that more perfect pattern should be better for him, and the more often we can make it available in the remedial situation, the better it should be. However, there are some educators who are arguing on the basis of consistency and reality that the child should just learn to wear his hearing aid, his personal hearing aid, wear it all the time—wear it in class and out of class and at home—and not mess around with group hearing aids at all. All I can say is that I visited some programs in which this philosophy is applied and the children are doing beautifully. I think they're probably doing beautifully for other reasons. It's probably the quality of the education program; but the point is that wearing their personal hearing aids is not standing in the way of these children.

Villchur:

If you're including the profoundly deaf in this simple hearing aid for the child, the lack of some kind of processing could prevent the child from hearing speech patterns. The child would only hear the tops of speech patterns, the most intense parts. If you simulate a very restricted dynamic range of hearing electronically, the rhythm of speech is destroyed: the first thing you notice is the destruction of the normal time pattern of the speech. You can convert, by multiband compression and equalization, the perceptually distorted speech to have a normal temporal pattern.

Børrild:

I have nothing against group hearing aids and speech trainers. They have been an eminent help for many years. You can use loops, infrared systems, AM or FM radio links, as you like, but in any case you should—in my opinion—end up the chain with the personal hearing aid normally used; not exclusively for acoustic reasons, but more to make it clear to the child that this device is just a part of the person, which has to be there and then, "just forget about it."

If we change too much during the day, we may risk directing too much attention to the different aids used and giving the child the impression that after all hearing is a very artificial and difficult thing, which might not be worth the trouble. The necessary equipment should be noticed as little as possible not only by the child, but by the teachers or parents as well.

That is one of the main reasons why I prefer not to change over the day, but to let the personal hearing aid act as the amplifying part of the system permanently. I think you can do it today without a serious bad conscience, as most modern hearing aids from the better manufacturers are quite good amplifiers, which does not mean that improvements should be impossible. Another thing is that I don't think I'd want to put a very sophisticated and special device on a child and train him with it, not knowing if I could get a similar one in 5 years or 3 years in case the training turned out to be a success. We had that ethical problem when we started training with the Johansson transposers. When we get a guarantee that we could have them as long as we wanted them, we started training them but you must have a guarantee that you can continue to get a similar device.

Ling:

I would like to come to another point of yours, Ira, which concerns aspects of visual input of speech. One of them is the unisensory (that is, auditory) versus the multisensory approach, which is audition plus vision plus anything else that goes. I think there's really no very good evidence about this sort of thing either way. In my work with speech development and hearing development in hearing-impaired kids, I work very much on an auditory-only approach for a large amount of the time. It is my clinical impression that if one puts a hearing aid on a child and then proceeds to attract his attention visually, either by getting him to look at you or by looking in a mirror, you are, in fact, focusing the attention on the visual rather than the auditory and saying that's where your information will be coming from: the visual side. It seems to me that time and time again when I work with hearing-impaired children, I see that where people have not focused on vision, manner distinctions, for example, are virtually always confused: /b/ and /m/. These sort of manner distinctions are audible to almost all but totally deaf kids, because there are manner cues in the low frequencies. With a lot of lipreading, which does not differentiate manner of production at all well (there are instances in which it does), the manner cues are confused visually. I teach manner distinctions in teaching speech to hearing-impaired kids before I teach place distinctions, because for the most part they are more readily audible to the majority of hearing-impaired kids: place cues lying principally above 1500 Hz and manner cues lying considerably below. That's one aspect of this visual argument. There's another one that I think is really quite important. When you use visual devices as part of a training process, usually speech training, they can provide inappropriate feedback. For example, in using a spectrograph to teach diphthongs, the feedback provided is about the formant transition, or formant movement. The child can give a response with a terrible voice and get a "fine, you're OK" response from the machine. One can produce exactly the right sort of formant pattern with lousy breathy voice, poor control of voice patterns and so on. These problems can thus be rehearsed into habitual production. There's also a feedback problem that relates to this point. In speech reception, we are concerned with audition and vision and touch, but in speech

Competition or Complementation of Visual Input

production these senses are used in a different way. They are used to provide feedback. Because of the neural and mechanical delay involved, feedback can only provide you with knowledge of correctness, that what one said was what one intended to say. It can't provide you with moment-by-moment control of speech. In normal speech one can produce several phonemes before one would be able to hear out any one of them, so that feed forward is very much more important than feedback in terms of speech production. Many of visual speech training machines are set up to train the child to try to exercise moment-by-moment control over production when in fact that's not what we should be setting out to do when we're really trying to teach production. We should be focusing on correct oral-sensory motor patterns and feed forward processes rather than concentrating on ongoing feedback. You really have quite a bunch of things here in terms of vision and its role in both perception and in speech. The questions are: is vision always an advantage? Does it always add or can it, in fact, detract from speech reception or certain aspects of speech reception? Second: What is the role of visual training devices? To provide feedback which is a post hoc evaluation of a response, or should one in fact use them to teach moment-by-moment control?

Hirsh:

On the first one my guess is that vision won't detract from auditory reception as long as it is redundant to the auditory pattern. It seems to me that there is a degree of redundancy that is in the speech mechanism itself. That is, both the lipread information and the auditory information are expressions of the same act. In that case I think there's sufficient redundancy so that there would not be confusion. (I recognize that except for the mirror the visual is not a way to monitor lipreading cues.) When you start to talk about auditory plus some of these fancy gadgets, I shouldn't think that that would be particularly helpful in receiving information, but if you want to use a gadget to underline a particular aspect of the speech act, then I don't see why that would be a difficulty.

Villchur:

I was once impressed by a paper that Arthur [Boothroyd] wrote about evaluations of visual systems. One of the things he pointed out was that the old fashioned system, in which the feedback system was the teacher saying, "yes, no, higher, lower, . . ." used with the same concentration of effort, worked about as well as the fancy electronic systems. However, there remains the residual benefit of the electronic system, particularly if it's a small one and a wearable one, that between clinic sessions the kid is on his own.

Boothroyd:

Can I respond for a moment to Dan's question about the competition between vision and audition? I think we should distinguish between a person who is perceiving with an established system (someone who has language and is looking for cues through visual and auditory modalities and has no difficulty integrating them because both cue the same message), and the child who is supposedly learning perceptual skills. Those people who initially promulgated a unisensory approach were talking only about orientation to the auditory component of speech in children who were visually dominant.

Hirsh:

I'm not so worried about this focus on the visual as you, because you don't turn off what ears you have left just because you are looking.

Ling:

I think you can. A couple of studies we've done in cued speech really underline the danger of this. After a couple of years training with visual cues, kids had switched off audition. Whether their hearing aids were on or off it made no difference to their speech reception scores. It's pretty convincing to me from looking at a whole lot of work that I've done clinically and also experimentally, that there are risks inherent in concentrating on vision at a very early stage.

Hirsh:

The consequence of the view, it seems to me, is to go back to something that you were arguing against a little while ago, and that is if you throw away the visual cues for the moment in a young child, then you are asking him to work on an impoverished stimulus, one that doesn't have as many cues as there are available. You're cutting off one channel of information.

Ling:

For particular training; for training on particular stuff, yes, but not all the time, not in communication situations.

Levitt:

What if the effects are symbiotic? That you have to have both together for speechreading, say.

Boothroyd:

Certainly in voiced-voiceless distinctions it's a combination of the two that's going to give you the information.

AUDITORY TRAINING

Ross:

I was interested when reading your [Ling] chapter, that you didn't mention all the research you've done on auditory training. Specifically, where does the work you've done on auditory coding fit into your present thinking?

Ling:

I'm in a really funny position about auditory training. About 5 years ago if somebody had asked me to give a couple of consecutive, full courses on auditory training, I would have done it with confidence and glee. However, I am now at the point where if you ask me to give a half-semester course, I'm slightly worried about what the content should be. The experiments I have done on discrimination are all very well. They attack possibilities for training skills that the child doesn't spontaneously acquire in the course of his auditory experience. However, I don't think they represent an adequate approach to auditory training.

Boothroyd:

I'd go along with that. I've gone through the same sequence of events. One of the reasons is that when you become involved in auditory training you are often dealing with children who are not auditorily turned on. They're at a higher level of development in other areas and they're just not tuned into their ears. One of the traditional approaches—teaching finer and finer discriminations (loud-soft, long-short, and so on)—was useful for getting the child back on the tracks again, getting him to realize that there is information in sound. One of the problems we have is that a lot of people have looked at that kind of work and thought that that was the way it should be done with the developing child. However, I think you can leave the child to do that for himself. If you structure the environment suitably, he's going to become aware of sound and become aware of differences. I can think of some particular examples where we've gone through activities that we were very pleased with and then discovered that they were totally unnecessary. All you have to do is create real meaningful situations to which you need to call the child's attention, and he will develop his auditory capacity.

Mention has been made of the inertia in the education of the deaf. It's very interesting to note that when attempts were made to first introduce group amplification there was tremendous resistence. One of the arguments against hearing aids was that lipreading skills would suffer. Everyone thought there would be interference of hearing on lipreading just as we are now concerned with interference in the opposite direction. Of course, it didn't happen. What happened was that amplification improved the total input, language skills improved, speech skills improved, educational achievement improved, and therefore lipreading improved.

Ling:

What I'm afraid of in that regard is that when you get rid of the inertia, you then have a bandwagon effect that leads to the acceptance of the new in favor of the old, instead of the better in favor of the poorer.

Boothroyd:

I'd like to mention an auditory study in which we deliberately adopted a global approach. Everything had to do with comprehension and communication. We did not use discrimination tasks or multiple choice responses. The children's reactions were interesting. These were all children whom we felt ought to be doing better auditorily than they were. They hated the training at first; but later they came to enjoy it, and they succeeded. When we tested their performance using both analytic discrimination tests and global comprehension tests, we didn't get any improvement in discrimination. The improvement was in the perception of words in sentences and not in isolated words. Something else of interest happened during that study, which is of relevance to what we talked about before. All this work was done with group hearing aids: ideal signal, ideal signal-to-noise ratio. Halfway through the study we felt guilty. Personal hearing aids were taking a back seat. Once again we were in danger of letting the children believe that hearing aids aren't important. So I asked the teacher to do some of the evaluations with their personal hearing aids and it was a complete disaster. Two of the children were in tears, and the rest were angry because they couldn't hear the message. Now whether that really means that they have to have the group amplification equipment or whether it means that they have to have additional training with hearing aids and learn how to function, I don't know, but it was an interesting occurrence.

Hirsh:

I have a worry about this emphasis on comprehension when it goes so far as to represent a suppression of instructional techniques that have been based on more analytic approaches. In fact it's clear that you don't want to throw them out completely. I hope that we don't swing around full cycle as they do in the history of reading, where look-see kinds of meaning associations with words seems now to be an insufficient training approach if you really want kids to read. What you do is emphasize the original alphabet-to-phoneme code. So I'm just a little worried about this antianalytic emphasis.

Ling:

Yes and no. I think I go into it very much more carefully in my book than in this chapter. I don't substitute repression of cues or jettison this type of analytic work. I think there's room for both. I think one has to go for comprehension in the way that I've suggested. On the other hand, there is a time when particular aspects demand more analytic procedures, for example, in speech teaching. I think the teacher should know when to be global and when to be analytical.

Hirsh:

She has to know lots of things, but I don't think you can represent it now as a shift where you don't use any training stimuli that don't have meaning, that don't have payoff in the social communication sense. I think that's going too far.

Speech versus Nonspeech Stimuli

May I come to the second point, which is the relation between training on nonspeech sounds and its application in perception of speech? It's quite clear that you can demonstrate huge learning effects in a great variety of auditory discrimination tasks that are nonspeech. The clearest one, for example, is the 600 msec initial limits for successions of unrelated sounds for which you can get down to about 100 or 200 msec with training. I can't believe that such training would not have an effect on, for example, the segmentation that involves similar durations in speech. You [Ling] tell us that the ability to discriminate the sequential order of speech sounds is certainly better than the ability to discriminate the order of nonspeech stimuli, both among normal hearing listeners and so on. The point is the relatedness of the sounds, not whether they are speech or nonspeech, in regards to discriminating their sequential order.

Ross:

Doesn't speech sequence engage a different kind of memory? Isn't it easier to group blocks of speech-sound in memory than nonsignificant type sounds?

Hirsh:

I think that's the point that's being made here. What I'm saying is that there certainly are rules of grouping that are imposed by your acquisition of the knowledge of the language, but there are also laws of grouping that belong to a more general phenomenon called auditory perception. I think this "speech is special" has carried us too far away from that view.

Villchur:

As far as the training with nonspeech sounds is concerned, it's sort of analogous to what used to be called "faculty" psychology in education theory. If you wanted a person to reason well, you taught him Latin and mathematics and that was supposed to train his reasoning faculty. Later it became generally accepted that if you wanted to train a person to reason in the field of politics what you did was have him practice reasoning in political subjects. He did much better by using the materials that he was actually going to work with.

Hirsh:

Before you leave that sly point, I have to comment on it. The point is that you're talking about training him in the tools, and the difficulty is that with respect to speech sounds, we don't know what all the tool dimensions are, particularly when you're using whole speech sounds together. If you want to make some hypotheses about what the tool dimensions are, then you do pull those out and demonstrate abilities to discriminate on dimensions, a, b, c, d, e without speech sounds because you don't know how to manipulate dimensions independently within speech sounds. Then you take those tools and apply them within the speech supertools, which become then the instruments.

Villchur:

I think the burden of proof is on the person who proposes to use training with abstracted stimuli; with nonspeech sounds.

Ling:

It's interesting that this has persisted without anyone ever showing any relationship to ability to perceive speech. I mean, there's a discussion point about it, but teachers use bells, drums, whistles, car horns, and things like that in auditory training because it has always been done that way and not because it has been shown to be effective.

Levitt:

I have the feeling that most of this is directed for the severely to profoundly deaf child, and a lot of people who will be reading this book will be working with hard-of-hearing children in regular schools. I think maybe the auditory training strategies are different. One seems to be concentrating on awareness of sound and gross distinction, whereas the hard-of-hearing child would have much finer distinctions to look for. For those kids, this cognitive approach may be more effective.

Ling:

I think it's more effective for all ranges of kids, but what I'm really trying to say is that the least intervention is the best intervention, and that what you do is work on the comprehension side until you find out what it is that the kid can't do and then you devise a specific analytic training procedure. Children with more hearing may well be able to learn without any sort of artificial training intervention at all. The more severely hearing impaired the child, the more structured your approach has to be.

Levitt:

The nature of the lesson should emphasize the cognitive aspect. Where you have certain words and you systematically reduce the redundancy for the words or phrases that you're trying to get the child to recognize. The child doesn't know this, but the teacher is choosing the words is very much aware of the specific contrasts that ought to be taught. You don't teach the child that this is voiced and this is voiceless. You teach the child as part of the context, but you're very careful to choose the stimuli accordingly.

Boothroyd:

I think that generalizes to other areas as well. I think the structure that we inevitably come down to in trying to write about and discuss these things is something that needs to exist in the mind of the teacher, but not in the activities done with the student. This is true of teaching language. You don't teach language to a deaf child by teaching him the rules of the sentence, but you have to know them yourself.

Ling:

There are many sort of things related to that, which I think are really quite important. One of them is strategies. I haven't talked about strategies at all here, but in working with hearing-impaired kids, if you want them, for example, to produce an *r* and they cannot hear an *r-w* distinction, it's very, very easy to teach it through whispering rather then speaking. This is because the formant change becomes very audible in a whisper when it's inaudible in voice. So you're cutting out the categoricality of perception and you're allowing a much more analytic approach. The interesting thing about whispered voice is that what you're doing is really cutting out a lot of the low frequency energy and putting in much more energy further up the frequency range as you hold the microphone closer. There are dozens of these sort of techniques that one can talk about in auditory training.

Boothroyd:

I'd like to raise a very important point, which I think is understood by people working in the area of reading, but not by those working on speech perception by the hearing impaired. I believe we take as much information from the stimulus as we need in order to satisfy ourselves that we are perceiving what we expect to be perceiving at any particular time. In listening to speech we don't in fact analyze every sound or every feature, just as when reading we don't look at every letter. Therein lies the hope for the hearing-impaired child. Given sufficient meaningful input, and lots of experience with the global message, he has a chance to learn how to get from the stimulus to the appropriate linguistic interpretation without having all the information available to him. We have it and don't use it. He doesn't have it, but he has to learn how, to get to an end point without going through the stages that we went through. We have access to complete information, and we have freedom of strategy in perception. When we are listening to speech, we can take in more or less of the acoustic information as we need it. If we're in trouble, we can go to greater depths and the information is there. If the content is very difficult, we can take in more of the acoustic information. If there is noise present, we can manage with a little bit less and it is really not too difficult. The hearing impaired, on the other hand, whether he's lipreading entirely or whether he's hearing with defective hearing, doesn't have that freedom of strategy. There's a limit to the amount of analysis that is possible for him. He has to learn strategies that permit him to keep on going even when there is not enough information available. For example, accepting his own interpretation of a particular sentence at a particular time and hoping that even though he isn't absolutely sure what he heard, it will become apparent as the discussion continues. He may not be exactly sure what somebody said to him, but he'll answer anyway as though he did understand and risk making himself look silly. One of the problems with the person who becomes deaf and has to rely more on lipreading than on hearing, is that he is afraid of exactly that kind of situation. He needs practice in acquiring these new strategies in situations that are more global and less analytic. In one sense we are painting a bleak picture for the hearing impaired by suggesting that they don't have all the available acoustic information, but there is the chance for them to get it in other ways. There are many children who demonstrate that they can in fact learn these skills, even given the defective input mechanism from the start.

As I look back over the history of education of the deaf, I see about three significant events. One was the realization that the deaf could be educated and, with that, the introduction of signed languages to make it feasible. The second was the demonstration that with a lot of effort you could in fact teach the deaf to use verbal language rather than manual alternatives. The third was the demonstration that all the deaf aren't deaf, that hearing can be used to accomplish these ends in a large number of cases. I think we're still waiting for the full implications of the last development to be realized. We see it with individual children and with individual programs but not in terms of its mass application. I can't resist a tongue in cheek comment, which also provides food for thought. The results of my many years of research in this field are often expressed in terms of correlations between various quantities. They can, however, be summarized as follows:

The deafer you are, the worse you hear. The worse you hear, the worse you speak, and the worse you speak, the more difficulty you have in making yourself understood. This is not as facetious as it may seem. Its corollary is: The more effectively a hearing-impaired child can learn to use his hearing, the less handicapped he will be.

APPENDICES

GUIDELINES FOR AUDIOLOGY PROGRAMS IN EDUCATIONAL SETTING FOR HEARING-IMPAIRED CHILDREN

Developed by the Joint Committee on Audiology and Education of the Deaf
Approved by: The American Speech and Hearing Association
The Conference of Executives of American Schools for the Deaf

Many preschool and school-age children have hearing impairments severe enough to affect their ability to function normally in an educational setting. Although each child has a legal, constitutional right to comprehensive quality services in educational settings, fewer than 50 percent are currently receiving appropriate services (Weintraub, Abeson, and Braddock, 1971). The position taken in these guidelines is that audiology programs should be an integral part of comprehensive services to hearing-impaired children in educational settings (ASHA, 1973).

These guidelines are not intended to cover identification audiometry programs. Although identification audiometry should be an integral part of a total audiological service for all children within any given school system, these guidelines are for programs in which children have already been identified as having a hearing impairment and requiring special educational and habilitative services. The American Speech and Hearing Association adopted Guidelines for Identification Audiometry in November 1974 (ASHA, 1975).

The term educational settings refers to organized programs of instruction, in private or public and residential or nonresidential environments, for hearing-impaired children who manifest special educational needs as a result of their hearing impairment. The rationale for organizing comprehensive and intensive audiology programs in these settings is based on three interlocking factors:

1. The auditory channel is the route through which speech and language development normally takes place. The human being's

development of speech and language appears to be based on innate, biologically programmed factors (Lenneberg, 1967; Fry, 1966) which can be exploited most effectively through an auditory input (Liberman, et al., 1967). The use of other approaches for teaching initial language and speech skills to hearing-impaired children must be considered inadequate, though frequently necessary, substitutes for the "real thing."

2. Most hearing-impaired children possess significant residual hearing capacity (Goodman, 1949; Huitzing, 1959; Eliott, 1967; Boothroyd, 1972; Hirsh, 1973). Interpreted pessimistically, these studies show that from one-half to two-thirds of the children enrolled in schools for the deaf have potentially useful residual hearing. This is precisely the population of hearing-impaired children expected to manifest the most severe hearing losses.

3. Efforts to employ maximally the residual hearing of most hearing-impaired children generally have met with little success. The evidence clearly demonstrates that at any one time, at least half the children's hearing aids can be malfunctioning; that many of the children who possess hearing aids do not routinely wear them; and that children who can potentially benefit from amplified sound do not even own a hearing aid (Gaeth, Lounsberry, 1966; Zink, 1972; Findlay, Winchester, 1972; Coleman, 1972; Northern, et al., 1972; Skalka, Moore, 1973; Porter, 1973). Classroom auditory trainers frequently fare little better than personal hearing aids (Matkin, Olsen, 1970a; Matkin, Olsen, 1970b; Wilson, Hoversten, Thies, 1972; Sung, Sung, Angelelli, 1973; Matkin, Olsen, 1973), and the poor acoustic conditions existing in classroom environments limit the effectiveness of even appropriate amplification (Ross, 1972). Finally, the great care needed to ensure individualized electroacoustic packaging to the impaired ear is seldom realized (Ling, 1964; Genge, 1971; Gengel, Pascoe, Shore, 1971; Sung, Sung, Angelelli, 1971; Danaher, Osberger, Pickett, 1973; Erber, 1973). These problems are understandable in view of the understaffed and ill-equipped audiology programs typically found in educational settings, and they are not likely to be remedied without a dedicated effort to strengthen these programs.

These guidelines attempt to describe the audiological conditions necessary for the exploitation of the auditory channel for speech and language development to the degree permitted by the residual hearing capacity of a hearing-impaired child. Schools and society are investing large sums of money in hearing aids, auditory trainers, and other audiological equipment. This investment is a wasteful expenditure unless this equipment is properly used and performing according to specifications. It is unrealistic to expect overburdened administrators and teachers to supervise the full exploitation of residual hearing in addition to their many other responsibilities. In regular and special education programs, the assistance of such resource personnel as psychologists, media specialists, guidance counselors, remedial-reading specialists, and learning disability teachers is welcomed. All of these specialists are finding a fruitful field for their endeavors. In educational programs for the hearing impaired, however, the audiologist, a resource person with skills to ensure the maximal exploitation of residual hearing is either absent, in short supply, or inadequately supported. The inclusion of well-educated audiologists is necessary to implement the commitment of educators to use optimally the residual hearing most hearing-impaired children possess.

Not all educational settings may be in a financial position to implement the entire program immediately. Possibly some of the suggested functions of audiologists will seem uselessly esoteric while others may need to be added or modified. Nevertheless, unless there is agreement on an eventual goal and informed commitment to high standards, improvement in audiological services is not likely to occur. It is expected that each step in the implementation of these guidelines will justify and support further steps until the entire program can be implemented. Certainly, modifications in the guidelines should be made as experience with their use accumulates. Some educational settings may find it financially desirable and convenient to contract for some or all audiology services with already existing facilities in their communities. In these instances, it is important that the spirit of these guidelines be adhered to, in that such arrangements should result in comprehensive and coordinated services to the child, parents, and educational staff. In any event, community-wide and inter-agency planning is desirable to minimize unnecessary duplication of professional services. It is emphasized that vastly improved audiological services will not be a panacea for speech and language problems. Miraculous cures are not likely to result, but improved performance in a significant number of children should occur. Intensive audiological intervention is deemed appropriate regardless of the "educational method" being used. There is no intent in these guidelines to favor, explicitly, or implicitly, any particular education approach.

PERSONNEL

1. One audiologist with a Certificate of Clinical Competence (CCC) in Audiology or its equivalent for approximately every 75 hearing-impaired children receiving special instructional and habilitative services in the educational setting.
2. A Director of Audiology (with either M.A. or Ph.D.) with a CCC in Audiology or its equivalent in any program where there are three or more audiologists. The Ph.D. degree is advisable in settings committed to a program of research.
3. One electronics technician for every 100 to 150 hearing-impaired children.
4. One full-time secretary/clerk for programs with three or more individuals on the staff. Part-time assistance will be needed in programs with one staff audiologist.
5. One or more audiometric assistants.
6. One or more consulting otolaryngologists.

EQUIPMENT

1. One sound-treated double room for programs with one audiologist and two sound-treated double rooms for every three audiologists employed. The dimensions of the test rooms should be sufficiently large to permit pediatric and hearing-aid evaluations in the sound field.
2. One two-channel clinical audiometer will be needed for each sound-treated double room, including the associated sound-field speakers and amplifiers.
3. A stock of loaner hearing aids in good working condition, along with extra cords, batteries, and receivers. It is assumed that all children will have their own hearing aids and that classroom auditory training units will be available.
4. Equipment for analyzing the electroacoustic characteristics of hearing aids and auditory training systems.
5. Instrumentation for impedance audiometry.
6. A sound-level meter and appropriate equipment for calibration of pure-tone and speech audiometers.
7. Ear-impression material kit, instamold kit, stock earmolds, hand grinder, earmold cleaners, and other miscellaneous earmold equipment.

JOB DESCRIPTIONS

Audiologist

1. Conduct comprehensive and periodic audiological assessments for each child. Younger children should be assessed as often as necessary to establish consistent, valid measures. Other children should be tested annually or whenever questions arise. Newly enrolled hearing-impaired students should be given a complete audiologic assessment. Additional audiological assessments may be needed when a new hearing aid is being considered, when otological examination is positive, when impedance audiometry indicates a change in the middle ear status or when teachers or parents notice a change in the child's auditory behavior.

2. Administer specific audiometric measures appropriate to the hearing-impaired child's needs and status. Children with recurring middle-ear problems may require only pre- and post-treatment pure-tone and impedance measures. The audiologist should be prepared to administer, when indicated, such assessments as: pure-tone audiometry; carefully graded speech discrimination measures; middle-ear impedance tests; tolerance and comfortable listening levels; speechreading tests; combined modality tests; aided and unaided sound-field measures; electroacoustic analysis of hearing aids; comparative hearing-aid evaluation; comparative intelligibility functions under different degrees of filtering; binaural versus monaural evaluations; dichotic listening measures; and other psychoacoustic measures that appear appropriate; for example, synthetic formant discriminations, difference limens for frequency, intensity and time, temporal integration, and effects of masking.

3. Advise school administrators and educators regarding the selection and purchase of auditory training equipment, and further be responsible for the electroacoustic evaluation of such equipment once it is placed within the classroom. Subsequent to purchasing such equipment, conduct or provide for periodic electroacoustic evaluations of it at least once per school year.

4. Assess and monitor classroom acoustics and the proper use of amplifying equipment, with consideration of the possible effects upon speech understanding.

5. Conduct auditory training programs for individual students or groups using or developing appropriate materials for the

particular children involved. The auditory training program should be based on the children's auditory status and development, and it should be developed in consultation with classroom teachers. Results of such programs should be evaluated and shared with teachers and others working with the children.

6. Participate in and/or conduct speech and language development programs based on an auditory approach.

7. Conduct inservice workshops for teachers and other staff members on such topics as microphone technique, intensity and articulation of input speech, relevance of language to topic, checking hearing aids daily, trouble-shooting of hearing aids and classroom equipment, significance of audiogram in terms of acoustics of speech, speech perception, and prosodic phenomena. Periodic classroom visits and teacher consultations may be considered inservice training too.

8. Conduct inservice training with electronics technician on the significance of the audiogram in relation to the characteristics and use of amplification equipment. Review electroacoustic data collected by the technician.

9. Make impressions for earmolds and teach earmold care to all staff members and students.

10. Participate in the admission procedures and placement procedures. Help develop criteria for early decisions regarding educational methodology to be employed with each child.

11. Participate in out-patient audiological program as appropriate in terms of community needs and time available.

12. Participate in parent-guidance and instructional counseling programs. Serve as a resource person in such programs to provide information on hearing loss, audiograms, hearing aids, acoustic environment, speech and language activities for home programs.

13. Conduct audiological research when possible and discuss its significance with staff and community leaders.

14. Evaluate quality and effectiveness of all aspects of audiology program.

Electronics Technician

1. Assess the status of hearing aids and classroom auditory training equipment at least three times during each school year.

2. Repair and maintain all auditory amplification and the speech or language training devices being used with the hearing-impaired children.

3. Assist with audiovisual equipment and videotape equipment as skills and experience permit.
4. Conduct or assist in the calibration and repair of audiometers.
5. Develop instrumentation required for research projects and programs of auditory training.

Secretary/Clerk

1. Maintain the records of the audiology program.
2. Answer telephone, make appointments, and maintain a schedule for each staff member.
3. Complete correspondence tasks required for the staff members.
4. Perform other tasks required for the operation of the audiology department under the direction of the staff members.

Audiometric Assistant

1. Perform specific tasks for which they are trained and supervised on the job by the audiologist in accordance with the American Speech and Hearing Association Guidelines on the Role, Training, and Supervision of Communication Aides adopted in November 1969 (ASHA, 1970).
2. Such tasks might include the administration of routine audiometric assessments, first echelon hearing aid maintenance, and acting as a test assistant for assessing preschool children or children who have behavior that makes them difficult to test.

Director of Audiology

1. Supervise and administer complete audiology program under the general direction of the school's chief administrator and on a coordinated basis with other department heads in the school.
2. Assign or conduct any portion of the program described above.
3. Participate in community public relations in terms of the audiology program.
4. Serve as a liaison with personnel in clinics, colleges, and universities or in the public school setting, using audiological programs. Act as audiology coordinator for any program that feeds children into the educational setting or into which children are assigned.
5. Supervise audiology practicum when school is affiliated with a college or university training program. May teach course work related to audiology services in an educational setting in the event of such an affiliation.

6. Direct or delegate research projects relative to use of amplification, effects of auditory training, and communication skills development.

REFERENCES

American Speech and Hearing Association (ASHA). Guidelines for identification audiometry. ASHA, 17:94–99, 1975.

American Speech and Hearing Association (ASHA). Guidelines on the role, training, and supervision of the communication aids. ASHA, 12: 78–80, 1970.

American Speech and Hearing Association (ASHA). Standards and guidelines for comprehensive language, speech, and hearing programs in the schools. The American Speech and Hearing Association, 9030 Old Georgetown Road, Washington, D.C. 20014, 1973–74.

Boothroyd, A. Distribution of hearing levels in Clarke School for the Deaf students. SARP #3, Clarke School for the Deaf, Northampton, Mass., 1972.

Coleman, R. F. Hearing aid stability in an acoustic preschool nursery program. Bill Wilkerson Hearing and Speech Center, Nashville, Tenn., 1972.

Danaher, E. M., Osberger, M. J., and Pickett, J. M. Discrimination of formant frequency transitions in synthetic vowels. J. Speech Hearing Res., 16:439–451, 1973.

Elliot, L. L. Descriptive analysis of audiometric and psychometric scores of students at a school for the deaf. J. Speech Hearing Res., 10:21–40, 1967.

Erber, J. P. Body-baffle and real-ear effects in the selection of hearing aids for deaf children. J. Speech Hearing Res., 38:224–231, 1973.

Findlay, R. C. and Winchester, R. A. Defects in hearing aids worn by preschool and school age children. Paper presented at the Annual Convention of the American Speech and Hearing Association, Detroit, Mich. 1973.

Fry, D. B. The development of the phonological system in the normal and the deaf child. In F. Smith and G. A. Miller (Eds.), The Genesis of Language, Cambridge: The MIT Press, 1966.

Gaeth, J. H. and Lounsbury, E. Hearing aids and children in elementary schools, J. Speech Hearing Dis., 31:551–562, 1966.

Gengel, R. W. and Pascoe, D. and Shore, I. A frequency-response procedure for evaluating and selecting hearing aids for severely hearing impaired children. J. Speech Hearing Dis., 36:341–353, 1971.

——— Acceptable speech-to-noise ratios for aided speech discrimination by the hearing impaired. J. Aud. Res., 11:219–222, 1971.

Goodman, A. I. Residual capacity to hear of pupils in schools for the deaf. J. Laryng., 63:551–662, (1949).

Hine, W. D. How deaf are deaf children? Brit. J. Aud. 7:41–44, 1973.

Huizing, H. C. Deaf mutism: Modern trends in treatment and prevention. Annals Oto-Rhino-Laryng 5:74–106, 1959.

Lenneberg, E. H. Biological Foundations for Language. New York, N.Y.: John Wiley & Sons, 1967.

Liberman, A. M., Cooper, F. S., Shankweiler, D. P. and Studdert-Kennedy, M. Perception of the speech code. Psychol. Rev., 7:431–461, 1967.

Ling, D. Implications of hearing aid amplification below 300 cps. Volta Rev. 66:723–729, 1964.

Matkin, N. D., and Olsen, W. O. Induction loop amplification systems. Classroom performance, ASHA 12:239–244, 1970A.

———— Response of hearing aids with induction loop amplification systems, Amer. Ann. Deaf, 115:73–78, 1970B.

———— An investigation of radio frequency auditory training units. Amer. Ann. Deaf, 118:25–30, 1973.

Montgomery, G. W. G. Analysis of pure-tone audiometric responses in relation to speech development in the profoundly deaf. J. Acoust. Soc. Amer., 41:53–59, 1967.

Northern, J. L., McChord, W., Fischer, E. and Evans, P. Hearing services in residential schools for the deaf. Maico Aud. Libr. Ser., 11, Report 4, 1972.

Porter, T. A. Hearing aids in a residential school. Amer. Ann. Deaf, 118:31–33, 1973.

Ross, M. Classroom acoustics and speech intelligibility. In J. Katz (Ed.) Handbook of Clinical Audiology, Williams and Wilkins: Baltimore, Md., 1972.

Skalka, E. C. and Moore, J. P. A program for daily "troubleshooting" of hearing aids in a day school for the deaf. Paper presented at the Annual Convention of the American Speech and Hearing Association, Detroit, Mich., 1973.

Sung, R. J., Sung, G. S., Hodgson, W. R., and Angelelli, R. M. Performance of hearing aids with an induction loop amplification system; laboratory vs. classroom setting. Paper presented at the Annual Convention of the American Speech and Hearing Association, Detroit, Mich., 1973.

Sung, G. C., Sung, R. J., and Angelelli, R. M. Effect of frequency-response characteristics of aids on speech intelligibility in noise. J. Aud. Res., 11:318–321, 1971.

Weintraub, F. J., Abeson, A. R., and Braddock, D. L. State Law and education of handicapped children issues and recommendations. Arlington, Va., Council for Exceptional Children, 1971.

Wilson, M. D., Hoversten, G. H., and Thies, T. L. Applications of acoustical analysis equipment in maintaining an auditory training system in a program for the deaf and hard of hearing. Paper presented at the Annual Convention of the American Speech and Hearing Association, San Francisco, Calif., 1972.

Zink, G. D. Hearing aids children wear: A longitudinal study of performance. Volta Rev., 74:40–41, 1972.

APPENDIX II

GUIDELINES FOR IDENTIFICATION AUDIOMETRY

Editor's Note: The set of "Guidelines for Identification Audiometry" was approved by the ASHA Legislative Council in November 1974. The following members of the ASHA Committee on Audiometric Evaluation developed these guidelines: J. B. Chaiklin, N. T. Hopkinson, J. I. Graham, Z. G. Shoeny, F. L. Sonday, V. W. Byers, R. M. McLauchlin, and W. R. Wilson, Chairman. ASHA encourages the professional community to use these guidelines in clinical practice. —K.O.J.

The set of *Guidelines for Identification Audiometry* is the second of a series developed by the Committee on Audiometric Evaluation, under the Office of Vice-President for Clinical Affairs of the American Speech and Hearing Association (ASHA).

Each of the guidelines presents a recommended set of procedures based on existing clinical practice and research findings. The spirit of these guidelines is not to mandate a single way of accomplishing the clinical process; rather the intent is to suggest standard procedures that, in the final analysis, will benefit the persons we serve. The intention is to improve interclinician and interclinic comparison of data thereby allowing for a more effective transfer of information.

The specific purpose of these guidelines is to detail procedures for accomplishing rapid and efficient identification of hearing impairment, particularly for use with young children.[1] As such, they represent an update of the procedures for identification audiometry for school-age children specified in the *Journal of Speech and Hearing Disorders* Monograph Supplement Number 9, "Identification Audiometry" (Darley, 1961). The current need for these guidelines is apparent with the development of increasing numbers of identification audiometry programs administered by state departments of education

---

Reproduced with permission from the American Speech and Hearing Association.

[1] The *Guidelines for Identification Audiometry* is written with emphasis on the testing of children; however, the approach is also appropriate for use with adults. A method of identification audiometry using a tracking procedure, sometimes called self-recording monitoring audiometry, is also used with adults in military and industrial settings. ASHA considers *Guidelines for Identification Audiometry Using a Threshold Tracking Procedure* deserving of a separate document. When the writing task is undertaken ASHA recommends that representatives of military and industrial groups should be included.

or health, the development of state mandatory special education statutes, and Medicaid guidelines for Early and Periodic Screening, Diagnosis, and Treatment (EPSDT).

For the most part, the philosophy and procedures laid out in these guidelines are based on and supported by published data. ASHA invites data-based input for future modifications of the guidelines.

SCOPE

A primary goal of identification audiometry using pure-tone air-conduction stimulation is to identify persons who have hearing impairments that interfere with or that have potential for interfering with communication. These guidelines focus on use with children of nursery-school age through grade three because early identification of communicative problems in this age group will permit maximum habilitation and avoidance of potential educational problems. Belkin, et al. (1964) have reported successful large scale individual pure-tone screening tests with children as young as three years of age. In addition, it is this age group which, in our society, is most often involved in the formal educational process through preschools and regular schools. While these guidelines focus on use with young children, they are equally applicable for use with older children and adults.

The guidelines are designed for rapid and efficient identification of hearing impairment. A basic assumption behind the guidelines is that identification audiometry is usually conducted in the relatively poor acoustic environments of schools and offices. Consequently, the procedures recommended are designed to be robust enough to be valid in a wide range of test settings. Naturally, it would be desirable for all identification audiometry to be conducted in acoustic environments that are controlled, but such environments are seldom available.

Identification audiometry is only one component of a hearing conservation program. A well-balanced program will include screening, rescreening, threshold audiometry, referrals for audiologic and medical evaluations, education and habilitation planning, and counseling for parents and teachers. Too often the sole goal is referral for medical evaluation rather than referral for consideration of communicative needs of those who fail screening procedures. Once people have been identified by the program, they should be followed regularly to insure that their communication and medical needs are met. It is pointless to identify people who have hearing impairments unless there is a concurrent follow-up program to handle their habilitative, educational, and medical needs.

Finally, these guidelines apply only to the use of pure-tone air-conduction screening for the purpose of identifying persons who have hearing impairment that interferes with or that has the potential for interfering with communication. Research (Eagles, 1961; Eagles, Wishik, and Doerfler, 1967; Roberts, 1972) demonstrates that pure-tone air-conduction screening is inefficient for the purpose of identifying many persons who have conductive ear pathology. Thus, if the purpose of an identification audiometry program is also to identify persons with conductive ear pathology, ASHA suggests the simultaneous use of otologic screenings, or supplemental procedures such as impedance (otoadmittance) measurements of pure-tone bone-conduction measurements. However, ASHA cannot specify any standardized screening procedures that employ impedance or bone-conduction measures because sufficient research data on such procedures are unavailable at the present time.

IDENTIFICATION AUDIOMETRY

The following recommendations emphasize identification audiometry for children using a manually administered, individual, pure-tone air-conduction screening procedure.

Children To Be Screened

Individual limited-frequency screening should be administered annually to children of nursery-school age through grade three and to high-risk children.[2] The time the program saves by emphasizing the lower grades permits appropriate attention for the high-risk group and focuses the program's efforts during the years when identification of communication problems can lead to intervention that will forestall serious educational, psychological, and social problems. Some school systems may elect to screen routinely after grade three at three- or four-year intervals (Darley, 1961). Others may find that a cost vs benefit analysis does not justify routine screening beyond grade three (Downs, Doster, and Wever, 1965). To determine the merit of routine screening after grade three, more data appear to be necessary.

---

[2] Examples of high-risk children are those who: (a) repeat a grade, (b) require special education programs, (c) are new to the school system, (d) were absent during a previously scheduled screening exam, (e) failed a threshold test during the previous year, (f) have speech problems, language problems, or obvious difficulty in communication, (g) are suspected of hearing impairment or have a medical problem associated with hearing impairment (children with recurrent or chronic problems such as allergies may require audiometric monitoring). Additional examples of high-risk children are given in Darley (1961, p. 36).

Procedure

Individual Screening   Individual as opposed to group screening is recommended. The Massachusetts Test (Johnston, 1948) is an example of a group pure-tone test that achieved great popularity and is still used in some states. It requires written responses and, consequently, like most group screening tests is limited to children above the second grade. Other limitations of group tests are calibration and maintenance problems of multiple earphones, increased set-up time and excessive time spent in retesting false-positive failures. All of these factors combine to increase the total time required for the screening program without increasing accuracy. Many group tests may appear to save time but the time taken to set up, check calibration, score answer sheets, and retest excessive failures may result in no saving of time.

Manual Method   A manual versus an automatic method is recommended because it is applicable with children down to three years of age. There is no known evidence that a self-recording or other type of automatic method is possible and effective with young children. Certainly, if an effective and more rapid automatic method is developed, its use should be considered.

Signal

Type   Pure-tone signals shall be used. Many different stimuli have been used to screen children and adults for the purpose of identifying persons with hearing impairment. Before audiometers were widely available, phonograph recordings were used to produce repeatable stimuli as in the Western Electric Fading Numbers Test. The Fading Numbers Test had a variety of defects: the most notable was its tendency to pass children with hearing deficits in the range above 500 Hz. Other screening tests that employ speech signals are vulnerable to the same defect.

Test Frequencies   Test frequencies shall be 1000 Hz, 2000 Hz, and 4000 Hz. The Conference on Identification Audiometry (Darley, 1961) recommended the frequencies 1000, 2000, 4000, and 6000 Hz. The recommendation for 500 Hz was ambiguous but the conference's intent appears to have been to eliminate 500 Hz except for very quiet test environments.

Melnick, Eagles, and Levine (1964), in a study which tested the conference's recommendations, used 500 Hz; however, all of their tests were conducted inside double-walled audiometric rooms. Melnick, Eagles, and Levine found that the conference's recommended test was highly efficient except at 6000 Hz, which produces too many failures. The variable interactions between earphones and ears at 6000 Hz (Villchur, 1970) among other considerations, make 6000 Hz a poor choice for inclusion in an identification audiometry program. The use of 500 Hz in order to assuage the user that he will discover all middle ear pathologies in a group of children is contraindicated by the hard data that is available (Eagles, 1961; Eagles, Wishik, and Doerfler, 1967; Roberts, 1972).

When an inordinate number of failures is expected at 4000 Hz, then 3000 Hz at 20 dB HL might be considered as the alternate test signal. There is insufficient research data at the present time to validate that the information obtained warrants the routine inclusion of 3000 Hz.[3]

Screening Levels Screening levels shall be 20 dB HL (re: ANSI-1969) at 1000 Hz and 2000 Hz and 25 dB HL at 4000 Hz. It is acceptable to screen at 20 dB HL at all three frequencies, but if 4000 Hz is not heard, output should be increased to 25 dB HL. Since most children will hear all three tones at 20 dB, the hearing level dial can remain at one setting for the entire test. It is important to remember, however, that 25 dB is the specified level at 4000 Hz.[4]

Results

Failure Criterion Failure to respond at the recommended screening levels at any frequency in either ear shall constitute failure.

Mandatory Rescreening All failures should be rescreened preferably within the same session in which they failed but definitely within one week after the initial screening. Removing and repositioning the phones, accompanied by careful reinstruction, markedly reduces the number of failures. Wilson and Walton (1974) reported a 52% reduction in failures by rescreening. The rescreening, using the same frequencies, levels, and failure criterion, is an essential procedure for improving the efficiency of a screening program.

Disposition of Failures Failures on rescreening should be referred for audiologic evaluation by an audiologist. Some persons, particularly young children, will fail both the screening and rescreening procedures and then yield normal thresholds on an audiometric

---

[3] ASHA invites active research on the addition of 3000 Hz to the screening format. Research studies also would be helpful to determine whether 3000 Hz could be substituted for 4000 Hz as a better predictor of subtle communicative problems among school-age children.

[4] ASHA is interested in active research concerning screening levels, since there is a great deal of strong feeling expressed concerning the issue, but very little hard data are available.

evaluation. Therefore, a hearing impairment should not be identified until after receiving an audiometric evaluation by an audiologist. An example of a program employing this referral format has been described by Campanelli, Krucoff, and DiLosa (1964). The following referral priority for audiologic evaluation is recommended for those children who fail the screening and rescreening procedures:

a. Binaural loss in both ears at all frequencies
b. Binaural loss at 1000 and 2000 Hz only
c. Binaural loss at 1000 or 2000 Hz only
d. Monaural loss at all frequencies
e. Monaural loss at 1000 and 2000 Hz
f. Binaural or monaural loss at 4000 Hz only.

The constraints placed on individual programs will determine the referral format, but the hearing conservation program supervisor should be responsible for providing case management necessary to guarantee appropriate referral for audiologic and medical consultation. In addition, the supervisor should secure educational assistance, if necessary, for students during and after medical therapy or audiologic habilitation. These duties are emphasized because the primary goal of school hearing conservation programs is to reduce the negative effects of communicative problems that are secondary to hearing loss, rather than simply to identify children who pass or fail a screening test.

PROCEDURAL CONSIDERATIONS

Adherence to the following procedural recommendations should facilitate successful implementation of the ASHA guidelines for identification audiometry.

Personnel

Identification audiometry programs should be conducted or supervised by an audiologist. After appropriate training, support personnel may administer audiometric screenings and rescreenings under the supervision of an audiologist. If properly trained professionals are not involved in supervising an identification audiometry program, an inordinate number of false-positive failures and false-negative passes may occur, this undermining the validity of the program. Without reservation, the audiologic evaluation should be administered by the audiologist.

Instructions

Instructions are critical in all audiometric procedures but particular care must be taken in instructing children. Instructions should emphasize the importance of responding "right away even when the beeps sound far away." Groups of children can be instructed at one time. Those waiting for the test profit from watching others being tested. Pantomime may have to accompany verbal instructions for the very young child or the difficult-to-test person, particularly if a conditioned play response is required rather than a hand or verbal response. Careful reinstruction is an important part of the rescreening process. Frequently children fail because they have misunderstood instructions. This is particularly true of children in the three- to six-year age range.

Time

At the third-grade level the entire screening, including earphone placement, occupies less than one minute. For younger children more time may be necessary. To avoid unnecessary failures with younger children, it is sometimes desirable to present more than one signal per frequency if there is no response. The net effect is a saving of time because the more careful screening process reduces the number of children who fail and require rescreening.

Acoustic Environment

The acoustic environment is an important variable in screening audiometry. Usually school environments are not too noisy for screening at frequencies above 1000 Hz, but sometimes ambient noise will interfere with screening at 1000 Hz. The 1000-Hz to 4000-Hz range was selected for the ASHA guidelines because it is less vulnerable to invalidation by ambient noise and because most significant hearing impairment will include failure in this range. The allowable ambient noise levels in the region of the test tone are shown in Table 1. Although screening at 500 Hz is not recommended, there is nothing inherently wrong in screening at 500 Hz in an appropriate environment such as a double-wall test room (Melnick, Eagles, and Levine, 1964). If an individual wishes to include 500 Hz, the allowable ambient noise levels are also included in Table 1.

Careful snug placement of the earphones increases attenuation of ambient noise by the earphone-cushion assembly. On the other hand, ASHA does not encourage the use of large sound-attenuating circumaural earphone assemblies (for example, Auraldomes and Otocups). Below 1000 Hz, these devices provide limited improvement in

Table 1.   Approximate allowable octave band ambient noise levels (SPL re: 20 micropascals for threshold measurements at Zero HL (re: ANSI-1969) and for screening at the ASHA recommended levels (re: ANSI-1969). In test environments that have fluctuating noise levels, caution must be used in applying the maximum value shown in this table. The committee has used the best information available in the literature to support the levels, and is basing its recommendation on these levels until additional information is available.

Test Frequency Octave Band Cutoff Frequencies	500 300 600	1000 600 1200	2000 1200 2400	4000 2400 4800
Allowable ambient noise for threshold at Zero HL (re: ANSI-1969)*	26	30	38	51
Plus ASHA screening level re: ANSI-1969	20	20	20	25
Resultant maximum ambient noise allowable for ASHA screening	46	50	58	76

* The allowable ambient noise levels for ANSI-1969 Zero HL threshold measurements were calculated by subtracting from the maximum allowable noise levels specified in the ANSI standard (S3.1, 1960) the difference between the ANSI-1951 and ANSI-1969 standards for pure-tone audiometers. In effect, the lower SPLs specified at Zero HL in the 1969 standard require quieter test spaces to measure normal listeners' thresholds.

attenuation of ambient noise relative to the attenuation produced by the MX-41/AR cushion (Webster, 1954; Cox, 1955; Benson, 1971). The advantage provided above 1000 Hz is not needed because ambient noise is generally weak above 1000 Hz and the MX-41/AR cushion provides relatively good attenuation of the weak high-frequency ambient noise. Furthermore, the large earphone assemblies are awkward for small children, and they increase test-retest variability in the higher frequencies.

Some persons have mistakenly assumed that sound-attenuating headsets eliminate the need for a quiet test environment, or worse, that they substitute for a sound-isolated audiometric test booth. In extremely noisy environments an audiometric test booth is often the only means of providing an environment quiet enough for screening audiometry. The sound-attenuating headsets provide the least benefit in the frequency range where it is needed most.

Audiometric Equipment and Calibration

Audiometers used for screening purposes shall meet the ANSI S3.6-1969 requirements for either a limited-range or narrow-range audiometer. Audiometers used for audiometric evaluation shall meet the ANSI S3.6-1969 requirements for a wide-range audiometer. Audiometric calibration to ANSI S3.6-1969 specifications should occur regularly at least once every year, following the initial determination that the audiometer meets specifications.[5] All of the ANSI specifications should be met, not just sound pressure level. Frequency errors, overshoot, and transient clicks are just a few of the problems that may invalidate a screening test. The sound pressure output of each audiometer should be checked at least every three months (preferably more often) in a 6 cc coupler. In addition, a daily listening check should be performed to determine that the audiometer is grossly in calibration and that no defects exist in major components.

Reports to Parents

Recommendations for audiologic and medical evaluations should be based on local realities. The language used in notices sent to parents about screening or rescreening results should avoid diagnostic conclusions and alarming predictions. Remember that the hearing impairment is not confirmed until the audiometric evaluation is administered. Personal contact would be preferable to sending notices, if possible. Some persons become overly concerned, others express no concern, and still others would like to cooperate but fear the expense that may be involved. If parents believe that their child can "hear," despite what a hearing screening suggests, tact and persuasion will be required to convince them that they may be in error. The word "fail" probably should be avoided in reporting screening results. The reporting aspect of programs for identification audiometry requires more time and thought than some programs have provided in the past.

SUMMARY

ASHA recommends a manually administered, individual, pure-tone, air-conduction screening procedure for accomplishing identification

---

[5] Studies on audiometer calibration suggest that, upon receipt, most audiometers may never have been in complete calibration (Eagles and Doerfler, 1961; Thomas, et al., 1969; Walton and Williams, 1972). This information underscores the importance of initial calibration of audiometers, and indicates that they should be checked to meet ANSI specifications before they are used in a screening program. It has been shown that when specifications are met initially, the audiometers generally remain stable (Walton and Wilson, 1974).

audiometry. The purpose of this procedure is to identify rapidly and effectively those persons with hearing impairment that interferes with communication or that has the potential for interfering with communication. The procedure is designed to be used with children as young as three years old, although it is applicable for use with adults.

The recommended identification audiometry procedure is as follows. Audiometric screening should be at 20 dB HL (re: ANSI-1969) at the frequencies of 1000 Hz and 2000 Hz and 25 dB HL at 4000 Hz. Failure to respond at the screening level at one or more frequencies in either ear is the criterion for failure. An audiometric rescreening should be administered the same day or no later than within one week to all persons failing the initial screening. An audiologist should administer an audiologic evaluation to persons failing the rescreening. If a hearing impairment is identified by audiometric evaluation, referrals should be made to meet the person's habilitative, educational, and medical needs.

Several procedural considerations are vital to implementing successfully the ASHA *Guidelines for Identification Audiometry*. An audiologist should conduct or supervise an identification audiometry program, although nonprofessional support personnel may be used for the screening procedures after appropriate training. Careful instructions are very important, particularly for young children. Ambient noise levels should not exceed 50 dB SPL at 1000 Hz, 58 dB SPL at 2000 Hz, and 76 dB SPL at 4000 Hz using a sound level meter with octave band filters centered on the screening frequencies. Audiometric equipment should initially meet all the ANSI S3.6-1969 specifications and be rechecked at least annually. The sound pressure output at the phones should be checked at least every three months, and listening checks for any gross malfunctions should be made daily. Finally, appropriate reporting of screening results should avoid diagnostic conclusions and encourage further evaluation for persons not passing the screening procedures.

Note: When the following Standards referred to in this document are superseded by an approved revision, the revision shall apply:
1. *American National Standard Specifications for Audiometers S3.6-1969; and*
2. *American Standard Criteria for Background Noise in Audiometer Rooms S3.1-1960.*

REFERENCES

American National Standard Specifications for Audiometers (ANSI S3.6-1969), New York: American National Standards Institute, Inc. (1970).
American Standard Criteria for Background Noise Audiometer Rooms

(ANSI S3.1-1960), New York: American National Standards Institute, Inc. (1960).

American Standard Specification for Audiometers for General Diagnostic Purposes (ANSI Z24.5-1951), New York: American National Standards Institute, Inc. (1951).

Belkin, M., Suchman, E., Bergman, M., Rosenblatt, D., and Jacobziner, H., A demonstration program for conducting hearing tests in day care centers. J. Speech Hearing Dis., 29:335-338 (1964).

Benson, R., "Auraldomes" for audiometric testing. Nat. Hearing Aid J., 24:14, 42 (1971).

Campanelli, P., Krucoff, M. and DiLosa, L., Hearing-screening of school children. Med. Ann Dist. of Columbia, 33:309-314 (1964).

Cox, J., How quiet must it be to measure normal hearing? Noise Control 1:25-29 (1955).

Darley, F. (ed.), Identification audiometry. J. Speech Hearing Dis., Mono. Suppl. 9 (1961).

Downs, M., Doster, M., and Wever, M., Dilemmas in identification audiometry. J. Speech Hearing Dis., 30:360-364 (1965).

Eagles, E., Hearing levels in children and audiometer performance. Appendix B in J. Speech Hearing Dis., Mono. Suppl. 9 (F. Darley, Ed.) 52-62 (1961).

Eagles, E., and Doerfler, L., A study of hearing in children: II. Acoustic environment and audiometer performance. Trans. Amer. Acad. Ophthal. Otolaryng., 283-296 (1961).

Eagles, E., Wishik, S., and Doerfler, L., Hearing Sensitivity and Ear Disease in Children: A Prospective Study. St. Louis: The Laryngoscope, 274 pp. (Tables pp. 146 and 163) (1967).

Johnston, P., The Massachusetts Hearing Test. J. Acoust. Soc. Amer., 20:697-703 (1948).

Jordan, R., and Eagles, E., The relation of air conducton audiometry to otological abnormalities. Ann. Otol. Rhinol., 70:819-827 (1961).

Melnick, W., Eagles, E., and Levine, H., Evaluation of a recommended program of identification audiometry with school-age children. J. Speech Hearing Dis., 29:3-13 (1964).

Roberts, J., Hearing sensitivity and related medical findings among children in the United States. Trans., Amer. Acad. Ophthal. Otolaryng., 355-359 (1972).

Thomas, W., Preslar, M., Summers, R., and Stewart, J., Calibration and working condition of 100 audiometers, Pub. Hlth. Rep., Wash., 84:311-327 (1969).

Villchur, E., Audiometer-earphone mounting to improve intersubject and cushion-fit reliability. J. Acoust. Soc. Amer., 48:1387-1396 (1970).

Walton, W. and Williams, P., Stability of routinely serviced portable audiometers, Lang. Speech Hearing Serv. Schools, 3:36-43 (1972).

Walton, W., and Wilson, W., Stability of pure-tone audiometers during periods of heavy use in identification audiometry. Lang. Speech Hearing Serv. Schools, 5:8-12 (1974).

Wilson, W. and Walton, W., Identification audiometry accuracy: Evaluation of a recommended program for school-age children, Lang. Speech Hearing Serv. Schools, 5:132-142 (1974).

Webster, J., Hearing losses of aircraft repair shop personnel. J. Acoust. Soc. Amer., 26:782-787 (1954).

Author Index

Subject Index